W9-BXY-901

HISTORICAL DICTIONARIES OF
INTERNATIONAL ORGANIZATIONS SERIES
Edited by Jon Woronoff

1. *European Community,* by Desmond Dinan. 1993
2. *International Monetary Fund,* by Norman K. Humphreys. 1993. *Out of print. See No. 17*
3. *International Organizations in Sub-Saharan Africa,* by Mark W. DeLancey and Terry M. Mays. 1994. *Out of print. See No. 21*
4. *European Organizations,* by Derek W. Urwin. 1994
5. *International Tribunals,* by Boleslaw Adam Boczek. 1994
6. *International Food Agencies: FAO, WFP, WFC, IFAD,* by Ross B. Talbot. 1994
7. *Refugee and Disaster Relief Organizations,* by Robert F. Gorman. 1994. *Out of print. See No. 18*
8. *United Nations,* by A. LeRoy Bennett. 1995
9. *Multinational Peacekeeping,* by Terry Mays. 1996. *Out of print. See No. 22.*
10. *Aid and Development Organizations,* by Guy Arnold. 1996
11. *World Bank,* by Anne C. M. Salda. 1997
12. *Human Rights and Humanitarian Organizations,* by Robert F. Gorman and Edward S. Mihalkanin. 1997
13. *United Nations Educational, Scientific and Cultural Organization (UNESCO),* by Seth Spaulding and Lin Lin. 1997
14. *Inter-American Organizations,* by Larman C. Wilson and David W. Dent. 1997
15. *World Health Organization,* by Kelley Lee. 1998
16. *International Organizations,* by Michael G. Schechter. 1998
17. *International Monetary Fund, 2nd Edition,* by Norman K. Humphreys. 1999
18. *Refugee and Disaster Relief Organizations, 2nd Edition,* by Robert F. Gorman. 2000
19. *Arab and Islamic Organizations,* by Frank A. Clements. 2001
20. *International Organizations in Asia and the Pacific,* by Derek McDougall. 2002
21. *International Organizations in Sub-Saharan Africa, 2nd Edition,* by Terry M. Mays and Mark W. DeLancey. 2002
22. *Multinational Peacekeeping, 2nd Edition,* by Terry M. Mays. 2004.

Historical Dictionary of Multinational Peacekeeping

Second Edition

Terry M. Mays

Historical Dictionaries of
International Organizations, No. 22

The Scarecrow Press, Inc.
Lanham, Maryland, and Oxford
2004

SCARECROW PRESS, INC.

Published in the United States of America
by Scarecrow Press, Inc.
A wholly owned subsidiary of
The Rowman & Littlefield Publishing Group, Inc.
4501 Forbes Boulevard, Suite 200, Lanham, Maryland 20706
www.scarecrowpress.com

PO Box 317
Oxford
OX2 9RU, UK

British Library Cataloguing in Publication Information Available

Library of Congress Cataloging-in-Publication Data

Mays, Terry M.
  Historical dictionary of multinational peacekeeping / Terry M. Mays.—
2nd ed.
    p. cm. — (Historical dictionaries of international organizations ; no. 22)
  Includes bibliographical references.
  ISBN 0-8108-4874-0 (alk. paper)
  1. United Nations—Peacekeeping forces—History—Dictionaries. 2.
Peacekeeping forces—History—Dictionaries. I. Title. II. Series: Historical
dictionaries of international organizations series ; no. 22.
JZ6374 .M38 2004
341.5'84—dc21

                                                                    2003013056

For Dr. Mark W. DeLancey,
teacher, mentor, friend

Contents

Editor's Foreword

It is getting so that hardly a day passes without the media reporting on one peacekeeping operation or another, and sometimes several. The public is becoming increasingly familiar with alphabetic bodies like UNEF, UNOSOM, and UNPROFOR and their activities. This certainly comes as a big surprise to the many observers who thought that international organizations would never be more than a talk shop and could never really "do something" to solve crises and enhance the prospects of peace. What is most surprising is that by now, each time a new crisis breaks out, public opinion vocally demands that something be done and, more than ever, something is done.

Much of this multiplication of peacekeeping operations is relatively new, occurring only since the end of the Cold War. But these operations reach much further back, to the early days of the United Nations and even its predecessor, the League of Nations. And it is not only the United Nations that intervenes but an expanding circle of other organizations. Nor are the peacekeeping bodies that appear most often in the media the only ones at work throughout the world. There are many more trying to resolve less-known problems and keep them out of the news.

That much can be gathered from this amazingly broad and deep study. *The Historical Dictionary of Multinational Peacekeeping* provides an extraordinary survey of the subject, including information on more operations, organizations, and crises than any other book. It also covers the actions of significant countries and persons who have contributed meaningfully to the accomplishment of always complex and occasionally hazardous missions. The list of acronyms will be precious for those who despair of ever sorting out the various bodies. And the comprehensive bibliography enables readers to find further information on aspects of particular interest.

This historical dictionary was compiled by Terry M. Mays, one of the few to actually teach a course on multinational peacekeeping. This he does, along with other subjects, at The Citadel in Charleston, South Carolina. Professor Mays writes regularly on peacekeeping, and his works include *Africa's First Peacekeeping Operation: The OAU in Chad, 1981–1982* and *The 1999 United Nations and 2000 Organization of African Union Formal Inquiries: A Retrospective Examination of Peacekeeping and the Rwandan Crisis of 1994*. He has also written numerous book chapters, academic journal articles, and conference papers on multinational peacekeeping. Professor Mays travels regularly to observe or research peacekeeping operations; his journeys have taken him to Canada, Egypt, Great Britain, Ireland, Israel, Nigeria, and Norway. He is also the coauthor of the *Historical Dictionary of International Organizations in Sub-Saharan Africa*. Still, how he managed to draw so many divergent strands into a comprehensible whole remains impressive.

Jon Woronoff
Series Editor

Preface

Multinational peacekeeping is increasingly being utilized as a tool in support of conflict management across the globe. Forty-three new peacekeeping operations have been mandated and fielded in the seven years between the submission dates of the first and second editions of this book. In other words, there has been an average of five new peacekeeping missions mandated annually between July 1995 and May 2003. Over one-third of these peacekeeping operations were mandated by regional or subregional international organizations. A second edition of the *Historical Dictionary of Multinational Peacekeeping* became a necessity to keep up with the multitude of new operations as well as to track the multiple missions fielded in the same countries. In areas of prolonged conflict, multiple international organizations have fielded peacekeeping operations in the same country. At the same time, single international organizations have mandated numerous missions in one country. Seven peacekeeping operations have been fielded in Lebanon since 1958; five in Haiti since 1993; five in Croatia since 1992; four in Bosnia and Herzegovina since 1992; four in Angola since 1988; and four between Egypt and Israel since 1948. Three different organizations fielded peacekeeping operations in Georgia at the same time. The organization of this book allows researchers to sort through these operations and gain a better understanding of how they are related.

This book takes a broad definition of multinational peacekeeping in order to provide a basis for comparison and permit researchers to review operations labeled as "peacekeeping" by international organizations. Many scholars do not agree on a single definition of peacekeeping and there are operations in this book that some will argue are not peacekeeping. The purpose of this book is not to generate debate on what is and is not a peacekeeping operation. The goal of this work is simply to assist researchers and others to sort through the myriad of peacekeeping or peace operations since 1920 and think about some of the trends and issues behind these missions. Every operation listed in the dictionary has been declared a peacekeeping mission or "peace operation" by an international organization or institute.

Much has changed in peacekeeping research since 1995. In the first edition of this book, I noted that the United Nations Operation in the Congo (ONUC) and the United Nations Emergency Force I (UNEF I) were probably the most heavily researched peacekeeping operations. Seven years later, I would argue that the most heavily researched missions are the United Nations Protection Force (UNPROFOR), United Nations Assistance Mission in Rwanda (UNAMIR), and the United Nations Operation in Somalia (UNOSOM). I also lamented the lack of research in regional and subregional organization mandated operations. While research in the latter peacekeeping missions is still lacking, there has been a small flurry of work on the Economic Community of West African States Monitoring Group (ECOMOG) mission in Liberia in recent years. While United Nations (UN) operations remain a favorite among researchers, there is still a void among the small UN missions as scholars concentrate on the large controversial forces. The success of a small UN operation can tell us as much about peacekeeping theory as the large controversial missions.

The goal of this book is not to write the complete history of every military operation referred to as "peacekeeping" by someone since 1920. Rather, the goal is to present enough information on the major multinational operations to allow readers to cut through any confusion and gain a better understanding of the many military missions fielded by international organizations since 1920. In the process, a few unilateral peacekeeping missions are also included in the dictionary to allow readers an opportunity to compare these to the operations mandated by international organizations.

The book is organized into several distinct categories. First, there is a list of acronyms and abbreviations. Like many military establishments around the globe, peacekeeping has a language of its own. Most missions have their own shortened names or acronyms which are more commonly heard than the actual name of the operation. In addition, although not covered in the list of acronyms, it should be noted that the UN and many regional organizations have a unique way of abbreviating the names of contingents assigned to the multinational operations.

Peacekeeping units are normally built around battalion- or company-sized units. The UN tends to refer to these units based upon their size and origin. Therefore, a battalion from Nigeria is referred to by the world body as NIGBATT. A country like France, which had four battalions in an operation such as UNPROFOR, had its units labeled as FREBATT1, FREBATT2, FREBATT3, and FREBATT4.

The next category in this book is a chronology of peacekeeping operations and related events since 1920. This list allows researchers to compare what is happening in the realm of peacekeeping at the same time around the globe. For instance, the UN mandated four different peacekeeping operations between April and May 1991. The chronology is followed by the dictionary itself. References are included for peacekeeping operations, key military and civilian individuals, political crises requiring intervention by peacekeeping operations, international organizations, and specific events during the multinational missions. The next category of the book is an appendix with three examples of peacekeeping mandates. A select but comprehensive bibliography of peacekeeping follows the appendix. While there is considerable literature on peacekeeping in other languages, this work contains sources in English due to size limitations. Only specialized works with inadequate English language coverage are included.

Acknowledgments

Many individuals have provided assistance for this project and I would like to acknowledge a few without minimizing the contributions of others. First, I would like to thank Jon Woronoff who, as always, has served as a great series editor. Kim Tabor of Scarecrow Press has consistently been of valuable assistance. Libraries and librarians at the Pearson Peacekeeping Centre (Heather Wharton), the University of Toronto, University of South Carolina, and The Citadel (Deborah Causey) provided valuable assistance. Stephen Foland helped with some of the basic mechanics of assembling this work. The Citadel Foundation provided funding for a research trip and a student assistant during the last year of the book's preparation. I would also like to thank the Krause Foundation for its support of The Citadel. Last, but far from least, I wish to thank my wife, Leslee, for her valuable support for this and all of my academic projects.

Acronyms and Abbreviations

ACRI	African Crisis Response Initiative
ADF	Arab Deterrent Force
ADL	Armistice Demarcation Line
AMIB	African Mission in Burundi
ANAD	Non-Aggression and Assistance Accord
AP	Assembly Point
AOL	Area of Limitation
AOS	Area of Separation
ASEAN	Association of South East Asian Nations
ASF	Symbolic Arab Security Force
AU	African Union
CEMAC	Economic and Monetary Community of Central African States
CIS	Commonwealth of Independent States
CMF	Commonwealth Monitoring Force
CMO	Chief Military Observer
COMESSA	Community of Sahel-Saharan States
CPF	Collective Peacekeeping Forces
CPLP	Community of Lusophone Countries
CSCE	Conference on Security and Cooperation in Europe
DOMREP	Mission of the Representative of the Secretary-General in the Dominican Republic
DPKO	Department of Peacekeeping Operations
EC	European Community
ECMM	European Community Monitoring Mission
ECOFORCE	Economic Community of West African States Force in Côte d'Ivoire
ECOMICI	Economic Community of West African States Mission in Côte d'Ivoire

ECOMOG	Economic Community of West African States Monitoring Group
ECOWAS	Economic Community of West African States
EIMAC	Egypt–Israel Mixed Armistice Commission
EU	European Union
EUMM	European Union Monitoring Mission
EUPM	European Union Police Mission
EURFOR	European Force
FAWEU	Forces Available to the West European Union
FC	Force Commander
FIA	Inter-African Force
FMP	Multinational Protection Force
FMR	Force Mobile Reserve
FNLA	Frente Nacional de Libertação de Angola/National Front for the Liberation of Angola
FPA	Non-Aggression and Assistance Accord Peace Force
FYROM	Former Yugoslav Republic of Macedonia
GA	General Assembly
IAF	Inter-African Force
IAF	Inter-American Force
IAPF	Inter-American Peace Force
IPF	Indian Peacekeeping Force
ICC	International Criminal Court
ICCS	International Commission of Control and Supervision
ICISS	International Commission on Intervention and State Sovereignty
IFOR	Implementation Force
IJMAC	Israel–Jordan Mixed Armistice Commission
ILMAC	Israel–Lebanon Mixed Armistice Commission
IMU	International Monitoring Unit
IPMT	International Peace Monitoring Team
IPTF	United Nations International Police Task Force
ISAF	International Security Assistance Force
ISMAC	Israel–Syria Mixed Armistice Commission
JTF	Joint Task Force
KFOR	Kosovo Force
MAC	Military Armistice Commission
MFO	Multinational Force and Observers

MICIVH	International Civilian Support Mission in Haiti
MINUCI	United Nations Mission in Côte d'Ivoire
MINUGUA	United Nations Verification Mission in Guatamala
MINURCA	United Nations Mission in the Central African Republic
MINURSO	United Nations Mission for the Referendum in the Western Sahara
MIPONUH	United Nations Civilian Police Mission in Haiti
MISAB	Inter-African Force in the Central African Republic
MNF	Multinational Force
MNF I	Multinational Force I
MNF II	Multinational Force II
MOG	Military Observer Group
MOMEP	Mission of Military Observers Ecuador–Peru
MONUA	United Nations Observer Mission in Angola
MONUC	United Nations Organization Mission in the Democratic Republic of the Congo
MOT	Military Observer Team
MPLA	Movimento Popular de Libertação de Angola/Popular Movement for the Liberation of Angola
MSC	Military Staff Committee
MTC	Mission Training Cells
NATO	North Atlantic Treaty Organization
NMOG I	Neutral Military Observer Group I
NMOG II	Neutral Military Observer Group II
OAS	Organization of American States
OAU	Organization of African Unity
OAUPKF	Organization of African Unity Peacekeeping Force
ODD	Observer Detachment Damascus
OECS	Organization of East Caribbean States
OGB	Observer Group Beirut
OGE	Observer Group Egypt
OGG	Observer Group Golan
OGL	Observer Group Lebanon
OMIB	Organization of African Unity Mission in Burundi
OMIC	Organization of African Unity Observer Mission in the Comoros Islands
ONUC	United Nations Operation in the Congo

ONUCA	United Nations Observer Group in Central America
ONUMOZ	United Nations Operation in Mozambique
ONUSAL	United Nations Observer Mission in El Salvador
ONUVEH	United Nations Observer Group for the Verification of the Elections in Haiti
OOTW	Operations Other Than War
PAPF	Pan-African Peacekeeping Force
PfP	Partnership for Peace
PLO	Palestinian Liberation Organization
PMG	Peace Monitoring Group
POLISARIO	Frente Popular para la Liberación de Saguila el-Hamra y de Rio de Oro
QRF	Quick Reaction Force
RECAMP	Renforcement des Capacités Africaines de Maintien de la Paix
ROE	Rules of Engagement
RV	Rendezvous Point
SADC	Southern African Development Community
SAM	Sanctions Assistance Mission
SASF	Symbolic Arab Security Force
SC	Security Council
SFOR	Stabilisation Force
SG	Secretary-General
SGTM	Standardized Generic Training Modules
SHIRBRIG	Stand-By Forces High Readiness Brigade
SPPKF	South Pacific Peacekeeping Force
TES	Training and Evaluation Service
TIPH	Temporary International Presence Hebron
TMG	Bougainville Truce Monitoring Group
UN	United Nations
UNAMET	United Nations Mission in East Timor
UNAMIC	United Nations Advance Mission in Cambodia
UNAMIR	United Nations Assistance Mission in Rwanda
UNAMSIL	United Nations Assistance Mission in Sierra Leone
UNAVEM I	United Nations Angola Verification Mission I
UNAVEM II	United Nations Angola Verification Mission II
UNAVEM III	United Nations Angola Verification Mission III
UNCCP	United Nations Conciliation Commission for Palestine

UNCIP	United Nations Commission for India and Pakistan
UNCIVPOL	United Nations Civilian Police
UNCK	United Nations Commission on Korea
UNCRO	United Nations Confidence Restoration Mission in Croatia
UNDOF	United Nations Disengagement Observer Force
UNEF I	United Nations Emergency Force I
UNEF II	United Nations Emergency Force II
UNFICYP	United Nations Peacekeeping Force in Cyprus
UNGCI	United Nations Guards Contingent in Iraq
UNGOMAP	United Nations Good Offices in Afghanistan
UNHCR	United Nations High Commissioner for Refugees
UNHUC	United Nations suboffices and Humanitarian Centers
UNIFIL	United Nations Interim Force in Lebanon
UNIIMOG	United Nations Iran–Iraq Military Observer Group
UNIKOM	United Nations Iraq–Kuwait Observation Mission
UNIPOM	United Nations India–Pakistan Observation Mission
UNITA	União Nacional para a Indepéndençia Total de Angola/ National Union for the Total Independence of Angola
UNITAF	Unified Task Force
UNMEE	United Nations Mission in Ethiopia and Eritrea
UNMGOIP	United Nations Military Observer Group in India and Pakistan
UNMIBH	United Nations Mission in Bosnia and Herzegovina
UNMIH	United Nations Mission in Haiti
UNMIK	United Nations Interim Administration Mission in Kosovo
UNMISET	United Nations Mission of Support in East Timor
UNMOP	United Nations Mission of Observers in Prevlaka
UNMOT	United Nations Mission of Observers in Tajikistan
UNOGIL	United Nations Observation Group in Lebanon
UNOMIG	United Nations Observer Mission in Georgia
UNOMIL	United Nations Observer Mission in Liberia
UNOMSA	United Nations Observer Mission in South Africa
UNOMSIL	United Nations Observation Mission in Sierra Leone
UNOMUR	United Nations Observer Mission Uganda–Rwanda
UNOSOM I	United Nations Operation in Somalia I
UNOSOM II	United Nations Operation in Somalia II

UNPA	United Nations Protected Areas
UNPF-HQ	United Nations Peace Forces—Headquarters
UNPREDEP	United Nations Preventive Deployment Force
UNPROFOR	United Nations Protection Force
UNPSG	United Nations Police Support Group
UNSAS	United Nations Stand By Arrangement System
UNSCOB	United Nations Special Committee on the Balkans
UNSF	United Nations Security Force
UNSMIH	Untied Nations Support Mission in Haiti
UNTAC	United Nations Transitional Authority in Cambodia
UNTAES	United Nations Transitional Administration in Eastern Slavonia, Baranja, and Western Sirmium
UNTAET	United Nations Transitional Administration in East Timor
UNTAG	United Nations Transition Assistance Group
UNTCOK	United Nations Temporary Commission on Korea
UNTEA	United Nations Temporary Executive Authority
UNTMIH	United Nations Transition Mission in Haiti
UNTSO	United Nations Truce Supervision Organization
UNV	United Nations Volunteers
UNYOM	United Nations Yemen Observation Mission
USMNF	United States Multinational Forces
USSSM	United States Sinai Support Mission
WEU	West European Union

Chronology

January 1920   League of Nations Plebiscite forces provide security in Schleswig and Upper Silesia.

10 January 1920   League of Nations is established.

July 1920   League of Nations Plebiscite forces provide security in Allenstein and Marienwerder.

October 1920   League of Nations Plebiscite forces provide security in the Klagenfurt Basin.

21 November 1920   Council of the League of Nations proposes the establishment of an international force to oversee the Vilna plebiscite.

19 December 1920   Lithuania, due to Soviet pressure, withdraws its acceptance of the League of Nations' Vilna International Force.

5 December 1934   Saar International force is officially proposed at a meeting of the Council of the League of Nations.

22 December 1934   The majority of the Saar International Force is in place in the Saar.

13 January 1935   Saar plebiscite is held.

28 January 1935   Saar International Force completes its withdrawal from the Saar.

22 March 1945   League of Arab States is established.

26 June 1945   UN Charter is signed.

20 January 1948   UN mandates UNCIP.

21 April 1948   UN mandates UNMOGIP.

30 April 1948   OAS is founded.

21 May 1948   The Truce Commission requests military personnel to assist in the supervision of the truce between the Israelis and their Arab neighbors.

11 August 1949   UN mandates the Mixed Armistice Commissions in the Middle East.

2 November 1950   First use of the Uniting for Peace Resolution.

30 March 1951   UN votes to retain UNMOGIP following a cease-fire in the Kashmir region.

1 March 1954   India, citing a perceived lack of United States neutrality, orders the removal of American observers assigned to UNMOGIP.

5 November 1956   UN mandates UNEF I.

15 November 1956   The first elements of UNEF I arrive.

11 June 1958   UN mandates UNOGIL.

12 June 1958   UNOGIL begins arriving.

9 December 1958   UNOGIL departs.

December 1959   General P. S. Gyani of India becomes the first officer from a Third World state to command a UN peacekeeping operation (UNEF I).

12 July 1960   President Joseph Kasa-Vubu and Prime Minister Patrice Lumumba of the Congo request UN military assistance.

14 July 1960   UN mandates ONUC.

15 July 1960   ONUC begins deploying.

26–28 April 1961   Forty-eight ONUC peacekeepers are massacred in Port-Francqui.

10 June 1961   Kuwait achieves independence.

20 July 1961   League of Arab States pledges assistance to guarantee Kuwait's independence.

12 August 1961   The agreement establishing the Arab League Force for Kuwait is signed.

September 1961   Arab League Force begins deployment to Kuwait.

18 September 1961   UN Secretary-General Dag Hammarskjöld dies in a plane crash during a mission in support of ONUC.

3 October 1961   Arab League Force completes deployment to Kuwait.

11 November 1961   Italian peacekeepers assigned to ONUC are massacred at Kindu.

24 November 1961   UN Resolution 169 permits ONUC to use force in the removal of mercenaries from Katanga in the Congo.

21 September 1962   UN mandates UNSF.

1 October 1962   West Irian is transferred to UNTEA.

3 October 1962   UNSF begins its deployment.

20 January 1963   ONUC peacekeepers enter the Kongolo Pocket.

February 1963   Arab League Force is withdrawn from Kuwait following the installation of a more moderate government in Iraq.

30 April 1963   UNSF withdraws.

1 May 1963   UNTEA transfers West Irian to Indonesia.

11 June 1963   UN mandates UNYOM.

4 July 1963   UNYOM begins arriving in Yemen.

4 March 1964   UN mandates UNFICYP.

13 March 1964   UNFICYP begins deployment to Cyprus.

30 June 1964   ONUC departs the Congo.

4 September 1964   UNYOM withdraws.

28 April 1965   American forces intervene in the Dominican Republic.

14 May 1965   UN establishes DOMREP.

23 May 1965   Inter-American Peace Force begins arriving in the Dominican Republic.

20 September 1965   UN mandates UNIPOM.

23 September 1965   UNIPOM begins deploying.

22 March 1966   UNIPOM is terminated.

21 September 1966   Inter-American Peace Force completes its withdrawal from the Dominican Republic.

22 October 1966   DOMREP departs the Dominican Republic.

16 May 1967   Egypt orders UNEF I to withdraw.

25 October 1973   UN mandates UNEF II.

31 May 1974   UN agrees to deploy UNDOF.

3 June 1974   UNDOF officially begins its mission.

April 1975   Lebanese civil war erupts.

15 October 1975   League of Arab States meets in an extraordinary session to discuss the crisis in Lebanon.

1 June 1976   Syrian armed forces intervene in Lebanon.

8 June 1976   League of Arab States votes to establish a Symbolic Arab Security Force to replace the Syrians in Lebanon.

15 June 1976   Lebanon announces that it will accept the deployment of the Symbolic Arab Security Force.

21 June 1976   Symbolic Arab Security Force begins arriving in Beirut.

18 October 1976   Attendees at the Riyadh Summit Conference announce their desire to transform the Symbolic Arab Security Force into the Arab Deterrent Force.

26 October 1976   League of Arab States votes to transform the Symbolic Arab Security Force into the Arab Deterrent Force.

8 March 1977   Shaba I begins.

8 April 1977   Morocco dispatches troops with French assistance to counter rebels during Shaba I.

25 July 1977   Lebanese, Syrian, and PLO delegates sign the Chtaura Agreement.

19 March 1978   UN mandates UNIFIL. Peacekeepers begin deployment on the same day.

13 May 1978   Shaba II begins.

19–20 May 1978   French and Belgian soldiers intervene in Zaire during Shaba II.

4 June 1978   Inter-African Force begins arriving to replace the French and Belgians in Zaire during Shaba II.

29 September 1978   UN mandates UNTAG, a decade prior to its deployment.

15 October 1978   Beiteddine Conference is convened.

March 1979   Gulf States threaten to terminate funding for the Arab Deterrent Force.

7 March 1979   Nigerian soldiers deploy to Chad under a unilateral peacekeeping mandate.

4 June 1979   Nigerian soldiers withdraw from Chad.

24 July 1979   The mandate of UNEF II lapses.

15 November 1979   Lancaster House Agreement is signed, mandating the CMF.

27 December 1979   CMF begins arriving in Zimbabwe.

6 January 1980   CMF in Zimbabwe completes the transportation of Patriotic Front armed personnel to Assembly Points.

18 January 1980   Congolese forces with the OAU Peacekeeping Force in Chad I arrive in N'djamena.

24 January 1980   Commonwealth Observer Group arrives in Zimbabwe.

30 March 1980   Congolese forces of the OAU Peacekeeping Force in Chad I withdraw.

15 November 1981   The OAU Peacekeeping Force in Chad II begins arriving in N'djamena.

30 June 1982   The OAU withdraws the OAU Peacekeeping Force in Chad II.

10 July 1982   France announces conditional willingness to deploy soldiers to Beirut.

15 August 1982   Israel agrees to accept an international peacekeeping force in Beirut to oversee the evacuation of the PLO.

19 August 1982   Lebanon officially requests soldiers from the United States, France, and Italy to form a peacekeeping operation to monitor the evacuation of the PLO from Beirut.

25 August 1982   U.S. Marines arrive in Beirut for MNF I.

6 September 1982   Fez Summit Conference convenes. The League of Arab States officially terminates the Arab Deterrent Force following a request from Lebanon.

10–12 September 1982   American, French, and Italian soldiers of MNF I depart Beirut.

20 September 1982   Lebanon asks the United States, France, and Italy to redeploy their peacekeeping forces to Beirut.

27–28 September 1982   American, French, and Italian soldiers of MNF II deploy to positions around Beirut.

20 December 1982   Great Britain announces that it will field a contingent with MNF II.

1 February 1983   British forces arrive in Beirut for MNF II.

23 October 1983   Suicide truck bombers kill 241 U.S. Marines and 58 French soldiers of MNF II.

24 October 1983   American and OECS forces intervene in Grenada under an OECS mandate.

22 November 1983   American forces hand security control on Grenada to the OECS contingents.

15 December 1983   American forces depart Grenada.

20 February 1984   Italy withdraws most of its soldiers assigned to MNF II.

21–16 February 1984   U.S. Marines of MNF II redeploy to ships off the coast of Lebanon.

22 March 1984   British contingent of MNF II is withdrawn from Lebanese waters.

31 March 1984   France removes its remaining soldiers assigned to MNF II from Beirut.

9 August 1988   UN mandates UNIIMOG.

19 August 1988   UNIIMOG begins deployment.

31 October 1988   UN mandates UNGOMAP.

10 December 1988   UN accepts the Nobel Peace Prize for its peace-keepers.

20 December 1988   UN mandates UNAVEM I.

1 April 1989   UNTAG begins deployment.

7 November 1989   UN mandates ONUCA.

7 December 1989   ONUCA begins arriving.

15 March 1990   UNGOMAP is terminated.

21 March 1990   UNTAG withdraws.

1 May 1990   EU enacts the Amsterdam Treaty

6–7 August 1990   ECOWAS Standing Mediation Committee recommends the fielding of ECOMOG in Liberia.

24 August 1990   ECOMOG begins arriving in Liberia.

10 October 1990   UN mandates ONUVEH.

9 April 1991   UN mandates UNIKOM.

29 April 1991   UN mandates MINURSO.

6 May 1991   UNIKOM is declared operational

19 May 1991   UNGCI begins arriving in Iraq.

20 May 1991   UN mandates ONUSAL.

30 June 1991   UNAVEM I officially transforms into UNAVEM II.

17 October 1991   UN mandates UNAMIC.

21 December 1991   Former Soviet Republics form the Commonwealth of Independent States.

31 December 1991   UN modifies the mandate of ONUSAL to include cease-fire observation.

31 January 1992   Security Council requests Secretary-General Boutros Boutros-Ghali to prepare what became known as "An Agenda for Peace."

21 February 1992   UN mandates UNPROFOR.

28 February 1992   UN mandates UNTAC.

15 March 1992   UNPROFOR begins operations. UNTAC becomes operational and absorbs UNAMIC.

21 April 1992   UN mandates UNOSOM I.

8 June 1992   UN votes to expand UNPROFOR and deploy an element in Bosnia and Herzegovina.

15 June 1992   An advance UNPROFOR team arrives in Bosnia and Herzegovina. Japanese Diet votes to allow Japanese soldiers to participate in UN peacekeeping operations.

19 June 1992   WEU develops the Petersberg Declaration.

24 June 1992   South Ossetia Joint Force established.

1 July 1992   UN Secretary-General Boutros Boutros-Ghali delivers "An Agenda for Peace."

August 1992   OAU deploys the NMOG I. UN mandates UNOMSA.

14 September 1992   UNOSOM I begins arriving.

December 1992   CIS deploys peacekeepers to Tajikistan.

3 December 1992   UN mandates UNITAF.

9 December 1992   UNITAF begins arriving in Somalia.

4 February 1993   CSCE mandates its mission to Moldova.

5 April 1993   WEU finalizes an agreement with Bulgaria, Hungary, and Romania to enforce an embargo on Serbia.

4 May 1993   UNOSOM I transforms into UNOSOM II.

6 May 1993   UN establishes six safe areas for Muslims in Bosnia and Herzegovina.

5 June 1993   Twenty-four Pakistani peacekeepers of UNOSOM II are killed by forces loyal to Mohammed Farah Aidid.

August 1993   NMOG I is transformed into NMOG II.

18 August 1993   UNOMUR begins deploying.

24 August 1993   UN mandates UNOMIG.

23 September 1993   UN mandates UNMIH.

24 September 1993   CIS mandates its Peacekeeping Forces in Tajikistan.

3 October 1993   UNITAF personnel clash with the forces of Aidid in Somalia.

5 October 1993   UN mandates UNAMIR.

December 1993   CSCE votes to deploy observers to Nagorno-Karabakh.

1 December 1993   CSCE mandates its mission to Tajikistan.

7 December 1993   Eleven OAU members sign the Mechanism for the Prevention, Management, and Settlement of African Disputes.

10 December 1993   UNAMIR begins arriving in Rwanda.

11 January 1994   NATO members reach a compromise on air strikes in support of UNPROFOR in Bosnia and Herzegovina.

19 February 1994   CSCE mission to Tajikistan begins operations.

31 March 1994   TIPH is mandated.

15 April 1994   CIS mandates the CIS Peacekeeping Forces in Georgia.

25 May 1994   Presidential Decision Directive Twenty-Five is released.

23 June 1994   French military intervenes to protect civilians in Rwanda.

31 July 1994 UN authorizes the use of force to remove the military leaders of Haiti.

8 August 1994 TIPH departs Palestinian territory.

21 August 1994 French forces complete their withdrawal from Rwanda and surrounding states.

19 September 1994 American forces intervene in Haiti.

3 October 1994 SPPKF arrives on Bougainville.

5 October 1994 Personnel from Barbados, Belize, Jamaica, and Trinidad join American forces in Haiti.

22 October 1994 SPPKF departs Bougainville.

4 November 1994 UN announces its intention to withdraw the peace-keepers of UNOSOM II by the end of March 1995.

21–23 November 1994 NATO planes conduct their largest air strikes against Serb positions in Bosnia and Herzegovina.

21–30 November 1994 Serb forces detain several hundred peace-keepers to deter NATO air strikes in Bosnia and Herzegovina.

14 December 1994 UN mandates UNMOT.

8 February 1994 UNAVEM II mission ends as the UN mandates UNAVEM III.

17 February 1994 MOMEP is mandated.

31 March 1994 UN mandates UNCRO.

31 March 1994 UN mandates UNPREDEP. UN mandates UNPRO-FOR as a separate operation in Bosnia and Herzegovina.

14 December 1994 Dayton Accord signed and mandates IFOR.

20 December 1994 IFOR begins operations.

21 December 1994 UN mandates UNMIBH.

1 February 1996 UN mandates UNMOP.

28 June 1996 UN mandates UNSMIH to replace UNMIH.

20 December 1996   IFOR transforms to SFOR.

20 January 1997   UN mandates MINUGUA.

21 January 1997   TIPH is remandated.

25 January 1997   Bangui Agreements mandate MISAB.

8 February 1997   MISAB deploys to the Central African Republic.

28 March 1997   UN endorses FMP.

15 April 1997   FMP arrives in Albania.

May 1997   ANAD establishes the FPA.

17 May 1997   MINUGUA departs Guatamala.

25 May 1997   Nigeria reinforces its troops in Sierra Leone under the ECOMOG banner following a coup in Freetown on this day.

30 June 1997   UN mandates MONUA as UNAVEM III ends its mission.

30 July 1997   UN mandates UNTMIH.

12 August 1997   FMP departs Albania.

30 September 1997   UNOMIL departs Liberia.

November 1997   Bougainville TMG mandated.

28 November 1997   UN mandates MIPONUH.

19 December 1997   UN mandates UNPSG.

27 March 1998   UN mandates MINURCA.

30 April 1998   Bougainville PMG is mandated and replaces the Bougainville TMG.

13 July 1998   UN mandates UNOMSIL.

15 October 1998   UNPSG's mandate expires.

26 February 1999   MONUA departs Angola.

28 February 1999   UNPREDEP mandate not extended by a Chinese veto.

March 1999   ECOMOG forces arrive in Guinea-Bissau.

14 May 1999   SADC forces depart Lesotho.

7 June 1999   ECOMOG forces depart Guinea-Bissau.

8 June 1999   OSCE mandates the Kosovo Task Force.

11 June 1999   UN mandates UNAMET.

12 June 1999   KFOR enters Kosovo.

17 June 1999   MOMEP departs Ecuador and Peru.

1 July 1999   OSCE mandates OMIK.

13 July 1999   UN mandates UNOMSIL.

6 August 1999   UN mandates MONUC.

12 September 1999   INTERFET is mandated.

20 September 1999   INTERFET arrives in East Timor.

22 October 1999   UN mandates UNAMSIL to replace UNOMSIL.

25 October 1999   UN mandates UNTAET.

28 February 2000   INTERFET transfers military operations to UN-TAET.

15 May 2000   UNMOT ceases operations.

31 June 2000   UN mandates UNMEE.

16 September 2000   CIS mandates the CIS Collective Peacekeeping Force.

15 October 2000   IPMT is mandated.

22 December 2000   ECCM becomes the EUMM.

15 August 2001   NATO mandates Operation Essential Harvest.

17 August 2001   Operation Essential Harvest arrives in FYROM.

26 September 2001   NATO mandates Operation Amber Fox and terminates Operation Essential Harvest.

27 October 2001   South African peacekeepers begin arriving in Burundi.

2 December 2001   Community of Sahel-Sahran States mandates a peacekeeping operation for Central African Republic.

1 January 2002   ISAF begins arriving in Afghanistan.

17 May 2002   UN mandates UNMISET.

2 October 2002   Economic and Monetary Community of Central African States mandates a peacekeeping operation for Central African Republic.

15 December 2002   United Nations Mission of Observers in Prevlaka is terminated.

16 December 2002   Operation Allied Harmony begins operations.

1 January 2003   European Union Police Mission arrives in Bosnia and Herzegovina.

12 February 2003   AU Cease-Fire Observer Mission in Burundi arrives.

17 March 2003   UN withdraws and remandates UNIKOM.

April 2003   United States begins to assemble the Iraq Stabilization Force.

1 April 2003   EURFOR begins operations in Macedonia.

12 May 2003   UN requests France and other states to form a Congo International Force.

13 May 2003   UN mandates MINUCI.

23 May 2003   Poland closes a conference that completes the international pledges for the Iraq Stabilization Force.

Introduction

What is peacekeeping and how can we categorize and compare these operations? These are not simple questions as some might think. Like the definition for "power," every scholar, international organization, and international institute seems to have a separate definition for peacekeeping. Fortunately, the differences between the definitions are usually minor. How can we categorize and compare peacekeeping missions once we define them? Should researchers compare them by generational periods, mandating organizations, or functions? While some might argue vehemently for one over the other, it is a matter of choice based on the requirements of the project.

DEFINITION

What is peacekeeping? When researching peacekeeping operations, one should take the time to consider this question. There have been a multitude of military operations mandated by international organizations since 1945. Most are classified by the organizations as "peacekeeping," a few are referred to as "collective security" or "peace enforcement," and several seem to float between these extremes. For example, how does one properly classify the Unified Task Force (UNITAF), led by the United States and mandated by the United Nations (UN)? Is it "peacekeeping" or what some refer to as "peace enforcement"? Few seem willing to accept the definitions offered by others. However, it is not the purpose of this book to open a debate on the meaning of "peacekeeping" but rather to present options and offer a set of more comprehensive definitions for understanding why multinational operations are included in this book.

UN Secretary-General Boutros Boutros-Ghali, in *An Agenda for Peace: Preventive Diplomacy, Peacemaking, and Peacekeeping* (1992), defined peacekeeping as "the deployment of a United Nations presence in the field, hitherto with the consent of all the parties concerned, normally involving United Nations military and/or police personnel and frequently civilians as well." The key to this definition is the word "hitherto." Thus, the UN recognizes that peacekeeping forces might not have the consent of all belligerents

This book uses a broad interpretation in order to cover the many multinational operations that have been labeled as "peacekeeping" since 1920. For the purpose of the dictionary, the American Department of Defense 1993 definitions for "peacekeeping" and "peace enforcement," as listed in the *Report of the Bottom-Up Review* (1993), are utilized. The Department of Defense has not only defined "peacekeeping" but has also subdivided the term into "traditional peacekeeping" and "aggravated peacekeeping," thus adding considerable clarity for understanding.

Peacekeeping is defined by the Department of Defense as "military operations, undertaken with the consent of all major belligerents, that are designed to monitor and facilitate implementation of an existing truce agreement in support of diplomatic efforts to reach a political settlement to a dispute." There are two types of peacekeeping operations—traditional peacekeeping and aggravated peacekeeping. The Department of Defense defined traditional peacekeeping as the "deployment of a UN, regional organization, or coalition presence in the field with the consent of all parties concerned, normally involving UN, regional organization, or coalition military forces, and/or police and civilians. Non-combat military operations (exclusive of self-defense) that are undertaken by outside forces with the consent of all major belligerent parties, designed to monitor and facilitate implementation of an existing truce agreement in support of diplomatic efforts to reach a political settlement to the dispute." This definition centers on the role of acceptance by the belligerents and the noncombat (neutral) role of the operation. One additional critical fact should be highlighted by the definition. The Department of Defense has correctly indicated that peacekeeping is not an attempt to settle a dispute. Peacekeeping is a tool to assist a separate negotiation process normally undertaken by the same international organization that mandated the neutral military operation.

The second type of peacekeeping mission is an aggravated peacekeeping operation. The Department of Defense defines aggravated peacekeeping as "military operations undertaken with the nominal consent of all major belligerent parties, but which are complicated by subsequent intransigence of one or more of the belligerents, poor command and control of belligerent forces, or conditions of outlawry, banditry, or anarchy. In such conditions, peacekeeping forces are normally authorized to use force in self-defense, and in defense of the missions they are assigned, which may include monitoring and facilitating implementation of an existing truce agreement, or supporting or safeguarding humanitarian relief efforts." In the case of aggravated peacekeeping, the peacekeepers may use force to fulfill their mandated mission even though they have been initially and minimally accepted by the belligerents. Recent peacekeeping operations, including the former Yugoslavia, Rwanda, Sierra Leone, and Somalia, have reminded international organizations and contingent providers that belligerents do not always welcome the presence of peacekeepers.

The Department of Defense uses the term "peace enforcement," which is defined as "military intervention to compel compliance with international sanctions or resolutions designed to maintain or restore international peace and security." While peacekeeping missions are mandated to oversee an existing cease-fire, peace enforcement operations are asked to actually restore the status quo, by force if necessary. UNITAF and the Economic Community of West African States Monitoring Group (ECOMOG) operations in Liberia and Sierra Leone could be placed into the definition of peace enforcement. While many peace enforcement operations are often referred to as "peacekeeping," researchers should keep their unique mandates in mind.

GENERATIONAL CATEGORIES

Once defined, how can researchers categorize peacekeeping operations? One useful method is to utilize generational periods. John Mackinlay and Jarat Chopra, in "Second Generation Multinational Operations" (1992), examined peacekeeping operations in terms of "first" and "second" generational missions. First Generation missions usually observed cease-fires between belligerents and were fielded sometime between 1956 and 1989. Second Generation operations emerged in 1989 and carried more elaborate mandates including election oversight, refugee assistance, disarmament, and other humanitarian tasks. If adopted as a means to categorize peacekeeping operations, this author would argue that a Third Generation of missions emerged after 1995 as the crises in Somalia, Rwanda, and the former Yugoslavia actually ended the optimistic Second Generation. The Third Generation represents a shift to Third World-dominated missions that are generally more cautiously deployed, at least by the UN.

Dividing peacekeeping missions into "first," "second," and even "third" generations does not solve every problem in the attempt to categorize peacekeeping operations as Mackinlay and Chopra indicate. How should one distinguish between the First Generation operations UNEF I and the United Nations Military Observer Group in India and Pakistan (UNMOGIP)? The United Nations Emergency Force I (UNEF I) was a large mission that physically separated Egypt and Israel through the establishment of a peacekeeper-manned neutral zone. UNMOGIP is a much smaller operation with a mission simply to observe and report violations of the cease-fire in the Kashmir region between India and Pakistan.

FUNCTION

Peacekeeping operations can also be categorized by their functions. Why were they mandated? Mackinlay and Chopra offer nine categories of peacekeeping operations in their study. While these can be useful, they can also be cumbersome as someone attempts to fit a peacekeeping mission into one of nine diverse categories. For ease in classification attempts, this author prefers to use three simplified categories: "observation," "interposition," and "law and order."

  Observation: Observation missions are mandated to oversee cease-fires between belligerents. The peacekeepers normally operate from both sides of the cease-fire line but have been known to only work from one side. Although they may patrol a neutral zone, the peacekeepers are not stationed within the area as a barrier between the opponents. UNMOGIP is a classic example of an observation force.
  Interposition: Barrier or interposition missions are peacekeeping operations mandated to physically enter a neutral zone between bel-

ligerents in order to form a "barrier" between them. One opponent can not attack the other without involving the neutral peacekeepers, thus helping to keep the peace while peace negotiations continue. UNEF I, the United Nations Emergency Force II (UNEF II), the United Nations Disengagement Observation Force (UNDOF), and the Multinational Force and Observer (MFO) operations are classic interposition missions.

Law and order: Law and order operations include more elaborate mandates asking the peacekeepers to go beyond observing a cease-fire or stationing themselves between armed opponents. These missions perform a variety of functions such as election oversight, disarmament, human rights, refugee and humanitarian assistance, and even monitoring the peacekeeping operations of other international organizations. The United Nations Transition Assistance Group (UNTAG) is an example of a law and order operation.

Some peacekeeping operations do not fit clearly into one of the three categories and seem to be mandated to function in multiple categories. For example, the placement of the United Nations Congo Operation (ONUC) into a single category can be challenging. In such cases, there are alternative ways to compare such missions.

MANDATING ORGANIZATION

Another method for categorizing peacekeeping operations is by comparing their mandating organizations. From where does the peacekeeping operation derive its legal basis for intervening in or between sovereign countries? The mandate provides this international legal authorization for military intervention in a conflict. Most peacekeeping operations have been mandated by the UN or some regional or subregional international organization. However, several internationally recognized peacekeeping missions have not been mandated by international organizations.

League of Nations

The League of Nations ultimately failed in its goal to preserve the peace following World War I. However, the organization did mandate and field several international military operations to oversee plebiscites in areas claimed by more than one state after the war. Although the majority of these operations were manned exclusively by the victorious Allied powers who controlled the league, two missions reflected a greater degree of neutrality. The first, the Vilna International Force, was mandated and planned in 1920 but never fielded due to a direct threat of Russia, which feared having Allied troops on its western border. One must remember that the Allied powers intervened in Russia during the late stages of the war and did not leave until 1920 (and afterwards, in the case of the Japanese). In 1935, the league mandated and fielded the Saar International Force. Although the Saar force is frequently not included in lists of multinational peacekeeping operations, it should be pointed out that its mandated mission would mirror many UN operations in recent postconflict areas.

United Nations

The United Nations has fielded more peacekeeping operations than all of the other international organizations combined despite the fact that the body prefers regional and subregional organizations to solve crises before they are referred to the global organization. As such, the world body tends to receive the vast majority of attention by researchers in the field of peacekeeping. In fact, when people think of "peacekeeping" they probably automatically equate the term with the UN.

Regional Organizations

Regional international organizations generally include members from a single continent or perhaps two continents. Examples of regional international organizations include the European Union (EU), Organization of African Unity (OAU) and its successor the African Union (AU), Organization of American States (OAS), the League of Arab States, and the North Atlantic Treaty Organization (NATO). Several regional international organizations have fielded peacekeeping operations or have assisted the operations of other organizations. Only one regional peacekeeping operation, the League of Arab States' Arab League Force in Kuwait, was fielded to separate two belligerent states in a classic barrier mission. All of the other regional operations deployed into civil war situations.

The League of Arab States deployed the first true regional peace-keeping operation after World War II with its Arab League Force in Kuwait in 1961. This was followed the next decade by the Symbolic Arab Security Force/Arab Deterrent Force in Lebanon. The OAU bowed to pressure and fielded two unsuccessful peacekeeping operations in Chad between 1980 and 1982. The next decade witnessed more successful small OAU observation missions. It is yet to be seen if the AU, the OAU's successor organization, will be able to return the continent to regionally mandated peacekeeping operations. NATO members, along with the Organization of Security and Cooperation in Europe (OSCE), have turned their attention to European peacekeeping in recent years following the end of the Cold War. The future will probably see larger and more elaborate European Union (EU) peace-keeping operations. The Commonwealth of Independent States (CIS) and the Organization of American States (OAS) have deployed military operations that many have declared to be peacekeeping. However, these operations tended to be dominated politically and militarily by a single state. The CIS has deployed two operations under its banner—each dominated by Russian political and military strategy. The OAS fielded the Inter-American Peace Force (IAPF) in the Dominican Republic. Although mandated by the OAS, the IAPF was also dominated by the United States.

There has been only one area noticeably without a regional international organization that has mandated a peacekeeping operation—Asia. This region lacks a single regional-level international organization. The largest comprehensive international organization in Asia is the Association of Southeast Asian Nations (ASEAN). Technically, ASEAN is a subregional organization since it concentrates on Southeast Asia and lacks membership from South and North Asia.

Subregional Organizations

Africa is the center of subregional international organization peace-keeping activities. A major reason for this was the reluctance of the regional organization, the OAU, to get involved in large peacekeeping operations following the failure of its multinational missions in Chad between 1980 and 1982. The Economic Community of West African States (ECOWAS) has deployed four peacekeeping operations in West Africa. However, two of these missions (Liberia and Sierra Leone) are often argued to be more in line with peace enforcement missions than true peacekeeping. The Southern African Development Community (SADC) mandated a South African-proposed peace operation in Lesotho. Many other African subregional international organizations have added peacekeeping protocols to their charters. However, they have not fielded peacekeeping operations . . . yet. It is also still to be seen whether the AU will be able to persuade African states to mandate and field peacekeeping operations under the regional banner. If so, subregional organization-mandated peacekeeping operations could be on the decline in Africa.

The Organization of East Caribbean States (OECS) represents small island states primarily located in the eastern Caribbean. The OECS mandated the invasion of Grenada as a multinational peacekeeping mission although it was actually overtly dominated by the United States, which is not a member of the organization.

State-Led Coalitions

Although most peacekeeping missions are mandated by international organizations, a number of multinational operations have been state-led coalitions of willing participants that are endorsed by the UN. The French intervention in Rwanda is a classic example of such missions. Western states displayed reluctance at deploying contingents with a re-mandated United Nations Assistance Mission in Rwanda (UNAMIR) after the massacres in Rwanda. In response, France offered to field a military force to safeguard refugee camps in the country. While not mandated by the UN, the French operation received an official endorsement by the Security Council giving the mission international legitimacy. France helped dispatch African contingents to the area as well and these units formed the nucleus of a new UNAMIR. France, again, repeated these procedures with its intervention in the Central African Republic. The United States-led Unified Task Force (UNTAF) in Somalia was another coalition of the willing as was the Australian-led mission to assist the UN in East Timor.

International Treaties

There are a small number of peacekeeping operations not mandated by international organizations nor formed as state-led coalitions under a UN endorsement. The Multinational Force and Observers (MFO) in the Sinai looks and acts like a traditional interposition peacekeeping mission. However, MFO is not mandated by an international organization but is the child of the United States. The basic mandate of the MFO was written into the Camp David peace treaty between Egypt and Israel. The three Australian and New Zealand-led peacekeeping operations in the South Pacific (Bougainville and Guadalcanal) were mandated by treaties negotiated with the conflict belligerents. Thus, each organization derives its international legitimacy from multilateral treaties.

Bilateral Arrangements

There is one final, unique, category of operations. These were mandated by bilateral agreements between the contingent providing states and the host country. Multinational Forces I (MNF I) and MNF II fit into this category. For example, MNF II consisted of contingents from the United States, France, Great Britain, and Italy. Each contingent providing state concluded a bilateral agreement with the Lebanese government permitting its troops to enter the country and occupy a specific zone or location. Although the four states nominally formed a single operation, legally they operated under bilateral agreements. The Russian peacekeeping mission in Georgia is technically a bilateral agreement between the two states.

PEACEKEEPING TRENDS

Many peacekeeping trends can be identified between 1948 and 2003. Several are listed here for review. This section does not present a complete collection of trends but rather a representative selection to help develop an understanding of multinational peacekeeping operations.

Change in Contingent Providers

Each generation of UN peacekeeping has been accompanied by a change in the main contingent providers. First Generation operations were dominated by the Nordic states (Norway, Sweden, and Denmark), South Asian countries (India, Pakistan, and later Bangladesh), and Western countries perceived as being neutral in most international relations (Ireland and Canada). The Cold War dominated this period of UN peacekeeping history. The Permanent Five (P5) members of the Security Council avoided participation in peacekeeping operations with limited exceptions including the United Kingdom in the United Nations Forces in Cyprus (UNFICYP), France in the United Nations Interim Force in Lebanon (UNIFIL), and the United States in the United Nations Truce Supervision Organization (UNTSO). Involvement of P5 states could taint a perception of neutrality for the peacekeeping operation.

The thawing of the Cold War led to the introduction of the P5 members of the Security Council to UN peacekeeping during the Second Generation. In fact, the P5 states of France, the United Kingdom, and the United States represented three of the top seven contingent providers to UN operations toward the end of the Second Generation. Russia provided only limited resources to UN peacekeeping after 1989 and concentrated its efforts within CIS and bilateral peacekeeping among the states of the former Soviet Union. The People's Republic of China has yet to become a significant player in UN peacekeeping. The Chinese have provided a limited number of observers to UN operations and do keep promising to become more involved in future peacekeeping missions.

The transformation of UN peacekeeping to the Third Generation included another shift in participants. The P5 states turned their focus to non-UN operations, especially those mandated by the North Atlantic Treaty Organization (NATO). The largest participants in UN Third Generation operations are South Asian and African states. The six largest contributors to UN operations are from these two regions. The P5 are not the only states to withdraw the majority of their support from UN peacekeeping operations in the Third Generation. Ireland, a major contributor during UN First Generation missions, now maintains only a small number of personnel with UN peacekeeping operations but provides more support to NATO-mandated missions and the European Union (EU). The following chart illustrates the transition of contingent providers from the Second to Third Generation UN peacekeeping operations.

December 1993 (Second Generation)

Country	Number of Peacekeepers Provided to the UN
France	6,370
India	5,904
Pakistan	5,089
Bangladesh	3,451
Italy	3,434
United Kingdom	2,765
United States	2,622
Egypt	2,200
Canada	2,088
Nepal	1,992

April 2003 (Third Generation)

Country	Number of Peacekeepers Provided to the UN
Pakistan	4,245
Nigeria	3,316
India	2,735
Bangladesh	2,658
Ghana	2,060
Kenya	1,806
Uruguay	1,690
Jordan	1,611
Ukraine	1,046
Nepal	921

(Source: United Nations, April 2003)

Increase in the Number of Peacekeeping Operations

The number of peacekeeping operations has grown at a tremendous rate since 1988. Between 1948 and 1988, the UN mandated 15 peace-keeping operations (average of one mission every three years). This number mushroomed to 39 missions between 1989 and 2002 (average of three missions every year). The end of the Cold War is one reason for the growth of peacekeeping operations since 1988. Missions can now be fielded in areas that were considered "off limits" to outside inter-vention in the Cold War. For example, during the early years of the An-golan civil war, Mozambican civil war, and Ethiopian-Somali conflict, the superpowers were more concerned with assisting their proxies and proteges than bringing true peace, assisted by a peacekeeping operation, to the region. Nearly every regional and subregional peacekeeping operation has been fielded after 1988 for similar reasons.

Increase in the Number of Participants in Each Peacekeeping Operation

Before 1989, most UN peacekeeping operations included contingents from a small number of states. For example, the initial fielding of UNEF I consisted of personnel from 11 states, the United Nations Force in Cyprus (UNFICYP) initially included peacekeepers from ten countries, and the United Nations India-Pakistan Observation Mission (UNIPOM) was formed with peacekeepers dispatched by ten members. Most Second and Third Generation missions have many more contingents, although the individual contingents are often smaller in size. UNTAG consisted of peacekeepers from 51 countries, the United Nations Angola Verification Mission III (UNAVEM III) included personnel from 39 states, and the UNOSOM II numbered 35 UN member states within its ranks.

Shift to Regional and Subregional Organizations

Although the UN mandates more peacekeeping operations than all other international organizations combined, there has been a noticeable increase in regional and subregional missions with UN encouragement. If one counts the OECS mandated military intervention in Grenada and the OAS mandated military intervention in the Dominican Republic, there have been six peacekeeping operations mandated by regional or subregional international organizations during the 40-year period between 1948 and 1988. In the 11-year period between 1989 and 2002, there has been a minimum of seven peacekeeping missions mandated by this group of organizations. This trend is likely to continue.

Shift from Interstate to Intrastate Conflict

During the First Generation of UN peacekeeping, the organization tended to deploy operations in support of attempts to resolve interstate conflict (wars between two or more sovereign states). This trend changed as the Second Generation of peacekeeping emerged in 1989.

Intrastate conflicts (war/rebellion within a single sovereign state) became the main focus of peacekeeping missions. This new trend continued into the Third Generation. During the First Generation (1948–1988), the UN fielded peacekeeping operations after ten interstate conflicts and five intrastate conflicts. The Second and Third Generations (1989–2003) have witnessed three UN peacekeeping operations after interstate conflicts and 39 missions during intrastate conflicts. One reason for this reversal is an increase in global intrastate conflict. A second and related reason results from the end of the Cold War.

Integrated Peacekeeping Units

Many states have shown reluctance in recent years to become involved in peacekeeping operations due to the problems experienced in Rwanda, Somalia, the former Yugoslavia, and Sierra Leone. A solution has been to field smaller units that are integrated with those of other countries to form composite formations. The Nordic states led the way with their innovative integrated units dating back to the First Generation of UN peacekeeping. The Czech Republic and Slovakia have fielded a unit comprising a contingent from each state. The Irish integrated their company in the United Nations Mission in Ethiopia-Eritrea with the Netherlands. Western states offering to participate in UN peacekeeping operations but not wanting to field battalion sized units have been urged to combine their contingents. This trend is likely to continue and become more popular.

Phased Deployments

Reaction to the failure of belligerents to adhere to cease-fires in Somalia, Rwanda, the former Yugoslavia, and Sierra Leone led to the development of a new deployment strategy for UN peacekeeping operations in the Third Generation. Instead of fielding all of the assigned contingents at the same time, the UN now utilizes a phased deployment schedule in many of its mandates. The belligerents have to demonstrate their seriousness in accepting the cease-fire and negotiation requirements (such as disarmament or troop withdrawals) throughout a series of stages. As the belligerents demonstrate their commitment to the peace process, UN peacekeepers deploy to help stabilize the situation. For example, the deployments of peacekeepers with the United Nations Mission in Ethiopia and Eritrea (UNMEE) and United Nations Observer Mission in the Democratic Republic of the Congo (MONUC) were based on three phases beginning with UN liaisons in each belligerent's capital. As the belligerents in each conflict demonstrated serious commitment to the peace process, the UN increased the number of peacekeepers and provided them with more comprehensive mandates.

Increase in Single State-Led Coalitions

There has been a small but noticeable increase in single state-led coalitions with the endorsement of international organizations in lieu of peacekeeping operations mandated by the same organizations. This occurs when the member states of the organization demonstrate reluctance to mandate and field a peacekeeping operation into a potentially dangerous conflict. However, a single member may have particular interests in the conflict and be willing to militarily intervene. The international organization then endorses the operation providing it with international legitimacy. What would have once been seen as a unilateral military intervention then becomes an internationally sanctioned peace operation. France has launched such operations in Rwanda and the Central African Republic; the United States in Somalia; Australia in East Timor; the United Kingdom in Sierra Leone; and South Africa in Burundi.

PEACEKEEPING ISSUES

Many issues have divided peacekeeping contingent providers, international organizations, or academic scholars over the years. A few are provided here for consideration.

Third World Demand for Increased Western Participation

Western aversion to peacekeeping operations on the African continent emerged following the problematic UN missions in Somalia and

Rwanda. Western peacekeepers were the targets of one or more factions in both operations despite their humanitarian mandate. Peacekeepers assigned to UNOSOM I faced kidnapping and sniper attacks prompting an armed intervention by American and allied forces under the UNITAF banner. The Rwanda crisis of 1994–1995 proved to be as troublesome for the UN as its peacekeepers, small in number and citing their mandate, did not intervene to prevent massacres throughout the country. Western states turned away from participating in UN operations as a result of these problems. A frustrated Secretary-General Kofi Annan referred to the American and European reluctance to participate in a renewed UNAMIR II as "the post-Somalia syndrome." Many Third World states have criticized the West for its willingness to commit Third World soldiers to conflict areas but not their own, which are reserved for NATO or EU missions within Europe.

Financing

Most UN peacekeeping operations are financed by all organizational members based on a scale. This system has led to considerable controversy over the years. The United States has complained that it pays an unfair share of the financial burden while economically strong states such as Saudi Arabia are still included in lower brackets and paying a much smaller percentage of operational costs. At various times the United States has withheld its payments to the UN. The United States has also criticized the organization in the past for not counting American airlift resources toward its financial contributions to peacekeeping operations. The refusal of major states, including the Soviet Union and France, to pay for controversial operations such as ONUC nearly collapsed the UN during the "Article 19 Crisis." The UN has paid for a limited number of operations via its regular budget. In other words the peacekeeping mission is added to the budget in a similar fashion as regular needs for daily operation. The United Nations Peacekeeping Force in Cyprus (UNFICYP) has been paid by voluntary contributions in the past and ONUC was partially paid with bond sales.

Many regional and subregional international organizations face similar financial problems. The OAU failed to persuade its members to deliver on promised financial support to cover the costs of its peacekeeping mission in Chad leaving the contingent providers to pay their own expenses and request assistance from Western states. Western states helped pay for the ECOMOG mission in Liberia and Sierra Leone. One should note that outside financial resources in peacekeeping operations often ride on the coattails of outside political influence. As an African scholar pointed out to the author as regards OAU peacekeeping, "He who pays the piper calls the tunes."

Casualties

Casualties have been an issue of contention in many UN and regional/subregional peacekeeping operations. Peacekeeping has proven to be a dangerous endeavor. Anytime a soldier steps between two or more belligerents, a life is placed on the line. As of April 2003, 1,817 UN personnel have lost their lives while assigned to peacekeeping operations. Approximately 300 UN peacekeepers died between the release of the first edition of this book and the completion of the second edition. Many of these deaths are the results of accidents but many more died at the hands of the belligerents they intended to separate and aid as part of a peace process. The total number of deaths in operations such as those fielded by the ECOWAS and the CIS may never be known due to the desire of contingent-providing states to maintain the wrap of secrecy around casualty figures. The author arrived in Nigeria in 1991 to research the issues behind Nigeria's participation in the ECOMOG mission in Liberia. An interesting media battle developed between the relatively free Nigerian press and the authoritarian government over casualty figures. While it was later proven that the press estimates were inflated and the government figures underreported, the intense fight demonstrated the political sensitivity of governments about casualty figures. This debate renewed itself in 2002 when a former Nigerian ECOMOG commander claimed to have secretly buried hundreds of Nigerian casualties from Liberia.

The most dangerous UN peacekeeping operation was ONUC. However, as of April 2003, UNIFIL had suffered only four fewer fatalities than ONUC. Unfortunately, UNIFIL is still an active peacekeeping mission and there is a very good chance it will surpass ONUC as the most costly UN peacekeeping operation in terms of human lives lost. The five highest casualty figures for UN operations, as of April 2003, are listed in the table on the next page:

Operation	Fatalities
United Nations Operation in the Congo (ONUC)	250
United Nations Interim Force in Lebanon (UNIFIL)	246
United Nations Protection Force (UNPROFOR)	211
United Nations Force in Cyprus (UNFICYP)	170
United Nations Operation in Somalia II (UNOSOM II)	151

(Source: United Nations, April 2003)

Third World Resources

The withdrawal of Western states from deployment with UN peace-keeping missions in the Third World has placed a greater burden on Third World states to provide their own contingents. For example, African states are willing to participate in UN peacekeeping operations within their own continent. In fact, 90 percent of the over 9,600 African peacekeepers in UN missions are assigned to operations on the African continent. However, African states often lack the resources required for peacekeeping and the UN is financially strapped to meet all of its requirements. Western aid often arrives reluctantly and slowly. Despite the American African Crisis Response Initiative (ACRI) and French Renforcement des Capacités Africaines de Maintien de la Paix (RECAMP) training programs for African states, many contingent providers firmly believe that the West is not providing enough support for their contingents in UN operations. They view the West as being ready to commit Third World soldiers to conflicts where they do not want to venture. But the Third World soldiers are sent without the equipment they require to be successful. On the other hand Western states have complained that Third World countries often dispatch their contingents without any equipment including items readily available in their home states. There have been many cases of Third World contingents arriving with nothing more than the clothes on their backs and asking for the UN to provide everything for them including weapons and underwear.

The Role of International Organization Member States

Who organizes multinational peacekeeping operations? While we tend to look to the international organizations that mandate them, these organizations do not have a life of their own. Decisions within international organizations are the products of the collective membership. A UN peacekeeping operation is mandated because the majority of the Security Council approved it, without a veto by one of the P5. (There have been at least three exceptions to this rule utilizing the General Assembly under the Uniting for Peace Resolution.) This is how the UN can remandate UNAMIR in Rwanda yet months tick by and Rwandan deaths continue before UN member states agree to provide contingents. Although paying for UN peacekeeping operations is theoretically mandatory, contributing contingents to the missions is totally voluntary. SADC mandated a peacekeeping operation in Lesotho because a majority of its members backed the South African proposal. However, SADC did not mandate an operation in the Democratic Republic of the Congo when a majority of the members narrowly defeated a proposal from Zimbabwe.

What Was the First Peacekeeping Operation?

Canadian Lester Pearson received the 1956 Nobel Peace Prize for his concept of a neutral barrier force to separate the Israelis and Egyptians after the 1956 Suez War. Many writers point to this mission, UNEF I, as the birth of peacekeeping. If this is the case, how should we describe the planned League of Nations operation in Vilna (1920), the League mission deployed to the Saar (1935), UNTSO (1948), and UNMOGIP (1949)? The latter two peacekeeping operations are still in place. Some writers have implied that the international units fielded by the Concert of Europe in the 19th century were forms of peacekeeping! It is not the purpose of this book to enter this controversial debate. However, this book does recognize the League of Nations missions as legitimate peacekeeping operations with the understanding that some scholars will not agree with this point. Readers are encouraged to make their own decisions after reviewing the cases.

FACTORS FOR SUCCESS

Many scholars have offered factors for success for peacekeeping operations. Several factors considered essential by this author are listed below:

Effective Cease-Fire and Acceptance by the Belligerents

Perhaps the greatest problem faced by peacekeepers is the refusal of belligerents to honor cease-fire agreements and peace negotiations. The UN's most troublesome peacekeeping operations in Africa, including the Congo, Somalia, Rwanda, and Sierra Leone, have faced breakdowns in cease-fires resulting in the deaths of UN peacekeepers and civilians. The collapse in the Congo faced by ONUC resulted in the withdrawal of UN peacekeeping from Africa for a 25-year period. The failure of belligerents to adhere to cease-fires in Somalia and Rwanda abruptly ended the post-UNTAG Second Generation of UN peacekeeping and initiated a Third Generation.

The effectiveness of peacekeeping is in correlation with the acceptance of the belligerents to the peace process. In cases where all of the belligerents genuinely accepted the peace process and deployment of peacekeepers, the peacekeeping missions have been very successful. UNTAG, possibly the most successful UN peacekeeping operation ever fielded, benefited immensely from the cooperation of the belligerents. The UN observer mission in the Aouzou Strip between Chad and Libya needed only 15 personnel to fulfill its mandate and withdraw on schedule thanks to the cooperation of the belligerents.

When the belligerents refused to adhere to negotiated cease-fires, peacekeepers have frequently found themselves targets or watching helplessly as civilians were murdered. Somalia, Rwanda, and Sierra Leone emerged as three of the most controversial peacekeeping operations fielded by the UN after belligerents turned on the peacekeepers. Peacekeepers have three options when this situation occurs. First, they can simply stand aside or withdraw as in Rwanda. Second, member states can field a relief mission, normally with UN blessing but separate from the peacekeeping mission. Two examples include the British paratroopers rushing to aid United Nations Assistance Mission in Sierra Leone (UNAMSIL) peacekeepers and the American intervention in Somalia on behalf of UNOSOM I. Third, the UN peacekeepers can convert their mission to one of peace enforcement as with ONUC.

Neutrality

Peacekeepers must remain neutral in the conflict. If any of the belligerents perceive the peacekeepers as favoring the other party, the impartiality of the peacekeepers is destroyed and their mission in jeopardy. India perceived the United States as favoring Pakistan in their conflict. In response, the Indian government ordered the United States to remove its peacekeepers from UNMOGIP. As a result of the neutrality issue, Sweden, Ireland, India, and Pakistan emerged as major contingent contributors during the First Generation of UN peacekeeping since they were viewed as politically neutral in conflicts across the Cold War dominated globe. Peacekeepers in ONUC lost their impartiality as a result of turning to assist the Congolese government against rebellious provinces. However, despite provocations from both sides, the OAU peacekeepers in Chad surprisingly remained highly neutral while fielded. The Chadian government expressed frustration with the OAU's neutrality and refusal to help fight the rebels. At the same time, the rebels counted on the OAU's neutrality to stabilize the southern front while they turned their forces against the government in the northern area of the country.

Mandate

A mandate provides three important items for a peacekeeping operation. First, it declares the basis for the international legitimacy of what is essentially a military intervention. Second, it states the mission of the peacekeeping operation. These mission statements can be very clear and to the point allowing the Force Commander to successfully interpret his mission and organize his operations. However, some are vague and leave too much room for interpretation. This type of mandate is often written to satisfy arguing belligerents who refuse to agree on the details of a peacekeeping mission. The international organization provides a vague statement of purpose allowing each belligerent independent interpretation of the mission. This, in turn, leads to trouble on the ground as a Force Commander is not sure what he should do. An action acceptable to one belligerent is perceived as a violation of neutrality by another. UNPROFOR in Bosnia and Herzegovina regularly faced these problems. Also, the mandated mission can be too restrictive and demand exact compliance by the Force Commander. Such mandates tie the hands of the Force Commander. UNAMIR contingents argued that their mandate did not include a mission to prevent mass acts of violence in Rwanda. Third, the mandate should provide an exit strategy. The peacekeepers are withdrawn when certain events occur or a time frame is completed. For example, peacekeepers could be withdrawn after the completion of national elections or belligerents are disarmed or they may be in the country for a specific period of time such as one year. Examples of peacekeeping mandates are included with the appendices of this book.

Status of Forces Agreement

Status of forces agreements are usually negotiated between the mandating international organization and the host country before a peacekeeping operation is fielded. The agreements provide the legal provisions concerning the soldiers assigned to the peacekeeping operation. The documents include issues such as mail, identification of peacekeepers, international transit, importation of supplies, evacuation of casualties and fatalities, application of local laws to the peacekeepers, and many other provisions. In one unique case, the UN did not negotiate a status of forces agreement with Egypt for UNEF II but rather utilized the UNEF I agreement. These agreements are important for all peacekeeping missions. Without them, the mandating international organization leaves the peacekeepers subject to local laws and potential problems with local officials in the host state.

Rules of Engagement

Rules of engagement provide peacekeepers with their guidelines on when/when not to use force and how much force can be utilized in a given situation. Theoretically, peacekeepers should not have to use force but we live in an imperfect world. Rules of engagement must be clear and permit peacekeepers the range of actions required for the particular situation. Too liberal rules of engagement can result in the loss of peacekeeper neutrality while too restrictive rules can prevent the peacekeepers from providing required protection for themselves or others. Generally, rules of engagement always permit self-defense. However, controversy often erupts when the rules of engagement are vague as regards the protection of others. Some UNAMIR contingents argued that their rules of engagement did not permit the physical protection of Rwandan civilians during the outbreak of genocide in that country.

Intelligence

Peacekeepers require solid intelligence on the conflict and belligerents when they deploy to an area. For example, in intrastate conflict situations, the peacekeepers need information on all of the belligerents, their leaders, and intentions. Western states often have the best intelligence gathering assets. Some Third World states have complained that their peacekeepers are not provided the information collected by Western states in the host state. One example of this problem occurred in Sierra Leone when arriving UN contingents stated that Western states were reluctant to share their intelligence on the rebel forces in the field.

CAN PEACEKEEPING MAKE A DIFFERENCE?

Many peacekeeping missions seem to have been fairly successful while many have tragically collapsed and failed leading to considerable controversy and criticism. Can peacekeeping missions make a difference and are they worth their costs?

Peacekeeping Can Save Lives

The presence of peacekeepers has prevented violence against individual civilians during missions. For example, despite the problems faced by the UN contingents in Rwanda, there are documented cases of peacekeepers saving the lives of Rwandan civilians. Despite criticism against their governments, many Belgian and Senegalese peacekeepers heroically protected Rwandan civilians under their immediate care until given direct orders to abandon them to their fate.

Peacekeeping Can Stabilize a Crisis

The presence of peacekeepers can be instrumental in stabilizing a crisis. The introduction of UN observer missions in Liberia, Central African Republic, and Sierra Leone were instrumental in providing stability during the withdrawal of African-mandated operations following negotiations with the belligerents. UN peacekeepers also provide a "face saving" service when they are utilized in conjunction with a neutral zone to separate two warring states as classically demonstrated by the UNEF II. The mere presence of neutral peacekeepers offers a symbolic barrier between the armed belligerents that should not be crossed.

Peacekeeping Can Prevent the Spread of Conflict to Neighboring States

The presence of peacekeepers has played a factor in preventing the spread of conflict to neighboring states although this can be difficult to prove if successful. The United Nations Observer Mission in Uganda and Rwanda (UNOMUR) watched the border between the two states to prevent the smuggling of weapons into Rwanda. Although Rwanda would later erupt into a situation of genocide, UNOMUR did help slow the cross border flow of weapons while it was deployed. MONUC is an attempt to bring order to a conflict that has involved many Central African states and has threatened to spread to Angola and Burundi and other countries.

The Dictionary

– A –

ABIN, MAJOR-GENERAL RAIS. Abin, a native of Indonesia, served as the **Force Commander** of the **United Nations Emergency Force II** (UNEF II) between December 1976 and the operation's successful termination in September 1979. Abin was the only non-Scandinavian Force Commander of UNEF II.

ACHESON PLAN. *See* UNITING FOR PEACE RESOLUTION.

ACLAND, MAJOR-GENERAL J. H. B. Acland, a British officer, commanded the **Commonwealth Monitoring Force in Zimbabwe**. In his position, he also served as the chair of the **Commonwealth Ceasefire Commission** that oversaw the peace and disarmament process. Acland assumed the difficult role of "neutral middleman" as the Patriotic Front soldiers left the bush and entered camps organized by the Commonwealth Force. His job included protecting Patriotic Front soldiers from possible retribution by white Rhodesians as well as ensuring that the former entered the **Rendezvous Points** and **Assembly Points** peacefully.

ADVISORY COMMITTEE. The **United Nations** (UN) Security Council established the Advisory Committee in November 1956 to assist Secretary-General **Dag Hammarskjöld** with the development of the **United Nations Emergency Force I** (UNEF I) deployed to the Middle East. The committee consisted of Brazil, Canada, Sri Lanka, Colombia, India, Norway, and Pakistan. Canada was an important player in the group since it was **Lester Pearson**, a Canadian, who developed the idea for UNEF I, which became the first **interposition**

1

force deployed by the UN. The Secretary-General served as the chairman of the committee. The committee handled issues such as the regulations behind UNEF I's operations, the rules of engagement, and the issuing of medals. Minutes of the committee's proceedings were maintained but considered confidential. The Security Council granted the committee the authority to convene the General Assembly. *See also* COMMITTEE OF THREE; UNITING FOR PEACE RESOLUTION.

AFGHANISTAN. *See* INTERNATIONAL SECURITY ASSISTANCE FORCE; UNITED NATIONS GOOD OFFICES IN AFGHANISTAN AND PAKISTAN.

AFRICAN CRISIS RESPONSE INITIATIVE (ACRI). In November 1995, the **United Nations** (UN) called for the international community to place a greater emphasis on solving crisis situations before they had to be debated by the global organization. At the same time, the Western powers were searching for alternatives to sending their peacekeepers into explosive situations such as **Somalia** and **Rwanda**. The **United States** developed the African Crisis Response Initiative (ACRI) as a means of training African military units for the rigors of peace operations on the African continent. ACRI was first proposed in September 1996 and the training of the first African battalion under the program commenced in 1997. Small teams of special forces soldiers have conducted training for troops in Benin, **Côte d'Ivoire**, Ghana, Kenya, Malawi, Mali, **Nigeria**, Senegal, and Uganda. ACRI is a type of **standby force** arrangement involving African contingents with Western equipment and financial backing. *See also* RENFORCEMENT DES CAPACITES AFRICAINES DE MAINTIEN DE LA PAIX.

AFRICAN MISSION IN BURUNDI (AMIB). **South Africa** dispatched a unilateral peacekeeping mission to **Burundi** in 2001 in an effort to support the peace efforts in that state. Following the signing of a power sharing agreement in the state, Ethiopia and Mozambique agreed to join South African forces in the formation of a new 3,500-man peacekeeping operation known as the African Mission in Burundi (AMIB). South African troops in Burundi were joined by the first small detachment of peacekeepers from Mozambique on April 9, 2003. The initial Ethiopian detachment arrived on May 19, 2003. Ethiopia and Mozambique, citing funding difficulties and logistical problems, have not increased their contingents to the sizes originally pledged. The **African Union** (AU) fielded the 35-man **AU Cease-fire Observer Mission in Burundi** to assist with the cease-fire observance.

AFRICAN STANDBY FORCE. The **African Union** (AU) proposed the establishment in 2002 of an African Standby Force. The body of troops would be a type of **Rapid Reaction Force** of African states. The AU would mandate a peacekeeping operation and call upon member states to deploy military units in support of the mission. Units designated as part of the African Standby Force would be earmarked for short notice deployments with the AU. *See also* EUROPEAN UNION RAPID REACTION FORCE; NORTH ATLANTIC TREATY ORGANIZATION RAPID REACTION FORCE; UNITED NATIONS STAND BY ARRANGEMENT SYSTEM.

AFRICAN UNION (AU). The **Organization of African Unity** (OAU) was transformed into the African Union (AU) in July 2002. The AU Constitutive Act reserves the right of the organization to "intervene in a member state pursuant to a decision of the Assembly in respect of grave circumstances, namely: war crimes, genocide, and other crimes against humanity." In other words, the act authorizes the AU to militarily intervene in situations such as the genocide in **Rwanda** even if the host government refuses permission for the deployment. The organization has proposed the establishment of an **African Standby Force** for peacekeeping operations under an AU mandate. In early 2003, the AU mandated its first peacekeeping operation, a small observer mission known as the **African Union Cease-fire Observer Mission in Burundi**. It is yet to be seen if the AU will be any more effective than the OAU at mandating, fielding, and sustaining peacekeeping operations on the continent or if the lead will remain with subregional organizations such as the **Economic Community of West African States** (ECOWAS) and the **Southern African Development Community** (SADC).

AFRICAN UNION (AU) CEASE-FIRE OBSERVER MISSION IN BURUNDI. A **South African** unilateral peacekeeping force arrived in **Burundi** in 2001 to oversee the peace process in that country. Following a breakdown of the existing cease-fire, a new agreement was signed by the government and the rebel factions in December 2002. The new peace process resulted in the mandating of two peacekeeping operations in the country. The first is an expansion of the original South African mission with the addition of peacekeepers from Ethiopia and Mozambique. This new group is known as the **African Mission in Burundi** (AMIB). The second is a small 35-man **African Union** (AU) force known as the AU Cease-fire Observer Mission in Burundi. While South Africa, Ethiopia, and Mozambique provide the majority of the peacekeeper personnel in the country for security duties, the separate AU mission is mandated to observe the maintenance of the cease-fire in the country. The AU observers are from Burkina Faso, Gabon, Togo, and Tunisia and began arriving in Burundi on February 12, 2003. The operation is funded by the **European Union** (EU).

AGGRAVATED PEACEKEEPING. The **United States** Department of Defense adopted this term for **peacekeeping** operations deployed in areas where the neutral forces may be required to use force to carry out their mandate. The Department of Defense defined the term as "Military operations undertaken with the nominal consent of all major belligerent parties, but which are complicated by subsequent intransigence of one or more of the belligerents, poor command and control of belligerent forces, or conditions of outlawry, banditry, or anarchy. In such conditions, peacekeeping forces are normally authorized to use force in self-defense, and in defense of the missions they are assigned, which may include monitoring and facilitating implementation of an existing truce agreement in support of diplomatic efforts to reach a political settlement, or supporting or safeguarding humanitarian relief efforts." *See also* TRADITIONAL PEACE-KEEPING.

AGREEMENT ON DISENGAGEMENT BETWEEN ISRAELI AND SYRIAN FORCES. This document, signed in May 1974, provided for the disengagement of Syrian and **Israeli** forces after the

1973 Yom Kippur War. The Protocol of this agreement called for the deployment of a neutral peacekeeping operation to separate the belligerents and oversee the disengagement process. This operation became known as the **United Nations Disengagement Observer Force** (UNDOF). **Lieutenant-General Ensio P. H. Siilasvuo,** the **Force Commander** of the **United Nations Emergency Force II** (UNEF II) in the Sinai, witnessed and signed the document on behalf of the **United Nations** (UN).

AHTISAARI, MARTTI. Ahtisaari, a native of Finland, filled the position of **Special Representative** during the long negotiations for Namibian independence and the operations of the **United Nations Transition Assistance Group** (UNTAG) between July 1978 and March 1990. Following Namibian independence, Ahtisaari became the Undersecretary for Administration and Management. In this position he exercised considerable influence during the development of the leadership structure for the **United Nations Mission for the Referendum in Western Sahara** (MINURSO). Because of his frustration with a military deputy while in Namibia, Ahtisaari recommended that the **United Nations** alter the leadership structure being established for the Western Sahara. Due to the personal intervention of Ahtisaari and the opposition of the Secretariat, the organization accepted a plan with one Under Secretary General and two Assistant Secretaries General. One of the latter would be a civilian position titled the Deputy Special Representative and the other a military position known as the **Force Commander**.

AIDID, MOHAMMED FARAH. Aidid, a Soviet-trained general in the Somali army and leader of the Haber Gedir sub-clan, ousted President Siad Barre in 1991. Aidid is noted for his opposition to the **United Nations Operation in Somalia I** (UNOSOM I) and **United Nations Operation in Somalia II** (UNOSOM II). When forces loyal to Aidid ambushed a **United Nations** (UN) patrol in Mogadishu, killing 24 Pakistani soldiers, the organization placed a bounty on his head and ordered his arrest. Continuing confrontation between the UN troops, especially **United States** units, and Aidid led to a series of bloody clashes resulting in Washington re-examining its objectives in the peacekeeping operation.

AKASHI, YASUSHI. Akashi, a native of **Japan**, served as the Secretary General's **Special Representative** of the **United Nations Transitional Authority in Cambodia** (UNTAC). The **United Nations** (UN) has been accused of selecting Akashi as a means of ensuring Japanese monetary contributions to the operation. Akashi arrived in Cambodia on March 17, 1992. Prior to his selection to head the peacekeeping mission in Cambodia, Akashi was the UN Under Secretary-General for Disarmament Affairs. Akashi often criticized his country for not participating in UN peacekeeping operations. However, as the UN Special Representative in Cambodia, Akashi had to defend his countrymen in their first peacekeeping mission. Japanese soldiers were accused of deserting their posts during hostile conditions and four were even reported to have taken their vehicles and driven to Thailand where they showed up at the Japanese embassy in Bangkok. Other contingents also questioned the lavish facilities the Japanese government built for their soldiers in Cambodia. Akashi referred to the incidents as "teething experiences." Following the assignment in Cambodia, the Secretary-General named Akashi as the Special Representative with the **United Nations Protection Force** (UNPROFOR) and then the follow-on **United Nations Peace Forces** (UNPF). In this capacity, Akashi has been in the shadow of the military commanders in Bosnia and Herzegovina who tended to criticize the UN and Secretary-General **Boutros Boutros-Ghali** for the shortcomings of the mission. In his position as Special Representative, Akashi had to be in agreement with the military commander before the Secretary-General would authorize air strikes in support of the peacekeepers by aircraft of the **North Atlantic Treaty Organization** (NATO).

ALBANIA. *See* MULTINATIONAL PROTECTION FORCE.

AMSTERDAM TREATY. European Union (EU) members enacted the Amsterdam Treaty on May 1, 1999. The document applied the **Petersberg Missions** of the **West European Union** (WEU) to the EU. The latter organization utilized this new mandate for crisis management, including peacekeeping, and to develop plans for the **European Union Rapid Reaction Force**. Title V of the treaty lists the provisions of a common foreign and security policy for the EU. The EU assumed the Petersberg Missions in Article 17 of Title V. The opening of Article 17 reads:

1. The common foreign and security policy shall include all questions relating to the security of the [European] Union, including the progressive framing of a common defence policy, in accordance with the second subparagraph, which might lead to a common defence, should the European Council so decide. It shall in that case recommend to the Member States that adoption of such a decision in accordance with their respective constitutional requirements. The Western European Union (WEU) is an integral part of the development of the [European] Union providing the [European] Union with access to an operational capability notably in the context of paragraph 2. It supports the Union in framing the defence aspects of the common foreign and security policy as set out in this Article. The Union shall accordingly foster closer institutional relations with the WEU with a view to the possibility of the integration of the WEU into the Union, should the European Council so decide. . . .

2. Questions referred to in this Article shall include humanitarian and rescue tasks, peacekeeping tasks, and tasks of combat forces in crisis management in the field of armaments.

3. The [European] Union will avail itself of the WEU to elaborate and implement decisions and actions which have defence implication.

"AN AGENDA FOR PEACE." The **United Nations** (UN) Security Council requested Secretary-General **Boutros Boutros-Ghali**, on January 31, 1992, to prepare this document as a report to the Security Council not later than July 1, 1992. The name "An Agenda for Peace" derives from the title of Section X of the document. The document recommended numerous changes to UN peacekeeping operations. The Secretary-General called for the following:

1. The establishment of peacekeepers for "**preventive deployment**" to areas prior to the outbreak of hostilities.
2. The use of **demilitarized zones** (DMZ) in the "preventive deployment" of peacekeepers.
3. The establishment of a new category of peacekeeping force to be known as "**peace enforcement**" operations.

4. The establishment of a **standing army** for the United Nations.
5. The setting up of a $50 million revolving peacekeeping reserve fund.
6. Improved training, especially language enhancement, for peacekeeping personnel.
7. Pre-positioning of basic peacekeeping equipment.

ANGOLA. *See* UNITED NATONS ANGOLA VERIFICATION MISSION I; UNITED NATONS ANGOLA VERIFICATION MISSION II; UNITED NATONS ANGOLA VERIFICATION MISSION III; UNITED NATIONS OBSERVER MISSION ANGOLA.

ANNAN, KOFI. Annan, a native of Ghana, served as the **United Nations** (UN) Assistant Secretary General for Peacekeeping from February 1992 to December 1993 and Undersecretary General for Peacekeeping from March 1993 to December 1996. Annan was a vocal advocate of maintaining an American presence in the **United Nations Operation in Somalia I** (UNOSOM I). He oversaw the attempt to make a major overhaul of how the UN coordinates peacekeeping operations and was an avid supporter of the calls for the establishment of a **standby force**. Annan has openly criticized states, especially the **United States**, for their failure to pay peacekeeping dues to the UN. He has been quoted as reminding states that peacekeeping is "cheaper than war." He has served as Secretary General of the UN since January 1997.

ANTICIPATORY PEACEMAKING. *See* PREVENTIVE DEPLOYMENT.

ARAB DETERRENT FORCE (ADF). In October 1976, the **Symbolic Arab Security Force** faced difficulties in **Lebanon**. The civil war had intensified, the Syrian army was on the offensive, and the Arab force was too small and lacked the **mandate** to contain the spread of hostilities. In response, Saudi Arabia called Syria, Kuwait, Egypt, Lebanon, and the Palestinian Liberation Organization (PLO) to a meeting in Riyadh during October 1976. The six parties agreed at the **Riyadh Summit Conference** to transform the Arab force into a larger peacekeeping organization with more authority to act in countering hostilities. The resulting **Riyadh Resolution** was accepted by the **League of Arab States** at the **Cairo Summit Conference** held during the same month. The states elected to increase the size of the mission to 30,000 soldiers, with the majority being Syrian. The new Arab Deterrent Force would oversee a cease-fire in Lebanon, disengage the belligerents, and deter any violation of the former two points. The Lebanese President became the overall commander of the multinational operation and he selected the military commander.

On November 5, 1976, President Ilyas Sarkis selected Colonel Ahmed al-Hajj, a Lebanese officer, as the first commander of the league's peacekeeping mission. President Sarkis also determined the size of each participating contingent. Over the objections of the PLO, he requested the Syrians to contribute 25,000 soldiers to the force. Egypt refused to participate and Syria vetoed a contingent from the PLO. Libyan (700 soldiers), Saudi Arabian (1,200 soldiers), and Sudanese (1,000 soldiers) units assigned to the Symbolic Arab Security Force were incorporated into the new operation. The United Arab Emirates (UAE) provided 1,000 soldiers and South Yemen fielded 700 troops.

Units of the Arab Deterrent Force, led by Syrian soldiers, deployed across Lebanon in an attempt to curb hostilities. They were prevented from entering southern Lebanon due to the presence of Israeli military units and eastern Beirut by Christian forces. The ADF could not move south of the **Litani River,** known as the **red line,** due to Israel's opposition to having a large Arab army so close to its border. Periodically, the league's troops used force, including heavy shelling of villages such as **Zahle**, to force belligerents to halt their fighting. The deployment of the **United Nations Interim Force in Lebanon** (UNIFIL) in March 1978 introduced a political problem for the Arab Deterrent Force. Syria regarded the **United Nations** (UN) peacekeeping operation as a challenge to the league's mission. In the eyes of Damascus, the deployment of the globally mandated operation indicated that the UN viewed the league mission as being too weak to curb hostilities across Lebanon.

As the civil war continued, contingent providers began to question the wisdom of fielding military units with the Arab Deterrent Force. As early as November 1976, Libya withdrew its soldiers from the operation. South Yemen brought its soldiers home in December 1977. Sudanese troops departed in February 1979. Saudi Arabian forces left in March 1979, and the UAE contingent withdrew in April 1979. The departure of the three contingents left Syria as the sole supplier of military units for the operation, thus underscoring the lack of confidence displayed by league members in the operation.

The league's Gulf States provided the majority of funding for the Arab Deterrent Force. Kuwait and Saudi Arabia each paid 20 percent of the tab, while the UAE and Qatar contributed 15 percent and 10 percent, respectively. Despite the uneasiness of the Gulf States toward the force, they continued to fund it due to the lack of alternatives. Lebanon took the first step toward dismantling the ADF by requesting the termination of the force's mandate (which had not been renewed after its expiration on July 27, 1982) at the **Fez Summit Conference** in September 1982. A compromise with Syria, now engaged in an undeclared war with Israel in Lebanon, allowed for the termination of the mandate but did not order the immediate withdrawal of Syrian forces. However, the Gulf states announced that they would not fund the Syrian units since the peacekeeping mandate was officially terminated. The possible vacuum in Beirut was filled by the troops assigned to the **Multinational Forces I** peacekeeping operation, while Syrian soldiers remained unilaterally in eastern Lebanon. Some have called the operation controversial because it moved from being a mandate of **peacekeeping** (Symbolic Arab Security Force) to one of **peace enforcement** (Arab Deterrent Force). It was also one of three separate multinationally mandated operations fielded at the same time in Lebanon. Toward the end of the force's mandate the UN fielded a peacekeeping operation in southern Lebanon and the United States organized a mission to oversee the removal of the PLO from Beirut.

ARAB LEAGUE. *See* LEAGUE OF ARAB STATES.

ARAB LEAGUE FORCE IN KUWAIT. In 1961, the Council of the **League of Arab States** requested its Secretary-General to organize a multinational operation to preserve the independence of Kuwait. Iraq had threatened to invade Kuwait, and the league wanted to replace the small British unit that was attempting to guarantee the independence of the new state. The league passed a resolution on July 20, 1961, calling for the removal of British troops from Kuwait and offering assistance from the organization to guarantee the independence of the new state. The league did, however, state in the same resolution that it would support any decision of Kuwait to voluntarily merge with any other member (i.e., Iraq). The Iraqi delegation walked out of the meeting and the organization pressed forward with the preparations for a peacekeeping force.

The regional body signed an agreement with Kuwait on August 12, 1961, establishing the status of the proposed force. Libya and Lebanon declined invitations to contribute contingents, while the United Arab Republic (Egypt and Syria), Saudi Arabia, Sudan, Jordan, and Tunisia agreed to provide units to the mission. The force consisted of 3,300 troops, with the majority coming from Saudi Arabia and the United Arab Republic. Each promised 1,200 soldiers. Jordan eventually fielded over 1,000 soldiers, while Sudan provided 400 and Tunisia moved 200 to the Kuwait border. A special fund was established to finance the operation, with Kuwait providing most of the monetary resources. Major-General Abdullah Al-Isa of Saudi Arabia was selected as the **Force Commander.** The contingents began arriving in September and the deployment was complete by October 3, 1961. The United Arab Republic quickly elected to withdraw from the operation after the last British soldiers departed Kuwait. The losses were replaced by Jordan and Saudi Arabia. The total numbers were increased to approximately 5,000 troops but were reduced in December 1962. A February 1963 coup brought a more moderate government to power in Iraq and the remaining contingents of the force were withdrawn the during same month.

ARAB LEAGUE FORCE IN LEBANON. *See* ARAB DETERRENT FORCE; SYMBOLIC ARAB SECURITY FORCE.

AREA OF LIMITATION (AOL). The AOL extends from both sides of the **Area of Separation** (AOS) on the Golan Heights between **Israeli** and Syrian military forces. Each AOL is divided into three zones. The first zone extends outward from the AOS for ten kilometers. Within this zone, the opponents may station up to 6,000 soldiers, 75 tanks, and 36 artillery pieces. The second zone runs from the ten-kilometer mark out to 20 kilometers from the AOS. In this zone, a state may post a maximum of 450 tanks and 162 artillery pieces. The third zone runs from 20 to 25 kilometers beyond the AOS. Each side is not allowed to post military units within this third zone. Beyond the 25-kilometer limitation, each side may keep whatever forces it desires. Although the **United Nations Disengagement Observer Force** (UNDOF) patrols the AOS, the AOL is watched by personnel assigned to the **United Nations Truce Supervision Organization** (UNTSO).

AREA OF SEPARATION (AOS). In generic terms, an Area of Separation (AOS), sometimes known as a Buffer Zone, is a neutral band of territory established to separate belligerents. **Peacekeeping** forces often move into an AOS to help guarantee that each belligerent will remain on its side of the zone. In more specific terms, the neutral barrier zone between **Israeli** and **Syrian** forces on the Golan Heights is known as the AOS. This neutral territory marks the disengagement line established between the two belligerents after the 1973 Yom Kippur War. The **United Nations Disengagement Observer Force** (UNDOF) maintains positions within and patrols the AOS. *See also* AREA OF LIMITATION.

ARMISTICE DEMARCATION LINE (ADL). The Armistice Demarcation Line is the "border" surveyed between **Israel** and its neighbors following the 1948 War of Independence. The Line is observed by peacekeepers assigned to the **United Nations Truce Supervision Organization** (UNTSO). The name derives from the fact that Israel has not signed peace treaties with all of its neighbors. Israel is officially in an armistice with the states of Syria and **Lebanon**. Despite Israel's peace treaty with Egypt, UNTSO observers still maintain posts along the common border of the two states in cooperation with the **Multinational Force and Observers** (MFO) peacekeeping operation.

ARTICLE 19 CRISIS. The crisis evolved from the refusal of several states, including the Soviet Union and **France**, to pay their share of the **peacekeeping** assessments for early **United Nations** (UN) operations, including the **United Nations Truce Supervision Organization** (UNTSO), the **United Nations Emergency Force I** (UNEF I), and the **United Nations Operation in the Congo** (ONUC). Article 19 of the UN charter declares that if a state is behind in its dues to an amount equivalent to two years of regular contributions, its vote can be suspended in the General Assembly. The Soviet Union threatened to withdraw from the UN if its ability to vote in the General Assembly was suspended. The **United States** brought the crisis to an end by offering a compromise that permitted the states in arrears to decide which portions of the UN budget they would fund and which they would not pay. In turn, the United States also declared that it would adopt the same procedures. The United States still reserves the right to deny funding for UN actions with which it does not agree.

ARTICLE 43 FORCES. This is a term derived from Article 43 in the Charter of the **United Nations** (UN), which discusses the use of military force to accomplish goals of the organization. The charter implies that the permanent members of the Security Council would provide the bulk of the military personnel in Article 43 forces, as they did during the **Korean War** and **Persian Gulf War.** However, early peacekeeping operations did not abide by this concept. The permanent members of the Security Council were excluded from participation in most of the missions until the late 1980s. French involvement in the **United Nations Interim Force in Lebanon** (UNIFIL) and British participation in the **United Nations Force in Cyprus** (UNFICYP) are notable exceptions. However, other than the **United Nations Truce Supervision Organization** (UNTSO), American, Chinese, and Soviet personnel were excluded from United Nations peacekeeping operations until the end of the Cold War.

ASSEMBLY POINT (AP). Assembly Point is the name given to collection areas for armed elements of the Zimbabwe African National Liberation Army and the Zimbabwe People's Revolutionary Army during the peace process in Zimbabwe from December 1979 to March 1980. The **Commonwealth Monitoring Force in Zimbabwe** planned to manage 16 Assembly Points during this period. However, the tactical situation allowed the force to open only 14 Assembly Points. Each contingent was responsible for the operation of at least one location [Great Britain (5), Australia (4), New Zealand (3), Kenya (1), and Fiji (1)]. Normally, Patriotic Front troops reported to **Rendezvous Points** located primarily along Zimbabwe's borders with Zambia and Mozambique. After a brief stay, they were then bussed to the Assembly Points, which were better equipped to handle large numbers of individuals. However, some Patriotic Front units reported directly to the Assembly Points due to their close proximity to the secondary locations. All Patriotic Front soldiers were scheduled to be moved to the Assembly Points by January 5, 1980. Numbers in each camp ranged greatly from 30 to over 6,000. By January 9, 1980, approximately 20,600 soldiers had reported to the Assembly Points and the total rose to over 22,000 by the time the Commonwealth peacekeepers ended their mandate in March.

AUSTRALIAN PEACEKEEPING. Since 1995, Australia has emerged as one of the largest contributors to **United Nations** (UN) peacekeeping. In March 2003, Australia was the only Western industrialized country among the ten contributors to UN peacekeeping. While other Western states, including the **United States**, have concentrated their peacekeeping efforts in Europe, Australia serves as the primary contributor to UN and non-UN peacekeeping missions in the Pacific Ocean region. *See also* BOUGAINVILLE PEACE MONITORING GROUP; BOUGAINVILLE TRUCE MONITORING GROUP; INTERNATIONAL FORCE IN EAST TIMOR; INTERNATIONAL PEACE MONITORING TEAM; SOUTH PACIFIC PEACEKEEPING FORCE; UNITED NATIONS MISSION IN EAST TIMOR; UNITED NATIONS MISSION OF SUPPORT IN EAST TIMOR.

– B –

BARIL, MAJOR-GENERAL MAURICE. A Canadian officer, Baril served as a military adviser to the **United Nations** (UN) for peacekeeping operations. He was selected for the position in 1992 and has peacekeeping experience as a regimental commander with the **United Nations Peacekeeping Force in Cyprus** (UNFICYP). In

1994, Baril was named as the commander of the **United Nations Assistance Mission in Rwanda** (UNAMIR).

BARREL INCIDENT. United Nations Truce Supervision Organization (UNTSO) personnel assigned to Jerusalem regularly inspected **Israeli** supplies being transported through a neutral zone to Mount Scopus, a Jewish enclave. During one inspection, a test rod being run into a barrel of oil touched a metal object. The UNTSO inspectors demanded the removal of the barrel from the truck and further inspection to determine if weapons were being smuggled into Mount Scopus in violation of the cease-fire agreement. The drivers backed their trucks out of the neutral zone and then demanded the return of the barrel since they were no longer in a neutral zone patrolled by the **United Nations** (UN). Lieutenant-General William E. Riley, the Chief of Staff of UNTSO, agreed to the request. This incident confirmed the Israeli assertion that peace observation and inspections by UNTSO depended on the consent of the parties involved.

BARRIER FORCE. *See* INTERPOSITION FORCE.

BASIC LAW. The Basic Law is a term applied to the **German** Constitution written after World War II. The Basic Law contained a provision limiting the use and overseas deployment of the German military. The German government used the Basic Law to justify its decision not to contribute soldiers to **United Nations** (UN) peacekeeping operations. Further interpretations of the Basic Law after German reunification reversed the decision, and German soldiers deployed to Somalia with the **United Nations Operation in Somalia II** (UNOSOM II).

BEITEDDINE CONFERENCE. The Beiteddine Conference was a meeting of all troop-contributing states and/or financial backers of the **Arab Deterrent Force** and the host state, **Lebanon**. The conference, convened on October 15, 1978, included the foreign ministers of Syria, Saudi Arabia, Lebanon, and Kuwait, as well as representatives from Qatar, the United Arab Emirates, and Sudan. The meeting called for the strict adherence to the **Riyadh Resolution** and **Cairo**

Resolution, the curbing of "armed manifestations," and the collection of all weapons retained contrary to the **Cairo Agreement**. The agreement also requested the ending of "information campaigns" and the prohibition of illegal radio and television broadcasts and newspapers. The Arab Deterrent Force would assume limited responsibilities for monitoring the latter provision. The conference also realigned some units of the Arab Deterrent Force stationed in Beirut. *See also* CHATAURA AGREEMENT.

BELGIAN PEACEKEEPING. *See* FRENCH PEACEKEEPING.

BERNADOTTE, COUNT FALKE. Count Bernadotte of Sweden served as Mediator with the **United Nations Truce Supervision Organization** (UNTSO) from May to September 1948. On September 17, 1948, Jewish terrorists assassinated Bernadotte in Jerusalem. He was replaced by **Ralph Bunche** who assumed the title of Acting Mediator.

BEST PRACTICES UNIT. The Best Practices Unit is an office within **the Department of Peacekeeping Operations** of the **United Nations** (UN). The UN established the organization in 2001 by merging its Lessons Learned Unit and Policy Planning Unit. The Best Practices Unit coordinates the evaluation and assessment of UN peacekeeping operations and develops guidelines to assist future missions.

BIHAC. The town of Bihac and its surrounding area in **Bosnia and Herzegovina** was a **United Nations** (UN) **safe area**. Muslim refugees were flowing into Bihac as a result of a local Serb offensive. Serb aircraft attacked Bihac on November 18, 1994. **North Atlantic Treaty Organization** (NATO) aircraft struck a Serb airfield located in a **United Nations Protection Area** within Croatia in retaliation for the air strike against Bihac. Serb forces shelled Bihac on November 25, 1994, and eventually seized high ground overlooking the town. A stand-off in the area continued until the signing of the Dayton Accords in 1995. *See also* SREBRENICA.

BIR, LIEUTENANT-GENERAL CEVIK. Bir, a native of Turkey, was selected as the first **Force Commander** of **United Nations Op-**

eration in **Somalia II** (UNOSOM II) in 1993. A major factor in the selection of Bir, who had experience as a senior commander for the **North Atlantic Treaty Organization** (NATO), revolved around the refusal of the **United States** to place its soldiers under the command of officers from other states. The United States did agree to place their forces under Bir as long as an American officer would serve as his deputy. Bir complained in October 1993 that the contingents under his command reported to their home countries prior to carrying out his orders. He completed his tour of duty in January 1994.

BLUE BERETS. *See* BLUE HELMETS.

BLUE HELMETS. A nickname given to **United Nations** (UN) peacekeepers because of the blue paint applied to their helmets for identification as neutral soldiers. UN peacekeepers are also issued blue berets and are thus called "Blue Berets." Peacekeepers first used the blue helmets during the **United Nations Emergency Force I** (UNEF I) following the Suez Crisis in 1956. The Egyptians were concerned that the Canadians looked like the British soldiers who had invaded the Suez Canal area. In addition, many of the other UNEF I contingents wore uniforms manufactured in the United States. The UN needed to develop a clothing plan that would allow belligerents to be able to immediately recognize the neutrality of the peacekeepers. Arm bands and patches were ruled out since they could not be identified except at close range. The group working on the problem first thought of dyeing berets light blue. However, berets that could be properly dyed and retain the light blue color were not available. In response to the next day departure of peacekeepers assigned to UNEF I, the UN elected to use surplus American helmet liners that could be easily painted blue. The solution to UNEF I's problem has become a regular practice in UN peacekeeping and now all assigned personnel are provided with blue helmets and blue berets.

BONEO, HORACIO. Boneo held two critical positions in **United Nations** (UN) peacekeeping operations. He served as the Deputy Chief of election observers for the **United Nations Observation Mission for the Verification of Elections in Nicaragua** (UNOMVEN) and later as the Chief of election observers for the **United**

Nations Observer Group for the Verification of the Elections in Haiti (UNOGVEH).

BOSNIA AND HERZEGOVINA. *See* EUROPEAN UNION POLICE MISSION; IMPEMENTATION FORCE; STABILIZATON FORCE; UNITED NATIONS INTERNATIONAL POLICE TASK FORCE; UNITED NATIONS MISSION IN BOSNIA AND HERZEGOVINA; UNITED NATIONS PROTECTION FORCE; UNITED NATIONS PROTECTION FORCE IN BOSNIA AND HERZEGOVINA.

BOUGAINVILLE. *See* BOUGAINVILLE PEACE MONITORING GROUP; BOUGAINVILLE TRUCE MONITORING GROUP.

BOUGAINVILLE PEACE MONITORING GROUP (PMG). A cease-fire agreement signed on April 30, 1998, led to the transition of the **Bougainville Truce Monitoring Group** (TMG) to the Bougainville Peace Monitoring Group (PMG). The PMG is mandated by the Lincoln Agreement and given the missions to monitor the compliance in the peace process, promote confidence among the groups, and provide the people of Bougainville with information on the peace process. The maximum authorized strength of the PMG is approximately 325 military and civilian personnel. The mission is officially led by **Australia** which provided 250 personnel. Additional personnel have been dispatched by Fiji, New Zealand, and Vanuatu to serve in PMG. The peacekeepers are unarmed. Australia and New Zealand provide logistical assistance and training. The operation costs approximately $13 million annually.

BOUGAINVILLE TRUCE MONITORING GROUP (TMG). The Northern Solomons island of Bougainville, part of Papua New Guinea (PNG), experienced political turmoil and an armed insurrection beginning in the late 1980s. Many islanders resented being part of Papua New Guinea and preferred their own independent state. Another problem involved the attitudes of the islanders to a large copper mine. Many believed that they should share more from the mine's profits and were concerned about the environmental and land damage caused by the mine's operation. The Bougainville Revolutionary

Army (BRA) emerged in 1988 and forced the mine to close. PNG removed its military forces from Bougainville in 1990 but returned them in 1991 and 1992. A 1994 peace conference was overseen by the **South Pacific Peacekeeping Force**. Continued discussions between PNG and various Bougainville groups led to peace talks in Burnham, New Zealand. The Burnham Declaration, resulting from the November 1997 discussions, served as the mandate for a new peacekeeping operation to be known as the Bougainville Truce Monitoring Group (TMG). The peacekeepers arrived in December 1997.

TMG's mandate included the monitoring of the truce agreement signed in Burnham in order to promote an atmosphere for continued negotiations. A cease-fire agreement signed on April 30, 1998, led to the transition of the TMG to the **Bougainville Peace Monitoring Group** (PMG). The maximum authorized strength of the TMG was approximately 325 military and civilian personnel. The mission was officially led by New Zealand. Additional personnel were provided by **Australia**, Fiji, and Vanuatu. Australia and New Zealand provided logistical assistance and training. The peacekeepers were unarmed. The operation cost approximately $4 million.

BOUTROS-GHALI, BOUTROS. Boutros-Ghali, an **Egyptian**, served as the Secretary General of the **United Nations** (UN) from 1992 to 1995. His leadership was marked by controversy in the field of peacekeeping. He held the post of Secretary General during the difficult periods of the **United Nations Protection Force** (UNPROFOR) in the Balkans, **United Nations Operation in Somalia** (UNOSOM), and the **United Nations Assistance Mission in Rwanda** (UNAMIR). He has been criticized for shaming the West for its involvement in European peacekeeping and ignoring the Third World. He demanded the commitment of peacekeepers in Somalia despite the lack of an effective peace process. In turn, Boutros-Ghali is also seen as a victim of Western politics within the UN.

BRAHIMI REPORT. *See* PANEL ON UNITED NATIONS PEACE OPERATIONS.

BRIQUEMONT, LIEUTENANT-GENERAL FRANCIS. Briquemont, a native of Belgium, served as the commander of the **United**

Nations Protection Force (UNPROFOR) element assigned in **Bosnia and Herzegovina** between June 1993 and January 1994. Briquemont replaced French General **Philippe Morillon** in June 1993 and faced the difficult task of maintaining the peace among Muslim, Serb, Croat, and Bosnian Serb forces while ensuring the delivery of humanitarian aid to civilians trapped during the civil war. Secretary-General **Boutros Boutros-Ghali** requested the replacement of Briquemont due to the latter's criticism of the **United Nations** (UN). Briquemont reportedly declared that the organization needed more action in Bosnia and fewer resolutions. He stated that there was a gap between the resolutions of the Security Council, the will to execute the resolutions, and the means available to commanders to carry out resolutions. He also referred to Bosnia as a soldier's nightmare and commented that peacekeepers assigned to the region felt humiliated at not being able to complete their mission. British Lieutenant-General **Michael Rose** officially replaced Briquemont in January 1994. *See also* JEAN COT.

BRITISH METHOD. The **rules of engagement** in the first half of the 20th century utilized by the **British** army when assisting civilian governments. The British Method, adopted by the **Saar International Force** in 1935, involved maintaining highly visible military patrols before trouble erupted. When tensions increased, the military forces were hidden from view, but kept in a large mobile reserve, while local police attempted to maintain order. *See also* CONTINENTAL METHOD.

BRITISH PEACEKEEPING. Great Britain participated heavily in the various **League of Nations** multinational missions after World War I including the **Saar International Force**. The state, as one of the Permanent Five members of the **United Nations** (UN) Security Council, played a minimal role in UN peacekeeping operations during the **Cold War** with the exception of the **United Nations Peacekeeping Force in Cyprus** (UNFICYP). The British held Cyprus as a colony prior to its independence and still maintained military bases on the island that could be utilized for logistics. After the Cold War, Great Britain increased its role in UN peacekeeping operations but in recent years has tended to participate more heavily in **North Atlantic**

Treaty Organization (NATO) missions rather than those of the UN. *See also* BRITISH METHOD.

BUFFER ZONE. *See* AREA OF SEPARATION (AOS).

BULL, LIEUTENANT-GENERAL ODD. Bull, a Norwegian officer, was the "Executive Member in charge of military observers" for the **United Nations Observation Group in Lebanon** (UNOGIL) during its brief tenure of June to December 1958. In this capacity, Bull performed the same job that came to be titled Chief Military Observer in future peacekeeping operations. He was also the Chief of Staff of the **United Nations Truce Supervision Organization** (UNTSO) from June 1963 to July 1970. Bull's seven-year position as commander of the mission is unique for the operation as well as for peacekeeping in general. Usually, the **United Nations** (UN) replaces its commanders within three years and many commanders serve for approximately one year. Bull was Chief of Staff during the Six-Day War in 1967 when **Israel** denounced all of the Mixed Armistice Commissions manned by UNTSO personnel. He faced the delicate task of persuading the belligerents to accept peacekeepers along the cease-fire line at the conclusion of hostilities.

BUNCHE, RALPH J. Bunche, a former American diplomat, fulfilled the role of Acting Mediator for the **United Nations Truce Supervision Organization** (UNTSO) after the murder of **Count Folke Bernadotte** of Sweden on September 17, 1948. Bunche held this position until August 1949. He was also the first **Special Representative** of the **United Nations Operation in the Congo** (ONUC). He served in this post from July to August 1960. In February 1963, Bunche, now an Undersecretary, flew to Yemen to see first hand the crisis in that state following an Egyptian-backed coup against the Saudi-supported royalist government. Bunche's work helped result in the establishment of the **United Nations Yemen Observation Mission**. Bunche received the **Nobel Peace Prize** in 1950 for his negotiation of the truce between **Israel** and the Arab states in 1949.

BUNIA. *See* CONGO INTERNATIONAL FORCE.

BURNS, LIEUTENANT-GENERAL E. L. M. Burns, a native of Canada, served as the Chief of Staff of the **United Nations Truce Supervision Organization** (UNTSO) from August 1954 to November 1956. Immediately following this assignment, Burns became the first **Force Commander** for the **United Nations Emergency Force I** (UNEF I) and held that position until December 1959. He was selected for the latter assignment due to his experience with UNTSO, immediate availability, and knowledge of the area and issues. In addition, Burns had earned the respect of the military commanders of **Israel** and **Egypt** while serving with UNTSO. France and Great Britain also respected the Canadian since he had been a senior Allied officer during World War II and had worked with fellow officers from both states.

BURUNDI. Conflict between the Hutu and Tutsi raged in Burundi since independence. Despite continued negotiations, successful cease-fires eluded the belligerents. At a regional conference in Arusha, Tanzania, in June 1996, the government of Burundi requested foreign military intervention to accompany the peace negotiation process. A technical meeting in July 1996 reaffirmed the request and Uganda and Tanzania pledged troops for the peacekeeping operation. Kenya offered to deploy police officers with the mission. The **United Nations** (UN) endorsed the efforts of the three states. If deployed, the operation would have been officially mandated by the Arusha peace process rather than an international organization. However, further discussions between the contingent pledging states and the belligerents failed to secure agreement on a mandated mission for the proposed operation. The mission collapsed before it was ever fielded.

Five years later, **South Africa** heeded a second call for an international peacekeeping force and deployed a 700-man contingent to Burundi. **Nigeria** and Senegal originally pledged contingents but did not deploy them. Following a breakdown in the peace process, the government and rebels signed a new cease-fire in December 2002. This agreement resulted in the formation of two separate peacekeeping operations to oversee the new peace process. The first was an expansion of the South African unilateral peacekeeping mission to include troops from Ethiopia and Mozambique known as the **African Mis-**

sion in Burundi (AMIB). While these three states provide the security needed to ensure the peace process worked, the second peace-keeping mission actually oversees the cease-fire itself and is known as the **African Union (AU) Cease-fire Observer Mission in Burundi**. *See also* ORGANIZATION OF AFRICAN UNITY MISSION IN BURUNDI.

– C –

CAIRO SUMMIT CONFERENCE. The conference, held on October 25–26, 1976, examined the unanswered question of funding for the **Arab Deterrent Force** that was to be fielded in **Lebanon.** The resolution resulting from the meeting called for the establishment of a special fund. Each member of the **League of Arab States** would pay an unspecified amount into the fund, which would be supervised by the President of Lebanon, in consultation with the Secretary-General of the league and the states that contributed at least 10 percent of the total. The conference granted the fund a six-month renewable mandate. Saudi Arabia and Kuwait contributed 20 percent apiece, the United Arab Emirates offered to fund 15 percent, and Qatar pledged to pay 10 percent of the costs. The remaining league members did not offer to fund the upkeep of the force, leaving Saudi Arabia and Kuwait to pay the balance. The attendees, with the exception of Iraq, also approved the resolutions and statements issued by the parties at the **Riyadh Summit Conference** on October 18, 1976. This action officially granted league endorsement to the decisions made at the Riyadh Summit which included the transformation of the **Symbolic Arab Security Force** into the Arab Deterrent Force.

CALLAGHAN, LIEUTENANT-GENERAL WILLIAM. Callaghan, a native of Ireland, was the Acting Chief of Staff (while in the grade of Colonel) of the **United Nations Truce Supervision Organization** (UNTSO) from April 1978 to June 1979. He held the position of **Force Commander** of the **United Nations Interim Force in Lebanon** (UNIFIL) from February 1981 to May 1986. In 1982, Callaghan arranged an agreement between **Israel** and its opponents in **Lebanon** which stated that each party would show the maximum restraint when confronting a breach in the cease-fire. Following this assignment he became the Chief of Staff of UNTSO and remained in that post until June 1987.

CAMBODIA. *See* UNITED NATIONS ADVANCED MISSION IN CAMBODIA; UNITED NATIONS TRANSITIONAL AUTHORITY IN CAMBODIA.

CARLSSON REPORT. *See* INDEPENDENT INQUIRY INTO THE ACTIONS OF THE UNITED NATIONS DURING THE 1994 GENOCIDE IN RWANDA.

CENTRAL AFRICAN REPUBLIC. *See* COMMUNITY OF SAHEL-SAHARAN STATES PEACEKEEPING OPERATION IN CENTRAL AFRICAN REPUBLIC; ECONOMIC AND MONETARY COMMUNITY OF CENTRAL AFRICAN STATES PEACEKEEPING OPERATION IN CENTRAL AFRICAN REPUBLIC; FRENCH OPERATIONAL ASSISTANCE UNITS; FRENCH PEACEKEEPING; INTER-AFRICAN FORCE IN CENTRAL AFRICAN REPUBLIC; UNITED NATIONS MISSION IN CENTRAL AFRICAN REPUBLIC.

CHAD. *See* NIGERIAN PEACEKEEPING; ORGANIZATION OF AFRICAN UNITY PEACEKEEPING FORCE I; ORGANIZATION OF AFRICAN UNITY PEACEKEEPNG FORCE II.

CHAND, LIEUTENANT-GENERAL DEWAN PREM. Chand, an Indian officer, was the **Force Commander** of the **United Nations Peacekeeping Force in Cyprus** (UNFICYP) between December 1969 and December 1976. He was named the Force Commander designate for the **United Nations Transition Assistance Group in Namibia** (UNTAG) in January 1980. He held that position until March 1989, when he assumed the title of Force Commander upon the deployment of the peacekeeping mission. He held the latter post during the duration of the operation which ended in March 1990.

CHAPTER SIX PEACEKEEPING. The **United Nations** (UN) charter does not specifically provide a provision for the mandating of

peacekeeping operations. In response, the Security Council has tended to mandate these missions, especially those sometimes referred to as **First Generation Peacekeeping,** under chapter six of the charter, which provides for the "pacific settlement of disputes." *See also* CHAPTER SIX-AND-A-HALF PEACEKEEPING; CHAPTER SEVEN PEACE ENFORCEMENT.

CHAPTER SIX-AND-A-HALF PEACEKEEPING. The **United Nations** (UN) charter does not specifically provide a provision for the mandating of **peacekeeping** operations. Chapter Six-and-a-Half Peacekeeping is a term sometimes applied to peacekeeping operations that go beyond the simple separation of belligerents following a successful cease-fire and have to use some type of force to ensure mission accomplishment. *See also* CHAPTER SIX PEACEKEEPING; CHAPTER SEVEN PEACE ENFORCEMENT.

CHAPTER SEVEN PEACE ENFORCEMENT. The **United Nations** (UN) charter does not specifically provide a provision for the mandating of **peacekeeping** operations. Chapter seven of the charter allows the international organization to conduct collective security military operations. However, the United Nations did mandate the **United Nations Operation in Somalia II** (UNOSOM II) under chapter seven to ensure that the peacekeepers had the authorization to defend themselves and carry out their humanitarian mission. *See also* CHAPTER SIX PEACEKEEPING; CHAPTER SIX-AND-A-HALF PEACEKEEPING.

CHARDIGNY COMMISSION. *See* VILNA MILITARY COMMISSION.

CHATAURA AGREEMENT. The agreement, concluded on July 25, 1977, involved representatives from **Lebanon**, Syria, and the Palestinian Liberation Organization (PLO). The agreement added additional responsibilities to the **Arab Deterrent Force** deployed in Lebanon. The document placed restrictions on the Palestinians by persuading them to comply with earlier agreements that limited their possession of weapons and their presence in southern Lebanon. The force was given the authorization to collect Palestinian heavy weapons, banned by the Cairo Agreement, and to launch unannounced inspections of Palestinian camps. The **League of Arab States** did not endorse the agreement, but it was generally accepted since the President of Lebanon, responsible for overall command of the force in accordance with the **Riyadh Agreement**, and the **Force Commander** were present for the negotiations. *See also* BEITEDDINE CONFERENCE.

CHIEF MILITARY OBSERVER (CMO). This title is given to the military commander of a **United Nations** (UN) observation mission. This term should not be confused with **Force Commander** although they perform similar duties.

CHINESE PEACEKEEPING. *See* PEOPLE'S REPUBLIC OF CHINA PEACEKEEPING.

CIVILIANIZATION OF PEACEKEEPING. *See* PRIVATIZATION OF PEACEKEEPING.

COLD WAR AND PEACEKEEPING. During the Cold War, the permanent members of the **United Nations** (UN) Security Council played minimal roles in the deployment of troops in support of the organization's **peacekeeping** operations. This was due to many reasons including the need to reduce perceptions of peacekeeper impartiality among belligerents and the desire to avoid large power confrontation in Third World conflicts. The permanent members are **France**, **Great Britain**, **People's Republic of China** (PRC), **Russia** (Soviet Union), and the **United States**. After the end of the Cold War, around 1990, each state, with the exception of the PRC, increased its direct participation in UN peacekeeping. However, by 1996, each state was concentrating more on regional peacekeeping missions rather than those of the UN.

COLLECTIVE PEACEKEEPING FORCE. Collective Peacekeeping Force is the generic term of the **Commonwealth of Independent States** (CIS) and applied to any temporary coalition of military units mandated and fielded by the organization as a **peacekeeping** type operation.

COMMITTEE OF THIRTY-FOUR. *See* UNITED NATIONS SPECIAL COMMITTEE ON PEACEKEEPING OPERATIONS.

COMMITTEE OF THREE. The **League of Nations** appointed the committee to develop recommendations in reference to the functions, composition, organization, and financing of the **Saar International Force**.

COMMONWEALTH. The Commonwealth, also known as the Commonwealth of Nations, is a free association of sovereign states which include former British colonies, Great Britain, and current British dependencies. The organization, established in 1931, numbers about 60 members. The purpose of the organization is to promote trade and other forms of cooperation among the member states. The Commonwealth does not have a defense protocol but has organized under British leadership to field one peacekeeping operation known as the **Commonwealth Monitoring Force in Zimbabwe.** *See also* COMMONWEALTH CEASE-FIRE COMMISSION; COMMONWEALTH OBSERVER GROUP; ORGANIZATION OF EAST CARIBBEAN STATES PEACEKEEPING.

COMMONWEALTH CEASE-FIRE COMMISSION. The commission, chaired by Major-General **J. H. B. Acland,** examined breaches of the cease-fire in **Zimbabwe**. The group also included a Rhodesian general, a Rhodesian Air Force officer, General Dabengwa of the Zimbabwe People's Revolutionary Army, and General Nhongo of the Zimbabwe National Liberation Army. The commission met every two weeks during the mandate of the **Commonwealth Monitoring Force in Zimbabwe.** Major-General Acland requested and received permission to use the commission to tour the **Assembly Points** in order to ensure that all of the armed groups understood the necessity of cooperation during the tense early period of the peace process.

COMMONWEALTH MONITORING FORCE IN ZIMBABWE (CMF). Zimbabwe, known as Rhodesia prior to gaining full independence in 1980, faced an internal conflict that began when white settlers refused to allow Great Britain to implement a program for majority rule in the territory. When negotiations between Great

Britain and the settler regime led by Ian Smith collapsed, the latter announced a unilateral declaration of independence in November 1965. The **United Nations** (UN) placed economic sanctions on Rhodesia, but they were ineffective due to the assistance provided to Smith by South Africa and Portugal. The two major African parties, the Zimbabwe African National Union (ZANU) and the Zimbabwe African People's Union (ZAPU), declared a war of independence against the Smith regime in April 1966. As early as December 1966, Great Britain attempted to negotiate with Smith in order to peacefully implement a plan for majority rule in Rhodesia. The settler regime refused to budge and the conflict intensified. The two African nationalist groups formed the Patriotic Front in 1976 in order to coordinate their military campaign and provide a united front for negotiations. In 1978, Smith signed an internal settlement as a last attempt to preserve white rule in Rhodesia. Bishop Abel Muzorewa won a majority in the parliament, but the Patriotic Front refused to accept the settler-dictated internal settlement and increased its offensive operations. Muzorewa did not implement expected internal reforms in the country and never exercised control of the armed forces.

Both parties in the conflict were persuaded to attend an independence conference in London. This led to the signing of the Lancaster House Agreement, which ended the conflict and established the Commonwealth Monitoring Force in Zimbabwe to oversee the transitional process. The **Commonwealth** states agreed to field a multinational peacekeeping force, officially named the Commonwealth Monitoring Force in Zimbabwe, to assist in the disarming of the armed opponents in the conflict. The Force was mandated by Annex E of the Lancaster House Agreement. Annex E also stated that the cease-fire would become effective at midnight on December 21, 1979. At this time all military movement would cease, and at midnight on December 28, 1979, all hostilities would cease. Rhodesian Security Forces were to regroup under the authority of the new **British**-selected governor, and Patriotic Front units were to move to **Rendezvous Points** manned by the Commonwealth Monitoring Force. All Patriotic Front forces would then be transported to **Assembly Points** by midnight on January 4, 1980. The Patriotic Front demanded that the monitoring force be comprised of Commonwealth and not only British soldiers. The Patriotic Front felt that its soldiers would be too vulnerable gathered in large camps and also wanted a large multinational unit to guarantee their security. The British originally envisioned deploying approximately 300 of their own soldiers. In compliance with this Patriotic Front request, the Commonwealth built the force around 1,250 British soldiers but also added approximately 300 troops from other members of the organization. The states volunteering to participate in the peacekeeping mission included Australia (150 soldiers), New Zealand (74 soldiers), Kenya (50 soldiers), and Fiji (24 soldiers).

Great Britain financed the entire force, including the needs of the other contingents. London also provided the majority of the logistics and transportation. The United States offered assistance in the movement of the peacekeepers to Zimbabwe. The British built their element around Headquarters 8 Field Force, named Major-General **J. H. B. Acland** as the overall military commander, and nicknamed the mission Operation Agila. The Commonwealth Force established its headquarters in Salisbury, the capital of Zimbabwe, and dispatched its teams to over 100 locations, including 16 Assembly Points and 22 Rendezvous Points, scattered across the country. The peacekeepers eventually set up only 14 Assembly Points, of which four were operated primarily by Australians, three by New Zealanders, and one each by Kenya and Fiji. To distinguish themselves as peacekeepers and not Rhodesian forces, the Commonwealth troops flew large British Union Jacks, used loudspeakers and bright lights, and wore white armbands. The Patriotic Front also stationed liaison officers at each Commonwealth location to ensure that their soldiers did not mistake the area as being hostile.

The Monitoring Force faced great difficulties in accomplishing its tasks. It frequently experienced tense encounters as Patriotic Front soldiers reported to the camps. Each side was nervous and suspicious of the other. Many of the camps lacked adequate water sources, which tested the logistical system of the Commonwealth soldiers. In addition, the countryside still harbored uncharted mines that occasionally took their toll on vehicles operated by the peacekeepers. Despite the logistical difficulties in caring for and transporting over 22,000 former guerilla soldiers between December 1979 and March 1980, the Commonwealth Force has been credited with completing

its mission in a highly successful manner. *See also* COMMON-
WEALTH OBSERVER GROUP; UNITED NATIONS ZIMBABWE
FORCE.

COMMONWEALTH OBSERVER GROUP. The **Commonwealth**
established the Observer Group in order to oversee the election
process in **Zimbabwe**. The observers arrived in Zimbabwe on January 24, 1980. The group, chaired by Rajeshwar Dayal of **India**, consisted of 11 senior advisers and 22 assistant advisers. The senior advisers were selected from the Commonwealth states of **Australia**,
Bangladesh, Barbados, Canada, Ghana, Jamaica, **Nigeria**, Papua New
Guinea, Sierra Leone, and Sri Lanka. Each senior adviser formed a
team with two of the assistant advisers. The teams were sent to observation locations on an ad hoc basis to ensure that all parties in the
peace process followed the rules of the election process. At one point,
the group caught a Rhodesian air unit dropping anti-Communist
leaflets in a remote rural area. The group is noted for being the first
Commonwealth election observation group to work alongside a
peacekeeping organization, in this case the **Commonwealth Monitoring Force in Zimbabwe.** The Observer Group unanimously declared that the elections in Zimbabwe were free and fair.

COMMONWEALTH OF INDEPENDENT STATES (CIS). The former Soviet republics formed the Commonwealth of Independent States
(CIS) on December 21, 1991, in conjunction with the dissolution of the
Soviet Union. The organization, originally comprising all of the former
republics of the former Soviet Union except Georgia (which joined the
organization in 1993 following the introduction of **Russian** soldiers in
the Georgian civil war), Estonia, Latvia, and Lithuania, was established
as a military and economic umbrella organization and has its coordination center (headquarters) in Minsk, Belarus. All of the CIS member
states except Turkmenistan signed an agreement on "Groups of Military Observers and Collective Peacekeeping Forces in the CIS" in
March 1992. Ukraine did reserve the right to review each peacekeeping operation on a case-by-case basis.

The CIS has officially mandated and deployed peacekeepers to
two areas of the former Soviet Union, although it can be easily argued that the international units are actually carrying out Russian for-

eign policy along its periphery. Several CIS members, including Ukraine, have objected to Russia's interventions in the name of peacekeeping despite the March 1992 agreement. Marshal Evgenii Shaposhnikov, the former Commander in Chief of the CIS Joint Armed Forces General Staff, commented in December 1992 that the CIS needed to show greater coordination in security issues, especially peacekeeping, in order to ensure that the **North Atlantic Treaty Organization** (NATO) did not adopt a position of establishing peacekeeping operations along Russia's borders. In December 1993, this concern materialized when the **Conference for Security and Cooperation in Europe** (CSCE) voted to deploy 1,000 military observers to Nagorno-Karabakh. *See also* COLLECTIVE PEACE-KEEPING FORCE; COMMONWEALTH OF INDEPENDENT STATES COLLECTIVE PEACEKEEPING FORCE; COMMONWEALTH OF INDEPENDENT STATES PEACEKEEPING FORCES IN GEORGIA; RUSSIAN PEACEKEEPING.

COMMONWEALTH OF INDEPENDENT STATES COLLECTIVE PEACEKEEPING FORCE. Tajikistan declared its independence from the Soviet Union on September 9, 1991. Economic and social instability, along with disagreements among clans and other regional groups, prevailed after independence. At the same time, tensions between Tajik secularists and Islamic fundamentalists increased. In May 1992, an anti-government coalition managed to gain control of the government following two months of unrest within the state. A civil war ensued that resulted in a defeat of the coalition by the end of 1992, forcing them to take refuge in Afghanistan. Tajikistan and **Russia** signed an agreement permitting Russian soldiers to deploy along the border with Afghanistan.

On September 24, 1993, the **Commonwealth of Independent States** (CIS) mandated the Commonwealth of Independent States Collective Peacekeeping Force (also known as the CIS Tajikistan Buffer Force). The operation consists of 6,631 soldiers from Russia and Kazakhstan. It is interesting to note that the operation officially commenced in August 1993, a month prior to the mandate. The formal CIS mandate expired on September 16, 2000. The Russian 201st Motorized Rifle Division has remained to continue the mission, without an official CIS mandate but under a bilateral agreement between

Russia and Tajikistan. The number of fatalities has not been openly reported. The cost of the operation is difficult to determine. The Stockholm International Peace Research Institute (SIPRI) reported that the operation cost 583.9 million rubles in 1999.

COMMONWEALTH OF INDEPENDENT STATES PEACE-KEEPING FORCES IN GEORGIA. Georgia faced an attempt by Abkhazia to separate itself from the country soon after independence following the collapse of the Soviet Union. Abkhazia is located in the northwestern part of the country. The unrest devolved into open fighting by the summer of 1992 after Georgia deployed 2,000 soldiers to the region. **Russia** negotiated a cease-fire agreement between the two parties on September 2, 1992. The agreement collapsed on October 1, 1992. Abkhazia allied itself with elements in Russia that sought political autonomy from that state. The **United Nations** (UN) became involved in the conflict resolution process along with the **Conference for Security and Cooperation in Europe** (CSCE), later renamed the **Organization for Security and Cooperation in Europe** (OSCE). On July 27, 1993, the belligerents agreed to sign a new cease-fire document. The agreement called for the deployment of international observers to monitor the cease-fire. The UN Security Council mandated the **United Nations Observer Mission in Georgia** (UNOMIG) with Resolution 850 (1993) on August 24, 1993. The purpose of the operation is to verify the cease-fire of July 27, 1993, between the government of Georgia and the rebel province of Abkhazia as well as monitor the Commonwealth of Independent States (CIS) peacekeeping operation.

The CIS peacekeepers in Georgia, actually 1,700 Russian troops, are currently under a CIS mandate from April 15, 1994. The CIS peacekeepers arrived in June 1994. There have been 75 fatalities among the peacekeepers between 1994 and 2000. The cost of the operation is difficult to determine. The Stockholm International Peace Research Institute (SIPRI) reported that the operation cost 198.1 million rubles in 1999.

COMMONWEALTH OF INDEPENDENT STATES TAJIKISTAN BUFFER FORCE. *See* COMMONWEALTH OF INDEPENDENT STATES COLLECTIVE PEACEKEEPING FORCE.

COMMUNITY OF LUSOPHONE COUNTRIES (CPLP). The Community of Lusophone Countries (CPLP) is an international organization grouping Portugal and former Portuguese colonies (Angola, Brazil, Cape Verde, Guinea-Bissau, Mozambique, and Sao Tome and Principe). In May 1999, CPLP defense ministers agreed to establish a mechanism for mandating and fielding a CPLP peacekeeping force when required. The mechanism included provisions for the joint training of national military units as a single peace force capable of conducting humanitarian operations. Little has been reported on the CPLP initiative since 1999.

COMMUNITY OF SAHEL-SAHARAN STATES (COMESSA) PEACEKEEPING OPERATION IN CENTRAL AFRICAN REPUBLIC. On May 28, 2001, former **Central African Republic** (CAR) president Andre Kolingba unsuccessfully attempted to overthrow his country's government. A small group of Libyan soldiers arrived to help maintain President Ange-Felix Patasse in power. Instability continued in the country following the coup attempt and additional Libyan soldiers deployed to CAR in early November 2001. To add legitimacy to its military intervention in CAR, Libya called for a gathering of states belonging to the Community of Sahel-Saharan States (COMESSA) to meet in Sudan on December 2, 2001. At the meeting, the delegates agreed to mandate a peacekeeping operation for the CAR. Troop totals included 200 Libyans, 50 Sudanese, and an undetermined small number from Djibouti. The presence of the Libyans unsettled many of the regional states. The, members of the **Economic and Monetary Community of Central African States** (CEMAC) gathered in Gabon on October 2, 2002, and mandated their own peacekeeping operation to replace the Libyan-dominated COMESSA mission. However, little action was taken until later in the month when an invasion from Chadian territory nearly toppled the Patasse regime. CEMAC peacekeepers began arriving in December 2002. In response, COMESSA personnel departed the CAR by December 28, 2002.

CONFERENCE FOR SECURITY AND COOPERATION IN EUROPE (CSCE). The Conference for Security and Cooperation in Europe (CSCE) consisted of the European states, the **United States**,

Canada, and the former Soviet Union. In 1992 the body sent 20 observers to the Serbian province of Kosovo but withdrew them when the Serbs ordered the group to depart the state. The CSCE established Sanctions Assistance Missions (SAMs) in the countries bordering the Federal Republic of **Yugoslavia** in order to assist with the sanctions imposed by the **United Nations** (UN). In 1994, the CSCE transformed itself into a more permanent body known as the **Organization for Security and Cooperation in Europe** (OSCE).

CONFERENCE FOR SECURITY AND COOPERATION IN EUROPE MISSION TO GEORGIA. *See* ORGANIZATION FOR SECURITY AND COOPERATION IN EUROPE MISSION TO GEORGIA.

CONFERENCE FOR SECURITY AND COOPERATION IN EUROPE MISSION TO MOLDOVA. *See* ORGANIZATION FOR SECURITY AND COOPERATION IN EUROPE MISSION TO MOLDOVA.

CONFERENCE FOR SECURITY AND COOPERATION IN EUROPE MISSION TO TAJIKISTAN. *See* ORGANIZATION FOR SECURITY AND COOPERATION IN EUROPE MISSION TO TAJIKISTAN.

CONFERENCE FOR SECURITY AND COOPERATION IN EUROPE SPILLOVER MONITOR MISSION TO SKOPJE. *See* ORGANIZATION FOR SECURITY AND COOPERATION IN EUROPE SPILLOVER MONITOR MISSION TO SKOPJE.

CONGO. *See* CONGO INTERNATIONAL FORCE; UNITED NATIONS OPERATION IN THE CONGO; UNITED NATIONS ORGANIZATION MISSION IN THE DEMOCRATIC REPUBLIC OF THE CONGO.

CONGO INTERNATIONAL FORCE. In May 2003, violence erupted in northeast Democratic Republic of the Congo as rival groups initiated a spat of murder and cannibalism following the withdrawal of Ugandan and other forces from the area around Bunia. The militia groups attacked civilians and **United Nations** (UN) peace-keepers stationed in the country as part of the **United Nations Organization Mission in the Congo** (MONUC). At least two UN peace-keepers died in the attacks upon their compounds. The UN called upon France and other states to form a "coalition of the willing" and dispatch an international force to halt the violence before it escalated to the level of a "second **Rwanda**." France sent a small military team to evaluate the local airport in preparations for the insertion of an international force. The UN envisions the international force as a separate mission from MONUC, endorsed but not mandated by the global body, and carrying a **peace enforcement** authorization to restore order to the area. Canada, Great Britain, Nigeria, Pakistan, and South Africa expressed interest in joining France in the operation.

CONTADORA GROUP. This informal group was formed in 1983 by Colombia, Mexico, Panama, and Venezuela. The group, later joined by Costa Rica, El Salvador, Guatemala, Honduras, and Nicaragua, developed the Procedure for the Establishment of a Firm and Lasting Peace in Central America in August 1987. The agreement paved the way for joint cooperation by the **United Nations** (UN) and the **Organization of American States** (OAS) and the eventual deployment of the United Nations Observer Group in Central America (ONUCA).

CONTINENTAL METHOD. The **rules of engagement** for working with civilian governments generally practiced by states on the European continent during the first half of the century. The practice involved displaying a large military presence at all times when assisting civilian authorities in order to maintain order. *See also* BRITISH METHOD.

COSTA DEL SOL DECLARATION. The declaration, also known as the Tesoro Beach Agreement, resulted from a meeting of representatives of Costa Rica, Guatemala, El Salvador, Honduras, and Nicaragua with the Secretary-General of the **United Nations** (UN) on February 8, 1989. The declaration dealt with coordination of the technical aspects behind supporting the Procedure for the Establishment of a Firm and Lasting Peace in Central America. The UN eventually deployed the **United Nations Observer Group in Central America** (ONUCA) to monitor the peace process in Central America.

COSTA RICA. *See* INTERNATIONAL COMMISSION FOR SUPPORT AND VERIFICATION.

COT, GENERAL JEAN. Cot, a **French** army officer, filled the position as **Force Commander** of the **United Nations Protection Force** (UNPROFOR) between July 1993 and March 1994. **United Nations** (UN) Secretary-General **Boutros Boutros-Ghali** requested the removal of Cot following the latter's criticism of the international organization in January 1994. Cot called for the use of **North Atlantic Treaty Organization** (NATO) aircraft in a close support role when needed by peacekeepers in **Bosnia and Herzegovina**. After NATO authorized the use of its aircraft in support of the peacekeeping operation, Cot asked Boutros-Ghali to request air strikes to protect peacekeepers in Sarajevo. In both cases, Boutros-Ghali did not forward the request to NATO authorities. Cot compared the peacekeeping force in Bosnia to a "goat tethered to a fence" and criticized Boutros-Ghali for not acting on his promises to call upon NATO air support when requested by the force commander. In response, Boutros-Ghali delegated the political authority to seek NATO air support to **Yasushi Akashi**, the Secretary-General's **Special Representative** in Bosnia and Herzegovina, and then asked France to replace Cot before the end of March 1994. *See also* UNITED NATIONS PROTECTION FORCE IN BOSNIA AND HERZEGOVINA.

COTE D'IVOIRE. *See* ECONOMIC COMMUNITY OF WEST AFRICAN STATES PEACEKEEPING FORCE IN COTE D'IVOIRE; FRENCH PEACEKEEPING; UNITED NATIONS MISSION IN COTE D'IVOIRE.

CROATIA. *See* UNITED NATIONS CONFIDENCE RESTORATION MISSION IN CROATIA; UNITED NATIONS MISSION OF OBSERVERS IN PREVLAKA; UNITED NATIONS POLICE SUPPORT GROUP; UNITED NATIONS PROTECTION FORCE; UNITED NATIONS TRANSITIONAL ADMINISTRATION IN EASTERN SLAVONIA, BARANJA, AND WESTERN SIRMIUM.

CYPRUS. *See* UNITED NATIONS PEACEKEEPNG FORCE IN CYPRUS.

– D –

DALLAIRE, BRIGADIER-GENERAL ROMEO A. Dallaire, a Canadian officer, was selected as the Chief Military Observer of the **United Nations Observer Mission in Uganda-Rwanda** (UNO-MUR) in 1993. He also became the **Force Commander** of the **United Nations Assistance Mission in Rwanda** (UNAMIR). Dallaire, in a well-documented case, attempted to warn the **United Nations** (UN) and the West that a potential massacre was brewing in Rwanda. He was ignored and the resulting genocide took the lives of approximately 800,000 people.

DAYAL, RAJESHWAR. Dayal, a native of **India**, was selected as one of the three members of the Observation Group headquarters assigned to the **United Nations Observation Group in Lebanon** (UN-OGIL) from June to December 1958. In addition, he served as the Special Representative of the **United Nations Operation in the Congo** (ONUC) from September 1960 to May 1961. He was the first non-American to hold this position. Dayal's selection displayed the concern of the **United Nations** (UN) to place someone in the position who was from a neutral Third World state.

DECLARATION OF SAN ISIDRO DE CORONADO. Costa Rica, El Salvador, Guatemala, Honduras, and Nicaragua issued the declaration on December 12, 1989. The five states requested an extension of the mandate for the **United Nations Observer Group in Central America** (ONUCA). The states asked the **United Nations** (UN) to verify both the cessation of hostilities and the demobilization of irregular forces throughout Central America. The task required the addition of combat units to ONUCA. The Security Council responded by passing Resolution 650 (1990) on March 27, 1990. In response, ONUCA, using a combat battalion deployed from Venezuela, demobilized Nicaraguan resistance members located in Honduras in April 1990.

DEMILITARIZED ZONE. An area, normally linear, in which the military forces of belligerents are forbidden to enter. In peacekeeping operations, the multinational soldiers normally operate within these established zones, if they have been established. *See also* INTERPOSITION FORCE.

DEPARTMENT OF PEACEKEEPING OPERATIONS (DPKO). The **United Nations** (UN) established the Department of Peacekeeping Operations (DPKO) in 1992 to serve as a permanent office within the organization for the planning and oversight of peacekeeping missions. DPKO is headed by an Undersecretary-General of the UN. The organization includes a Mine Action Service, a **Training and Evaluation Service** (TES), an Office of Operations, an Office of Mission Support, a Military Division, a Civilian Police Division, and a **Best Practices Unit**.

DIBUAMA, MAJOR-GENERAL TIMOTHY K. Dibuama, a native of Ghana, was the Military Adviser to the Secretary-General of the **United Nations** (UN) between 1977 and 1992. He headed a military group assigned to travel to the Western Sahara to gather information for the development of the **United Nations Mission for the Referendum in Western Sahara** (MINURSO). On July 12, 1992, Dibuama assumed command of the **United Nations Iraq-Kuwait Observation Mission** (UNIKOM).

DOMINICAN REPUBLIC. *See* INTER-AMERICAN PEACE FORCE; REPRESENTATIVE OF THE SECRETARY-GENERAL IN THE DOMINICAN REPUBLIC.

– E –

EAST TIMOR. *See* INTERNATIONAL FORCE IN EAST TIMOR; UNITED NATIONS MISSION IN EAST TIMOR; UNITED NATIONS MISSION OF SUPPORT IN EAST TIMOR; UNITED NATIONS TRANSITIONAL ADMINISTRATION IN EAST TIMOR.

ECONOMIC AND MONETARY COMMUNITY OF CENTRAL AFRICAN STATES (CEMAC) PEACEKEEPING OPERATION IN CENTRAL AFRICAN REPUBLIC. On December 2, 2001, the Community of Sahel-Saharan States (COMESSA) mandated the **Community of Sahel-Saharan States Peacekeeping Mission in Central African Republic.** Other states in the area felt uneasy about this mission which was dominated by Libyan troops. In response, the Economic and Monetary Community of Central African States (CEMAC) gathered in Gabon and mandated its own peacekeeping operation on October 2, 2002, to replace the COMESSA mission. Little action was taken until later in the month when an invasion by **Central African Republic** (CAR) rebels from Chadian territory nearly toppled President Ange-Felix Patasse. In response, there was a renewed effort by CEMAC to deploy a peacekeeping operation. Initially, the Libyan and CAR governments noted that Libyan troops would still remain in the country despite the presence of the CEMAC peacekeepers. However, Libya reversed its position and stated that its troops would depart when every contingent of the CEMAC operation arrived in CAR. Gabon agreed to lead the force and provide the **Force Commander** and largest contingent.

Initial plans called for a total of approximately 350 peacekeepers. The majority (200 in number) would come from Gabon and the rest from Cameroon, Republic of the Congo, Equatorial Guinea, and Mali. Cameroon later dropped its pledge due to border problems with **Nigeria**. Gabonese peacekeepers arrived on December 4, 2002, on transportation leased by **France**, and COMESSA peacekeepers from Djibouti, Libya, and Sudan departed the CAR at the end of December 2002. Troops from the Republic of the Congo and Equatorial Guinea arrived in late January 2003 to join the Gabonese peacekeepers in the CAR. Funding and equipment for the operation are provided by France, the **European Union** (EU), the **United States**, and the **People's Republic of China**. Although the CAR government fell in a coup on March 16, 2003, the CEMAC peacekeepers remained on the ground at the request of the new president.

ECONOMIC COMMUNITY OF WEST AFRICAN STATES (ECOWAS). The Economic Community of West African States is a subregional organization in Western Sub-Saharan Africa. The organization, established in 1975, has 16 member states. The basic purpose of the group is to liberalize trade between the members and establish a common market. The members signed a mutual defense protocol in 1981. This document was used to justify the mandating of subregional peacekeeping operations. *See also* ECONOMIC COMMUNITY OF WEST AFRICAN STATES MONITORING GROUP IN GUINEA; ECONOMIC COMMUNITY OF WEST AFRICAN STATES MONITORING GROUP IN GUINEA-BISSAU; ECONOMIC COMMUNITY OF WEST AFRICAN STATES MONITORING GROUP IN LIBERIA; ECONOMIC COMMUNITY OF WEST AFRICAN STATES MONITORING GROUP IN SIERRA LEONE; ECONOMIC COMMUNITY OF WEST AFRICAN STATES PEACEKEEPING FORCE IN COTE D'IVOIRE.

ECONOMIC COMMUNITY OF WEST AFRICAN STATES MISSION IN COTE D'IVOIRE. *See* ECONOMIC COMMUNITY OF WEST AFRICAN STATES PEACEKEEPING FORCE IN COTE D'IVOIRE.

ECONOMIC COMMUNITY OF WEST AFRICAN STATES MONITORING GROUP (ECOMOG) IN COTE D'IVOIRE. *See* ECONOMIC COMMUNITY OF WEST AFRICAN STATES PEACEKEEPING FORCE IN COTE D'IVOIRE.

ECONOMIC COMMUNITY OF WEST AFRICAN STATES MONITORING GROUP (ECOMOG) IN GUINEA. Conflict in **Liberia** and **Sierra Leone** continued to spill over into Guinea. The **Economic Community of West African States** (ECOWAS) had fielded the **Economic Community of West African States Monitoring Group (ECOMOG) in Liberia** and the **Economic Community of West African States Monitoring Group (ECOMOG) in Sierra Leone** in attempts to halt the spread of the civil conflict. In 1994, over 50,000 refugees had fled to Guinea from Liberia. At the same time Guinea provided training bases for groups who were fighting Charles Taylor, the main Liberian opposition figure. By 1998, there were over 297,000 refugees from Liberia and Sierra Leone in Guinea. In 1999, reports indicated that the Guinean army was operating within the territory of Liberia and Sierra Leone. Liberia retaliated and raided villages in Guinea. In order to halt the spread of the regional conflict, ECOWAS proposed the mandating of a peacekeeping operation for deployment to Guinea, a member of the organization. The ECOWAS states mandated the Economic Community of West African States Monitoring Group (ECOMOG) in Guinea and agreed to deploy 1,700 peacekeepers, most of them from **Nigeria**, in February 2001. However, February arrived and the peacekeepers were not able to deploy due to reluctance on the part of Guinea to allow them to enter its territory. ECOWAS continued negotiations with Guinea throughout much of 2001, but the state refused to permit the introduction of the peacekeepers on its soil. The peacekeepers never deployed to Guinea.

ECONOMIC COMMUNITY OF WEST AFRICAN STATES MONITORING GROUP (ECOMOG) IN GUINEA-BISSAU. Elements of the military rebelled against the government of Guinea-Bissau in June 1998. In response, Senegal dispatched 2,500 soldiers and Guinea sent 500 troops to the country in support of the government. Both countries acted out of concern for their national interests and did not deploy under an international peacekeeping mandate. In November 1998, the belligerents signed a peace agreement that called for a cease-fire, the departure of the troops from Senegal and Guinea, and the introduction of a peacekeeping operation from the **Economic Community of West African States** (ECOWAS).

Senegalese and Guinean troops departed the country in March 1999 as peacekeepers of the Economic Community of West African States Monitoring Group (ECOMOG) in Guinea-Bissau arrived to replace them. On April 6, 1999, the **United Nations** (UN) endorsed the ECOMOG operation. ECOMOG's mandate included providing security at the international airport; assisting with humanitarian aid deliveries; and disarming the belligerents. ECOMOG departed following the ouster of Guinea-Bissau's president by the rebel forces despite the cease-fire. The last ECOMOG forces left the country by June 7, 1999. The maximum strength of ECOMOG in Guinea-Bissau was 712 peacekeepers from Benin, Gambia, Niger, and Togo.

ECONOMIC COMMUNITY OF WEST AFRICAN STATES MONITORING GROUP (ECOMOG) IN LIBERIA. Master Sergeant Samuel Doe came to power in **Liberia** in 1980 following a military coup against the government of President William Tolbert. In 1984, President Doe, who had survived numerous assassination attempts and coups d'etat since 1980, charged his Director of the General Services Agency, Charles Taylor, with embezzling $900,000. When Taylor fled to the **United States**, the authorities arrested and held him in Massachusetts for extradition to Monrovia. However, Taylor escaped and made his way to Côte d'Ivoire, where he received sympathy and introduction to the leaders of Burkina Faso and Libya who would later aid him in forming a guerilla army. In January 1990, Taylor led his newly formed group into Nimba County, Liberia, from Côte d'Ivoire and initiated his war against the government of President Doe. The conflict took a new twist when Prince Johnson, one of Taylor's commanders, formed his own guerilla group and became Taylor's political and military rival. While the civil war intensified and neared Monrovia, President Doe's government began to crumble as the Taylor forces defeated his army and his government ministers began fleeing the country.

It was at this point that the **Economic Community of West African States** (ECOWAS) became involved. The ECOWAS Standing Mediation Committee met between August 6 and 7, 1990 to examine alternatives for settling the Liberian civil war. The committee recommended the establishment of an ECOWAS Monitoring Group (ECOMOG) to oversee a cease-fire in Liberia. ECOMOG would consist of contingents from the committee members (Gambia, Ghana, Mali, Nigeria, Togo) as well as Guinea and Sierra Leone. Officially, ECOMOG would supervise the implementation and compliance with a cease-fire by all parties until a freely elected government could be installed. The committee also recommended that ECOWAS set up a special emergency fund to finance ECOMOG. Mali and Togo backed out of the operation prior to its arrival in Liberia by sea on August 24, 1990. Ghana selected **Force Commander** Lieutenant-General Arnold Quainoo to lead the 3,500 peacekeepers who initially comprised the operation.

Taylor refused to accept ECOMOG's mission and declared that the peacekeepers were not neutral in the conflict. He attacked the ECO-

MOG forces in Monrovia, forcing the contingents to move from a pure peacekeeping mission to one more in line with **peace enforcement.** Nigeria charged that Quainoo was too conservative in using force and unilaterally replaced him with Major-General Joshua Dogonyaro. After Dogonyaro established control in Monrovia and its hinterland, the civil war settled into a stalemate of intermittent cease-fires between the belligerents and ECOMOG. Senegal joined ECOMOG in 1991 and Mali did the same the following year. By August 1992, ECOMOG's strength stood at approximately 9,000 soldiers. The next month, Taylor launched a major offensive against ECOMOG. The peacekeepers counterattacked with ground troops and air power. Senegal, disillusioned and suffering several fatalities, elected to withdraw from ECOMOG during January 1993. Estimates have placed the strength of ECOMOG at approximately 12,000 after Senegal's withdrawal. At this time, the **United Nations** (UN) recognized that Taylor would probably never view ECOMOG as a neutral tool for peace and increased its own deliberations on the subject of settling the civil war.

The belligerents signed what is known as the Cotonou Peace Agreement on July 25, 1993. This document called for a new cease-fire and proposed the introduction of military observers from the United Nations. Discussions at the UN led to the mandating of an all-African peacekeeping operation to assist ECOMOG and meet Taylor's demands for a truly neutral military force prior to free elections. This operation, known as the **United Nations Observer Mission in Liberia** (UNOMIL), deployed to Liberia in 1993. The Liberian civil unrest spread to **Sierra Leone** and Guinea as rebels crossed the border into each state. After many false starts, a peace process finally brought elections to Liberia. Taylor won the election for the presidency. ECOMOG departed Liberia by mid-1999 but did leave a small number of troops in the country to watch the border with Sierra Leone.

The financing of ECOMOG by ECOWAS proved to be a failure. The member states refused to contribute to the operation, and diplomats were not successful in their original attempts to secure cash at the UN. Nigeria paid the vast majority of the ECOWAS tab. Later, the United States began contributing a small sum annually to assist ECOMOG.

ECONOMIC COMMUNITY OF WEST AFRICAN STATES MONITORING GROUP (ECOMOG) IN SIERRA LEONE. Civil war erupted in **Sierra Leone** in March 1991 as the Revolutionary United Front (RUF), with assistance from rebels in Liberia, attempted to overthrow the government. Charles Taylor, the main rebel leader in Liberia, dimly viewed Sierra Leone's backing of the **Economic Community of West African States Monitoring Group (ECOMOG) in Liberia** which was under Nigerian leadership. The presence of diamond fields in Sierra Leone was another attraction for the rebel groups. ECOMOG dispatched a small force of peacekeepers from Liberia to Sierra Leone to assist the government. The ECOMOG force and the military of Sierra Leone managed to contain the RUF. On April 29, 1992, the military overthrew the government of Sierra Leone. The military stepped down four years later and Sierra Leone held its first democratic elections since 1967. On November 20, 1996, President Ahmed Tejan Kabbah signed a peace agreement with the RUF. On May 25, 1997, the military launched another coup and toppled President Kabbah. The military formed an Armed Forces Revolutionary Council (AFRC) under Major Johnny Koroma and invited the RUF to join it. Although Koroma remained the nominal head of government, the RUF essentially wrestled control of the government from the AFRC.

Nigerian soldiers were already in Sierra Leone under a bilateral agreement at the time of the May 1997 coup. Nigeria quickly reinforced its soldiers in Sierra Leone and actively engaged the AFRC forces. Guinean troops assisted Nigeria but those of Ghana chose to withdraw declaring they preferred a negotiated settlement. Nigeria found itself in a tough situation and many of its soldiers were taken hostage by the AFRC. Many of the **Economic Community of West African States** (ECOWAS) member states criticized Nigeria for acting without a mandate from the organization. However, by late 1997 Nigerian actions in Sierra Leone were being endorsed by the **Organization of African Unity**, the **Commonwealth**, and the **United Nations** (UN) as appropriate responses to military officers who had overthrown a democratically elected government.

In February 1998, a Nigerian-led ECOMOG offensive forced the AFRC and RUF to abandon Freetown, and President Kabbah returned to power in Sierra Leone. Fighting in the rural areas continued. The UN Security Council mandated the **United Nations Observer Mission in Sierra Leone** (UNOMSIL) on July 13, 1998, with Resolution 1181 (1998), to assist with the disarming of combatants and restructuring the military of Sierra Leone. UNOMSIL included an authorized 70 military observers and approximately 120 other personnel. However, the operation was slow in being manned and fielded, and approximately only half of its mandated strength was actually on the ground by the middle of 1999. In December 1998 RUF forces infiltrated Freetown, initiating the heaviest fighting in the country's civil war. ECOMOG regained the upper hand by late January 1999. UNOMSIL personnel evacuated Sierra Leone and traveled to Guinea during this period.

On July 7, 1999, the belligerents signed the Lome Accord. This agreement called for a cease-fire and disarmament/demobilization to be overseen by a new UN peacekeeping operation. On October 22, 1999, the Security Council mandated the new peacekeeping operation, the **United Nations Assistance Mission in Sierra Leone** (UNAMSIL), and ordered that the new organization absorb the mission and personnel of UNOMSIL. By early 2000, UNAMSIL absorbed the ECOMOG forces in Sierra Leone, and the African mission was phased out. The RUF forces did not completely adhere to the terms of the Lome Agreement prolonging the civil war.

It has been estimated that the maximum strength of ECOMOG forces in Sierra Leone stood at approximately 15,000 soldiers—the majority being Nigerian. Total ECOMOG fatalities in Sierra Leone have not been released and are still controversial in Nigeria where civilian groups claim the government continues to cover up the total number of casualties. The total cost of the ECOMOG operation has also not been released since Nigeria funded much of the mission. It is known that the United States and other Western countries contributed cash to help pay for ECOMOG.

ECONOMIC COMMUNITY OF WEST AFRICAN STATES PEACEKEEPING FORCE (ECOFORCE) IN COTE D'IVOIRE. On September 19, 2002, approximately 750 soldiers mutinied over plans to remove them from the armed forces of Côte d'Ivoire. The soldiers quickly gained control over the northern half of the country. **French** military forces, *Eléments français d'assistance* *opérationelle* (EFAO), based in Côte d'Ivoire, along with **British, Nigerian,** and **United States** troops, evacuated many individuals from towns behind rebel lines. Following the departure of the American, British, and Nigerian soldiers, the French military stabilized a zone between the rebels and government troops. Member states of the **Economic Community of West African States** (ECOWAS) opted to mandate a peacekeeping operation, the Economic Community of West African States Peacekeeping Force (ECOFORCE) in Côte d'Ivoire, to replace the French forces between the belligerents. However, members proved to be reluctant to field their contingents without a successful cease-fire in place. The situation deteriorated further when at least two new rebel groups entered the country from Liberia and initiated their own offensive against the government until checked by the French.

A small advance group of ECOFORCE officers arrived in Côte d'Ivoire in December 2002 to coordinate the arrival of the main body of peacekeepers. However, contingent providers still balked at fielding their troops without a cease-fire in the state. The original planned size of the peacekeeping operation is 1,200 troops with the majority, approximately 700, coming from Senegal. Nigeria originally pledged a small contingent but withdrew its offer by December 2002. The first small group of the main body flew into the country on January 3, 2003. Larger contingents from Ghana, Niger, Senegal, and Togo arrived in January and February 2003. In late February 2003, ECOFORCE peacekeepers deployed to the neutral barrier zone established and manned by French soldiers. Funding and equipment are provided by France, **Great Britain,** and the **United States** and are primarily directed to individual contingents rather than to the mission as a whole. ECOFORCE is sometimes referred to as the Economic Community of West African States Mission in Côte d'Ivoire (ECOMINCI).

ECUADOR. *See* MISSION OF MILITARY OBSERVERS ECUADOR-PERU.

EGYPT. *See* MIXED ARMISTICE COMMISSION; MULTINATIONAL FORCE AND OBSERVERS; OBSERVER GROUP EGYPT; UNITED NATIONS EMERGENCY FORCE I; UNITED NATIONS EMERGENCY FORCE II; UNITED NATIONS TRAN-

SITION ASSISTANCE GROUP; UNITED NATIONS TRUCE SU-PERVISION ORGANIZATION.

EL SALVADOR. *See* UNITED NATIONS OBSERVER MISSION IN EL SALVADOR.

ELEMENTS FRANCAIS D'ASSISTANCE OPERATIONELLE (EFAO). France has maintained permanent military garrisons in Africa since the end of the colonial period. These troops, known as *Eléments français d'assistance opérationelle* (EFAO), are based primarily in Côte d'Ivoire, Djibouti, Gabon, and Senegal. France has utilized the EFAO to protect its interests in Africa and maintain friendly governments in power. On two occasions, the EFAO stabilized a crisis situation and then handed the security duties to a French-organized peacekeeping operation fielded with African contingents. The first occurred in Zaire during 1978 when the EFAO was replaced by the **Inter-African Force.** The second incident happened in 1997 when the **Inter-African Force in the Central African Republic** assumed security from the French. In 2002, the EFAO, with reinforcements from France, planned to turn over security to the **Economic Community of West African States Monitoring Group (ECOMOG) in Côte d'Ivoire** during the civil crisis in Côte d'Ivoire. However, prolonged problems in securing a cease-fire and the deployment of the ECOMOG mission have delayed the change.

ELISABETHVILLE. Elisabethville, a town in secessionist Katanga province of the Congo, was a center of opposition to the **United Nations Operation in the Congo** (ONUC). **United Nations** (UN) Security Council Resolution 169 (1961) of November 24, 1961, authorized ONUC to use force in the removal of mercenaries in Katanga. On November 28, 1961, two UN officials were beaten. Over the next couple of days, several peacekeepers assigned to ONUC and based in Elisabethville were abducted and beaten. Other peacekeepers were killed or wounded in ambushes. ONUC peacekeepers in Elisabethville managed to hold on until December 14, when reinforcements were brought in to assist them. On December 15, the peacekeepers in Elisabethville were of sufficient strength to launch their own offensive.

ENCLAVES. *See* SAFE HAVENS.

ERITREA. *See* UNITED NATIONS MISSION IN ETHIOPIA AND ERITREA.

ERSKINE, LIEUTENANT-GENERAL EMMANUEL A. Erskine, an army officer from Ghana, was the first African to command a **United Nations** (UN) peacekeeping operation fielded outside of the African continent. He was the Chief of Staff of the **United Nations Truce Supervision Organization** (UNTSO) in the Middle East from January 1976 to April 1978 and from February 1981 to May 1986. He also served as the first **Force Commander** of the **United Nations Interim Force in Lebanon** (UNIFIL) from March 1978 and February 1981. Erskine was originally named as the first commander of the **Economic Community of West African States Monitoring Group (ECOMOG) in Liberia**. However, he did not take command of this operation. The reason for this change is not clear.

ETHIOPIA. *See* UNITED NATIONS MISSION IN ETHIOPIA AND ERITREA.

EUROPEAN COMMUNITY. *See* EUROPEAN UNION.

EUROPEAN COMMUNITY MONITORING MISSION. *See* EUROPEAN UNION MONITORING MISSION.

EUROPEAN FORCE (EURFOR). The **European Union** (EU) mandated and deployed the European Force (EURFOR) as a replacement for the **North Atlantic Treaty Organization's** (NATO) **Operation Amber Fox** in **Macedonia**. EURFOR officially replaced Operation Amber Fox on April 1, 2003. The EU mission consists of 380 soldiers from 27 European states, and its purpose is to keep the peace within Macedonia and prevent the country from sliding into the interethnic conflict witnessed in other Balkan states. The EU fielded EURFOR with an initial mandate of six months in duration. EURFOR is the EU's first nonpolice peacekeeping operation. The EU funds the operation.

EUROPEAN UNION (EU). The European Union (EU) unites 15 European states into a close economic, political, and social union although some individual countries do not participate as fully as others. There are 13 candidate members awaiting full membership within the EU. The EU evolved from the European Community on November 1, 1993, and members have a Common Foreign and Security Policy framework. Within this framework, the EU has discussed and deployed small peace operations. The EU planned to replace a **North Atlantic Treaty Organization** (NATO) mission in **Macedonia** known as **Operation Amber Fox** by January 1, 2003. However, difficulties delayed the transition of the security duties from NATO to the EU. The organization finally dispatched the **European Force** (EURFOR) to replace Operation Amber Fox on April 1, 2003. The EU has also offered to mandate a mission to replace NATO's **Stabilisation Force** (SFOR) in **Bosnia and Herzegovina**. *See also* AMSTERDAM TREATY; EUROPEAN UNION MONITORING MISSION; EUROPEAN UNION POLICE MISSION; EUROPEAN UNION RAPID REACTION FORCE; NICE TREATY; PETERSBERG MISSIONS.

EUROPEAN UNION MONITORING MISSION (EUMM). The European Community Monitoring Mission (ECCM) deployed to the Western Balkans in July 1991 following the outbreak of violence as the Federal Republic of Yugoslavia began to break up. The Council of the **European Union** (EU) passed a resolution on December 22, 2000, to convert the ECCM to **the European Union Monitoring Mission** (EUMM). The change in name reflects the earlier conversion of the European Community to the European Union. The EUMM monitors the political and security developments in **Albania**, **Bosnia and Herzegovina**, **Croatia**, Federal Republic of **Yugoslavia**, and the Former Yugoslav Republic of **Macedonia**. The EUMM consists of approximately 120 international civilian monitors and 75 local civilians. The mission headquarters is in Sarajevo and is funded by the European Commission. Some scholars do not acknowledge the EUMM as a peacekeeping mission. The Stockholm International Peace Research Institute (SIPRI) recognizes EUMM as a "peace operation" which the organization defines as being either an observer, peacekeeping, or peace-building mission.

EUROPEAN UNION POLICE MISSION (EUPM). The European Union (EU) mandated the European Union Police Mission (EUPM) to replace the **United Nations International Police Task Force** (UNIPTF) and **United Nations Mission in Bosnia and Herzegovina** (UNMIBH). EUPM assumed its duties on January 1, 2003, and oversees 16,000 police officers in the country's two autonomous regions—the Muslim–Croat federation and the Serb Republic. The organization also has oversight responsibility for the state border service and the Central Security Ministry. EUPM consists of 500 personnel with approximately 80 percent of these from EU states. The remaining officers are from non-EU European countries and Canada. The EU finances EUPM.

EUROPEAN UNION RAPID REACTION FORCE. The **European Union** (EU) asked its members to designate military units for inclusion in an EU **Rapid Reaction Force**. The 20,000 troops are designated, trained, and maintained by the member states for short-notice deployments under an EU **mandate**. The force would serve as the organization's response during the fielding of a **peacekeeping** operation. Each state has the right to refuse inclusion of its troops in any operation. *See also* AFRICAN STAND BY FORCE; NICE TREATY; NORTH ATLANTIC TREATY ORGANIZATION RAPID REACTION FORCE; UNITED NATIONS STAND BY ARRANGEMENT SYSTEM.

– F –

FEZ SUMMIT CONFERENCE. The **League of Arab States** convened the conference on September 6, 1982. During the meeting, the Lebanese officially requested the termination of the mandate of the **Arab Deterrent Force**. A compromise with Syria allowed its soldiers, fighting Israeli forces, to remain in **Lebanon** following the end of the mandate. At the same time, the Gulf State members, who contributed 65 percent of the funding, agreed to cease all financial contributions to the Syrian forces in Lebanon. The conference marked the official death of the Arab Deterrent Force, a **peacekeeping** operation that had generated a great deal of controversy as it moved into the category of **peace enforcement** in Lebanon. *See also* CAIRO SUMMIT CONFERENCE; RIYADH SUMMIT CONFERENCE.

FIRST GENERATION PEACEKEEPING. First Generation peacekeeping is a term sometimes applied to early **United Nations** peacekeeping operations that involved simply separating two belligerents following a cease-fire. These operations have also been called **Traditional Peacekeeping.** *See also* SECOND GENERATION PEACEKEEPING.

FORCE COMMANDER (FC). This term is applied to the military commander of a **United Nations** (UN) peacekeeping mission other than an **observation force.** This title should not be confused with Chief Military Observer, even though the two perform similar duties. Chief Military Observers command smaller contingents than a peacekeeping Force Commander. Secretary-General U Thant clarified the role of a Force Commander when he wrote in his aide-mémoire that the "Commander of the force, who is responsible to the Secretary-General, receives, as appropriate, directives from the Secretary-General on the exercise of his command and reports to the Secretary-General. The executive control of all units of the Force is at all times exercised by the Commander of the Force."

FORCE MOBILE RESERVE (FMR). The Force Mobile Reserve (FMR) evolved from the necessity to have highly mobile reserve units ready to assist peacekeepers assigned to the **United Nations Interim Force in Lebanon** (UNIFIL). Originally, each contingent's battalion provided its own reserve force. Early in 1987, UNIFIL underwent a major redeployment of its units, during which the FMR was established as a permanent organization drawing its assets from seven of the nine UNIFIL contingents. Each contributing contingent provides one platoon. The seven platoons, six mechanized infantry and one administrative, are organized into a mechanized company of approximately 175 soldiers. The mission of the force is to perform reconnaissance on all potential trouble spots within the UNIFIL area of operations, map routes to these trouble spots, demonstrate a high state of readiness, provide teams for patrols and escort duty, and operate as an integrated unit. The FMR maintains one platoon on alert at all times, which must be ready to move from its base in less than 15 minutes. The remaining five combat platoons have 30 minutes to mobilize and depart their base. Due to its base location, the FMR should be able to reach any location within the UNIFIL area of operation within one hour. The FMR has conducted several intensive combat operations in support of ambushed peacekeepers.

FORCES AVAILABLE TO THE WEST EUROPEAN UNION (FAWEU). The **West European Union** (WEU)'s Planning Cell maintained a list of conventional military forces available for use by the organization for peacekeeping, humanitarian operations, and peacemaking. These operations were named after their authorizing document and were often known as **Petersberg Missions**. The WEU referred to the list as the FAWEU.

FORMER YUGOSLAV REPUBLIC OF MACEDONIA. *See* MACEDONIA.

FOURTH COMMITTEE. The Fourth Committee is one of six main committees of the **United Nations** (UN) General Assembly and is also known as the Special Political and Decolonization Committee. The **Special Committee on Peacekeeping Operations** reports to the General Assembly through the Fourth Committee.

FRENCH OPERATIONAL ASSISTANCE UNITS (EFAO). *See* ELEMENTS FRANCAIS D'ASSISTANCE OPERATIONELLE (EFAO).

FRENCH PEACEKEEPING. France, which once held extensive colonies across northern, western, and central Africa, still maintains a military presence on the continent. The French military has soldiers based in Senegal, Côte d'Ivoire, **Central African Republic**, and Gabon, as well as a rapid deployment force in southern France. France has frequently used its military forces on the continent for unilateral interventions in support of governments considered friendly toward Paris. However, France has led several multinational military interventions that are considered in some circles to be peacekeeping operations. These missions include two in **Zaire** and one in **Rwanda**. The first operation in Zaire, often known as Shaba I, occurred in 1977.

On March 8, 1977, Zairian dissidents based in Angola entered Zaire's Shaba province, where government forces proved to be ineffective in offering resistance. President Sese Seku Mobutu of Zaire appealed for Western assistance before his military collapsed. King Hassan II of Morocco responded by dispatching 1,500 troops, with the first contingent arriving on April 8, 1977. The French provided logistical assistance to the Moroccans, who were then able to stabilize the situation in Shaba. On May 13, 1978, the Zairian rebels returned to Shaba and attacked the city of Kolwezi, a mining center with a considerable expatriate population of Westerners. The French responded to the crisis by deploying Legionnaires to Kolwezi on May 19, 1978. Belgium joined the military effort and dispatched a military unit the next day. After securing their immediate objectives, the French and Belgians extracted themselves from the conflict by introducing an **Inter-African Force** to replace them.

The French initiated a third multinational mission on June 23, 1994, in Rwanda. This operation, launched with the blessings of the **United Nations** (UN) and led by Commander Marin Gillier, included a mission of providing humanitarian assistance following the resumption of ethnic violence between the Hutus and Tutsi of Rwanda. The Tutsi rebellion against the Hutu-dominated government of Rwanda led to a series of massacres across the state. The **United Nations Assistance Mission in Rwanda** (UNAMIR) was not able to halt the hostilities and was encountering difficulty in protecting refugees from the fighting. The UN opted to increase its operation with peacekeepers from African states, but the mission faced difficulties in getting off the ground. In response, the French moved in its force to assist in the protection of civilians. The French operation consisted of 2,500 Legionnaires and Marines flown in from bases in other African states. The African response to the French intervention has been mixed. Uganda, Tanzania, and Burundi denied the French permission to stage military operations from their territory. Zimbabwe declared that the French actions endangered the All-African force being considered for Rwanda. On the other hand, Zaire granted France permission to use its territory, and Egypt pledged a military contingent to aid the French effort. Senegal dispatched 300 soldiers to join the French military units in Rwanda.

In 1996, France organized the **Inter-African Force in the Central African Republic** (MISAB) to help restore order in Central African Republic. At the end of 2002, French soldiers stabilized Côte d'Ivoire following an outbreak of civil war in that state. France established a neutral zone between government and rebel forces in order to promote the peace process and prepare for the arrival of the **Economic Community of West African States Peacekeeping Force in Côte D'Ivoire** (ECOFORCE). In May 2003, the UN requested France to help organize an international operation to restore order in the Democratic Republic of the Congo. *See also* CONGO INTERNATIONAL FORCE; ELEMENTS FRANCAIS D'ASSISTANCE OPERATIONELLE; RENFORCEMENT DES CAPACITES AFRICAINES DE MAINTIEN DE LA PAIX.

– G –

GAMBIEZ, COLONEL GERARD. Gambiez, a French army officer, was appointed by **United Nations** (UN) Secretary-General **Boutros Boutros-Ghali** in January 1993 to lead a team of diplomats attempting to secure pledges of military personnel and equipment for a **stand-by force** for **peacekeeping** operations fielded by the international organization. Traditionally, the UN must request military contingents from member states each time it fields a peacekeeping operation. Boutros-Ghali's plan was to establish a pool of military units and personnel from which the UN can call upon without having to request pledges. The personnel would remain in their home countries but would be ready to deploy on short notice upon receiving a request from the Secretary-General. This would save time in actually deploying the peacekeeping mission and would only be used for operations termed as **traditional peacekeeping**. Gambiez and six assistants traveled to approximately 50 countries and contacted 130 other states in their efforts to secure the equipment and personnel for the international organization. The team concluded its work in April 1994 and reported that they had received pledges from at least 15 states totaling approximately 54,000 soldiers and technical experts such as logisticians. Although impressive in numbers (the UN had 70,000 peacekeepers in the field in early 1994), the total was short of the goal of 100,000 personnel envisioned by Boutros-Ghali. The United States declined to earmark military forces for the UN.

GEORGIA. *See* COMMONWEALTH OF INDEPENDENT STATES PEACEKEEPING FORCES IN GEORGIA; ORGANIZATION FOR SECURITY AND COOPERATION IN EUROPE MISSION TO GEORGIA; SOUTH OSSETIA JOINT FORCE; UNITED NATIONS OBSERVER MISSION IN GEORGIA.

GERMAN PEACEKEEPING. Germany contributed additional funds beyond its assessments to support **United Nations** (UN) peacekeeping for many years. However, the country, citing its **Basic Law**, did not field personnel with the missions. Legislative reinterpretation of the Basic Law has permitted Germany to deploy peacekeepers in limited situations after the **Cold War**. Germany contributes to UN and **North Atlantic Treaty Organization** (NATO) peacekeeping missions and will potentially field contingents with the **European Union Rapid Reaction Force**.

GOMES, BRIGADIER-GENERAL PERICLES FERREIRA. Gomes, a Brazilian officer, served as the only commander of the **United Nations Angola Verification Mission I** (UNAVEM I) beginning in December 1988. Gomes held the title of Chief Military Observer. From September 3 to 23, 1989, Gomes, while still assigned to UNAVEM I, led a reconnaissance mission for the Secretary-General to Central America. His report, accepted by the Secretary-General, recommended the immediate deployment of the **United Nations Observer Group in Central America** (ONUCA).

GOOD FAITH AGREEMENT. This agreement, developed by **United Nations** (UN) Secretary-General **Dag Hammarskjöld**, confirmed the willingness of Egypt to accept the **United Nations Emergency Force I** on its territory. The UN operates under a principle that a **host state** must agree to allow a peacekeeping mission to be stationed on its territory. Egypt later requested the removal of UNEF I in 1967. The UN reluctantly complied with the request and the Six Day War erupted following the withdrawal.

GORAZDE. *See* SAFE AREAS.

GORGE, REMY. Gorge, a **Swiss** diplomat, was the acting **Special Representative** for **the United Nations Peacekeeping Force in Cyprus** (UNFICYP) between December 1977 and April 1978. This was an unusual selection since Switzerland held observer rather than full-member status in the **United Nations** and did not contribute military elements to peacekeeping operations.

GOULDING, MARRACK. Goulding, a **British** citizen, served as the Undersecretary-General for Peacekeeping in the **United Nations** (UN) from 1986 until March 1993. When he first assumed the title after replacing the retiring **Brian Urquhart**, the position was known as the Undersecretary-General for Special Political Affairs. Goulding initiated the efforts to improve UN coordination of peacekeeping operations, which were continued by his successor, **Kofi Annan**. He personally represented the Secretary-General in a fact-finding mission to the Middle East to determine the fate of American Lieutenant-Colonel William Higgins, who was kidnapped and murdered in **Lebanon** despite his assignment as a peacekeeper with the **United Nations Truce Supervision Organization** (UNTSO). Goulding held the post of "senior peacekeeper" when the UN peacekeepers were awarded the **Nobel Peace Prize** in 1988. Goulding moved from his peacekeeping position to the post of Undersecretary-General for Political Affairs in 1993. Between 1979 and 1983, Goulding represented his country in the UN and presided over the Trusteeship Council for a year.

GREAT BRITAIN AND PEACEKEEPING. *See* BRITISH PEACEKEEPING.

GREECE. *See* UNITED NATIONS SPECIAL COMMITTEE ON THE BALKANS.

GREEN LINE. The Green Line is a narrow boundary and neutral zone in the city of Nicosia on the island of Cyprus. The zone is patrolled by elements of the **United Nations Peacekeeping Force in Cyprus** (UNFICYP). The line separates the Turkish Cypriots who control the northern areas of Nicosia and the Greek Cypriots who inhabit the southern regions of the city. The British military stationed on Cyprus originally established the Green Line. In some locations, the neutral zone marked by the Green Line is only meters wide. *See also* RED LINE.

GRENADA. *See* ORGANIZATION OF EAST CARIBBEAN STATES.

GRIENDL, MAJOR-GENERAL GUNTHER G. Griendl, a native of Austria, served as the **Force Commander** of the **United Nations Disengagement Observer Force** (UNDOF) between April 1979 and February 1981. Like his predecessor, Major-General Hannes Philipp of Austria, Griendl arrived as a Colonel and was promoted directly to the rank of Major-General. The passing over of the rank of Brigadier General for both men may have been due to the requirement that the Force Commander be a Major-General. The two Brigadier-Generals who commanded the operation held the titles of "interim" and "acting" Force Commander. Griendl moved from the UNDOF position and became the Force Commander of the **United Nations Peacekeeping Force in Cyprus** (UNFICYP) in March 1981. He held that position until April 1989. Griendl later held the position as the first Force Commander of the **United Nations Iraq-Kuwait Observation Mission** (UNIKOM) until July 1992. With the completion of this assignment, Griendl can claim over twelve years of senior **United Nations** (UN) peacekeeping service.

GUADALCANAL. *See* INTERNATIONAL PEACE MONITORING TEAM; SOUTH PACIFIC PEACEKEEPING FORCE.

GUATAMALA. *See* UNITED NATIONS VERIFICATION MISSION IN GUATAMALA.

GUINEA. *See* ECONOMIC COMMUNITY OF WEST AFRICAN STATES MONITORING GROUP IN GUINEA.

GUINEA-BISSAU. *See* ECONOMIC COMMUNITY OF WEST AFRICAN STATES MONITORING GROUP IN GUINEA-BISSAU.

GYANI, LIEUTENANT-GENERAL P. S. Gyani, an Indian army officer, served as the **Force Commander** for the **United Nations Emergency Force I** (UNEF I) from December 1959 to January 1964. At the same time, he also held the position of Force Commander of the **United Nations Yemen Observation Mission** (UNYOM) from September to November 1963. In November 1963, the position was "downgraded" to the term Chief of Staff. Briefly dual-hatting Gyani was not unusual since UNYOM fell under UNEF I for logistical and personnel issues. In March 1964, Gyani, who held the position of Special Representative for the crisis on Cyprus since January, became the first Force Commander of the **United Nations Peacekeeping Force in Cyprus** (UNFICYP) and held that post until June 1964. Gyani had informed Secretary-General U Thant that he would only serve one three-month term in the position due to personal reasons.

– H –

HAGGLUND, MAJOR-GENERAL GUSTAV. Hagglund, an army officer from Finland, was the **Force Commander** of the **United Nations Disengagement Observer Force** (UNDOF) from June 1985 to May 1986. Following this assignment, Hagglund became the Force Commander of the **United Nations Interim Force in Lebanon** (UNIFIL) and remained in this position until June 1988.

HAITI. *See* MULTINATIONAL FORCE IN HAITI; UNITED NATIONS CIVILIAN POLICE MISSION IN HAITI; UNITED NATIONS MISSION IN HAITI; UNITED NATIONS OBSERVATION GROUP FOR THE VERIFICATION OF THE ELECTIONS IN HAITI; UNITED NATIONS SUPPORT MISSION IN HAITI; UNITED NATIONS TRANSITION MISSION IN HAITI.

HAMMARSKJOLD, DAG. Hammarskjöld, a Swede, served as the Secretary-General of the **United Nations** (UN) from April 10, 1953, to his death on September 18, 1961. He held the position of Secretary-General during two critical periods of peacekeeping history. First, he opted to utilize the **Uniting for Peace Resolution** to convene the General Assembly to mandate the **United Nations Emergency Force I** (UNEF I) in 1956. Second, he was active in negotiations related to the Congolese civil war and the mission of the **United Nations Operation in the Congo** (UNOC). Hammarskjöld died in a plane crash within the Congo while on a peace mission.

HONDURAS. *See* INTERNATIONAL COMMISSION FOR SUPPORT AND VERIFICATION.

HORN, LIEUTENANT-GENERAL CARL C. VON. Von Horn, a Swedish officer, was the Chief of Staff of the **United Nations Truce Supervision Organization** (UNTSO) between March 1958 and July 1960 and from January 1961 to May 1963. Between his two UNTSO assignments, Von Horn was named as the first **Force Commander** of the **United Nations Operation in the Congo** (ONUC) and held that position from July to December 1960. In July 1963, von Horn became the first Force Commander of the **United Nations Yemen Observation Mission** (UNYOM). He held that position until resigning in August 1963, following a major falling-out with Secretary-General U Thant. Reportedly, Von Horn charged that the operation was undermanned and short of supplies and equipment. General **Indar Rikhye**, the military adviser to the Secretary-General, reported that despite physical hardship, morale of the peacekeepers was high. Disagreements between Force Commanders and Secretaries-General are also evident in the **United Nations Protection Force** (UNPROFOR) in the former **Yugoslavia**.

HOST STATE. The host state is the country in which a peacekeeping operation is actually based during its operation. An agreement is normally reached between the mandating international organization and the host state prior to the deployment of the neutral operation. *See also* GOOD FAITH AGREEMENT.

– I –

IMPLEMENTATION FORCE (IFOR). In the 1980s, **Yugoslavia** began showing serious strains between the various ethnic groups comprising the state. In June 1991, **Croatia** and Slovenia declared their independence from Serb-dominated Yugoslavia. The Serb minorities in the new states called for assistance and fighting erupted. The European Community and **West European Union** (WEU) failed in their efforts to halt the conflict and the **United Nations** (UN) became actively involved in September 1991. The UN mandated the **United Nations Protection Force** (UNPROFOR) in February 1992 and deployed the operation by the summer of 1992. Hostilities continued and even spread to **Bosnia and Herzegovina**, another territorial entity of Yugoslavia. In April 1993, the **North Atlantic Treaty Organization** (NATO) agreed to enforce a no-fly zone over Bosnia and Herzegovina for the UN. In February 1994, NATO members, with the endorsement of the UN, authorized the organization to conduct air strikes in support of UNPROFOR. NATO conducted a short air campaign in Bosnia and Herzegovina in the summer of 1995.

The various parties to the conflict in Bosnia and Herzegovina met in Dayton, Ohio, to discuss the provisions of a peace plan. The groups signed the General Framework for Peace on December 14, 1995. The document, known as the Dayton Accord, was negotiated in the **United States** but actually signed in **France**. The UN Security Council, with Resolution 1031 (1995), endorsed NATO as the security force to oversee the implementation of the agreement. The document provided NATO with a mission to provide a safe and secure environment; separating the opposing parties; overseeing the movement of military forces and heavy weapons to approved sites; conducting patrols along the demilitarized Inter-Entity Boundary Line; and inspecting weapons storage sites. The NATO mission, known as the Implementation Force (IFOR), replaced the **United Nations Protection Force in Bosnia and Herzegovina**.

Officially, IFOR began operations on December 20, 1995, with a maximum allowance of 60,000 troops (50,000 were from NATO members but 10,000 were contributed by 18 non-NATO states). Many of the latter, as well as some NATO forces, transferred from UNPROFOR to IFOR. The NATO mission successfully carried out the mandate provided in the Dayton Accord. The operation provided the secure environment required for the first free elections held in Bosnia and Herzegovina (April 1996) since the end of the war. IFOR also helped provide the stability required for the September 1996 elections in the state. IFOR had a relatively short mandate of one year from implementation of the Dayton Accord to elections within the state. With IFOR's mandate completed, NATO members agreed to maintain a continued presence to oversee the peace process. The **Stabilisation Force** (SFOR) resulted from those meetings. NATO activated SFOR on December 20, 1996, the same date that IFOR's mandate expired. While IFOR *implemented* the peace, SFOR would *stabilize* the peace in Bosnia and Herzegovina. IFOR was funded by NATO and the states that contributed contingents to the operation.

INDEPENDENT INQUIRY INTO THE ACTIONS OF THE UNITED NATIONS DURING THE 1994 GENOCIDE IN RWANDA. United Nations (UN) Secretary-General **Kofi Annan** called for the UN to conduct formal reviews of the peacekeeping failures in **Rwanda** and **Srebrenica**. The Secretary-General's office opted to examine Srebrenica but chose to select an international panel for the Rwanda study. A Secretary-General convening an independent inquiry into the operations of the UN is an unusual occurrence. However, the Security Council expressed its support for the proposal. In May 1999, Annan appointed Swedish Prime Minister Ingvar Carlsson as chair of the Independent Inquiry. Annan tasked Carlsson to investigate the events surrounding the genocide of the Rwandan Tutsi and the failure of the **United Nations Assistance Mission in Rwanda** to halt the massacres. Carlsson's specific mandate asked him to establish the facts related to the UN's response to the genocide in Rwanda. The other panel members included Han Sung-Joo, former Foreign Minister of the Republic of Korea, and Lieutenant-General Rufus Kupolati of **Nigeria**.

The final document produced by the panel, known as the Carlsson Report, faulted the global body, its secretariat, and the Secretary-General, as well as many Western states including the **United States**, Belgium, and **France**, for the failure to check the genocide in Rwanda. The panel issued the Carlsson Report in December 1999. *See also* INDEPENDENT PANEL OF EMINENT PERSONALITIES TO INVESTIGATE THE 1994 GENOCIDE IN RWANDA AND THE SURROUNDING EVENTS.

INDIA. *See* INDIAN PEACEKEEPING; UNITED NATIONS COMMISSION FOR INDIA AND PAKISTAN; UNITED NATIONS

INDIA-PAKISTAN OBSERVER MISSION; UNITED NATIONS MILITARY OBSERVER GROUP IN INDIA AND PAKISTAN.

INDIAN PEACEKEEPING. India has launched two unilateral military operations in South Asia that are often classified as being in the realm of **peacekeeping**. The first involved a July 1987 intervention in Sri Lanka. Although the majority of the Tamil sub-ethnic group lives in India, approximately three million Tamils inhabit the island state of Sri Lanka, where they are a minority. The Sri Lankan Tamils revolted against the government in hopes of establishing a small independent Tamil state on the island. Sri Lanka requested the assistance of India, and the resulting agreement referred to the military aid as an "Indian Peacekeeping Contingent." India dispatched 3,000 soldiers to Sri Lanka and then increased its personnel to over 30,000 by the end of 1987. By 1988, the total number of Indian soldiers in Sri Lanka had grown to over 50,000. The Indian military managed to regain limited control over the Tamil-dominated regions of Sri Lanka. However, in the process, India suffered over 1,000 battle deaths. Non-Tamil governmental opposition demanded the removal of the Indian military. The government complied with the pressure and the Indians withdrew by the end of March 1990. Following the departure of the Indian military, the Tamil rebels regained control over the northern and eastern regions of Sri Lanka.

The second peacekeeping operation evolved from an attempted coup by mercenaries in the state of the Maldives in November 1988. The government of the Maldives appealed for Indian assistance, and the latter state deployed approximately 1,000 paratroopers to counter the 200 mercenaries hired by a Maldivian businessman. The mission was a success. Both military operations were funded by the Indian government.

INDONESIA. *See* INTERNATIONAL FORCE IN EAST TIMOR; UNITED NATIONS MISSION IN EAST TIMOR; UNITED NATIONS MISSION OF SUPPORT IN EAST TIMOR; UNITED NATIONS SECURITY FORCE; UNITED NATIONS TEMPORARY EXECUTIVE AUTHORITY.

INTER-AFRICAN FORCE (IAF). Zairian dissidents crossed into Zaire's Shaba province from Angola on May 13, 1978. The rebels attacked Kolwezi, a major mining center with over 2,500 Belgian, **French**, and **United States** expatriates. The French and Belgians responded by deploying military forces to Zaire. French troops began landing on May 19, 1978, and the Belgians followed the next day. After securing their immediate objectives of protecting Westerners, the two European powers needed a plan to allow them to depart Zaire while still ensuring the protection of President Sese Seku Mobutu's government. The French solved the problem at the 1978 Franco-African Summit during the month of May. Morocco, Senegal, Côte d'Ivoire, Togo, and Gabon agreed to field contingents as part of an "inter-African force" to replace the French and Belgian military personnel in Zaire. The inter-African force allowed the French and Belgians to depart while keeping the Zairian dissidents in check. Although unclear, the funding for the operation probably originated in France. *See also* FRENCH PEACEKEEPING.

INTER-AFRICAN FORCE IN THE CENTRAL AFRICAN REPUBLIC (MISAB). The **Central African Republic** (CAR) faced a political crisis in 1996 due to lengthy economic problems including the failure to pay salaries. Segments of the military initiated a series of mutinies against the government. The Presidents of Burkina Faso, Chad, Gabon, and Mali met the CAR leaders at the end of the year and secured a truce between progovernment and rebel forces in the state. On January 25, 1997, the belligerents signed the Bangui agreements as a step toward a political settlement. Provisions of the agreements called for the fielding of a joint French-African peacekeeping operation known as the Inter-African Force in the Central African Republic (MISAB).

The agreements contained a provision for an international military force to oversee the peace process. The mandate of MISAB included the restoration of peace and security by monitoring the implementation of the Bangui Agreements and disarming former rebels, militia, and other unlawfully armed groups. Thus, MISAB was not mandated by an international organization but by an international agreement. MISAB deployed to the CAR on February 8, 1997. The **United Nations** (UN) Security Council gave its approval to MISAB's operations on August 6, 1997, in Resolution 1125 (1997). The UN recognized the inability of the African states in MISAB to continue the operation after the pending withdrawal of **French** troops and logistical support. In response, the Security Council passed Resolution 1159 (1998) on March 27, 1998, and mandated the **United Nations Mission in the Central African Republic** (MINURCA) to replace MISAB.

MISAB consisted of approximately 800 soldiers from Burkina Faso, Chad, Gabon, Mali, Senegal, and Togo. Gabon provided the military command structure for the operation, and France contributed logistical assistance. Approximately 1,000 French soldiers based in the Central African Republic under a previous bilateral agreement provided support for MISAB. At one point, rebellious soldiers fired upon the African peacekeepers prompting a French helicopter reprisal against the barracks housing the mutineers. France funded MISAB.

INTER-ALLIED PLEBISCITE FORCES. *See* LEAGUE OF NATIONS PLEBISCITE FORCES.

INTER-AMERICAN FORCE (IAF). *See* INTER-AMERICAN PEACE FORCE (IAPF).

INTER-AMERICAN PEACE FORCE (IAPF). In 1965, civil conflict in the Dominican Republic attracted the attention of the **United States**, which had not intervened militarily in Latin America since 1933. The United States deployed troops to the island state on April 28, 1965, in order to protect American lives and other foreign nationals and escort them from the country. The **Organization of American States** (OAS) met to discuss the Dominican crisis and agreed to field an Inter-American Force (IAF) to replace the unilateral force from the United States. A committee later changed the name of the operation to the Inter-American Peace Force (IAPF). The IAPF began arriving on May 23, 1965. The non-American participants were organized into a Latin American Brigade consisting of two battalions. The first, the Brazilian Army Battalion, was comprised of approximately 1,000 soldiers from that state. The other battalion, known as the Fraternity Battalion, included a Brazilian Marine Company (approximately 150 marines), a Honduran Company (250 troops), a Nicaraguan Company (164 troops), a Paraguayan Company (178 troops), and a Costa Rican Platoon (25 policemen). Costa Rica does not have armed forces and thus opted to participate through the use of policemen. The 22,000 American troops on the island were reorganized under the title of United States Forces in the Dominican Republic and added to the IAPF as a separate unit from the Fraternity Battalion. A Brazilian, General Hugo Panasco Alvim, served as the **Force Commander**. Alvim assumed command on May 31, 1965, replacing American Lieutenant-General Bruce Palmer, Jr., who assumed the role of the Deputy Commander and commander of the American contingent.

The mandate of the IAPF called upon the force to assist "in the restoration of normal conditions in the Dominican Republic, in maintaining the security of the inhabitants and for inviolability of human rights, and in the establishment of an atmosphere of peace and conciliation that will permit the functioning of democratic institutions." Alvim answered not to the Secretary-General but to a committee comprising all of the contingent-contributing states, a common practice in early **United Nations** (UN) operations. Alvim exercised command over the contingents provided to the IAPF. General Alvaro Alves da Silva Braga of Brazil replaced Alvim on January 17, 1966, while American Brigadier-General Robert R. Linvill succeeded Palmer on the same day. The IAPF began its withdrawal from the Dominican Republic on June 28, 1966, and continued until September 21, 1966, when the last contingent departed. The funding of the IAPF, as set by the OAS, called for voluntary contributions from members of the regional organization. However, Brazil and the United States were the only countries that actually provided funding for the mission. The former paid approximately 6 percent and the latter approximately 94 percent of the total IAPF budget. Although the IAPF has been referred to as a neutral peacekeeping operation, the deployed forces tended to support the American-favored belligerent in the conflict. In many ways, IAPF resembled a cross between **peacekeeping** and **peace enforcement**. *See also* REPRESENTATIVE OF THE SECRETARY-GENERAL IN THE DOMINICAN REPUBLIC (DOMREP).

INTER-ENTITY BOUNDARY LINE. *See* STABILISATION FORCE.

INTERNAL PEACEKEEPING. Internal peacekeeping involves an operation that is fielded in an attempt to help settle an internal conflict in a state. In other words, the peacekeepers do not separate two conflicting countries but are involved in a civil war situation. Internal peacekeeping operations have been the most difficult missions for international organizations to manage due to the nature of the conflict. Frequently, more than two belligerents are involved in civil wars, and arranging agreement among all parties is very difficult.

INTERNATIONAL CIVILIAN SUPPORT MISSION IN HAITI (MICIVH). The International Civilian Support Mission in Haiti (MICIVH) was a joint operation of the **United Nations** (UN) and the **Organization of American States** (OAS). The UN General Assembly mandated MICIVH on April 20, 1993. However, monitors had deployed to Haiti as early as February 1993. MICIVH's mission included the verification of human rights in Haiti. The organization worked in very difficult political conditions. In late 2000, UN Secretary-General Kofi Annan called on the global body to not remandate MICIVH after February 2001 due to continued political problems in the country and the refusal of the UN's members to increase funding for the verification mission. MICIVH consisted of 200 UN and 133 OAS staff members. The majority of the personnel were classified as international monitors. Many scholars do not consider MICIVH as a peacekeeping operation. The mission is included in this book due to its mission, size, and arrangement as a joint UN/OAS operation.

INTERNATIONAL COMMISSION FOR SUPPORT AND VERIFICATION. The commission involved a joint **Organization of American States** (OAS) and **United Nations** (UN) operation to oversee the disarmament and resettlement of the Contra armed group in Nicaragua in 1991. The UN held the responsibility for both military and nonmilitary activities in Costa Rica and Honduras. The OAS was responsible for nonmilitary activities of the commission in Nicaragua. The commission established security zones within Nicaragua to provide the returning Contras a safe location to gather and turn in their weapons. It took months of mediation to finally persuade the Contras to surrender their weapons despite the fact that the Sandinistas had departed the government following their presidential electoral defeat to Violeta Chamorro.

INTERNATIONAL COMMISSION OF CONTROL AND SUPERVISION (ICCS). The 1973 Paris Accords, which allowed the **United States** to withdraw its forces from South Vietnam during the Vietnam War, included a provision for the establishment of the International Commission of Control and Supervision (ICCS). Although not a peacekeeping mission in the classic sense of the term, the ICCS operated along the lines similar to many later cease-fire observation missions fielded by the **United Nations** (UN). The mission of the ICCS included oversight of the cease-fire. Four states participated in the commission: Canada, Indonesia, Hungary, and Poland. The first two states favored the American position, while the latter two were sympathetic toward North Vietnam and the Viet Cong. The composition of the ICCS allowed for a balance of states sympathetic toward the belligerents in the Vietnam War. Each state provided 290 observers, half of whom were military officers. Canada withdrew its observers at the end of 1973 due to the refusal of all belligerents to adhere to the cease-fire and was replaced by Iran. The mission of the ICCS devolved into an exercise of providing verbal reprimands to both sides. The four main belligerents, the United States, South Vietnam, North Vietnam, and the Viet Cong, were supposed to pay for the ICCS. However, the latter two refused to provide funding when requested. The ICCS suspended its activities by the end of 1974, and the 1975 Communist victory officially brought the organization to a conclusion.

INTERNATIONAL COMMISSION ON INTERVENTION AND STATE SOVEREIGNTY (ICISS). In September 2000, Canada announced that it would fund a study first proposed by **United Nations** (UN) Secretary-General **Kofi Annan** in 1999. Annan alarmed many states when he declared that human rights should take precedent over national/state rights. In other words, the collective body of the UN members should have the right to intervene in a state without invitation to restore fragile democracies and protect human rights. Such an international authorization could permit the UN to field a **peace enforcement** operation in a state to halt acts of genocide without the invitation or approval of the recognized government. Opposition from many states within the UN prompted Canada to assume an independent lead in the body, known as the International Commission on Intervention and State Sovereignty (ICISS).

The ICISS consists of an Advisory Board tasked to facilitate global discussion and to build international support for the mission of the organization. The organization is headquartered at the offices of the Canadian Department of Foreign Affairs and International Trade in Ottawa and financed by grants from the Canadian government as well as the Carnegie, MacArthur, and Rockefeller Foundations.

INTERNATIONAL CRIMINAL COURT (ICC). The International Criminal Court (ICC) began operations on July 1, 2002. The ICC, established by 139 states through the **United Nations** (UN), is mandated to prosecute individuals suspected of war crimes committed anywhere in the world after July 1, 2002. The **United States** attempted to secure an exemption of ICC jurisdiction over Americans assigned to international peacekeeping missions. The United States expressed concern that American soldiers could be singled out for wrongful prosecution on political grounds. To make a point, the United States vetoed the mandate extension of the **United Nations Mission in Bosnia and Herzegovina** (UNMIBH). American allies criticized the move to tie the peacekeeping operation to the ICC debate. A compromise emerged on July 12, 2002. The Security Council unanimously approved a one-year temporary immunity for the peacekeepers of any country that did not sign the ICC treaty. The resolution permits the exemption to be renewed after the one-year expiration. Many states claimed that the compromise undermined the ICC. The controversy also affected the **United Nations Mission of Observers in Prevlaka** (UNMOP) which receives its funding from the UNMIBH budget. A temporary, or permanent, closure of UNMIBH would have actually impacted two peacekeeping operations.

INTERNATIONAL FORCE IN EAST TIMOR (INTERFET). The **United Nations** (UN) Security Council mandated the **United Nations Mission in East Timor** (UNAMET) on June 11, 1999, to help conduct a referendum in East Timor. Following an outbreak of violence on the island, UN negotiators met with Indonesian officials and signed an agreement on September 12, 1999, permitting the deployment of an international military force to assist in stabilizing the situation. The peacekeepers, known as the International Force in East Timor (INTERFET), arrived on September 20, 1999. Additional discussions between the UN, Indonesia, and Portugal resulted in the transfer of the territory to UN administration. The Security Council opted to replace UNAMET with a new operation, known as the **United Nations Transitional Administration in East Timor** (UNTAET). UNTAET was mandated on October 25, 1999, with Resolution 1272 (1999), to help the international organization administer the territory.

It should be noted that INTERFET was not a UN peacekeeping operation. The Security Council authorized Australia to organize INTERFET, with the participation of other countries, to provide security and help restore the peace. INTERFET peacekeepers arrived in East Timor on September 20, 1999. On September 28, 1999, Indonesia and Portugal agreed to transfer East Timor to UN administration while the territory prepared for independence.

INTERFET, led by Australia, consisted of nearly 10,000 soldiers. Australia provided 5,000 peacekeepers and 21 other states dispatched an additional 4,500 peacekeepers. INTERFET's mandate included the restoration of peace and security in East Timor; the protection of UNTAET personnel; and the facilitation of humanitarian operations. On February 28, 2000, INTERFET transferred command of military operations to UNTAET. Many of the INTERFET peacekeepers remained in East Timor as part of UNTAET. The East Timorese voted on a Constituent Assembly on August 30, 2001, which then drafted a new constitution on March 22, 2002. East Timor became an independent state on May 20, 2002. The Security Council mandated a new peacekeeping operation, the **United Nations Mission of Support in East Timor** (UNMISET) on May 17, 2002, with a mandate to provide assistance to the government during a transitional period.

INTERNATIONAL MONITORING UNIT (IMU) (SUDAN). The International Monitoring Unit (IMU) (SUDAN) is also referred to as the Sudan Verification Mission in some sources. The terrorist attack on the World Trade Center towers on September 11, 2001, prompted the **United States** and other countries to renew efforts to secure a cease-fire and successful peace negotiations in Sudan. Osama bin Laden and his followers utilized Sudan as a training base prior to 2001 and there was concern that the state could be a destination for those terrorists escaping the 2002 Allied assault on **Afghanistan**. The

Sudanese government has made pledges to not support terrorist organizations, and many Western governments viewed an end to that state's long civil war as one way to bring greater stability and ensure terrorists did not return. In March 2002, the United States announced plans to deploy a small number of international monitors to observe a new cease-fire between the Sudanese government and the Sudan People's Liberation Army (SPLA) in the southern area of the state. IMU (Sudan) is the product of joint United States/**Swiss** mediation and deployed to the Sudanese Nuba Mountains in April 2002. The mission of IMU (Sudan) includes observing the cease-fire; monitoring the disengagement of Sudanese and SPLA forces; and investigating violations of the cease-fire. Approximately nine countries provide 15 monitors to the operation. IMU (Sudan) is not mandated by an international organization but rather by an agreement known as the *Report of Sudan and SPLA Movement/Nuba* signed on January 19, 2002.

INTERNATIONAL PANEL OF EMINENT PERSONALITIES TO INVESTIGATE THE 1994 GENOCIDE IN RWANDA AND THE SURROUNDING EVENTS. In November 1997, Prime Minister Metes Zenawi of Ethiopia proposed the establishment of a formal **Organization of African Unity** (OAU) inquiry into the **Rwandan** genocide to the Central Organ of the **OAU Mechanism for Conflict Prevention, Management, and Resolution**. OAU Secretary-General Salim Ahmed Salim endorsed the proposal and submitted it to various organs of the OAU for consideration. The 67th Ordinary Session of the heads of state and government voted in favor of the proposal in February 1998 and appointed Sir Ketumile Masire, the former foreign minister of Botswana, as the panel chair. The group consisted of seven members—three of whom were not African. The panel produced a detailed final report in July 2000. Many of its conclusions and lessons mirrored those of the United Nations' **Independent Inquiry into the Actions of the United Nations During the 1994 Genocide in Rwanda**.

INTERNATIONAL PEACE COOPERATION LAW. After its entry into the **United Nations** (UN), **Japan** did not deploy personnel with peacekeeping operations. The Japanese government cited its post-

World War II constitution and declared that its military was permitted to only conduct self-defense missions. In 1992, three political opposition parties managed to persuade the legislature to pass the International Peace Cooperation Law permitting the use of Japanese military assets in peaceful endeavors outside of the country. The law outlines four conditions for the use of the Japanese military in peace operations:

1. There must be an existing cease-fire.
2. Belligerents must grant consent to the introduction of peacekeepers and specifically a Japanese contingent.
3. The peacekeeping operation must be impartial in the conflict.
4. The use of force must be either a last resort or self-defense.

INTERNATIONAL PEACE MONITORING TEAM (IPMT). Ethnic conflict erupted on Guadalcanal in the Solomon Islands in 1998. Local Guadalcanese had expressed concern about the migration of people from the island of Malaita to Guadalcanal. Guadalcanese believed the newcomers were taking land without compensation, disrespecting the local culture, and taking job opportunities away from the local inhabitants. Over 100 people died and approximately 30,000 others became internal refugees following the toppling of the local government. The country nearly collapsed as services dried up and the government faced bankruptcy. Australia and New Zealand, along with **Commonwealth** support, stepped in and offered to help mediate a settlement to the crisis. The resulting Townsville Peace Agreement, signed on October 15, 2000, ended the hostilities and established an international presence to monitor the cease-fire.

The International Peace Monitoring Team (IPMT) resulted from the Townsville Peace Agreement and has **United Nations** (UN) support. The mandate of the IPMT is to collect and store weapons and build confidence among the parties for a peaceful settlement to the crisis. The personnel assigned to IPMT are unarmed civilians. IPMT consists of six teams—four on Guadalcanal and two on Malaita. The authorized strength of IPMT is approximately 49 civilian monitors from Australia, the Cook Islands, New Zealand, Tonga, and Vanuatu.

INTERNATIONAL POLICE TASK FORCE. *See* UNITED NATIONS INTERNATIONAL POLICE TASK FORCE.

INTERNATIONAL SECURITY ASSISTANCE FORCE (ISAF). After the World Trade Center terrorist attack of September 11, 2001, an international coalition of forces, led by the **United States**, assisted the Afghan Northern Alliance to remove the Taliban government from power in Afghanistan. ISAF is mandated by the "Agreement on Provisional Arrangements in Afghanistan Pending Re-establishment of Permanent Governmental Institutions" signed in Bonn on December 5, 2001, between the Afghan Interim Authority and the states offering contingents. The document is also known as the Bonn Agreement. The new Afghan Interim Authority government assumed power on December 22, 2001. The Western powers organized the International Security Assistance Force (ISAF) to assist the interim government with military and police training as well as offering a measure of security for the new regime. A small reconnaissance team arrived in Afghanistan on January 1, 2002, and joined **British** forces earmarked for ISAF. The **United Nations** (UN) offered its backing for ISAF with Security Council Resolution 1386 (2001).

The mandate calls for ISAF contingents to train and conduct joint patrols in Kabul with the Afghan police; train units of the new Afghan National Guard; dispose of captured Taliban munitions; and provide humanitarian assistance. A Joint Coordinating Body provides for consultations between the contingent providers and the Afghan Interim Authority. In February 2002, ISAF provided assistance following an avalanche that struck the Salang Tunnel and in March 2002 responded to a major earthquake in northern Afghanistan. By June 2002, ISAF had completed the training for the first new battalion in the Afghan National Guard.

As of July 2002, the maximum fielded strength of ISAF was approximately 5,000 personnel from 19 countries based in Kabul. The British led ISAF for its first six months and then turned over the operation to Turkish leadership in June 2002. ISAF is financed by the contingent providers. Some scholars do not consider this a peacekeeping operation but rather an extension of the Allied coalition in Afghanistan.

INTERNATIONAL VERIFICATION AND FOLLOW-UP COMMISSION (CIVS). The commission, consisting of representatives of the **Organization of American States** (OAS), the **United Nations**

(UN), the Contadora Group, five Central American states, and a Support Group of Argentina, Brazil, Peru, and Uruguay, had the responsibility for verifying and monitoring the terms of the Procedure for the Establishment of a Firm and Lasting Peace in Central America. The UN later deployed the **United Nations Observer Group in Central America** (ONUCA) to carry out these duties.

INTERPOSITION FORCE. An Interposition Force, also known as a barrier force, is a form of **traditional peacekeeping** in which a neutral military unit places itself physically between two belligerents. A **demilitarized zone** is normally established in the process, within which the peacekeepers base themselves.

IRAN. *See* UNITED NATIONS IRAN-IRAQ MILITARY OBSERVER GROUP.

IRAQ. *See* UNITED NATIONS GUARDS CONTINGENT IN IRAQ; UNITED NATIONS IRAN-IRAQ MILITARY OBSERVER GROUP; UNITED NATIONS IRAQ-KUWAIT OBSERVATION MISSION; IRAQ STABILIZATION FORCE.

IRAQ STABILIZATION FORCE. In April 2003, the **United States** initiated serious planning for a peacekeeping operation to supplement and later replace American and coalition forces in Iraq following the toppling of Saddam Hussein's regime. The Iraq Stabilization Force is a peacekeeping operation that is not mandated by an international organization but results from a series of bilateral agreements with the United States and other sector leaders. The Iraq Stabilization Force divides the country into three large sectors. The United States, Great Britain, and Poland each control one of the three sectors. Poland will command a division consisting of its own troops along with those of other **North Atlantic Treaty Organization** (NATO) members. The Polish/NATO division will oversee northern Iraq although the United States will retain a limited presence in the area due to the Kurdish problem with Turkey. The United States will man the central sector with up to three divisions (two American and one consisting of other coalition troops). The British will manage the southern sector of the country with a division consisting of its forces and those of other states.

The mission of the force is to disarm and demobilize Iraqi military and civilians; patrol the border with Iran; guard major oil fields; secure strategic facilities; and provide protection for the transitional government. Other contributors of soldiers or specialists (medical, engineers, mine clearing, etc.) include Albania, **Australia**, Bulgaria, Czech Republic, Denmark, Fiji, Italy, Netherlands, Qatar, Philippines, Portugal, Romania, South Korea, Spain, and Ukraine.

ISRAEL. *See* MIXED ARMISTICE COMMISSION; MULTINATIONAL FORCE AND OBSERVERS; TEMPORARY INTERNATIONAL PRESENCE IN HEBRON; UNITED NATIONS DISENGAGEMENT OBSERVER FORCE; UNITED NATIONS EMERGENCY FORCE I; UNITED NATIONS EMERGENCY FORCE II; UNITED NATIONS INTERIM FORCE IN LEBANON; UNITED NATIONS TRUCE SUPERVISION ORGANIZATION.

ISRAEL-EGYPT MIXED ARMISTICE COMMISSION. *See* MIXED ARMISTICE COMMISSION.

ISRAEL-JORDAN MIXED ARMISTICE COMMISSION. *See* MIXED ARMISTICE COMMISSION.

ISRAEL-LEBANON MIXED ARMISTICE COMMISSION. *See* MIXED ARMISTICE COMMISSION.

ISRAEL-SYRIA MIXED ARMISTICE COMMISSION. *See* MIXED ARMISTICE COMMISSION.

– J –

JAPANESE PEACEKEEPING. Japan has played a minimal role in **United Nations** (UN) **peacekeeping** operations for a country of its population size and economic strength. For many years after World War II, Japan cited its Constitutional clause prohibiting the use of the military for operations other than self-defense as the rationale for not deploying contingents with peacekeeping missions. However, Japan did contribute additional money beyond its assessments to help fund

UN missions. The passage of the **International Peace Cooperation Law** by the Japanese legislature in 1992 proved to be an important step in transforming Japan's role in peacekeeping missions. Tokyo took its first leap into peacekeeping with the fielding of a contingent with the **United Nations Transitional Authority in Cambodia** (UNTAC). The results of this Japanese experiment were mixed. Japan does contribute small numbers of personnel to a limited number of UN peacekeeping operations.

JOINT CONTROL COMMISSION PEACEKEEPING FORCE. Following the breakup of the Soviet Union, the former Soviet Republic of Moldova became an independent state. Many people living in the Transdneister region of the country are of Romanian descent and seek measures of autonomy from Moldova. **Russia** is sensitive to insecurity within the former Soviet republics due the presence of ethnic Russians, economic connections, and the tendency of the crises to attract outside attention and interference. Under a bilateral agreement between Moldova and Russia signed on July 21, 1992, Russian troops still in the country assumed a peacekeeping role. The mission is known as the Joint Control Commission Peacekeeping Force and has also been referred to as the Moldova Joint Force. The mission consists of 1,312 troops from Russia, Moldova, and Transdneister. The **Organization for Security and Cooperation Mission to Moldova** is also in the country, partially to observe the Russian operation.

The number of fatalities, if any, have not been openly reported. The cost of the operation is difficult to determine. The Stockholm International Peace Research Institute (SIPRI) reported that the operation cost 44.7 million rubles in 1999. Some scholars do not view the Joint Control Commission Peacekeeping Force as a peacekeeping operation. SIPRI recognizes the Moldova mission as a "peace operation" which the organization defines as either being an observer, peacekeeping, or peace building mission.

JOINT NORDIC COMMITTEE ON MILITARY UNITED NATIONS MATTERS. This Scandinavian committee, representing Denmark, Finland, Norway, and Sweden, is responsible for advanced peacekeeping training courses for member states preparing to support **United Nations** (UN) peacekeeping operations.

JOINT TASK FORCE PROVIDE PROMISE. This is the **United States** term for its support and participation in the **United Nations Protection Force (UNPROFOR) in Macedonia**. The American contribution to this operation included 300 infantry soldiers. The initial American contingent originated from the soldiers assigned to the Berlin Brigade, which was being disbanded. American units were rotated in and out of **Macedonia** from the United States every six months.

JOINT TASK FORCE SOMALIA. The **United States** applied this term in November 1993 to its forces assigned with the **United Nations Operation in Somalia II** (UNOSOM II). The United States restructured its forces in Somalia following a series of confrontations with **Mohammed Farah Aidid's** forces within Mogadishu. The restructuring involved the addition of mechanized vehicles and supporting forces, including Marines located off shore. The move also led to the withdrawal of special operations units assigned to capture Aidid. The American forces also altered their mission in support of the **United Nations** (UN) operation and reduced their patrolling in Mogadishu. The United States assigned Major-General Carl F. Ernst to command the task force, which was still technically under the UN until withdrawn in early 1994.

JORDAN. *See* MIXED ARMISTICE COMMISSION; UNITED NATIONS TRUCE SUPERVISION ORGANIZATION.

– K –

KARACHI AGREEMENT. India and Pakistan, under the auspices of the **United Commission for India and Pakistan** (UNCIP), signed the Karachi Agreement on July 18, 1949. The agreement established a cease-fire line in the disputed territory of Kashmir and opened the possibility for the stationing of neutral **United Nations** (UN) peacekeepers with each belligerent to observe the cease-fire accord. The peacekeepers, 20 in number under the command of Lieutenant-General Maurice Delvoie of Belgium, were dispatched later to the cease-fire line. Later additions to the agreement included a list of prohibited activities that would be reported to the peacekeepers such as the crossing of the cease-fire line, any firing or use of explosives within five miles of the cease-fire line, the laying of new mines or wire along any positions, the reinforcement of any existing forward defense positions, the overflight of the cease-fire line by aircraft, and the forward movement of military personnel or equipment from Kashmir.

KASHMIR. *See* UNITED NATIONS OBSERVER GROUP IN INDIA AND PAKISTAN.

KASMIYAH BRIDGE. The bridge, located near Tyre in **Lebanon**, was scheduled in 1978 to be occupied by the French contingent of the **United Nations Interim Force in Lebanon** (UNIFIL). The Palestinian Liberation Organization (PLO) protested on the grounds that the area had not been occupied by Israeli forces during the latter's invasion and thus should not come under direct observation of peacekeepers. The **United Nations** (UN) agreed with the PLO claims and diverted the French units away from the bridge.

KATANGA. *See* UNITED NATIONS OPERATION IN THE CONGO.

AL-KHATIB, LIEUTENANT-COLONEL SAMI. President **Elias Sarkis** of **Lebanon** selected al-Khatib, a Lebanese officer, as the second commander of the **Arab Deterrent Force** (ADF). Al-Khatib assumed his post on April 11, 1977, and remained there until March 1983, when President Amin Gemayel eliminated the position following the deployment of the **Multinational Forces** I (MNF I) peacekeeping operation.

KINDU. Kindu, located in Kasai province of the **Congo**, was the site of a massacre of peacekeepers assigned to the **United Nations Operation in the Congo** (ONUC). On November 11, 1961, a 13-man Italian crew flew a C-119 transport plane into Kindu airfield. The plane carried two armored cars for the Malayan contingent. Soldiers of the Congolese National Army (ANC) seized the Italians and then murdered and dismembered them.

KISSINGER, HENRY A. Kissinger, the Secretary of State during the Richard Nixon and Gerald Ford administrations of the **United States**, initiated what became known as shuttle diplomacy at the conclusion of the 1973 Yom Kippur War between Israel and its Egyptian and Syrian neighbors. Kissinger's diplomatic negotiations helped lead to cease-fires between the belligerents and the introduction of two peacekeeping operations to the area. The first, the **United Nations Emergency Force II** (UNEF II), deployed between Egypt and Israel, while the second, the **United Nations Disengagement Observer Force** (UNDOF), separated Syrian and Israeli forces on the Golan Heights.

KNOX-ARMEE. Knox-Armee was the nickname given to the international police force recruited to assist in the monitoring of the civilian population during the **Saar Plebiscite**. The force, heavily recruited from the ranks of retired British policemen, was named after Geoffrey Knox.

KOKKINA. Kokkina is a Turkish Cypriot enclave in the western Greek Cypriot area of Cyprus. In August 1964, Greek Cypriot forces attacked the Kokkina enclave, prompting a response by the Turkish Cypriot and Turkish government troops on the island. The Turkish government launched air strikes to support the Turkish Cypriot forces in the enclave. The **United Nations** (UN) Security Council debated the crisis, which was the worst cease-fire violation since the arrival of the **United Nations Peacekeeping Force In Cyprus** (UNFICYP). On August 11, 1964, the Security Council bypassed the Secretary-General and directly informed the UNFICYP commander, General Kodendera Subgayya Thimayya, to supervise the cease-fire around Kokkina and reinforce the UNFICYP units in the areas of recent military operations. By communicating directly with Thimayya, the Security Council was violating the normal UN chain of command for peacekeeping operations. Normally, the Security Council issued instructions via resolutions to the Secretary-General, who then carried out the will of the body by contacting the **Force Commander**. *See also* MELOUSHA.

KOLWEZI. *See* FRENCH PEACEKEEPING; INTER-AFRICAN FORCE.

KOREAN WAR. Although not an example of **peacekeeping**, actions of the **United Nations** (UN) during the Korean War illustrate how an international organization can mobilize at least some of its members under a declaration of collective security. Despite **United States** dominance during the Korean War, the military actions were officially sanctioned by the United Nations just as in the **Persian Gulf War** four decades later. North Korea crossed the border and invaded South Korea on June 25, 1950. On June 27, 1950, the United States persuaded the Security Council, thanks to a boycott by the Soviet delegation, to urge members to contribute assistance to South Korea. American ground and naval forces went into action the same day against North Korea. On July 7, 1950, the Security Council recommended that member states provide military assistance to South Korea. Twenty states deployed military contingents of various sizes to assist the South Korean government. In all, 45 states sent some form of aid to South Korea based upon the resolution. The return of the Soviet delegate and his assumption of the presidency of the Security Council blocked further resolutions on the Korean War. In turn, the United States pushed the **Uniting for Peace Resolution** through the General Assembly on November 2, 1950. Also known as the Acheson Plan, the resolution provided a means of moving peace and security issues from a deadlocked Security Council to the General Assembly. The United States selected General Douglas MacArthur to command all United Nations forces during the Korean War. After stemming the North's offensive around what was known as the Pusan Perimeter, the United Nations forces counterattacked and launched an amphibious operation at Inchon. The successful United Nations drive ended when the Chinese intervened in large numbers on November 25, 1950. Following a withdrawal of United Nations forces, another offensive stabilized the lines roughly along the original border (38th Parallel of latitude) between North and South Korea. The belligerents finally signed an armistice on July 27, 1953, which is still in place.

KOSOVO. *See* KOSOVO FORCE; ORGANIZATION FOR SECURITY AND COOPERATION IN EUROPE KOSOVO TASK FORCE; ORGANIZATION FOR SECURITY AND COOPERATION IN EUROPE KOSOVO VERIFICATION MISSION; ORGANIZATION

FOR SECURITY AND COOPERATION IN EUROPE MISSION IN KOSOVO; UNITED NATIONS INTERIM ADMINISTRATION IN KOSOVO.

KOSOVO FORCE (KFOR). Kosovo is a territorial entity within the Federal Republic of **Yugoslavia**. The latter is dominated by Serbia and ethnic Serbs while the majority population in Kosovo is ethnic Albanian. Kosovo had considerable autonomy until 1989 when Serbian leader Slobodon Milosevic brought the region under direct Serbian control. By 1998, tensions were increasing between the ethnic Albanian majority and Serbian minority within Kosovo, and fighting between the Yugoslavian army and the Kosovo Liberation Army became daily occurrences. A humanitarian crisis erupted as Serbians forced people to flee Kosovo. Yugoslavian authorities refused to abide by international demands to end the crisis and the situation threatened to spread to other states in the region.

On October 13, 1998, the **North Atlantic Treaty Organization** (NATO) authorized air strikes to support diplomatic moves to force the Serbians to end the violence. The Serbs backed down and the **Organization for Security and Cooperation in Europe Kosovo Verification Mission** was established to monitor the situation. By March 1999, the situation began to collapse again and the monitors of the verification mission departed Kosovo. A final appeal to Milosevic was rebuffed and NATO commenced airstrikes after March 23, 1999. The campaign lasted until June 10, 1999, when the Serbs agreed to international demands. The **United Nations** Security Council, with Resolution 1244 (1999), endorsed the sending of a NATO ground force into Kosovo. This operation became known as the Kosovo Force (KFOR).

KFOR entered Kosovo on June 12, 1999, as the Serbs initiated a military withdrawal from the territory. The Serbian withdrawal was completed by June 20, 1999. KFOR is organized into five multinational brigades, and its authorized full strength was set at 50,000 military personnel with 40,000 of the troops actually in Kosovo. Every NATO member provided personnel for KFOR along with 18 non-NATO members. It is interesting to note that **Switzerland**, a traditionally neutral state that is rarely seen in any capacity in peacekeeping operations, is a participant in KFOR. Russia also dispatched a contingent for KFOR, and tensions ran high as Moscow and NATO found themselves in a race to gain control of the main airport. KFOR's mandate includes maintaining a secure environment in Kosovo; monitoring the compliance of the Serbians and Kosovo Liberation Army to the cease-fire agreement; and providing assistance to the **United Nations Mission in Kosovo**.

NATO openly describes KFOR as a **peace enforcement** mission. Thus, many scholars do not consider KFOR as a **peacekeeping** operation. KFOR is included here since it is a multinational peace operation mandated by an international organization and provides a basis of comparison with other missions.

KUPOLATI, MAJOR-GENERAL R. M. Kupolati, a Nigerian army officer, has participated in two major non-**United Nations** (UN) peacekeeping operations. During 1981–1982, Kupolati was selected as the Nigerian contingent commander in the **Organization of African Unity peacekeeping Force in Chad II**. In this capacity, he also served as the overall Chief of Logistics in the **Organization of African Unity** (OAU) mandated operation. In 1991, Kupolati was selected as the **Force Commander** of the **Economic Community of West African States Monitoring Group (ECOMOG) in Liberia**.

KUWAIT. *See* ARAB LEAGUE FORCE IN KUWAIT; UNITED NATIONS IRAQ-KUWAIT OBSERVATION MISSION.

– L –

LANCASTER HOUSE AGREEMENT. The agreement, signed in London on November 15, 1979, ended the conflict in Zimbabwe. The document included a provision that mandated the deployment of the **Commonwealth Monitoring Force in Zimbabwe** to oversee the peace process and collect Patriotic Front soldiers as they came in from the bush.

LASSO, GALO PLAZA. Lasso, a native of Ecuador, served as the Chairman of the **United Nations Observation Group in Lebanon** (UNOGIL) during its brief duration from June to December 1958. In this capacity, he carried out the duties attributed to the position now known as Special Representative. He later became the Mediator for the **United Nations Peacekeeping Force in Cyprus** (UNFICYP) and held that post from September 1964 to December 1965.

LEAGUE OF ARAB STATES. The League of Arab States, also known as the Arab League, was established on March 22, 1945. The purpose of the 21-state organization is to promote Arab unity in political, economic, and social issues. A Council consisting of all-member states coordinates peacekeeping activities of the league. *See also* ARAB DETERRENT FORCE; ARAB LEAGUE FORCE IN KUWAIT; SYMBOLIC ARAB SECURITY FORCE.

LEAGUE OF NATIONS. The League of Nations was established on January 10, 1920. The membership numbered up to 65 states, although the **United States** never joined. The league was an organization of very broad scope intended to preserve the peace and improve human welfare. The body maintained a permanent headquarters in Geneva, Switzerland. The Council of the organization, a precursor to the Security Council of the **United Nations** (UN), handled security issues that can be categorized as early attempts at multinational peacekeeping. *See also* LEAGUE OF NATIONAS PLEBISCITE FORCES; SAAR INTERNATIONAL FORCE; VILNA INTERNATIONAL FORCE.

LEAGUE OF NATIONS PLEBISCITE FORCES. The **League of Nations** supervised several plebiscites after World War I in order to settle territorial questions that had emerged with the demise, birth, and/or readjustment of European states. Although the military units fielded in support of these missions were multinational, they represented joint operations of the victorious Allied powers and are thus questionable as being representative of neutral peacekeeping forces. In 1920, 3,000 **British** and **French** soldiers provided security during a plebiscite to determine if Schleswig should be **German** or Danish. The **United States** originally committed a battalion to this operation but later withdrew its offer. In that same year, Great Britain, France, and Italy fielded over 15,000 soldiers in support of a plebiscite in Upper Silesia between Germany and Poland. In October 1920, fewer than 100 British, French, and Italian military officers oversaw the plebiscite in the Klagenfurt Basin that determined the status of the area as being Austrian and not Yugoslavian. Approximately 2,000 British, French, and Italian soldiers deployed to Allenstein and Marienwerder in 1920 during the plebiscite that determined whether these areas should be German or Polish. The league moved 450 soldiers from the international force in Upper Silesia to the Sopron region between Austria and Hungary. Following the plebiscite that transferred the area to Hungarian political control, the troops returned to duty in Upper Silesia. The League of Nations did propose one truly neutral plebiscite force to oversee the political process in Vilna. That operation, the **Vilna International Force**, was never fielded. In 1935, the league finally deployed a neutral peacekeeping operation, the **Saar International Force**, in the Saar region between France and Germany.

LEBANON. *See* ARAB DETERRENT FORCE; MIXED ARMISTICE COMMISSION; MULTINATIONAL FORCES I; MULTINATIONAL FORCES II; OBSERVER GROUP BEIRUT; OBSERVER GROUP LEBANON; SYMBOLIC ARAB SECURITY FORCE; UNITED NATIONS INTERIM FORCE IN LEBANON; UNITED NATIONS OBSERVATION GROUP IN LEBANON; UNITED NATIONS TRUCE SUPERVISION ORGANIZATION.

LEFKA. Lefka, a town in western Cyprus, was the destination of five Swedish members of the **United Nations Peacekeeping Force in Cyprus** (UNFICYP) who were attempting to smuggle weapons to the Turkish Cypriots in September 1965. The three enlisted personnel were exonerated and the two officers were returned to Sweden. The latter personnel were found guilty, removed from the military, and jailed. An earlier incident of arms smuggling to the Turkish Cypriots involved a British airman, although he was not assigned to UNFICYP. The Greek press used the incident to declare that the **North Atlantic Treaty Organization** (NATO) was behind the gunrunning of **United Nations** (UN) contingents on Cyprus. It has been speculated that this incident resulted in the reassignment of the Swedish contingent from western to eastern Cyprus in December 1964.

LESOTHO. *See* SOUTHERN AFRICAN DEVELOPMENT COMMUNITY OPERATION IN LESOTHO.

LESSONS LEARNED UNIT. *See* BEST PRACTICES UNIT.

LIBERIA. *See* ECONOMIC COMMUNITY OF WEST AFRICAN STATES MONITORING GROUP IN LIBERIA; UNITED NATIONS OBSERVER MISSION IN LIBERIA.

LILJESTRAND, MAJOR-GENERAL BENGT. Liljestrand, a native of Sweden, was the Chief of Staff of the **United Nations Truce Supervision Organization** (UNTSO) between April 1974 and August 1975, when he was named as the Force Commander of the **United Nations Emergency Force II** (UNEF II). He held that position until November 1976.

LINE OF CONTROL. The Prime Minister of **India** and the President of Pakistan established what is called the Line of Control in 1972 after agreeing to a cease-fire in a war that erupted between the two states in 1971. This line follows, with a few minor deviations, the cease-fire line of the Karachi Agreement of 1949 in Kashmir. The **United Nations Military Observer Group in India and Pakistan** (UNMOGIP) monitors the cease-fire along the Line of Control.

LITANI. The Litani River marks the northern boundary of the territory patrolled by the **United Nations Interim Force in Lebanon** (UNIFIL). The Litani also marks the southernmost line that could be occupied by forces of the **Arab Deterrent Force** (ADF). In addition, Litani is the name of the official UNIFIL magazine which is published in order to boost the morale of the personnel assigned to the operation.

LITHUANIA. *See* VILNA INTERNATIONAL FORCE.

– M –

MACEDONIA. *See* OPERATION ALLIED HARMONY; OPERATION AMBER FOX; OPERATION ESSENTIAL HARVEST; OR-

GANIZATION FOR SECURITY AND COOPERATION IN EUROPE SPILLOVER MONITOR MISSION TO SKOPJE; UNITED NATIONS PREVENTIVE DEPLOYMENT FORCE; UNITED NATIONS PROTECTION FORCE; UNITED NATIONS PROTECTION FORCE IN MACEDONIA.

MACKENZIE, BRIGADIER-GENERAL LEWIS. Mackenzie, a native of Canada, served the **United Nations** (UN) in a variety of positions as a peacekeeper. He served as the first commander of the **United Nations Protection Force** (UNPROFOR) element assigned to **Bosnia and Herzegovina**. A controversial officer, Mackenzie was reportedly removed from command due to his open opinions about the mismanagement of the situation in the former Yugoslavia by the UN.

MALDIVES. *See* INDIAN PEACEKEEPING.

MARITIME OPERATIONAL GROUP. *See* UNITED NATIONS TRANSITIONAL AUTHORITY IN CAMBODIA.

MELOUSHA. In July 1966, Greek Cypriot forces attacked the Turkish Cypriot village of Melousha. The **United Nations Peacekeeping Force in Cyprus** (UNFICYP) managed to place a group of peacekeepers between the two belligerents and informed the Greek Cypriots that the peacekeepers would oppose any armed attack through their lines into Melousha. The Greek Cypriots ended the attack and returned their troops to their barracks. This action is in contrast to an incident at **Kokkina** during which the **United Nations** (UN) withdrew its forces when fighting erupted between the two belligerents.

MILITARY OBSERVER GROUP (MOG). In 1990, a Tutsi military force crossed from Uganda into **Rwanda**. The majority Hutu dominated the political system of Rwanda and the minority Tutsi. Conflict erupted and many individuals became refugees as the fighting spread. Belgium and France airlifted paratroopers to Rwanda to evacuate foreign nationals. The **Organization of African Unity** (OAU) worked with the belligerents to secure a cease-fire and initiate a peace process in Rwanda. In April 1991, the OAU dispatched a small force of military observers, known as the Military Observer Group (MOG), to Rwanda in support of the peace process. Some sources refer to the operation as the Military Observer Team (MOT). The MOG personnel monitored the situation in Rwanda. Burundi, Uganda, and Zaire contributed military personnel to the small operation. The Rwandan groups did not view these states as neutral parties to the conflict, and the mission collapsed by late 1991 as a result of this perception. After another cease-fire, the OAU fielded a second peacekeeping mission known as the **Neutral Military Observer Group I** (NMOG I). Many sources, including governmental and international agency reports, have confused MOG, NMOG I, and the **Neutral Military Observer Group II** (NMOG II) and interchanged the facts of their composition and deployment dates.

MILITARY OBSERVER TEAM (MOT). *See* MILITARY OBSERVER GROUP (MOG).

MISSION OF MILITARY OBSERVERS ECUADOR-PERU (MOMEP). Ecuador and Peru maintained a territorial dispute that dated back to the 19th century. In January 1995, the dispute erupted into open conflict as air and ground units from Peru intruded several times into Ecuadorian territory. Ecuador resisted and called for a cease-fire and international support. Negotiations opened in Brazil the next month. On February 17, 1995, the two belligerents, along with the Guarantor States of Argentina, Brazil, Chile, and the **United States**, signed the Itamaraty Treaty. This agreement called for a cease-fire; the separation of the military forces of Peru and Ecuador along their border; the demilitarization of the conflict zone; and the dispatch of neutral military observers from the Guarantor States to monitor the cease-fire and withdrawal of armed forces. The parties signed a second agreement, the Montevideo Treaty, on March 28, 1995, which verified the provisions of Itamaraty.

The Guarantor States deployed the Mission of Military Observers Ecuador-Peru (MOMEP) in accordance with the peace process. The small mission conducted its operations based on four phases. First phase involved implementing the cease-fire. Second, MOMEP assumed control of the air space in the conflict zone and received the order of battle from Ecuador and Peru. Third, Ecuador and Peru removed their forces from the conflict zone. Fourth, MOMEP initiated its mission to monitor the cease-fire and conflict zone. MOMEP maintained base camps on both sides of the border and conducted its patrols by helicopter due to the remoteness of the area.

Originally, MOMEP consisted of military personnel from the Guarantor States. As conditions warranted, Ecuador and Peru were invited to contribute monitors to the operation. Ecuador and Peru signed a final border treaty on October 26, 1998, and MOMEP ended its mission on June 17, 1999. MOMEP was funded by Ecuador and Peru.

MISSION TRAINING CELL (MTC). The **Training and Evaluation Service** (TES), an organization within the **Department of Peacekeeping Operations** (DPKO) of the **United Nations** (UN), developed Mission Training Cells (MTC) in 2001–2002 to prepare "lessons learned" for future peacekeeping training and provide additional individual and unit level training for existing peacekeeping operations. MTCs are assigned to peacekeeping missions in the field in order to accomplish their assigned tasks.

MIXED ARMISTICE COMMISSION. The Mixed Armistice Commissions are part of the Armistice Commission that oversees the Israeli-Arab cease-fire. Observers of the **United Nations Truce Supervision Organization** (UNTSO) are assigned to the Mixed Armistice Commissions. The four commissions investigate and examine complaints of the various parties related to firing across or crossing the armistice demarcation line. The Egypt-Israel Mixed Armistice Commission (EIMAC) operated between both belligerents until 1956, when Israel unilaterally denounced the armistice agreement and refused to cooperate with the commission. After 1956, the commission remained in place but operated only on the Egyptian side of the frontier. The other commissions included the Israel-Syria Mixed Armistice Commission (ISMAC), Israel-Jordan Mixed Armistice Commission (IJMAC), and the Israel-Lebanon Mixed Armistice Commission (ILMAC). These organizations, despite armistice violations from all parties, remained in place until the Six-Day War in 1967, when Israel denounced the last three commissions. The **United Nations** (UN) refused to accept any of the unilateral withdrawals from the armistice agreements. However, the Israel-Egypt Mixed Armistice Commission was officially terminated in 1979 following the conclusion of a peace agreement between the two states.

MIYAZAWA, KIICHI. Miyazawa, a former **Japanese** prime minister, was instrumental in persuading the Diet (parliament) of his country on June 15, 1992, to vote for participation in **United Nations** (UN) peacekeeping operations. Japan dispatched military personnel to the **United Nations Transitional Authority in Cambodia** (UNTAC) shortly after the approval given by the Diet.

MOLDOVA. *See* JOINT CONTROL COMMISSION PEACEKEEPING FORCE; ORGANIZATION FOR SECURITY AND COOPERATION IN EUROPE MISSION TO MOLDOVA.

MORILLON, GENERAL PHILIPPE. Morillon, a **French** army officer, served as the commander of the **United Nations Protection Force** (UNPROFOR) element in **Bosnia and Herzegovina** after General **Lewis MacKenzie.** In July 1993, he was replaced by General **Francis Briquemont.** Morillon openly criticized Secretary-General **Boutros Boutros-Ghali** in January 1994 for the operation's problems. Morillon not only declared that the peacekeepers lacked the means, including the use of air support from the **North Atlantic Treaty Organization** (NATO), to counter snipers and artillery fire, but that they operated under an unclear mandate.

MOROCCO. *See* UNITED NATIONS MISSION FOR THE REFERENDUM IN WESTERN SAHARA.

MOZAMBIQUE. *See* UNITED NATIONS OPERATION IN MOZAMBIQUE.

MULTINATIONAL FORCE AND OBSERVERS (MFO). The **United States** proposed the deployment of a peacekeeping operation to oversee the peace process of the Camp David Accords signed in March 1979 by **Egypt, Israel,** and the United States. The mission, to be known as the Multinational Force and Observers (MFO), would operate as a multinational peacekeeping unit but would not be mandated by an international organization. Instead, the operational mandate stemmed directly from the Camp David Accords, and the United States offered to organize the mission. The **United Nations** (UN) had deployed the **United Nations Emergency Force II** (UNEF II) following the Yom Kippur War of October 1973. This peacekeeping operation helped pave the way for MFO since the latter organization benefited from the experience of the former in the Sinai between Egypt and Israel. Following the signing of the Camp David Accords, the UN withdrew UNEF II, whose mandate was completed by the conclusion of a peace treaty between Israel and Egypt. In turn, MFO would replace UNEF II in the Sinai. The United States Sinai Field Mission (SFM), located in the Sinai with UNEF II, was responsible for operating radar installations to prevent a surprise air attack by either Egypt or Israel. This organization remained in the Sinai with MFO.

The composition of MFO includes approximately 2,000 soldiers. Colombia, Fiji, and the United States provide the three combat battalions assigned to MFO. The Colombians are based in the northern, the Fijians in the central, and the Americans in the southern areas of the neutral zone between Egypt and Israel. Italy provides the naval element, and Australia and New Zealand contribute the air element of MFO. General Bull Hansen of Norway was selected as the first **Force Commander** of MFO due to his experience as a **North Atlantic Treaty Organization** (NATO) commander and United Nations Emergency Force commander and his linguistic ability. The headquarters of MFO is located in Rome, Italy. Operations in Rome are coordinated by a Director-General. His relationship to the Force Commander is similar to that of the United Nations Secretary-General to his Force Commanders. The command structure of MFO is also similar to that of the United Nations. MFO headquarters in the Sinai consists of a 31-member civilian observer unit that conducts reconnaissance and arms verification of the areas outside of the neutral zone where MFO battalions are based. MFO maintains liaison with the **United Nations Disengagement Observation Force** (UNDOF), the **United Nations Interim Force in Lebanon** (UNIFIL), and the **United Nations Truce Supervision Organization** (UNTSO).

The Camp David Accords divided the Sinai and western Israel into four zones. Egypt is allowed to post an unlimited number of troops and weapons west of the Suez Canal. Zone A, located in western Sinai, is the first arms-limitation area. Egypt may station a total of 230 tanks and 22,000 soldiers in this zone. Zone B is located in the central Sinai. Within Zone B, Egypt may post four infantry battalions. Zone C, MFO neutral barrier, extends along the eastern area of the Sinai. Only military forces of the MFO may enter Zone C. Zone D is a very narrow area immediately across the border inside Israel. The Israeli military may place four infantry battalions within Zone D. Outside of Zone D, Israel may have an unlimited number of troops and weapons. MFO has been an unqualified success due to the cooperation of Israel and Egypt following the Camp David Accords. It is interesting to note that MFO uses the color orange to designate its forces in contrast to the UN which equips its personnel in the color light blue. Egypt and Israel equally share the costs of MFO. However, the United States increased its economic aid to Egypt and Israel to allow them to cover their share of the funding for MFO.

MULTINATIONAL FORCE (MNF) IN HAITI. Haiti's democratically elected president, Jean Bertrand Aristide, lost power to a military coup on September 30, 1991. Violence erupted across the country as supporters of the coup murdered backers of President Aristide and committed numerous human rights violations. The **United Nations** (UN) began debating how to handle the issue and eventually imposed an arms and oil embargo in June 1993. This act was suspended after successful negotiations to end the crisis. On September 23, 1993, the Security Council passed Resolution 867 (1993) which mandated the **United Nations Mission in Haiti** (UNMIH) in cooperation with the **Organization of American States** (OAS). The government refused to cooperate and allow the peacekeepers to move into Haiti. In response, the Security Council mandated a Multinational Force (MNF) on July 31, 1994, to topple the illegal Haitian government. The MNF, consisting of units from 28 states, arrived unopposed in Haiti on September 19, 1994. The mission included seizing weapons and overseeing security on the island. The coup leaders departed on October 15, 1994. On March 31, 1995, the MNF transferred responsibility to UNMIH which completed its mandate and departed Haiti at the end of June 1996. Many scholars do not view MNF as a peacekeeping operation. At the least, it is clearly a **peace en-**

forcement mission mandated by the UN to assist a more **traditional peacekeeping** operation.

MULTINATIONAL FORCES I (MNF I). Israel invaded **Lebanon** in June 1982 following a series of attacks by the Palestine Liberation Organization (PLO). The Israeli military pushed the PLO northward until they were cornered in Beirut. At this point, the **United States** and other countries stepped in to prevent a large-scale clash between Israel and the PLO. The United States proposed a multinational military unit that would act as a peacekeeping operation in the same manner as the **Multinational Force and Observers** (MFO) in the Sinai. The **League of Arab States**, which had fielded the **Arab Deterrent Force** (ADF) in eastern Lebanon, agreed to the suggestion. It should be noted that, in June 1982, there were three peacekeeping operations in Lebanon: the ADF, the **United Nations Interim Force in Lebanon** (UNIFIL) located just north of the border with Israel, and personnel assigned with the **United Nations Truce Supervision Organization** (UNTSO). The proposed peacekeeping operation, to be known as the Multinational Forces I (MNF I), was not mandated by an international organization. It was based on a series of bilateral agreements between the contingent providers and the Lebanese government.

The mission of MNF I included providing assistance in evacuating the PLO from Beirut, guaranteeing the safety of PLO families remaining in Beirut, and denying access into civilian refugee camps by the Israeli military and Christian Phalange forces. The United States deployed 800 marines to the operation, while France offered an equal number of its personnel and Italy fielded 400 of its soldiers. The contingents arrived in August 1982 and departed the following month. Following the evacuation of the PLO, the contingents assigned to MNF I withdrew from Lebanon. The United States planned to request funding for MNF I by an unspecified international organization. However, the State Department covered the initial costs of the American participation and the United States never secured international backing for the operation. MNF I was a successful operation. However, massacres of civilians living in the Sabra and Shatilla refugee camps led to a return of the contingents in a new operation titled the **Multinational Forces II** (MNF II).

MULTINATIONAL FORCES II (MNF II). The Multinational Forces II (MNF II) peacekeeping operation followed on the heels of the successful **Multinational Forces I** (MNF I) fielded in Beirut in August 1982. After MNF I withdrew from Beirut, massacres of civilians at the Sabra and Shatilla refugee camps erupted following the assassination of a Lebanese Christian leader. The **United States** proposed a return to **Lebanon** in an operation to mirror the successful MNF I. The new international mission, MNF II, was similar to MNF I in that both missions lacked a mandate from an international organization and were funded by the contingent providers. The United States offered 1,400 marines while **France** agreed to field 1,500 personnel. Italy sent 1,400 soldiers, and **Great Britain** later joined the mission and dispatched 80 troops with armored cars. Again, each contingent provider signed a bilateral agreement with the government of Lebanon.

MNF II held a two-fold mandate. First, MNF II's mission included a short-term goal of providing a buffer between the **Israeli** forces, their opponents, and the refugee centers. The long-term objective of the operation included assisting the Lebanese government in expanding its control in the country. MNF II, like its predecessor, was unique in peacekeeping. A central headquarters for command, control, and coordination of the contingents did not exist. Each contingent did provide a liaison officer to the other contingents, but none of the four worked for a neutral command. In other words, each contingent responded directly to its home government. This issue damaged the credibility of MNF II since the operation was not perceived as being truly neutral in character. In addition, each contingent exercised its own agenda and **rules of engagement**. The Lebanese tended to perceive the Italians as being neutral in the conflict due to the latter's humanitarian projects. On the other hand, the Americans and French were viewed as "lackeys" of the Lebanese government and became the targets of various factions in the civil war. The American contingent increasingly received hostile fire. As casualties mounted, the Americans altered their rules of engagement from being highly restrictive to just the opposite as naval gunfire and air support joined the marines in returning fire. Car bombings of the American and French detachments on October 23, 1983, persuaded the contributing states to withdraw their units during February and March 1984. The

British and Italians departed after the withdrawal of the American and French detachments.

MULTINATIONAL PROTECTION FORCE (FMP). The Albanian government was dominated by Enver Hoxha, a self-proclaimed communist, between 1945 and 1985. During this 20-year period, the country had few contacts outside of its borders, and Hoxha ruled with an iron fist. Six years after his death, communism collapsed in Albania. The newly freed Albanian people adopted democratic institutions and a free market economy. Pyramid investment schemes attracted a large segment of the population with the hopes of high returns on their money. The pyramids began collapsing in 1996. The collapse of the pyramids and other economic heartbreaks such as criminal gangs helped lead to political unrest by early 1997. Riots erupted in the capital of Tirana and other areas of the country. By March 1997, the army folded and people began to loot military armories. Refugees began flooding Italy prompting the state to assume the lead in the future formation of an international peacekeeping force in Albania.

The **Organization for Security and Cooperation in Europe** (OSCE) appealed for a military force to stabilize Albania and provide protection for humanitarian relief efforts. Italy and Greece agreed to provide the leadership and bulk of the forces for a peacekeeping mission in support of OSCE and **European Union** (EU) humanitarian relief. The **United States** did not want to participate but was not against an all-European peacekeeping mission. Italy attempted to utilize the **West European Union** (WEU) as the mandating organization by citing the operation as a **Petersberg Mission**. However, the WEU, led by **Great Britain** and **Germany**, was not willing to provide strong support for a military operation in Albania. Italy turned to the **United Nations** (UN), and the Security Council agreed to endorse a "coalition of the willing" for Albania on March 28, 1997, with Resolution 1101 (1997). Thus, the Multinational Protection Force (FMP) deployed to Albania without the mandate of an international organization but held the endorsements of the UN, EU, and OSCE.

The FMP contributing states formed an Ad Hoc Political Steering Committee to oversee the operation. Austria, Denmark,

France, Greece, Italy, Romania, Spain, and Turkey offered up to 7,000 soldiers. Italy alone contributed 3,778 peacekeepers to the operation. France, with the second largest contingent in FMP, sent 1,000 soldiers. Greece dispatched 803 soldiers and 224 vehicles. Rumania provided 400 men, Denmark offered 100 peacekeepers, and the other states sent the remaining troops. FMP, also known as Operation Alba, was the first all-European peacekeeping mission fielded in Europe. The peacekeepers arrived on April 15 and 16, 1997. FMP's mission included providing a visible stabilization force for Albania, the protection of humanitarian relief work, and the protection of civilian election monitors. The peacekeepers withdrew on August 12, 1997, after completing their mandate. Part of the Italian contingent and one Greek company of 205 personnel remained in Albania under bilateral agreements between the states to help the Albanians reorganize their armed forces. Contributing states funded their own contingents during the peacekeeping operation.

– N –

NAMIBIA. *See* UNITED NATIONS TRANSITIONAL ASSISTANCE GROUP.

NAVAL PEACEKEEPING. This term is often applied to the utilization of naval assets to support **peacekeeping** missions. Peacekeeping primarily involves the use of personnel situated on the ground between or among belligerents. However, international organizations came to realize that many of the functions carried out on land must also be conducted on the open ocean or inland waterways. Naval assets in support of peacekeeping missions usually conduct a surveillance type missions. *See also* WEST EUROPEAN UNION PEACEKEEPING.

NEUTRAL MILITARY OBSERVER GROUP I (NMOG I). After the collapse of the **Military Observer Group** (MOG), the **Organization of African Unity** (OAU) fielded a second peacekeeping mission known as the **Neutral Military Observer Group I** (NMOG I) after the signing of another cease-fire in July 1992. Mali, Nigeria, Senegal, and Zimbabwe dispatched approximately 50 military observers to NMOG I. Many sources, including governmental and international agency reports, have confused MOG, NMOG I, and the **Neutral Military Observer Group II** (NMOG II) and interchanged the facts of their composition and deployment dates. The peacekeepers oversaw a four kilometer neutral zone within Rwanda and established three observation posts to monitor the cease-fire and report violations. A renewal of the conflict in February 1993 resulted in the arrival of reinforcements for a small French garrison based in the capital of Kigali since October 1990. NMOG I peacekeepers withdrew to the relative safety of Kigali. A request for 400 additional military observers was denied by the OAU. NMOG's mission was essentially over as the OAU and **United Nations** (UN) continued to work to return the belligerents to the peace process. Further negotiations would lead to the mandating of NMOG II. *See also* UNITED NATIONS ASSISTANCE MISSION IN RWANDA; UNITED NATIONS OBSERVER MISSION UGANDA-RWANDA.

NEUTRAL MILITARY OBSERVER GROUP II (NMOG II). **Neutral Military Observer Group I** (NMOG I) peacekeepers withdrew to the relative safety of Kigali, Rwanda, following the renewal of hostilities in February 1993. After the introduction of a new cease-fire, the **Organization of African Unity** (OAU) agreed to mandate a third peacekeeping mission in August 1993. The operation, known as the Neutral Military Observer Group II (NMOG II), consisted of approximately 130 military observers with a mission to monitor the new cease-fire. Many sources, including governmental and international agency reports, have confused MOG, NMOG I, and NMOG II and interchanged the facts of their composition and deployment dates. The OAU transferred NMOG II's personnel to the **United Nations Assistance Mission in Rwanda** (UNAMIR) when the latter mission arrived in Rwanda in December 1993. *See also* UNITED NATIONS OBSERVER MISSION UGANDA-RWANDA.

NICARAGUA. *See* INTERNATIONAL COMMISSION FOR SUP-
PORT AND VERIFICATION; UNITED NATIONS OBSERVER
GROUP IN CENTRAL AMERICA.

NICE TREATY. The **European Union's** (EU) Nice Treaty was developed in order to alter the structure of the organization to accommodate new members from Eastern Europe. However, Irish citizens opposed to the ratification of the treaty claimed it would negate the
country's neutral foreign policy and destroy its traditional standing as
a major participant in peacekeeping operations. The opposition ral-
lied sufficient support in 2001 to defeat a government referendum to
ratify the treaty. In 2002, the government launched an aggressive
campaign to inform Irish voters that the treaty did not alter Ireland's
neutrality or traditional stance on peacekeeping participation. Irish
citizens finally approved their country's ratification of the treaty in
October 2002.

NIEMBA. Niemba, a town in the Katanga province of the Congo, was
the site of a massacre of Irish peacekeepers assigned to the **United
Nations Operation in the Congo** (ONUC). On November 8, 1960,
the 11-man Irish patrol was ambushed, resulting in the deaths of nine
of the peacekeepers. *See also* KINDU; PORT FRANCQUI.

NIGERIAN PEACEKEEPING. The Nigerians, major participants in
multinational peacekeeping operations deployed by the **United Nations** (UN), the **Economic Community of West African States**
(ECOWAS), and the **Organization of African Unity** (OAU), have
fielded two unilateral "peacekeeping" operations. Nigeria's first unilateral peacekeeping operation was in Tanganyika. British soldiers
provided security for the government of Tanganyika after a mutiny
by the military in 1964. At the request of Tanganyika's government,
Nigeria dispatched a military force to replace the British and provide
security and stability within the country. The Nigerians arrived on
March 31, 1964, and departed without any incidents on September
26, 1964.

The second Nigerian unilateral peacekeeping operation deployed
to neighboring **Chad**, which had suffered from civil conflict since its
independence. The turmoil in Chad attracted several external coun-

tries, including France (the former colonial power) and Libya. The French military occupied the Chadian capital of N'Djamena, and Nigeria sought to have them removed. Nigeria opted to host what became known as the Kano Accord meetings between March and April 1979. During these meetings, the leaders of major Chadian factions met with Nigerian officials to develop a provisional government that would represent each group until popular elections. The Kano Accords included a provision for the introduction of peacekeepers from Nigeria to oversee the cease-fire. Nigerian soldiers, eventually numbering 800, began arriving in Chad on March 7, 1979 (actually three days prior to the first meeting under the Kano Accords).

The peacekeeping mandate, as recorded in the Kano Accord, included instructions to guarantee the demilitarization of N'Djamena and a 100-kilometer zone around the capital; protect the Chadian faction leaders; and guarantee the free movement of civilians in Chad. The Nigerian peacekeepers were also to replace the departing French forces. Because the Chadian factions viewed the Nigerian peacekeepers as an army of occupation, they refused to cooperate fully with the Nigerian military, despite signing the Kano Accords. The Nigerians also suffered from internal problems, as evidenced by the lack of sufficient funding and logistical support, including adequate amounts of food. The frustrated peacekeepers, commanded by Colonel M. Magoro, departed on June 4, 1979, at the request of the Chadian interim government.

NIMMO, LIEUTENANT-GENERAL R. H. Nimmo, an Australian officer, served as the Chief Military Observer of the **United Nations Military Observer Group in India and Pakistan** (UNMOGIP) from October 1950 to January 1966. In 1959, he was given the title Assistant Secretary-General to help in his negotiating duties. This was the first time that a peacekeeping commander, other than the Chief of Staff for the **United Nations Truce Supervision Organization** (UNTSO), had been awarded this title. Currently, all force commanders and chief military observers are assigned the title of Assistant Secretary-General for administrative purposes. In 1965, Nimmo was named as the interim commander of the newly established **United Nations India Pakistan Observation Mission** (UNIPOM) until the arrival of Major-General B. F. Macdonald of Canada.

Nimmo's 16 years with UNMOGIP is the **United Nations** (UN) record for a tour as a peacekeeping operation commander.

NOBEL PEACE PRIZE. The Nobel Peace Prize has been awarded twice for **United Nations** (UN) multinational peacekeeping-related activities. The prize, given annually to the individual(s) selected as having accomplished the most toward promoting global peace, was awarded in 1988 to all UN peacekeepers. Secretary-General Javier Perez de Cuellar accepted the award in Oslo on December 10, 1988, on behalf of all United Nations peacekeepers. Seventeen peacekeepers, representing the 17 operations fielded by the UN between 1948 and 1988, accompanied the Secretary-General to Oslo. The Secretary-General used the occasion to remind the world that 733 soldiers had died in the service of the UN. Egil Aarvik, Chairman of the Norwegian Nobel Committee, also asked listeners to remember those who died in the service of the UN and commented, "They came from different countries and had widely different backgrounds, but they were united in one thing: they were willing to devote their youth and their energy to the service, knowing that it could involve risk. It became their lot to pay the highest price a human can pay." In 1956, **Lester B. Pearson** received the Nobel Peace Prize for his development of the concepts that led to the establishment of the **United Nations Emergency Force I** (UNEF I).

NO-FLY ZONES. The **United Nations** (UN) established No-Fly Zones in the former **Yugoslavia** and **Iraq**. The term refers to areas where the UN only permits aircraft overflights by its own aircraft or those of another international organization in order to safeguard a protected population.

NON-AGGRESSION AND ASSISTANCE ACCORD PEACE FORCE (FPA). In May 1997, the members of the Non-Aggression and Assistance Accord (ANAD), an African subregional organization, endorsed a report establishing an ANAD Peace Force (FPA). FPA would be a banner under which ANAD members could dispatch military units in times of a crisis. A communique at the end of the meeting stated that FPA will support the prevention, management, and settlement of conflicts. In particular, members viewed FPA as a mechanism to conduct humanitarian operations. Members called for future peacekeeping operations under the FPA banner. Little has been reported on this initiative since 1997.

NORTH ATLANTIC TREATY ORGANIZATION (NATO). The North Atlantic Treaty Organization (NATO) emerged on April 4, 1949, as a Western alliance to counter any possible Soviet military threat to Western Europe. The North Atlantic Council is NATO's senior political authority and consists of permanent representatives from all full member states. Decisions in the body are based on consent. The Military Committee is the highest military body in the organization but is under the council and the civilian authorities. Each member holds a seat on the Military Committee. At the conclusion of the **Cold War**, NATO evolved to develop new missions including peacekeeping operations. Since the North Atlantic Council is based on consent, all members must agree to deploy NATO forces in a peacekeeping operation. However, members are not required to participate. NATO's first peacekeeping missions were sent to the new states of the former Yugoslavia including **Bosnia and Herzegovina**, **Croatia**, **Kosovo**, and **Macedonia**. The organization approved a **Rapid Reaction Force** in November 2002 to facilitate the speedy coordination and deployment of NATO assets during crisis situations. NATO has 19 full members and 27 **Partnership for Peace** (PfP) members. In November 2002, seven states were invited to become full members and will officially join in 2004. PfP is a program that coordinates and promotes cooperation between NATO and other states outside of the alliance. PfP members have fielded contingents alongside NATO forces in peacekeeping operations. *See also* IMPLEMENTATION FORCE; IRAQ STABILIZATION FORCE; KOSOVO FORCE; NORTH ATLANTIC TREATY ORGANIZATION RAPID REACTION FORCE; OPERATION ALLIED HARMONY; OPERATION AMBER FOX; OPERATION ESSENTIAL HARVEST; STABILISATION FORCE; UNITED NATIONS PROTECTION FORCE IN BOSNIA AND HERZEGOVINA.

NORTH ATLANTIC TREATY ORGANIZATION (NATO) RAPID REACTION FORCE. The **North Atlantic Treaty Organization** (NATO) established a **Rapid Reaction Force** in November 2002. One purpose of the force is to have military units designated, trained, and ready for short notice deployment for **peacekeeping** operations under a NATO **mandate**. NATO envisions its member states earmarking a total of 20,000 troops for the program. *See also* AFRICAN STAND BY FORCE; EUROPEAN UNION RAPID REACTION FORCE; UNITED NATIONS STAND BY ARRANGEMENT SYSTEM.

– O –

OAKLEY, ROBERT B. United States President Bush originally selected Oakley as the White House special envoy in Somalia in 1992. Oakley established the United States Liaison Office in Somalia in December 1992. In his capacity, Oakley served as the senior American civilian posted to Somalia and represented Presidents Bush and Clinton in the country. Robert Gosende replaced Oakley in March 1993. However, Clinton requested that Oakley return to Somalia before the end of 1993. Oakley was responsible for the negotiations with supporters of General **Mohammed Farah Aidid** following a series of bloody clashes between the latter's supporters and American rangers assigned to assist the **United Nations** (UN) military contingent in Somalia. Oakley's efforts resulted in a cease-fire between Aidid's forces and the UN peacekeepers.

OBSERVER DETACHMENT DAMASCUS (ODD). The approximately 35 peacekeepers assigned to the Observer Group Damascus perform support functions for the **Observer Group Golan** of the **United Nations Truce Supervision Organization** (UNTSO).

OBSERVER GROUP BEIRUT (OGB). The **United Nations** (UN) established the group in August 1982 following the **Israeli** invasion of **Lebanon** and attack upon Beirut. The personnel assigned to OGB were from the **United Nations Truce Supervision Organization** (UNTSO). The purpose of the group included monitoring the movements of the Israelis and Palestinians in and around Beirut. After the Israeli withdrawal in 1983, the strength of OGB was gradually reduced from a maximum of 50 to eight personnel who currently perform liaison duties for UNTSO.

OBSERVER GROUP EGYPT (OGE). The **United Nations Truce Supervision Organization** (UNTSO) established the Observer Group Egypt (OGE) following the lapse of the **United Nations Emergency Force II** (UNEF II) mandate and the termination of the **Israel-Egypt Mixed Armistice Commission** in 1979. The conclusion of the Israeli-Egyptian peace treaty made both operations obsolete. The **United Nations** (UN) established the OGE as a means of maintaining a neutral presence along the Israeli-Egyptian frontier. The group operates six static outposts as well as mobile patrols in the Sinai and an outpost at Ismailia. Areas under observation by the **Multinational Force and Observers** are not supervised by the OGE. The group consists of approximately 55 personnel and maintains its main headquarters in Cairo.

OBSERVER GROUP GOLAN (OGG). The **United Nations Truce Supervision Organization** (UNTSO) established the Observer Group Golan (OGG) in support of the **United Nations Disengagement Observer Force** (UNDOF) deployed between **Israel** and Syria in May 1974. The 90 **United Nations** (UN) peacekeepers assigned to UNTSO in the area were detailed to UNDOF and later organized under the title of OGG in 1979. The peacekeepers assigned to the group perform inspections to ensure that both sides are in compliance with the disengagement agreement. The group consists of approximately 138 observers.

OBSERVER GROUP LEBANON (OGL). The **United Nations Truce Supervision Organization** (UNTSO) discontinued its monitoring of the **Israeli-Lebanese** cease-fire line following the establishment of the **United Nations Interim Force in Lebanon** (UNIFIL) in March 1978. However the organization continued to monitor the armistice (dating to 1948) between the two states. The peacekeepers assigned to UNTSO along the Israeli-Lebanese border were organized as the Observer Group Lebanon and are under the operational control of UNIFIL. Approximately 65 OGL peacekeepers operate five static observation posts and conduct mobile patrols along the border. Lieutenant-Colonel William Higgins, an American Chief of OGL, was kidnapped and murdered while assigned to the organization.

OPERATION ABLE SENTRY. The **United States** military applied this name to its support of the **United Nations Protection Force (UNPROFOR) in Macedonia**. Fielded in July 1993, Operation Able Sentry originally consisted of 315 American soldiers who were part of a total **United Nations** (UN) strength of 1,000 peacekeepers in **Macedonia**. The majority of the soldiers in this operation were infantry transferred from the Berlin Brigade, which was scheduled for deactivation after the reunification of Germany. In 1994, the United States increased its contingent by approximately another 300 soldiers to allow a Scandinavian company to transfer to Bosnia and Herzegovina.

OPERATION ALBA. *See* MULTINATIONAL PROTECTION FORCE.

OPERATION ALLIED HARMONY. The **North Atlantic Treaty Organization** (NATO) planned to turn over peacekeeping responsibilities in **Macedonia** to the **European Union** (EU) at the end of 2002. However, the EU was not able to deploy a force as originally scheduled due to political issues including disagreement between Greece and Turkey. The former is a NATO and EU member while the latter is only a NATO member. NATO continued with plans to end its **Operation Amber Fox** mission in Macedonia but also agreed to field a new mission as a transition while awaiting the arrival of a EU force. This new mission, Operation Allied Harmony, assumed its duties on December 16, 2002. Its responsibilities included supporting international monitors and providing security advice to the Macedonian government. Operation Allied Harmony consisted of approximately 400 personnel. The EU officially replaced Operation Allied Harmony on April 1, 2003, with the introduction of its **European Force** (EURFOR).

OPERATION AMBER FOX. After **Operation Essential Harvest** departed from the Former Yugoslav Republic of **Macedonia** (FRYOM), the **North Atlantic Treaty Organization** (NATO) mandated Operation Amber Fox on September 26, 2001. The mandate for this mission included the protection of international monitors overseeing the peace plan within the FYROM. Germany led the mission consisting of approximately 1,000 NATO soldiers. The NATO troops assigned to the operation were known as Task Force Fox. The **United Nations** (UN) Security Council endorsed NATO's efforts by passing Security Council Resolution 1371 (2001).

Although NATO peacekeepers served as a security and extraction force for the international monitors, they could only act if requested by the FYROM government which maintained the primary security role for the teams. Operation Fox's mandate ended on December 15, 2002. NATO intended to turn over the peacekeeping duties of Macedonia to the **European Union** (EU) prior to the end of 2002. However, the EU was not prepared to assume the mission and postponed the plan. NATO mandated **Operation Allied Harmony** to replace Operation Amber Fox until the EU was ready to assume the peacekeeping mission. Operation Allied Harmony initiated its operations on December 16, 2002. *See also* UNITED NATIONS PREVENTIVE DEPLOYMENT FORCE.

OPERATION DESERT SHIELD. The American nickname for the movement of **United States** military forces, as well as units from other **United Nations** (UN) members, to the Persian Gulf area following the invasion of Kuwait by Iraq in 1990. Desert Shield's purpose included the protection of Saudi Arabia from possible military advances by Iraq. *See also* OPERATION DESERT STORM; PERSIAN GULF WAR.

OPERATION DESERT STORM. A code name applied by the **United States** to the **United Nations** (UN) air and ground strikes into Iraq and Kuwait during the 1991 **Persian Gulf War**. Desert Storm's purpose included the crippling of the Iraqi military and the removal of Iraqi forces from Kuwait. *See also* OPERATION DESERT SHIELD; PERSIAN GULF WAR.

OPERATION ESSENTIAL HARVEST. Civil strife between the Macedonian majority population and minority ethnic Albanians in the Former Yugoslav Republic of **Macedonia** (FYROM) resulted in serious clashes by mid-2001. On June 20, 2001, President Boris Trajkovski called upon the **North Atlantic Treaty Organization** (NATO) for assistance. NATO approved and produced a draft plan for a small peacekeeping operation, known as Operation Essential

Harvest, on June 29, 2001, with a requirement that the two sides agree to a political dialogue and respect a cease-fire. The NATO troops assigned to the operation were known as Task Force Harvest. NATO officially mandated the mission on August 15, 2001.

An advance party of 400 NATO peacekeepers arrived on August 17, 2001, and approximately 3,100 additional NATO troops deployed to FYROM by August 22, 2001, with a mandate to disarm the ethnic Albanians and destroy their weapons. However, NATO troops were to only destroy weapons and ammunition voluntarily given to them. They did not hold any authority to conduct searches and seize any weapons or ammunition. NATO declared the end of the operation on September 26, 2001, and most of the peacekeepers began departing the country. They were replaced with other NATO peacekeepers under **Operation Amber Fox**. *See also* UNITED NATIONS PREVENTIVE DEPLOYMENT FORCE.

OPERATION POISED HAMMER. When the **United Nations** (UN) assumed responsibility for humanitarian aid to the Kurds in northern Iraq after the **Persian Gulf War** in 1991, the allies established Operation Poised Hammer to provide air support in the event of Iraqi intervention into the **safe havens**. Forces assigned to the Operation were primarily based in western Turkey. *See also* OPERATION PROVIDE COMFORT; UNITED NATIONS GUARDS CONTINGENT IN IRAQ.

OPERATION PROVIDE COMFORT. The American nickname for Allied (**United States, France**, Italy, Canada, Belgium, Luxembourg, **Australia**, Spain, Netherlands, and **Germany**) humanitarian support for Kurds in northern Iraq following the **Persian Gulf War** in 1991. The military elements of Operation Provide Comfort were replaced by the **United Nations Guards Contingent in Iraq** (UNGCI) by July 1991. *See also* OPERATION POISED HAMMER; SAFE HAVENS.

OPERATION SMASH. This title, also known as Operation MOTHOR in the Hindi language, was a series of highly controversial **United Nations** (UN) offensives in the former Congo during September and December 1961 and December 1962. The three offensives were conducted by contingents assigned to the **United Nations Operation in the Congo** (ONUC). The first offensive, also known as Round One, lasted from September 13 to 21 1961. This operation is perhaps the most controversial act of ONUC during the Congolese civil war. ONUC has been accused of initiating the offensive without proper authority, exceeding its mandate and employing excessive force. The offensive lacked the element of surprise and was poorly executed and led. Secretary-General **Dag Hammarskjöld** died on September 18, 1961, in an aircraft crash on his way to Northern Rhodesia to arrange a cease-fire in Round One. The UN did secure a cease-fire by September 20th. However, the embarrassment to the global organization included the capture of a 200-man Irish company by forces loyal to secessionist Katanga. The second offensive, also known as Round Two, lasted between December 5 and 21, 1961. This offensive resulted from a series of incidents in **Elisabethville**. Although Round Two had better planning and military support, many UN member states opposed the offensive. These states included **France, Great Britain**, Congo, Portugal, Rhodesia, and **Central African Republic**. ONUC suffered 21 casualties during Round Two's move to end Katanga's attempt at secession from the Congo. Round Three lasted from December 28, 1962, to January 21, 1963. This offensive, spearheaded by **Indian** and Ethiopian troops, quickly occupied much of Katanga and forced the region to end its attempts at secession.

ORGANIZATION FOR SECURITY AND COOPERATION IN EUROPE (OSCE). The Organization for Security and Cooperation in Europe (OSCE) is a pan-European international organization that also links several non-European states to Europe. The organization has 55 members and nine partners for cooperation. The latter states include **Japan**, South Korea, and Thailand as well as six North African/Middle Eastern countries. The **United States** and **Russia** are full members. The OSCE emerged from the **Conference for Security and Cooperation in Europe** (CSCE). The CSCE was a Cold War organization, lacking a permanent secretariat, established in 1975 by the Helsinki Final Act as a means to discuss state behavior toward citizens and other countries. Members opted to form a more permanent structure for the organization at the end of the Cold War. In 1994, the CSCE changed its name to the OSCE and the organization established a permanent headquarters in Vienna.

The OSCE has fielded several international monitoring missions in Europe and the former Soviet Union. While most of these are clearly not **peacekeeping**, others can be placed into the category of peacekeeping. The classification of the latter OSCE missions as peacekeeping is based on their mandated international mission to monitor areas affected by conflict. A select few that are mandated to monitor conflicts are included in this dictionary. Some scholars do not acknowledge any of the OSCE missions as peacekeeping operations. The Stockholm International Peace Research Institute (SIPRI) recognizes all of the OSCE monitoring missions as "peace operations" which the organization defines as being either observer, peacekeeping, or peace building mission. Most OSCE monitors are unarmed civilians although a few are members of the military of their home states. While OSCE missions tend to be quite small, some have been fielded with a large number of observers/monitors. *See also* ORGANIZATION FOR SECURITY AND COOPERATION IN EUROPE KOSOVO TASK FORCE; ORGANIZATION FOR SECURITY AND COOPERATION IN EUROPE KOSOVO VERIFICATION MISSION; ORGANIZATION FOR SECURITY AND COOPERATION IN EUROPE MISSION IN KOSOVO; ORGANIZATION FOR SECURITY AND COOPERATION IN EUROPE MISSION TO GEORGIA; ORGANIZATION FOR SECURITY AND COOPERATION IN EUROPE MISSION TO MOLDOVA; ORGANIZATION FOR SECURITY AND COOPERATION IN EUROPE MISSION TO TAJIKISTAN.

ORGANIZATION FOR SECURITY AND COOPERATION IN EUROPE (OSCE) KOSOVO TASK FORCE. The **Organization for Security and Cooperation in Europe** established the Kosovo Task Force on June 8, 1999, as a three-week transition between the **Organization for Security and Cooperation in Europe Kosovo Verification Mission** and the **Organization for Security and Cooperation in Europe Mission in Kosovo.**

ORGANIZATION FOR SECURITY AND COOPERATION IN EUROPE KOSOVO VERIFICATION MISSION (KVM).

Kosovo is a territorial entity within the Federal Republic of **Yugoslavia**. The latter is dominated by Serbia and ethnic Serbs while the majority population in Kosovo is ethnic Albanian. Kosovo had considerable autonomy until 1989 when Serbian leader Slobodon Milosevic brought the region under direct Serbian control. By 1998, tensions were increasing between the ethnic Albanian majority and Serbian minority within Kosovo, and fighting between the Yugoslavian army and the Kosovo Liberation Army became daily occurrences. A humanitarian crisis erupted as Serbians forced people to flee Kosovo. Yugoslavian authorities refused to abide by international demands to end the crisis, and the situation threatened to spread to other states in the region. On October 13, 1998, the **North Atlantic Treaty Organization** (NATO) authorized air strikes to support diplomatic moves to force the Serbians to end the violence. The Serbs backed down, and the **Organization for Security and Cooperation in Europe** (OSCE) established its Kosovo Verification Mission.

By March 1999, the situation began to collapse again and the monitors of the verification mission departed Kosovo. A final appeal to Milosevic was rebuffed, and NATO commenced air strikes after March 23, 1999. The campaign lasted until June 10, 1999, when the Serbs agreed to international demands. The **United Nations** Security Council, with Resolution 1244 (1999), endorsed the sending of a NATO ground force into Kosovo. This operation became known as the **Kosovo Force** (KFOR). Some scholars do not view KVM as a peacekeeping operation. The Stockholm International Peace Research Institute (SIPRI) recognizes it as a "peace operation" which the organization defines as either being an observer, peacekeeping, or peace building mission.

ORGANIZATION FOR SECURITY AND COOPERATION IN EUROPE MISSION IN KOSOVO (OMIK). The **Organization for Security and Cooperation in Europe** (OSCE) mandated the **Organization for Security and Cooperation in Europe Kosovo Verification Mission** (KVM) prior to the commencement of air strikes in March 1999 by the **North Atlantic Treaty Organization** (NATO) against Serbia for human rights violations in **Kosovo**. After the conclusion of hostilities, the OSCE established a new operation, the OSCE Mission in Kosovo (OMIK), on July 1, 1999, with OSCE

Permanent Council Decision 305. The mission actually replaces the **Organization for Security and Cooperation in Europe Kosovo Task Force** set up as a transition between KVM and OMIK. The mandate includes monitoring the compliance of the Federal Republic of **Yugoslavia** with the **United Nations'** (UN) resolutions concerning Kosovo. The group also monitors the cease-fire, observes the movement of military forces, and promotes human rights and democracy. The joint OSCE-UN training of a new police force is also included in the mandate. The OSCE opened and operates the Kosovo Police Service School as part of this process.

The mission is the OSCE's largest operation and is authorized for up to 700 international monitors and 1,600 local staff members although the actual numbers are smaller. OMIK receives an annual budget of 70 million euros from the OSCE. The OSCE closely coordinates the operation of the monitors with the UN. The OSCE Head of Mission also serves as the **United Nations Interim Administration Mission in Kosovo** (UNMIK) Deputy Special Representative for Institution Building. This is the first time the OSCE has linked one of its missions with a UN operation. NATO's **Kosovo Force** (KFOR) provides security for the OSCE monitors to conduct their work. Some scholars do not consider this mission as a peacekeeping operation. The Stockholm International Peace Research Institute (SIPRI) recognizes OMIK as a "peace operation" which the organization defines as either being an observer, peacekeeping, or peace building mission.

ORGANIZATION FOR SECURITY AND COOPERATION IN EUROPE (OSCE) MISSION TO GEORGIA. Georgia faced an attempt by Abkhazia to separate itself from the country soon after independence following the collapse of the Soviet Union. Abkhazia is located in the northwestern part of Georgia. The unrest devolved into open fighting by the summer of 1992 after Georgia deployed 2,000 soldiers to the region. **Russia** negotiated a cease-fire agreement between the two parties on September 2, 1992. The agreement collapsed on October 1, 1992. The **Conference for Security and Cooperation in Europe** (CSCE) mandated an observer mission in December 1992 to monitor the situation in Georgia and along its borders. The objective of the mission is to encourage negotiations to settle the conflicts in Abkhazia and South Ossetia. In 1994, the name of the operation changed to reflect the transition of the CSCE to the **Organization for Security and Cooperation in Europe**.

The mission works to help develop methods of defining the political positions of South Ossetia and Abkhazia, which lie within Georgia. It also monitors the Russian-led peacekeepers in South Ossetia (**South Ossetia Joint Force**). On December 15, 1999, the OSCE expanded the mission to include observing the border between Georgia and the Chechen Republic of the Russian Federation. The observers also coordinate with the **United Nations Observer Mission in Georgia**.

Approximately 23 OSCE members provide approximately 44 unarmed observers for the operation. Most of the observers are civilians. The annual budget, as of 2000, is approximately 6,500,000 euros. Some scholars do not view this OSCE mission as a peacekeeping operation. The Stockholm International Peace Research Institute (SIPRI) recognizes it as a "peace operation" which the organization defines as either being an observer, peacekeeping, or peace building mission.

ORGANIZATION FOR SECURITY AND COOPERATION IN EUROPE (OSCE) MISSION TO MOLDOVA. The **Conference for Security and Cooperation in Europe** (CSCE) mandated the Mission to Moldova on February 4, 1993. The purpose of the operation is to monitor the political situation within the Transdniester region of Moldova. The CSCE was concerned about the proper definition of the region within a newly sovereign Moldova following the breakup of the Soviet Union. Many in Transdniester are of Romanian descent and seek measures of autonomy if not separation from Moldova. The name of the mission changed when the CSCE evolved into the **Organization for Security and Cooperation in Europe** in 1994.

The mandate of the operation includes assisting the parties in their negotiations as well as observing the **Joint Control Commission Peacekeeping Force** fielded by **Russia**. Only eight unarmed members are assigned to the operation. However, two of them are military. As of 2000, the annual budget for the operation was 720,400 euros. Some scholars do not view the OSCE Moldova mission as a peacekeeping operation. The Stockholm International Peace Research Institute (SIPRI) recognizes the Moldova mission as a "peace operation" which the organization defines as either being an observer, peacekeeping, or peace building mission.

ORGANIZATION FOR SECURITY AND COOPERATION IN EUROPE (OSCE) MISSION TO TAJIKISTAN. Tajikistan declared its independence from the Soviet Union on September 9, 1991. Economic and social instability, along with disagreements among clans and other regional groups, prevailed after independence. At the same time, tensions between Tajik secularists and Islamic fundamentalists increased. In May 1992, an anti-government coalition managed to gain control of the government following two months of unrest within the state. A civil war ensued that resulted in a defeat of the coalition by the end of 1992 and forcing them to take refuge in Afghanistan. Tajikistan and **Russia** signed an agreement permitting Russian soldiers to deploy along the border with Afghanistan.

On September 24, 1993, the **Commonwealth of Independent States** (CIS) mandated the **Commonwealth of Independent States Collective Peacekeeping Force**. The **Conference on Security and Cooperation in Europe** (CSCE) opted to work with the **United Nations** (UN) in its own conflict management process. As a result, the OSCE mandated its Mission to Tajikistan to assist the **United Nations Mission of Observers in Tajikistan** (UNMOT). The CSCE established the mission on December 1, 1993, and the group began operations on February 19, 1994. In 1994, the CSCE changed its name to the **Organization for Security and Cooperation in Europe**. A new opposition offensive nullified the cease-fire agreement by July 1996.

A second cease-fire was signed in December 1996 and a general peace agreement on June 27, 1997. The latter agreement initiated a transitional period that included the return of refugees and the demobilization of opposition fighters. Tajikistan held legislative elections for its lower house on February 27, 2000, which were monitored by the UN and OSCE Joint Electoral Observation Mission. The Joint Mission noted that the election did not meet minimum electoral standards. The upper house elections occurred on March 23, 2000.

The OSCE's mission was mandated to promote confidence building measures among the disputing parties in Tajikistan, promote respect for human rights, secure adherence to OSCE norms and principles, and assist in the establishment of democratic institutions. In 1995, the OSCE provided the monitors with a mission to also observe the conditions of returning refugees. The mission consists of approximately 15 personnel. The annual budget is approximately 1.8 million euros. Some scholars do not view the mission as a peacekeeping operation. The Stockholm International Peace Research Institute (SIPRI) recognizes it as a "peace operation" which the organization defines as either being an observer, peacekeeping, or peace building mission.

ORGANIZATION FOR SECURITY AND COOPERATION IN EUROPE (OSCE) SPILLOVER MONITOR MISSION TO SKOPJE. The Former Yugoslav Republic of **Macedonia** (FYROM) faced the potential of ethnic conflict spillover in 1992 as **Yugoslavia** split into several regions. Ethnic Serbs contested Croats and Bosnian Muslims in **Croatia** and **Bosnia and Herzegovina**. The **Conference for Security and Cooperation in Europe** (CSCE) mandated a multinational operation to monitor the border between Macedonia and Serbia in the attempt to prevent conflict spillover. The **European Community** planned to expand its **European Community Monitoring Mission** (ECMM) as an effort to prevent the spread of ethnic conflict in the region. The two organizations agreed to allow the CSCE to mandate and field the mission in Macedonia, an observer member of the latter organization. In 1994, the name of the operation changed to reflect the transition of the CSCE to the **Organization for Security and Cooperation in Europe**. Macedonia became a full member of the OSCE in October 1995.

The mandate of the operation calls for the monitoring of the border as well as promoting efforts for ethnic cooperation within the country and training/advising the Macedonian police. The number of personnel assigned to the operation has steadily increased from four in 1992 to over 150 monitors and police advisers/trainers at the end of 2001. The reported annual budget for 2000 was 598,600 euros. However, it can be assumed that the budget increased greatly with the addition of new personnel in 2001. Some scholars do not view the Skopje mission as a peacekeeping operation. The Stockholm International Peace Research Institute (SIPRI) recognizes this OSCE mission as a "peace operation" which the organization defines as either being an observer, peacekeeping, or peace building mission.

ORGANIZATION OF AFRICAN UNITY (OAU). The Organization of African Unity (OAU) was established on May 25, 1963. The 52 members represented all countries on the continent and several off-shore island states except Morocco. The purpose of the organization was to promote African unity, defend the sovereignty of member states, and improve living standards on the continent. The body has mandated four definite **peacekeeping** operations (two in **Chad**, one in **Rwanda**, and one in **Burundi**) and a mission in the Comoro Islands that some argue is too small to be a peacekeeping operation. The OAU transitioned into a new organization in 2002 known as the **African Union** (AU). While some have hoped that the new AU would be more active in security related issues, this has yet to be seen *See also* MILITARY OBSERVER GROUP; NEUTRAL MILITARY OBSERVATION GROUP I; NEUTRAL MILITARY OBSERVATION GROUP II; ORGANIZATION OF AFRICAN UNITY MISSION IN BURUNDI; ORGANIZATION OF AFRICAN UNITY MISSION IN THE COMORO ISLANDS; ORGANIZATION OF AFRICAN UNITY PEACEKEEPING FORCE IN CHAD I; ORGANIZATION OF AFRICAN UNITY PEACEKEEPING FORCE IN CHAD II; UNITED AFRICAN ACTION.

ORGANIZATION OF AFRICAN UNITY MISSION IN BURUNDI (OMIB). In 1993, the belligerents in **Rwanda** agreed to a new cease-fire and peace process. The **Organization of African Unity** (OAU) had supported the peace process in Rwanda since 1990 with the **Military Observer Group** (MOG), the **Neutral Military Observer Group I** (NMOG I), and the **Neutral Military Observer Group II** (NMOG II). The **United Nations** (UN) mandated the **United Nations Assistance Mission in Rwanda** (UNAMIR) and began fielding the operation in December 1993. The OAU transferred its personnel from NMOG II to UNAMIR during the same month. The OAU expressed concern that the civil war in Rwanda could spill over into neighboring **Burundi**. In February 1994, the OAU dispatched approximately 47 military observers to Burundi in an attempt to monitor the situation and prevent conflict spillover. The operation, known as the Organization of African Unity Mission in Burundi (OMIB), was originally envisioned as a larger force with 400 military observers. Burkina Faso, Mali, Niger, and Tunisia provided the personnel for the operation. Other sources report the contingents arrived from Burkina Faso, Cameroon, Guinea, Mali, Niger, and Tunisia. This could be due to rotating contingents or simply confusion among the sources. Even government and international agency reports have frequently confused and interchanged the facts of the various small OAU peacekeeping missions in Rwanda and Burundi. The operation departed in July 1996 following a coup.

ORGANIZATION OF AFRICAN UNITY OBSERVER MISSION IN THE COMORO ISLANDS (OMIC). Separatists on two islands demanded independence from the Comoros in 1997. The **Organization of African Unity** (OAU) quickly stepped in and offered to mediate the crisis. On November 6, 1997, the OAU mandated the Organization of African Unity Observer Mission in the Comoro Islands (OMIC) to monitor the situation and establish a climate of trust. The OAU deployed 20 military observers from Niger, Senegal, and Tunisia. At least one source credits Egypt with providing personnel as well. OMIC withdrew the military observers from the Comoros in May 1999 following a military coup on April 30, 1999. Three civilians remain to continue the OAU mission. The annual cost of OMIC is approximately $176,500.

ORGANIZATION OF AFRICAN UNITY (OAU) PEACEKEEPING FORCE (OAUPKF) IN CHAD I. The country of **Chad** had suffered from civil conflict since its independence in 1960. Several major factions were in competition for control of the Chadian government. The turmoil in Chad attracted several external countries including **France**, the former colonial power, and Libya, both of which had intervened militarily in Chad. As the civil strife continued and attempts at **Nigerian peacekeeping** failed, the **Organization of African Unity** (OAU) agreed to discuss the possibility of mandating a multinational peacekeeping operation. The OAU opted to use the newly signed Lagos Accords as the legal basis for the peacekeeping mission. The Lagos Accords, written by Nigeria and signed by the major Chadian factions, called for a multinational peacekeeping force to replace the French military in Chad. The international force would also supervise the Chadian cease-fire, protect the free movement of civilians, restore law and order, and help establish an integrated national army representing all of the major factions. The mandate of the neutral force terminated upon the completion of the training and fielding of the new integrated Chadian national army, which would then protect the new interim government of Chad.

The operation actually consisted on paper of two separate organizations. The first included the OAU peacekeeping force, and the second involved a Monitoring Commission consisting of two representatives from each of Chad's neighbors (Cameroon, **Central African Republic**, Libya, Niger, **Nigeria**, and Sudan); two from the four OAU observer states of Benin, Congo, Liberia, and Senegal; and two from each of Chad's major factions. In order to placate the Chadian factions that still resented the Nigerian attempt at unilateral peacekeeping, the Lagos Accords declared that participants in the military side of the operation could not be states that shared a border with Chad. Congo, Guinea, and Benin each pledged 500 soldiers for the peacekeeping force, while Algeria and Nigeria agreed to provide transportation and logistical support for the mission. The OAU requested each member state to contribute $50,000 toward the operational costs.

The contingent from the Congo was the only body of neutral soldiers to arrive in Chad. The approximately 550 Congolese troops began flying into Chad on January 18, 1980, six days after renewed hostilities in the civil war. Logistical problems arose quickly in this operation. Benin and Guinea announced that the lack of transport prevented the deployment of their units. The Congolese, who also experienced logistical difficulties, reportedly arrived in Chad on Algerian aircraft piloted by Angolans. Nigeria did offer to transport the contingent from Guinea but made it conditional on the departure of the French army from Chad. The French did not withdraw and the Nigerians did not assist Guinea. The Congolese contingent occupied a substandard barracks complex near the airport and reportedly only entered the capital to obtain supplies. The unit never received a mission, came under attack by at least one faction suffering at least one fatality, and departed out of concern for its safety four months later. OAU member states did not meet their contributions to the peacekeeping operation. OAU appeals to members of the **United Nations** (UN) also fell on deaf ears. Algeria, when not reimbursed for transporting the Congolese detachment, forwarded a bill to the Congo. Despite the miserable failure of this mission, the OAU did attempt to deploy a peacekeeping operation to Chad two years later. That force was known as the **Organization of African Unity Peacekeeping Force in Chad II**.

ORGANIZATION OF AFRICAN UNITY (OAU) PEACEKEEPING FORCE (OAUPKF) IN CHAD II. The Organization of African Unity (OAU) Peacekeeping Force (OAUPKF) II grew out of the failure of the **Organization of African Unity Peacekeeping Force I** that was fielded in 1980. By 1981, **French** forces in Chad had been replaced by Libyan troops. Many OAU members considered this situation even more intolerable than the one that existed in 1980 when they had to contend with French forces in Chad. The OAU mandated a new attempt at peacekeeping with Resolution AHG/102 (XVIII) in June 1981. The peacekeeping operation included the mission of ensuring the defense and security of Chad while awaiting the integration of a new government army. **Nigeria**, Senegal, and Zaire offered combat battalions for the OAU peacekeeping operation. **France** assisted in equipping and fielding the Senegalese; the **United States** helped the battalion from Zaire; and both the United States and **Great Britain** worked with Nigeria. Algeria, Guinea-Bissau, Kenya, and Zambia provided detachments of military observers. Nigeria provided the **Force Commander**, Major-General Geoffrey Obiaje Ejiga.

One hundred parachutists from Zaire were the first soldiers fielded under the OAU mandate in Chad. The contingent from Zaire began arriving on November 15, 1981, in an attempt to fill the vacuum created by the departing Libyan army and, eventually, approximately 800 troops from Zaire flew to Chad in support of the OAU. The Senegalese soldiers began arriving on November 27 and by mid-December numbered approximately 700 troops. Nigerian soldiers initiated their crossing into Chad on December 7. Deployment of the contingents to their operational zones commenced after the arrival of the Nigerian units. Originally, the OAU envisioned fielding six contingents to six zones, each stretching from the capital, N'Djamena. With the reduced manpower and a rebel army on the offensive in the east, the OAU was forced to quickly develop a new deployment plan. Troops from Nigeria and Zaire were rushed to the town of Ati in central Chad to block the rebels' westward advance from the town of Abeche. The Senegalese battalion deployed to Mongo, a town south of Ati, to block the south-central road to N'Djamena. A final Nigerian battalion, fielded in Chad on March 2, 1982, deployed to a series of small towns north of N'Djamena to prevent the rebels from outflanking the peacekeepers in central Chad.

The hasty deployment of the OAU contingents to block rebel forces and the Chadian government's frequent forays against its rival through the peacekeepers' lines demonstrated the failure of a cease-fire to take hold in Chad. The OAU attempted twice to force a cease-fire on the rival parties after fielding the peacekeeping unit. The government and rebels refused to abide by the previously adopted OAU resolutions and communiques so the OAU tried twice more in February and May 1982 to get the two rivals to agree to a conflict management process that the already fielded peacekeeping force could facilitate. The lack of finances and the rebels' ouster of President Oueddemimi Goukouni from N'djamena in June 1982 prompted the OAU to officially terminate the operation but not before a frustrated Nigeria began a unilateral withdrawal of its forces from the country.

The OAU sought funding for the peacekeeping operation from its member states. When these countries refused to contribute to the operation, Secretary-General Edem Kodjo and Chairman Daniel Arap Moi dispatched representatives to the **United Nations** (UN) to seek funding. A few members of the global body pledged small amounts of cash, but the OAU officially terminated the operation before any funds were received. The failure of the OAU's peacekeeping force can be seen as resulting from a lack of funding and the refusal of the belligerents to adhere to a cease-fire in the conflict. Logistically, the contingents established bilateral agreements with Western states. The OAU departed Chad with a negative feeling toward the concept of peacekeeping and did not attempt another such operation until 1993 with the fielding of the **Neutral Military Observer Group I** (NMOG I) in Rwanda.

ORGANIZATION OF AMERICAN STATES (OAS). The Organization of American States (OAS) was established in March 1948 and is headquartered in Washington, D.C. The organization has 31 members representing North, Central, and South America. It is a broad-based organization that handles issues involving regional security, economics, and social issues. The OAS has fielded one operation that is sometimes classified as **peacekeeping** in nature and assisted the **United Nations** (UN) with missions mandated by the latter. *See also* INTER-AMERICAN PEACE FORCE; REPRESENTATIVE OF THE SECRETARY-GENERAL IN THE DOMINICAN REPUBLIC; UNITED NATIONS MISSION IN HAITI.

ORGANIZATION OF EAST CARIBBEAN STATES (OECS). The Organization of East Caribbean States (OECS) was founded in 1981 and consists of states located in the eastern Caribbean Sea. The OECS has participated in one multinational military operation that can be classified as a form of collective security. The location of this operation was the island state of Grenada. Maurice Bishop had come to power in Grenada by a coup in 1979. On October 13, 1983, a faction of Bishop's ruling group staged another coup that ousted him from power. Six days later, Bishop's attempt to regain control of the government failed and he, along with several ministers, was executed. The OECS met on October 21 to discuss the situation on Grenada and its impact to the region, as well as the potential for greater violence within Grenada. The OECS opted to launch an armed intervention of Grenada and sought assistance from states outside of the organization. The **United States** accepted the invitation from the OECS. However, it is not clear if the United States had any role in prompting the OECS to elect to field an armed intervention into Grenada prior the extension of the invitation to Washington. The **British** Governor-General of Grenada was secretly contacted and informed that he should seek a multinational intervention. He made the request and American soldiers landed on the island on October 24, 1983.

Although the United States justified its participation with the OECS as a means to protect approximately 1,000 American citizens, mainly medical students, in Grenada, Washington exhibited a desire to remove the island from the political orbit of Cuba. Approximately 2,000 American paratroopers and marines were joined by 300 soldiers and policemen from Antigua, Barbados, Dominica, the Grenadines, St. Lucia, and St. Vincent. Offers by Montserrat and St. Kitts-Nevis were withdrawn due to "technical reasons." Other members of the OECS, including Barbados and Trinidad and Tobago, objected to the military action in the name of the international organization. Shridath Ramphal, the Secretary-General of the **Commonwealth**, called for the replacement of the OECS force with a Commonwealth peacekeeping unit. The United States officially handed security control of the island to the OECS contingents on November 22, 1983, which numbered approximately 392 at that point. All American combat forces were withdrawn by December 15, 1983.

OSORIO-TAFALL, BIBIANO F. Osorio-Tafall, a Mexican diplomat, held the position of Officer-in-Charge of the **United Nations Operation in the Congo** (ONUC) between April and June 1964. In February 1967, he was named the Special Representative for the **United Nations Peacekeeping Force in Cyprus** (UNFICYP) and held that post until June 1974.

OSSETIA. *See* SOUTH OSSETIA JOINT FORCE.

– P –

"PAINTING A COUNTRY BLUE." British Foreign Secretary Douglas Hurd coined this phrase to illustrate peacekeeping missions aimed at providing humanitarian aid, security, disarmament, and a jump-start for a political reconciliation in states whose governments have broken down such as **Somalia**. The **United Nations Transition Assistance Group** (UNTAG) and the **United Nations Transitional Authority in Cambodia** (UNTAC) are classic examples of this term in application. *See also* BLUE HELMETS.

PAKISTAN. *See* UNITED NATIONS COMMISSION FOR INDIA AND PAKISTAN; UNITED NATIONS GOOD OFFICES IN AFGHANISTAN AND PAKISTAN; UNITED NATIONS INDIA-PAKISTAN OBSERVER MISSION; UNITED NATIONS MILITARY OBSERVER GROUP IN INDIA AND PAKISTAN.

PALESTINE. *See* TEMPORARY INTERNATIONAL PRESENCE IN HEBRON.

PAN-AFRICAN FORCE. *See* ORGANIZATION OF AFRICAN UNITY PEACEKEEPING FORCE IN CHAD I; ORGANIZATION OF AFRICAN UNITY PEACEKEEPING FORCE IN CHAD II.

PAN-ARAB FORCE. *See* ARAB DETERRENT FORCE; ARAB LEAGUE FORCE IN KUWAIT; SYMBOLIC ARAB SECURITY FORCE.

PANEL ON UNITED NATIONS PEACE OPERATIONS. In March 2000, **United Nations** (UN) Secretary-General **Kofi Annan** established a panel to make a formal inquiry and offer recommendations to improve the global organization's **peacekeeping** capabilities following the release of the Carlsson Report by the **Independent Inquiry into the Actions of the United Nations During the 1994 Genocide in Rwanda** as well as a second study on the massacre of civilians in **Srebrenica**. Annan tasked former Algerian Foreign Minister Ladhdar Brahimi to chair the ten-member panel that consisted of members from all six inhabited continents. The Secretary-General requested the members of the inquiry panel to make a critical examination of past attempts to reorganize the structure and management of UN peacekeeping.

The resulting document, known as the Brahimi Report, made the following recommendations:

1. Utilize more conflict preventive measures such as fact-finding missions.
2. Enhance peace-building strategies.
3. Provide peacekeepers with "robust" **rules of engagement**.
4. Develop clear, credible, and achievable mandates.
5. Establish a Secretariat for Information and Strategic Analysis.
6. Develop an interim criminal code for use by peacekeeping operations pending the re-establishment of local rule of law and local law enforcement capability.
7. Define "rapid and effective deployment capacities" as the ability to fully deploy **traditional peacekeeping** operations within 30 days after the passage of a mandating Security Council resolution and within 90 days for more complex missions.
8. Strengthen the processes for the selection and assembling of leadership assigned to a peacekeeping operation.

9. Strengthen the **United Nations Standby Arrangements System**.
10. Enhance the selection and training of civilian police personnel assigned to peacekeeping operations.
11. Reform the recruitment and training of civilian specialists assigned to peacekeeping operations.
12. Increase mission budgets for public information.
13. Review and overhaul the logistics support and financial management systems for peacekeeping operations.
14. Increase the funding for peacekeeping support at the UN headquarters.
15. Integrate peacekeeping mission planning and support.
16. Restructure the **Department of Peacekeeping Operations**.
17. Establish an organization for the operational planning and support of public information at the UN headquarters.
18. Establish a peace-building organization within the UN Department of Political Affairs.
19. Enhance the field mission planning and preparation capacity of the Office of the United Nations High Commissioner for Human Rights.
20. Increase the acquisition and use of new information technology.

PAPUA NEW GUINEA. *See* BOUGAINVILLE PEACE MONITORING GROUP; BOUGAINVILLE TRUCE MONITORING GROUP.

PARTICIPATING STATE AGREEMENT. This document is an agreement between the **United Nations** (UN) and a member state to provide personnel and/or equipment for a **peacekeeping** operation.

PARTNERSHIP FOR PEACE (PfP). The **North Atlantic Treaty Organization** (NATO) established the Partnership for Peace (PfP) program to allow non-NATO members to cooperate militarily with members of the organization. There are 27 members in PfP and some of these will eventually become full NATO members. The PfP program is the basis for non-NATO members to participate in NATO mandated **peacekeeping** operations such as **Kosovo Force** (KFOR) and **Stabilisation Force** (SFOR).

PATRIOTIC FRONT COMMISSIONER TEAMS. These special teams, led by Patriotic Front officers in the grade of Lieutenant-Colonel, monitored the activities of the former Patriotic Front soldiers who were reporting to **Rendezvous Points** and **Assembly Points** in Zimbabwe. Each team included a liaison officer from the **Commonwealth Monitoring Force in Zimbabwe**.

PEACE ENFORCEMENT. The **United States** Department of Defense's October 1993 *Report of the Bottom-Up Review* defined peace enforcement as "military intervention to compel compliance with international sanctions or resolutions designed to maintain or restore international peace and security." The armed personnel of this type of operation would be allowed to go beyond the normal neutral stance of other peacekeepers and have permission to use force to restore a cease-fire or end a breach of the peace. Secretary-General **Boutros Boutros-Ghali** of the **United Nations** called for the establishment of this category of operations in his "**An Agenda for Peace.**" *See also* PEACEKEEPING; PREVENTIVE DEPLOYMENT.

PEACEKEEPING. The **United States** Department of Defense's October 1993 *Report of the Bottom-Up Review* defined peacekeeping as "military operations, undertaken with the consent of all major belligerents, that are designed to monitor and facilitate implementation of an existing truce agreement in support of diplomatic efforts to reach a political settlement to a dispute." The Department of Defense has also subdivided the term into "**traditional peace-keeping**" and "**aggravated peacekeeping**" because it recognizes that acceptance of peacekeeping operations by the belligerents does not always mean that the disputing parties will allow the peacekeepers to conduct their operations without being subject to harassment or violence. *See also* PEACE ENFORCEMENT; PREVENTIVE PEACEKEEPING.

PEARSON, LESTER B. Pearson, a former Foreign Minister of Canada, received the **Nobel Peace Prize** for his part in developing the **United Nations** (UN) concept of **peacekeeping** during the Suez crisis in 1956. Although the **League of Nations** mandated two peacekeeping missions between 1920 and 1935 (and fielded the one in 1935) and the UN fielded the **United Nations Truce Supervision Organization** (UNTSO) in 1948 and the **United Nations Military Observer Group in India and Pakistan** (UNMOGIP) in 1948, Pearson is often described as the "father of peacekeeping" for development of the **United Nations Emergency Force I** (UNEF I) in 1956 between **Egypt** and **Israel**. Pearson actually developed the concept of placing a **barrier force** between conflicting parties.

Pearson, representing Canada at the UN, opposed a resolution that called for a cease-fire in the Suez Crisis but did not include provisions to assist the peace process. Pearson suggested the establishment of an international force to replace the **British, French**, and Israeli troops that had invaded the area. Secretary-General **Dag Hammarskjöld** originally doubted that such a multinational force could be deployed to the Middle East. However, Ambassador Cabot Lodge of the **United States** informed Pearson that his idea had American support. Pearson worked on the details of the plan while Lodge submitted a resolution calling for the deployment of an international military force to oversee a cease-fire in the Suez Crisis. The discussions had to be moved to the General Assembly to avoid vetoes by **France** and Great Britain. The General Assembly approved the resolution and requested the Secretary-General to establish the peacekeeping operation in accordance with Pearson's plans. Many future UN peacekeeping operations were based on Pearson's concept. *See also* UNITING FOR PEACE RESOLUTION.

PEOPLE'S REPUBLIC OF CHINA PEACEKEEPING. The People's Republic of China (PRC) has played a very minimal role in multinational **peacekeeping**. During the **Cold War** four of the five permanent members of the **United Nations** (UN) Security Council participated in few peacekeeping operations. At the same time, the PRC viewed many peacekeeping operations as instruments of Western foreign policy and declined to deploy contingents with them. After the Cold War, the attitude of the PRC toward UN peacekeeping has softened but the state still has not deployed a large contingent with an operation. The PRC has dispatched small numbers of military observers with various missions. The Chinese government has pledged more than once to become more active in peacekeeping missions but still is a minimal participant.

PERSIAN GULF WAR. Although not a peacekeeping operation, the Persian Gulf War represents an example of the **United Nations** (UN) using collective security to mobilize its members in a military action against a state labeled as an aggressor. The **Korean War** is another example of this type of action. Iraq invaded the small state of Kuwait on August 2, 1990, following a period of diplomatic hostility between the two countries. When attempts at negotiation failed, the Security Council voted under the provisions of Chapter VII of the Charter on August 6 to initiate sanctions against Iraq. On August 7, American forces began arriving in Saudi Arabia under a bilateral agreement between the two states. **Egypt**, Morocco, and Pakistan also agreed to deploy military units to Saudi Arabia. A multitude of countries from around the world soon followed these states and deployed either combat or combat service support (logistics and medical) to the area.

The Security Council passed Resolution 678 (1990) on November 29, 1990, authorizing member states to use all necessary means (including force) if Iraq did not withdraw from Kuwait by January 15, 1991. UN forces were placed under the command of General Norman Schwarzkopf of the **United States**. The UN coalition forces launched air strikes against Iraq on January 16, 1991, and followed this action with a ground assault on February 25. A provisional cease-fire on March 2, 1991, was followed by the Iraqi acceptance of a formal truce on April 6. The Persian Gulf War resulted in the fielding of two peacekeeping operations after the conclusion of hostilities, including the **United Nations Iraq-Kuwait Observer Mission** (UNIKOM) and the **United Nations Guards Contingent in Iraq** (UNGCI).

PERU. *See* MISSION OF MILITARY OBSERVERS ECUADOR-PERU.

PETERSBERG MISSIONS. The **West European Union** (WEU) developed the Petersberg Declaration at its ministerial summit in Bonn on June 19, 1992. The Foreign Ministers of the WEU member states wanted to strengthen the organization. Europe was reliant upon American participation for military operations, and the **United States** demonstrated a reluctance to become involved in many European crises. Washington opted to not contribute soldiers for the **United Nations** (UN) missions in **Croatia** and **Bosnia and Herzegovina**.

Europeans realized they needed to develop their own ability to militarily intervene in crises outside of the **North Atlantic Treaty Organization** (NATO) framework.

As a result, WEU members pledged to make conventional military forces available for crisis situations under the authority and mandate of the WEU. The organization would field military units in support of humanitarian and rescue tasks, peacekeeping, and peacemaking. These categories became known as the "Petersberg Missions" and are sometimes known as the "Petersberg Tasks." The Petersberg Declaration provided the WEU with the mandate to conduct military operations without the participation of the United States. The WEU would carry out these operations in cooperation with the UN and **Conference for Security and Cooperation in Europe** (CSCE). This cooperation was later extended to the **European Union** (EU) and the **Organization for Security and Cooperation in Europe** (OSCE) when the OSCE replaced the CSCE. The WEU offered support for African peacekeeping efforts in cooperation with the EU.

In 1996, the WEU and EU conducted a summit with the resulting document known as the "WEU Contribution to the European Union Intergovernmental Conference of 1996." The Petersberg Missions were adopted into the EU's **Amsterdam Treaty** of May 1, 1999. The WEU reverted back to its primary objective of supporting NATO. The EU utilized its new military options from the Petersberg Missions to develop plans for the **European Union Rapid Reaction Force**. *See also* MULTINATIONAL PROTECTION FORCE.

PHILIPP, MAJOR-GENERAL HANNES. Philipp, a native of Austria, served as the Officer-in-Charge and later **Force Commander** of the **United Nations Disengagement Observer Force** (UNDOF) from December 1974 to April 1979. He held the title Officer-in-Charge from the beginning of his tour until July 1975 when he received his promotion from Colonel directly to Major-General. The same scenario occurred with **Gunther G. Greindl** of Austria. Passing over the rank of Brigadier-General for both men apparently resulted from the requirement that the Force Commander of UNDOF be a Major-General. The two Brigadier-Generals assigned to command the operation were referred to as "interim" or "acting." Philipp later served as the Force Commander designate of the **United Nations Transition Assistance Group** (UNTAG) in Namibia between September 1978 and January

1980. He never assumed the full title of Force Commander since the operation did not deploy until 1989.

PINK ZONES. Pink Zones were areas in **Croatia** held by Serbian forces but outside of the **United Nations Protected Areas** (UNPA) established by the global organization. The **United Nations** identified the latter as geographical areas with a Serbian majority population within Croatia. Before the arrival of the **United Nations Protection Force** (UNPROFOR) in Croatia, the Serbs had expanded their control from the UNPAs into adjacent territory, which then became known as the pink zones. These zones were a thorny issue in negotiations between the Croatian government and Serbs.

POLAND. *See* VILNA INTERNATIONAL FORCE.

POLICY PLANNING UNIT. *See* BEST PRACTICES UNIT.

PORT-FRANCQUI. A detachment of peacekeepers from Ghana, their British officers, and a Swedish movement control team assigned to the **United Nations Operation in the Congo** (ONUC) were based in the town of Port-Francqui in the Congo. During April 26–28, 1961, soldiers of the Congolese National Army (ANC) attacked the detachment and killed at least 48 of the peacekeepers including 44 Ghanaians. Actual casualties are still disputed because the bodies were thrown into a river by the ANC soldiers. General von Horn originally reported that approximately 120 peacekeepers were massacred in the attack. The incident prompted the **United Nations** (UN) to cease basing small detachments of peacekeepers at isolated posts in the Congo. *See also* KINDU; NIEMBA.

PRESIDENTIAL DECISION DIRECTIVE TWENTY-FIVE. The Clinton Administration released Presidential Decision Directive Twenty-Five on May 5, 1994. The document outlined American policy toward participating in multinational peacekeeping operations. The directive addressed six issues:

1. Establishing standards for the US to decide which **United Nations** (UN) peacekeeping operations to support and to which to contribute American troops.

2. Reducing of the U.S. contribution to UN peacekeeping operations.
3. Defining American policy regarding the command and control of U.S. personnel in UN operations.
4. Reforming the UN's capability to manage peace operations.
5. Improving the way the U.S. government manages and funds peace operations.
6. Establishing better forms of communication within the government and between the government and the public on peace operations.

See also PRESIDENTIAL REVIEW DIRECTIVE THIRTEEN.

PRESIDENTIAL REVIEW DIRECTIVE THIRTEEN. President Bill Clinton requested the preparation of the document in February 1993, and the group, headed by Deputy National Security Adviser Samuel R. Berger, completed the draft in July of the same year. The purpose of the document was to review **United States** participation in international peacekeeping operations. The document proposed supporting a greatly expanded American role with the **United Nations** (UN) and advocated placing American troops under international commanders. Congressional and public concern about the latter proposal, combined with American combat-related deaths in support of the **United Nations Forces in Somalia II** (UNOSOM II) operation, persuaded the Clinton Administration to redraft the Directive in October 1993. The resulting new document is known as **Presidential Decision Directive Twenty-Five**.

PREVENTIVE DEPLOYMENT. A proposed concept in which a threatened party could request the dispatch of a **United Nations** (UN) rapid deployment force. Secretary-General **Boutros Boutros-Ghali** called for the establishment of this type of operation in his "**An Agenda for Peace**." In theory, the fielding of this rapid deployment force would serve as a barrier and deter aggression. In order for this concept to be tested, the global body would need to create a **Standing Army**.

PRIVATIZATION OF PEACEKEEPING. There has been a trend among countries to privatize many functions previously carried out by military personnel. These functions range from basic facility maintenance to security duties. The same trend is occurring with **peacekeeping** operations. Rather than provide the airlift assets for some peacekeeping missions, the **United States** now contracts this role with civilian companies. Washington announced that it would fund the air assets of the proposed **Economic Community of West African States Monitoring Group (ECOMOG) in Côte d'Ivoire** operation by contracting a civilian company that flies Russian-built transport aircraft and helicopters. In addition, many of the American personnel serving with the **Stabilisation Force** (SFOR) are civilians working for private companies rather than the United States military or government. Their duties include serving as security guards at American posts.

– Q –

QUICK REACTION FORCE (QRF). The quick reaction force consisted of 1,700 American soldiers assigned to the **United Nations Operation in Somalia I** (UNOSOM I). The purpose of the unit included the quick movement to areas where other peacekeepers were under threat or actual attack in order to either reinforce or remove them. The **United Nations** (UN) tended to rely heavily on the QRF for nonemergency missions, including the escort of convoys and weapons sweeps, due to the efficiency of the American units as compared to soldiers of other peacekeeping contributing states. This heavy reliance led to criticism of the international organization in the **United States** Congress since the American forces lacked adequate armored support and began taking casualties in the conflict. *See also* FORCE MOBILE RESERVE; RAPID REACTION GROUP.

– R –

RAPID DEPLOYMENT FORCE. Military units that are designated to an international organization as being available for a quick deployment in peacekeeping operations. **Rapid Reaction Force** is the more common name for this type of program that is maintained by several international organizations.

RAPID REACTION FORCE. A Rapid Reaction Force, sometimes referred to as a **Rapid Deployment Force**, is established by an international organization as a means to have military units at its disposal for short notice operations such as **peacekeeping** missions. A rapid reaction force is not a military unit already deployed with a peacekeeping mission and earmarked for quick action to rescue or protect other units. Rather the units remain with their home countries and receive special training and designation to respond on short notice to a crisis situation. Rapid Reaction Forces are fielded only if the contingent-providing states agree to the request of the international organization. *See also* AFRICAN STAND BY FORCE; EUROPEAN UNION RAPID REACTION FORCE; NORTH ATLANTIC TREATY ORGANIZATION RAPID REACTION FORCE; UNITED NATIONS STAND BY ARRANGEMENT SYSTEM.

RED LINE. The "red line" represented the southernmost boundary of **Lebanon** within which **Israel** would tolerate the deployment of forces of the **Arab Deterrent Force** (ADF). ADF units could not move south of the **Litani River**, which later became the northern boundary of the area patrolled by the **United Nations Interim Force in Lebanon** (UNIFIL). Christian militia, armed by Israel, patrolled south of the Litani River. Names such as "red line" derive from the fact that an actual red line was drawn on a map of Lebanon and the boundary became known for the color pen used in the marking. *See also* GREEN LINE.

RENDEZVOUS POINT (RV). Rendezvous Point is the name given to the initial coordination areas for soldiers of the Patriotic Front who came in from the bush during the peace process in **Zimbabwe**. The **Commonwealth Monitoring Force in Zimbabwe** managed 22 Rendezvous Points from December 29, 1979, to January 6, 1980. The purpose of the temporary camps was to allow the Patriotic Front units to make their initial contact with representatives of their organization and the **Commonwealth** peacekeepers. After reporting to the Rendezvous Points, the Commonwealth soldiers bussed the Patriotic Front soldiers to more permanent camps known as **Assembly Points**. Due to the nature of the long conflict in Zimbabwe, initial contacts between the Patriotic Front forces and the peacekeepers were tense.

Many Patriotic Front soldiers also viewed the British contingent as being the equivalent of the Rhodesian Security Forces, a group they had been fighting for years. Despite the early tensions, the Commonwealth peacekeepers completed their mission at the Rendezvous Points by January 6 and moved on to the two-month Assembly Point phase of the operation. *See also* COMMONWEALTH OBSERVER GROUP.

RENFORCEMENT DES CAPACITES AFRICAINES DE MAINTIEN DE LA PAIX (RECAMP). In November 1995, **United Nations** (UN) Secretary-General **Boutros Boutros-Ghali** called for the international community to place a greater emphasis on solving crisis situations before they had to be debated by the global organization. At the same time, the Western powers were searching for alternatives to sending their peacekeepers into explosive situations such as **Somalia** and **Rwanda**. The **United States** developed the **African Crisis Response Initiative** (ACRI) as a means of training African military units for the rigors of peace operations on the African continent. **France** proposed the Renforcement des capacités Africaines de Maintien de la Paix (RECAMP) program at the same time. RECAMP is very different from ACRI. The French provide individual training to African officers and noncommissioned officers who return to work with their units. The French then coordinate subregional peacekeeping exercises to allow the units to practice their skills and operate in a multinational environment. France established peacekeeping training centers in Côte d'Ivoire and Benin. RECAMP also includes the stockpiling of large quantities of equipment at French overseas bases for the use by African peacekeeping units. It is interesting to note that RECAMP includes both francophone and anglophone states. *See also* FRENCH PEACEKEEPING.

REPRESENTATIVE OF THE SECRETARY-GENERAL IN THE DOMINICAN REPUBLIC (DOMREP). This operation, a three-man mission to the Dominican Republic, is classified by the **United Nations** (UN) as a peacekeeping operation. However, the size of the mission and the nature of its mandate leave one to question whether DOMREP should be listed as such by the global body. Civil war conditions in the Dominican Republic prompted an intervention by

United States military forces on April 28, 1965. The **Organization of American States** (OAS) opted to assume official responsibility for the operation the following month and issued a call to its members for contingents for a multinational peacekeeping mission. This operation, later named the **Inter-American Peace Force** (IAPF), consisted of approximately 14,000 United States and 1,700 Latin American soldiers. The latter group represented six member states of the OAS. The UN mandated a small observer mission in Security Council Resolution 203 (1965) on May 14, 1965, to monitor the OAS operation and the cease-fire process.

Secretary-General U Thant selected Jose Antonio Mayobre as his **special representative** in the Dominican Republic and appointed Major-General **Indar J. Rikhye** as the Military Adviser for the group. Rikhye's staff consisted of two military advisers. Brazil, Canada, and Ecuador provided one military adviser each to DOMREP. However, only two of these advisers were authorized to be assigned to DOMREP at any time. The OAS's Special Committee of the Tenth Meeting of Consultation complained that the presence of the UN personnel interfered with its mission of bringing peace to the Dominican Republic. Following a period of turmoil and elections in June 1966, the IAPF initiated a phased withdrawal from the state, which was completed on September 21, 1966. In response, the UN officially terminated DOMREP on October 22, 1966. DOMREP, headquartered in Santo Domingo, was funded by the regular budget of the UN and cost the organization $275,831 between May 1965 and October 1966.

RESERVE FUND. The **United Nations** (UN) maintains a peacekeeping reserve fund to help it finance the initial deployment of peacekeeping operations. The fund must be repaid when money arrives from member states under the **Special Assessment** program.

RHODESIA. *See* COMMONWEALTH FORCE IN ZIMBABWE; COMMONWEALTH OBSERVER GROUP.

RIAD, MAHMOUD. Riad, an Egyptian, held the post of Secretary-General of the **League of Arab States**. He conducted the negotiations with Lebanese President Frangieh that led to the latter's acceptance of the **Symbolic Arab Security Force** in 1976 and was instrumental in the discussions which transformed the operation into the **Arab Deterrent Force** (ADF). As Secretary-General, Riad "supervised" the two peacekeeping missions. Riad resigned from his post in 1979 following the conclusion of the Egyptian-Israeli peace treaty. The league expelled **Egypt** as a member and moved its headquarters from Cairo to Tunis. *See also* LEBANON.

RIKHYE, MAJOR-GENERAL INDAR JIT. Rikhye, an Indian officer, had a distinguished career with the **United Nations** (UN). Rikhye began as the Military Adviser to the Secretary-General. In 1963, Secretary-General U Thant dispatched Rikhye to Yemen following the resignation of General Von Horn, the **Force Commander** of the **United Nations Yemen Observation Mission** (UN-YOM). He reported that, despite physical hardships, the morale of the peacekeepers was high. Rikhye also reported that supplies, although often limited, were adequate for mission accomplishment. Rikhye, still in his capacity as Military Adviser, greatly assisted in the original establishment of the **United Nations Force in Cyprus** (UNFICYP) by purchasing equipment and developing airlift timetables. He later became the Military Adviser to Special Representative Jose Antonio Mayobre during the Mission of the **Representative of the Secretary-General in the Dominican Republic** (DOMREP) for the duration of the mission from May 1965 to October 1966. He served as the last Force Commander of the **United Nations Emergency Force I** (UNEF I) between January 1966 and June 1967. Rikhye faced the tremendous logistical difficulty of removing the peacekeepers from the Sinai following the Egyptian order for the neutral soldiers to depart the area. The Israeli-Arab Six-Day War erupted immediately after the departure of the peacekeepers.

RIYADH RESOLUTION. The resolution, adopted at the **Riyadh Summit Conference** on October 18, 1976, outlined the functions of the **Arab Deterrent Force** that evolved from the **Symbolic Arab Security Force**. The operation, according to the resolution, would ensure observance of the cease-fire, disengage belligerent soldiers, deter any violation of the agreement, implement the **Cairo Agreement**, maintain internal security, supervise the withdrawal of armed troops to positions held on April 13, 1975, supervise the collection of heavy weapons, and assist the **Lebanese** authorities when necessary. The document also included an elaborate schedule detailing how the mission should accomplish its mandate. *See also* BEITEDDINE CONFERENCE; CHATAURA AGREEMENT.

RIYADH SUMMIT CONFERENCE. Saudi Arabia, Kuwait, Syria, **Lebanon, Egypt**, and the Palestinian Liberation Organization (PLO) met in Riyadh, Saudi Arabia, during October 16–18, 1976. The conference, also known as the Six-Party Summit Conference, discussed the situation in Lebanon and agreed to send additional forces to strengthen the **Symbolic Arab Security Force** deployed under a mandate of the **League of Arab States**. The meeting also proposed changing the force to an **Arab Deterrent Force** by giving it more teeth in dealing with transgressions of the peace in Lebanon. At the same time, the force was placed under the personal command of the President of Lebanon. The resolutions of the conference were endorsed by the League of Arab States at the **Cairo Summit Conference** during the same month. *See also* RIYADH RESOLUTION.

ROSE, LIEUTENANT-GENERAL SIR MICHAEL. Rose, a British officer, was tapped to serve as the commander of the **United Nations Protection Force** (UNPROFOR) element in **Bosnia and Herzegovina**. He officially replaced General **Francis Briquemont** in January 1994. Within two weeks of assuming command, Rose faced a Serbian challenge to his command. Serbian militiamen placed a roadblock between Sarajevo and the main peacekeepers' base at Kiseljak. Rose ordered a **British** platoon "to press for the right of freedom of movement by negotiation initially, and by force if necessary." The Serb militia units backed down to Rose's counterchallenge. Rose was commander during the air strikes launched by the **North Atlantic Treaty Organization** (NATO) against Serb forces. Like his predecessors, Rose tended to criticize the international bureaucracy which hampered his operation. Although rumors stated that he might be removed due to his candid criticism, Rose completed his one-year term and was replaced by Major-General Rupert Smith in January 1995.

RULES OF ENGAGEMENT (ROE). Rules of Engagement (ROE) establish the conditions when peacekeepers are allowed to use force during their mission. Most ROEs call for the peacekeepers to use force only in defense of lives and property. Other ROEs allow the peacekeepers to use force against a belligerent who violates the cease-fire agreement. This type of mission is often called "**peace enforcement**." An example is the **United Nations Protection Force** (UNPROFOR) mission in the former **Yugoslavia**. In addition, the ROEs may call for a multinational unit to actively enter a conflict on behalf of one belligerent against another. Examples include the **Korean War** and the **Persian Gulf War**.

RUSSIAN PEACEKEEPING. During the **Cold War**, Russia (former Soviet Union) maintained minimal participation in peacekeeping operations. After the Cold War, the emphasis of Russian peacekeeping is with the **Commonwealth of Independent States** (CIS). Russian troops have participated with **United Nations** (UN) and **North Atlantic Treaty Organization** (NATO) mandated operations. The Russians have fielded peacekeepers within the borders of the former Soviet Union four times. Twice, the CIS mandated peacekeeping operations under Russian domination (**Commonwealth of Independent States Collective Peacekeeping Force** and **Commonwealth of Independent States Peacekeeping Forces in Georgia**). The Russians have also fielded two additional missions that they label as peacekeeping under bilateral agreements with multinational contingents.

The Russians have two terms for what is often called "**peacekeeping**." The first is *voiska po podderzhaniyu mira* and translates as "forces for the maintenance of peace" while the second, *mirotvorcheskie voiska*, means "peacemaking forces." The first term is more in line with **traditional peacekeeping** concepts, while the second refers to the use of military forces to actively impose a peaceful settlement on belligerents, which is also known in English as "**peace enforcement**." Because the Russians use the terms interchangeably, an academic review of peacekeeping operations in which they are contributing soldiers is difficult. The composition of the peacekeeping operations is controversial. In the two Russian bilateral operations, the units contain contingents from the belligerent states. In the case of Ossetia, both North and South Ossetians have joined the Russians, while the Moldovans are included in the operation in their state. *See also* JOINT CONTROL COMMISSION PEACEKEEPING FORCE; SOUTH OSSETIA JOINT FORCE.

RWANDA. *See* FRENCH PEACEKEEPING; MILITARY OBSERVER GROUP; NEUTRAL MILITARY OBSERVER GROUP I; NEUTRAL MILITARY OBSERVER GROUP II; UNITED NATIONS ASSISTANCE MISSION IN RWANDA; UNITED NATIONS OBSERVER MISSION UGANDA-RWANDA.

– S –

SAAR. *See* SAAR INTERNATIONAL FORCE; SAAR PLEBISCITE.

SAAR INTERNATIONAL FORCE. The **League of Nations** proposed the Saar international force in 1934 as a means to ensure law and order during the **Saar plebiscite** scheduled for January 1935. The proposed force, primarily organized by Great Britain, overcame stiff opposition in the **British** government thanks to the firm backing of Prime Minister Anthony Eden. British support and agreement to participate allowed the league to propose the international force as an alternative to a reintroduction of **French** troops, which would have antagonized **Germany**. As a means of winning acceptance from Germany and France, the league requested contingents from states which lacked an interest in the Saar plebiscite. The multinational unit consisted of 3,300 soldiers from Great Britain (1,500), Italy (1,300), Netherlands (250), and Sweden (250). The units were deployed to the Saar by December 22, 1934. Each contingent provided for its own logistics needs and forwarded the tab to the league, which in turn required France, Germany, and the Saar to share the costs of the operation. Major-General J. E. S. Briand of Great Britain served as the military commander and the entire operation fell under the authority of the Saar Governing Commission.

The force adopted the **British method** of military assistance to civilian governments as its **rules of engagement**. The Saar international force performed well in its mission despite the cold weather and less-than-adequate housing and was withdrawn by January 28, 1935, following the conclusion of the plebiscite. The international force is noted for the concern for neutrality displayed by the League of Nations. Until this operation, other multinational units fielded by the league were essentially coalitions of the Allied powers from World War I. **Switzerland** declined to participate in order not to jeopardize its position as a neutral state, while the Netherlands, neutral during World War I, refused to contribute a contingent unless Sweden also provided a unit to the international force.

SAAR PLEBISCITE. The Saar is a region located along the **French** and **German** border southeast of Luxembourg. German by language and culture, the area was coveted by France following World War I due to an abundance of rich coal mines. The other Allied states did not want to provide Germany with a grievance against them and thus refused to openly support the French claims on the Saar. The **League of Nations** prepared the 1920 Compromise that established a five man Saar Governing Commission to administer the region for 15 years. Following this period, the league would supervise a plebiscite to determine if the inhabitants desired to remain a ward of the international organization or unite with either France or Germany. French troops, numbering 2,000, would police the region during the period of league administration. In 1927, the French troops were replaced by an allied force of 800 soldiers from Great Britain, Belgium, and France, who were in turn removed in 1930.

The league faced potential difficulties with the impending plebiscite due to France's desire to hold the area and right-wing German elements that were organizing support for returning the Saar to Germany. The league needed to restrain France from returning its soldiers to the area under the pretense of maintaining law and order. However, the league did insist that it could handle any violence that might break out during the plebiscite. The solution materialized when Prime Minister Anthony Eden of Great Britain persuaded his government to provide **British** soldiers as an element of a **Saar International Force** that would maintain order during the voting process. The plebiscite, held on January 13, 1935, overwhelmingly confirmed the opinion of the population to reunite with Germany.

SAFE AREAS. The **United Nations** (UN) established six safe areas in **Bosnia and Herzegovina** in 1992 in an attempt to protect Muslims from Bosnian Serbs. The safe areas were protected by units assigned to the **United Nations Protection Force (UNPROFOR) in Bosnia and Herzegovina**. The peacekeepers moved to six Muslim-dominated towns, including Sarajevo, Gorazde, Zepa, **Srebrenica**, Tuzla, and **Bihac**. The first five towns are located in eastern Bosnia near the border with Serbia while Bihac is on the border with **Croatia**. The use of safe areas did not eliminate the shelling of Muslims in these towns. Sbrebrenica was overrun by Serbs resulting in a massacre of Muslim men and boys. The **North Atlantic Treaty Organization** (NATO) offered the use of its aircraft in support of the UN peacekeepers who were often targets of the same shelling aimed at the Muslims.

SAFE HAVENS. Areas established in northern Iraq by the **United Nations** (UN) for the protection of Kurds following the **Persian Gulf War** in 1991. The operation, under the UN suboffices and Humanitarian Centers program and protected by the **United Nations Guards Contingent in Iraq**, offered humanitarian assistance and protection of the Kurds from the Iraqi forces of Saddam Hussein. The safe havens extended from Iraq's northern border to the 36th parallel. Iraq was prohibited from using either fixed-wing aircraft or helicopters north of the 36th parallel into the safe havens. The term "safe havens" replaced "enclaves" in order to preserve Iraqi territorial integrity.

SAHNOUN, MOHAMMED. Sahnoun, an Algerian, was the **United Nations** (UN) **Special Representative** in **Somalia** during the initial fielding of the **United Nations Operation in Somalia I** (UNOSOM I) in 1992. He is credited with the difficult negotiations, especially with Mohammed Farah Aidid, to gain acceptance of the various warlords for the fielding of the peacekeepers. Sahnoun is also noted for his diplomacy in persuading Ethiopia, Eritrea, Sudan, and Djibouti that an international force in Somalia would not threaten their security. Sahnoun openly stated that the UN did not understand either the conflict in Somalia or Somali culture. He gained the respect of the local warlords and relief workers for his understanding of the political situation and his criticism of the way the United Nations handled the crisis. Secretary-General **Boutros Boutros-Ghali** dismissed Sahnoun in October 1992, after only five months on the job, for criticizing the UNOSOM. He was replaced by **Ismat Kattani**. Sahnoun's previous assignments included serving as his country's ambassador to the UN, **France**, **Germany**, and the **United States**.

SANCTIONS ASSISTANCE MISSION (SAM). *See* CONFERENCE FOR SECURITY AND COOPERATION IN EUROPE (CSCE).

SARAJEVO. *See* SAFE AREAS; UNITED NATIONS PROTECTION FORCE (UNPROFOR) IN BOSNIA AND HERZEGOVINA.

SARKIS, PRESIDENT ELIAS. The Six-Party Arab Summit Conference concluded that the envisioned **Arab Deterrent Force** (ADF) should be under the personal command of the President of **Lebanon**. President Sarkis, in order to counter the heavy Syrian influence in the force as well as within Lebanon, selected Lebanese officers who were neutral in the civil war to command the operation. The restricted selection criteria meant that the two Lebanese commanders of the force, Colonel Ahmed al-Hajj (1976–1977) and Lieutenant-Colonel **Sami al-Khatib** (1977–1983), were junior in rank to the Syrian and Saudi generals appointed to assist them. *See also* SYMBOLIC ARAB SECURITY FORCE.

SECOND GENERATION PEACEKEEPING. Second Generation peacekeeping is a term applied to **United Nations** (UN) peacekeeping operations fielded primarily after 1989. In contrast to earlier missions sometimes referred to as **First Generation peacekeeping** or **traditional peacekeeping**, which simply separated two belligerents, Second Generation peacekeeping missions include the duties of state building, election monitoring, and humanitarian assistance. They are sometimes given the authority to use force to ensure compliance with an existing cease-fire.

SECRETARY-GENERAL. The Secretary-General is the full time civil servant in charge of an international organization's permanent headquarters. The Secretary-General provides recommendations on peacekeeping operations and how to organize them. At the **United**

Nations (UN), the Security Council or General Assembly normally requests the Secretary-General to recommend the composition and organization of peacekeeping operations. The **Force Commander** of an operation responds to the directions of the Secretary-General who, in turn, answers to the Security Council or General Assembly.

SHABA. *See* FRENCH PEACEKEEPING.

SHAHEEN, BRIGADIER-GENERAL IMITIAZ. Shaheen commanded the initial Pakistani battalion fielded as the **United Nations Operation in Somalia I** (UNOSOM I). In addition, he served as the UNOSOM I **Force Commander**. As UNOSOM I commander, Shaheen had to cope with the early **United Nations** (UN) logistical problems in the operation and the humiliation of having well-armed locals rob and disarm small parties of his soldiers. It has been reported that logistics were so poor when the Pakistanis first arrived that Shaheen had to use his personal credit card to order rice for his soldiers to eat.

SHARM-EL-SHEIKH. Sharm-el-Sheikh is a town located on the southern tip of the Sinai peninsula. It is of strategic importance because it overlooks the entrance to the Strait of Tiran, which leads to the **Israeli** port of Elath. Prior to the Suez Conflict in 1956, **Egypt** used the location to prevent Israeli shipping from entering or leaving the Strait of Tiran. After the war, the **United Nations Emergency Force I** (UNEF I) stationed a small group of peacekeepers at Sharm-el-Sheikh to ensure the free passage of Israeli shipping to and from the port of Elath. The peacekeeping detachment consisted of 43 Swedish and nine Canadian soldiers. Conflicting sources state that Finns and not Swedes manned the observation posts at Sharm-el-Sheikh. The Israelis requested that the **United Nations** (UN) station a naval contingent at Sharm-el-Sheikh to ensure free passage of the Strait of Tiran. However, Secretary-General U Thant declined to act on the suggestion, saying that the proposal was outside of UNEF I's mandate. This request was the first time that the UN considered a naval arm to a peacekeeping operation. Many future missions would have a naval arm to assist in carrying out their mandates. The detachment withdrew when UNEF I was ordered out of the Sinai by Egypt in 1967.

SIERRA LEONE. *See* ECONOMIC COMMUNITY OF WEST AFRICAN STATES MONITORING GROUP IN SIERRA LEONE; UNITED NATIONS ASSISTANCE MISSION IN SIERRA LEONE; UNITED NATIONS OBSERVER MISSION IN SIERRA LEONE.

SIILASVUO, LIEUTENANT-GENERAL ENSIO P. H. Siilasvuo, a native of Finland, served as the Chief of Staff of the **United Nations Truce Supervision Organization** (UNTSO) between August 1970 and October 1973, when he was named as the first **Force Commander** of the **United Nations Emergency Force II** (UNEF II). He held the title of interim commander from October to November 1973 and then commander from November 1973 until August 1975. On behalf of the **United Nations** (UN), he helped negotiate and then signed the Egyptian-Israeli cease-fire at Kilometer 101. In January 1974, Siilasvuo officially witnessed the signing of the disengagement agreement between **Egypt** and **Israel**. Due to his extensive experience, Secretary-General Kurt Waldheim named Siilasvuo the Chief Coordinator of the United Nations Peacekeeping Missions in the Middle East. In this capacity, he negotiated with the Israeli and Lebanese governments for the deployment of a peacekeeping operation that would become known as the **United Nations Interim Force in Lebanon** (UNIFIL). He also negotiated the Israeli withdrawal from **Lebanon** in 1978 on behalf of the UN.

SINAI. *See* MULTINATIONAL FORCE AND OBSERVERS; UNITED NATIONS EMERGENCY FORCE I; UNITED NATIONS EMERGENCY FORCE II; UNITED NATIONS TRUCE SUPERVISION ORGANIZATION.

SOLOMON ISLANDS. *See* INTERNATIONAL PEACE MONITORING TEAM; SOUTH PACIFIC PEACEKEEPING FORCE.

SOLOMON ISLANDS PEACE MONITORING TEAM. *See* INTERNATIONAL PEACE MONITORING TEAM.

SOMALIA. *See* UNIFIED TASK FORCE; UNITED NATIONS OPERATION IN SOMALIA I; UNITED NATIONS OPERATION IN SOMALIA II.

SOUTH AFRICAN PEACEKEEPING. Most of South Africa's post-apartheid peacekeeping attention has been directed through the **Southern African Development Community** (SADC). However, South Africa has fielded one peacekeeping operation under the endorsement of the **Organization of African Unity** (OAU). **Burundi** has suffered violence between its Hutu and Tutsi groups for many decades. A new round of violence erupted in 1993. Negotiations, led by former South African president Nelson Mandela, showed promise by 2001. South Africa agreed to field a peacekeeping contingent, mandated by the peace process and endorsed by the OAU, to protect returning exile leaders and train elements of the Burundi army to fulfill the same mission. Despite the lack of a successful cease-fire, 700 South African troops began arriving in Burundi on October 27, 2001. Many groups in Burundi resented the South African presence and threatened the peacekeepers. **Nigeria** and Senegal originally offered to field contingents but not until after an effective cease-fire was in place. Peacekeepers from these states never arrived. Individual European countries provided South Africa with the funding required to maintain the peacekeepers in Burundi.

Following a breakdown in the peace process, the government of Burundi signed a new cease-fire with the rebel factions in December 2002. The document resulted in the fielding of two separate peacekeeping operations. The first is an expansion of the South African unilateral mission. Soldiers from Ethiopia and Mozambique began arriving in Burundi in early 2003 to provide the security required to guarantee the peace process. A second operation, known as the **African Union (AU) Cease-fire Observer Mission in Burundi**, began arriving in February 2003 to oversee the actual cease-fire in the country. *See also* UNITED NATIONS OBSERVER MISSION IN SOUTH AFRICA; UNITED NATIONS TRANSITION ASSISTANCE GROUP.

SOUTH OSSETIA JOINT FORCE. While North Ossetia is situated in **Russia**, the ethnically related South Ossetians are located within the borders of Georgia. Stalin originally divided the area between the two former Soviet republics but the dissolution of the Soviet Union left the two areas split into separate countries. The South Ossetians have expressed a desire to join their Northern cousins and become a part of Russia but have been overruled by Georgia. The Southerners launched a guerilla war against the government of Georgia, while the latter imposed an economic blockade on the area. Russia signed a bilateral agreement with Georgia and the other belligerents on June 24, 1992, establishing the South Ossetia Joint Force. The force consists of 1,385 soldiers from Russia, Georgia, North Ossetia, and South Ossetia. The troops officially deployed in July 1992. The number of fatalities, if any, has not been openly reported. The cost of the operation is difficult to determine. The Stockholm International Peace Research Institute (SIPRI) reported that the operation cost 46.9 million rubles in 1999. Some scholars do not view the South Ossetia Joint Force as a peacekeeping operation. SIPRI recognizes the Ossetia mission as a "peace operation" which the organization defines as either being an observer, peacekeeping, or peace building mission. *See also* ORGANIZATION OF SECURITY AND COOPERATION IN EUROPE MISSION TO GEORGIA; UNITED NATIONS OBSERVER MISSION IN GEORGIA.

SOUTH PACIFIC PEACEKEEPING FORCE (SPPKF). The Northern Solomons island of Bougainville, part of Papua New Guinea (PNG), experienced political turmoil and an armed insurrection beginning in the late 1980s. Many islanders resented being part of Papua New Guinea and preferred their own independent state. Another problem involved the attitudes of the islanders to a large copper mine. Many believed that they should share more from the mine's profits and were concerned about the environmental and land damage caused by the mine's operation. The Bougainville Revolutionary Army (BRA) emerged in 1988 and forced the mine to close. PNG removed its military forces from Bougainville in 1990 but returned them in 1991 and 1992. The BRA and PNG agreed to a cease-fire agreement on September 8, 1994, and to attend a Bougainville Peace Coference.

Australia, New Zealand, Tonga, Fiji, and Vanuatu offered to dispatch a peacekeeping force to provide security and ensure a neutral environment for the peace conference. The operation was mandated by an international treaty between the belligerents and contingent providers that also served as the mission's **status of forces agreement**. The peacekeepers arrived in Bougainville on October 3, 1994.

Talks between the belligerents failed to materialize after a BRA member was killed and the PNG reportedly did not withdraw all of its forces from areas designated as neutral zones. A small splinter group of the BRA did meet with the government. The talks resulted in the establishment of the Bougainville Transitional Government. The peacekeepers departed by October 22, 1994. Additional discussions in 1997 would lead to the deployment of the **Bougainville Truce Monitoring Group**.

The maximum authorized strength of SPPKF was approximately 400 military personnel. Fiji provided the bulk of the force and dispatched 232 soldiers. The remaining peacekeepers came from Tonga (130) and Vanuatu (50). Australia and New Zealand provided logistical assistance and training. SPPKF was financed by the Papua New Guinea government.

SOUTH WEST AFRICA. *See* UNITED NATIONS TRANSITION ASSISTANCE GROUP.

SOUTHERN AFRICAN DEVELOPMENT COMMUNITY (SADC). The Southern African Development Community (SADC) is a 14-member subregional international organization comprising states in southern Africa and the Indian Ocean and is sometimes dominated by South Africa. The primary purpose of the organization involves economic development but SADC does have a defense protocol allowing the body to mandate peacekeeping operations. In 1998, members mandated the **Southern African Development Community Operation in Lesotho**.

SOUTHERN AFRICAN DEVELOPMENT COMMUNITY ADVISORY TEAM. *See* SOUTHERN AFRICAN DEVELOPMENT COMMMUNITY OPERATION IN LESOTHO.

SOUTHERN AFRICAN DEVELOPMENT COMMUNITY OPERATION IN LESOTHO. A May 1998 disputed election led to protests in Lesotho. Related to ongoing demonstrations, junior military officers forced 15 senior officers to resign and flee to **South Africa** in September 1998. The **Southern African Development Community** (SADC), with prodding from South Africa, mandated a military operation. Officially, the King of Lesotho requested the SADC intervention. South Africa dispatched 600 soldiers, followed later by 200 (some sources say 300) from Botswana, to Lesotho. South African reinforcements arrived later to join the mission. After securing the country, the SADC forces departed on May 14, 1999. Many scholars do not consider this operation a peacekeeping mission. It is clearly a **peace enforcement** mission at the least. The operation is included here because it was mandated by an international organization, consisted of multinational units, and organized to protect a government that was a member of the organization.

SPECIAL ACCOUNT. A special account is established as a way to financially support a peacekeeping operation. The term is primarily used by the **United Nations** (UN) in support of a **special assessment** on member states. *See also* SUSPENSE ACCOUNT.

SPECIAL ASSESSMENT. Special Assessment is a method used to finance peacekeeping operations. With a special assessment, all member states of an international organization contribute a fixed amount to help cover the expenses of the operation. *See also* RESERVE FUND; SPECIAL ACCCOUNT; SUSPENSE ACCOUNT.

SPECIAL COMMITTEE OF THE TENTH MEETING OF CON-SULTATION. This **Organization of American States** (OAS) committee consisted of Argentina, Brazil, Colombia, Guatemala, and Panama. Its mission involved finding a solution to the political crisis that had erupted in the Dominican Republic in 1965. The OAS officially replaced a unilateral **United States** intervention in the state with a multinational mission known as the **Inter-American Peace Force** (IAPF). The **United Nations** (UN) deployed a three-man mission, known as the **Representative of the Secretary-General in the Dominican Republic** (DOMREP), to monitor the IAPF and the cease-fire process. The Special Committee complained that the presence of the UN in the Dominican Republic interfered with efforts to bring peace to the island. The committee also requested that the Security Council withdraw DOMREP. The UN refused to abide by the committee's request and kept DOMREP in the Dominican Republic until the IAPF departure.

SPECIAL COMMITTEE ON PEACEKEEPING OPERATIONS. The **United Nations** (UN) General Assembly established the Special Committee on Peacekeeping Operations on February 18, 1965, with Resolution 2006 (XIX). The mandate of the committee includes conducting a comprehensive review of all aspects of peacekeeping. The committee reports directly to the General Assembly through the **Fourth Committee** (Special Political and Decolonization Committee). The committee consists of 100 member states although the other UN members do participate in the work of the organization as well as sit in working groups as observers.

SPECIAL REPRESENTATIVE. A term applied to the individual selected to represent the Secretary-General in negotiations for the fielding and continued operations of peacekeeping missions.

SPINELLI, P. P. Spinelli, an Italian, was the **Special Representative** assigned to the **United Nations Yemen Observation Mission** (UNYOM). Prior to this selection, he held the position as the Undersecretary and Director of the European Office of the **United Nations** (UN). Although the operation deployed in July 1963, Spinelli's tour as Special Representative lasted from November 1963 to September 1964. In addition, he held the position of acting Special Representative for the **United Nations Peacekeeping Force in Cyprus** (UNFICYP) from January to February 1967.

SREBRENICA. Srebrenica was one of the **safe areas** established by the **United Nations** (UN) in **Bosnia and Herzegovina** on April 16, 1993. The UN assigned a 150-man Dutch contingent of the **United Nations Protection Force (UNPROFOR) in Bosnia and Herzegovina** to protect Bosnian Muslims in and around Srebrenica from Bosnian Serbs. The small Dutch detachment was overwhelmed by a 2,000-man Serb unit that overran the town in July 1995. Following the fall of Srebrenica, thousands of Muslim men and boys were massacred by the Serbs. The massacre at Srebrenica stands as one of the worst moments in UN peacekeeping history.

A comprehensive investigation in 1999 faulted many in the massacre. First, those responsible among the Serbs were identified for arrest and prosecution. The Dutch were faulted for not defending the safe area. Dutch requests for air support were denied on several occasions by UN-PROFOR headquarters. The Dutch commander reported more than once to superiors that his small force, with small arms, would not be able to halt a determined Serb advance with heavy weapons and armored vehicles. The UN failed to fully comprehend the Serb war aims. In other words, the Serbs did not have the intention of withdrawing from around the safe areas simply because the UN declared them to be "safe." A Dutch investigation of the incident was not completed until the spring of 2002. In response, the Dutch government resigned but this was only a symbolic gesture since elections were already scheduled for the country.

SRI LANKA. *See* INDIAN PEACEKEEPING.

STABILISATION FORCE (SFOR). When the **Implementation Force** (IFOR) of the **North Atlantic Treaty Organization** (NATO) had completed its mission in Bosnia and Herzegovina, the members of the organization agreed to maintain a continued presence to oversee the peace process. The Stabilisation Force (SFOR) resulted from those meetings. NATO activated SFOR on December 20, 1996, the same date that IFOR's mandate expired. While IFOR *implemented* the peace, SFOR would *stabilize* the peace. The **United Nations** (UN) Security Council, with Resolution 1088 (1996), endorsed the establishment of SFOR under NATO leadership. SFOR's mission includes deterring or preventing a renewal of hostilities; promoting a climate for peace; and offering support to civilian humanitarian organizations. Non-NATO members, including Russia, were invited to join SFOR. As of March 2002, 17 non-NATO states had dispatched peacekeepers under the SFOR banner. Operational decisions are made by NATO's North Atlantic Council with the participation of nonmember countries which have contributed troops to SFOR.

SFOR has been fairly successful in meeting its mandated mission. The operation provided a secure environment for local elections in 1997 and 2000 and national elections in October 1998. The NATO peacekeepers have developed and maintained a close working relationship with the **Organization for Security and Cooperation in Europe** (OSCE) and the latter's operations in the area as well as the

United Nations Mission in Bosnia and Herzegovina. SFOR has also detained numerous individuals who have been indicted for war crimes.

The initial maximum authorized strength of SFOR was 32,000 troops but this was reduced as the situation warranted. As of March 2002, NATO and non-NATO members contributed approximately 18,000 troops for SFOR. Some 17,500 are located in Bosnia and Herzegovina and approximately 500 are in Croatia. Another 2,000 soldiers are in National Support Elements. SFOR is funded by NATO and the states contributing contingents to the operation.

STAND BY FORCE. This concept is an alternative to the efforts to build a **standing army** for the **United Nations** (UN). A stand by force would consist of military personnel and equipment earmarked for service with the UN or another international organization. The personnel would remain based in their home states and would deploy for international service upon receiving authorization from their governments following a request from the UN. In 1993, Secretary-General **Boutros Boutros-Ghali** requested the member states of the UN to pledge military personnel and equipment for a stand by force. He appointed Colonel Gerard Gambiez of France as his negotiator in this process. By April 1994, Gambiez reported that 15 states had pledged a total of 54,000 personnel for the stand by force. The establishment of this type of force would reduce the time required by the UN to deploy a peacekeeping operation since military units would be earmarked for international service with the global body. Boutros-Ghali has stated that the personnel of a stand by force would only serve in "**traditional peacekeeping**" operations. The terms "stand by force" and "**standing army**" are often mistakenly confused.

STAND BY FORCES HIGH-READINESS BRIGADE (SHIR-BRIG). Austria, Canada, Denmark, the Netherlands, Norway, and Sweden (with the Czech Republic, Finland, and Ireland as observers) formed the Stand By Forces High-Readiness Brigade (SHIRBRIG) in 1997. The purpose of SHIRBRIG is to pool military resources that are maintained at a high state of readiness to meet crisis situations. Planners could form a brigade-sized **rapid reaction force** from the contingents earmarked by the members for deployment by the **United Nations** (UN). Each country retains command of its contingents and the option of whether to deploy them as part of SHIRBRIG when requested.

STANDARDIZED GENERIC TRAINING MODULES (SGTM). The **Training and Evaluation Service** (TES), an organization within the **Department of Peacekeeping Operations** (DPKO) of the **United Nations** (UN), developed Standardized Generic Training Modules (SGTM) to provide member states with generic training modules for peacekeeping operations. The purpose of the project is to standardize peacekeeping training and provide it in an exportable package for the training of contingents in member states. *See also* MISSION TRAINING CELL.

STANDING ARMY. This term is applied to the concept of assigning national military units directly to **United Nations** (UN) command. Although the units would remain based in their home countries, they would respond directly to the UN and could be deployed, in theory, without consultation of their respective national governments. Many countries, including the **United States**, have expressed grave reservations about this concept and have ensured that it has never been implemented. As an alternative, the UN has developed the plan to designate a **stand by force** of military personnel and equipment that would be earmarked for international service. The terms "standing army" and "stand by force" are often confused.

STATUS OF FORCE AGREEMENT. This document is developed based upon close coordination between the mandating international organization and the **host state** of a peacekeeping operation. The agreement details specific privileges and responsibilities of the peacekeepers while on the territory of the host state. For example, the Status of Force Agreement examines issues such as legal jurisdiction over peacekeepers, freedom of movement, distinctive markings for peacekeepers and their vehicles, settlement of disputes or claims, and evacuation of deceased peacekeepers. The **United Nations Emergency Force I** (UNEF I) was the first **United Nations** (UN) peacekeeping operation to use a Status of Force Agreement, and this document became the model for future missions mandated by the global body. Although many of the future peacekeeping operations in the Middle East did not have agreements due to political reasons, the

UNEF I document became the unofficial standard for dealing with issues in these missions.

SUDAN. *See* INTERNATIONAL MONITORING UNIT (SUDAN).

SUDAN VERIFICATION MISSION. *See* INTERNATIONAL MONITORING UNIT (SUDAN).

SUSPENSE ACCOUNT. An account established to receive voluntary financial contributions from states in order to support a peacekeeping operation. Normally, a suspense account is set up in the attempt to cover a deficit resulting from the refusal of some states to contribute to a **special account** due to political or financial reasons.

SWISS PEACEKEEPING. Switzerland maintained its fairly strict neutrality after World War II and refused to formally join the **United Nations** (UN) until 2002. As a UN observer state, Switzerland refused to offer troop contingents but did provide funding and non-lethal aid (medical and evacuation aircraft) to many UN peacekeeping operations. In recent years, even before admission to the UN as a full member, Switzerland has slowly increased its participation in peacekeeping operations and has even assisted the **North Atlantic Treaty Organization** (NATO) in the latter's **Kosovo Force**. *See also* GEORGE, REMY; SAAR INTERNATIONAL FORCE; TEMPORARY INTERNATIONAL PRESENCE IN HEBRON; UNITED NATIONS MISSION IN ETHIOPIA AND ERITREA; UNITED NATIONS MISSION OF OBSERVERS IN PREVALAKIA; UNITED NATIONS TRANSITIONAL ASSISTANCE GROUP.

SYMBOLIC ARAB SECURITY FORCE (ASF). The **League of Arab States** mandated the force, also known as the Token Arab Security Force, on June 8, 1976, at an extraordinary session in Cairo. The league's members were concerned about the Lebanese civil war as well as the Syrian intervention in **Lebanon** on June 1, 1976. The Syrians had cited the pretext of responding to an appeal for assistance from the Maronite Christian population of Qoubaiyat and Aandqet. The mandating resolution gave the ASF the authority to maintain security and stability in Lebanon. The league members also envisioned it as a replacement for the Syrian forces in the country. However, the force would have Syrian participation. The league modified the mandate the next day and granted the Secretary-General the responsibility for determining the size of the contingents.

The league organized the ASF along the lines of **United Nations** (UN) peacekeeping operations. Algeria, Libya, Saudi Arabia, Sudan Syria, and the Palestinian Liberation Organization (PLO) offered to provide contingents. After initial objection, League Secretary-General Mahmoud Riad persuaded Lebanese President Solomon Frangieh to accept the international mission. Libya and Syria each deployed a 500-man unit to Beirut under the agreement on June 21, 1976. Over the next few weeks, additional peacekeepers from Syria and Libya, as well as smaller units from Saudi Arabia and Sudan, arrived in Lebanon, raising the total strength of the force to 2,500 men by mid-July 1976. The presence of Libyan soldiers created controversy within the Lebanese government, but they remained until November, when Tripoli decided to remove them. The Syrian contingent included 600 men of the Palestine Liberation Army. **Egyptian** Major-General Muhammad Ghoneim was selected to command the force.

The Symbolic Arab Security Force established itself around the international airport, while Syrian forces not assigned to the league's operation were withdrawn from the city. The force was limited by its size and the refusal of Lebanese Christians to allow it to deploy to Christian areas of east Beirut. In addition, the Syrians refused to allow the ASF to replace all of its units in Lebanon and actually increased the number of its non-league soldiers in Lebanon after the deployment of the peacekeepers. The Lebanese civil war intensified over the summer and into the early fall as Syrian forces went on the offensive around Beirut in September and October. The ASF was not able to contain the hostilities due to its mandate and size. In response, Saudi Arabia called for a conference to discuss the crisis situation. The meeting, known as the **Riyadh Summit Conference**, proposed a strengthened peacekeeping operation and transformed the original Symbolic Arab Security Force into the larger **Arab Deterrent Force**.

SYRIA. *See* MIXED ARMISTICE COMMISSION; OBSERVER GROUP DAMASCUS; OBSERVER GROUP GOLAN; UNITED

NATIONS DISENGAGEMENT OBSERVER FORCE; UNITED NATIONS TRUCE SUPERVISION ORGANIZATION.

– T –

TAJIKISTAN. *See* COMMONWEALTH OF INDEPENDENT STATES COLLECTIVE PEACEKEEPING FORCE; ORGANIZATION FOR SECURITY AND COOPERATION IN EUROPE MISSION TO TAJIKISTAN; UNITED NATIONS MISSION OF OBSERVERS IN TAJIKISTAN.

TANGANYIKA. *See* NIGERIAN PEACEKEEPING.

TASHKENT AGREEMENT. This agreement, signed by the Prime Minister of **India** and President of Pakistan on January 10, 1966, in Tashkent in the former Soviet Union, called for the withdrawal of each belligerent to the positions held prior to the initiation of hostilities in 1965. The agreement, negotiated with the assistance of the **United Nations** (UN), set the rules for the withdrawal and requested verification by representatives from the **United Nations Military Observer Group in India and Pakistan** (UNMOGIP) and **United Nations India-Pakistan Observation Mission** (UNIPOM). The completion of the withdrawals in February 1966 allowed the United Nations to officially terminate the mission of UNIPOM the following month. At the same time, the strength of UNMOGIP was reduced from 103 to 45 peacekeepers.

TASK FORCE 160. The operational name for **United States** special operations forces sent to Somalia in an attempt to capture **Mohammed Farah Aidid**. The task force was carrying out **United Nations** (UN) orders to capture the Somali warlord following an ambush that killed 24 Pakistani soldiers assigned to the **United Nations Operation in Somalia II** (UNISOM II). Approximately 100 Rangers of Task Force 160 were pinned down for nine hours following a raid to capture several of Aidid's lieutenants at the Olympic Hotel in Mogadishu. The Rangers were embroiled in a firefight that left 15 Americans and approximately 400 Somalis dead. Aidid's forces captured an American helicopter pilot and already held a **Nigerian** peace-keeper. The event led to considerable debate in Washington, D.C., and persuaded President Clinton to redefine American goals in Somalia and helped prompt many in Congress to demand a reduced American role in Somalia, if not a total withdrawal. *See also* UNIFIED TASK FORCE.

TASK FORCE 212. The operational name for the initial American contribution to the **United Nations Protection Force** (UNPRO-FOR). The American support included the 212th Mobile Army Surgical Hospital from which the task force name evolved. As the American participation grew to include the **United Nations Protection Force (UNPROFOR) in Macedonia**, the name was changed to **Joint Task Force Provide Promise**.

TASK FORCE FOX. *See* OPERATION AMBER FOX.

TASK FORCE HARVEST. *See* OPERATION ESSENTIAL HARVEST.

TEL-EL-QADI INCIDENT. The incident involved the **Armistice Demarcation Line** (ADL) between **Israel** and Syria in 1964. The Israelis decided to construct a track and parallel drainage ditch along the ADL and initiated a survey project prior to construction. The **United Nations Truce Supervision Organization** (UNTSO) had completed a partial survey of the ADL in 1963. When the Israelis moved beyond the line surveyed by UNTSO, the Syrians claimed they had encroached on Syrian territory and commenced firing on the party. The resulting fire and counter fire resulted in considerable death and destruction on both sides before the issue was submitted to the **United Nations** Security Council which stalemated over the issue. The incident served to show that UNTSO's mission accomplishment relied on the consent and cooperation of the two belligerents.

TEMPORARY INTERNATIONAL PRESENCE IN HEBRON (TIPH). Following the murder of 29 Palestinians by an **Israeli** citizen on February 25, 1994, the **United Nations** Security Council passed Resolution 904 condemning the attack and authorizing a neutral international presence in the Hebron area of the West Bank. Palestinian Chairman Yasser Arafat demanded Israeli acceptance of the international observers as a condition for returning to the negotiating table. The Israelis and Palestinians signed an agreement on March 31, 1994, requesting Denmark, Italy, and Norway to provide observers for the mission to be known as the Temporary International Presence in Hebron (TIPH). The observers arrived in April 1994 but withdrew on August 8, 1994, following the inability of the belligerents to agree on a mandate extension.

The interim Oslo peace agreement of September 28, 1995, called for a new international observer team. The original plan asked for an all-Norwegian team until a new agreement could be negotiated. The new mission was established on May 12, 1996. After the January 1997 withdrawal of Israeli forces from Hebron, the parties signed the Protocol Concerning the Redeployment in Hebron on January 21, 1997. This document mandated an expanded TIPH. Observers from Denmark, Italy, Sweden, **Switzerland**, and Turkey joined the Norwegians. Approximately 85 individuals were assigned to TIPH in 2002.

Approximately 85 observers are assigned to TIPH. The operation costs an estimated $2 million annually, and costs are paid by the observer contributing states. Although a provision exists for the observers to carry pistols, they are unarmed at the request of the Israelis and Palestinians. The team members are strictly observers and do not have any enforcement or police powers. TIPH is led by Norway and organized into three divisions. The Operations Division coordinates the observer teams; the Staff Division provides legal advice, liaison functions, research, and public relations; and the Support Division oversees transportation, communications, and administrative and financial needs.

Some scholars do not view TIPH as a peacekeeping operation. The Stockholm International Peace Research Institute (SIPRI) recognizes TIPH as a "peace operation" which the organization defines as either being an observer, peacekeeping, or peace building mission.

TOKEN ARAB SECURITY FORCE. *See* SYMBOLIC ARAB SECURITY FORCE.

TRADITIONAL PEACEKEEPING. The **United States** Department of Defense adopted this term for peacekeeping operations accepted by all parties in a conflict. The official Department of Defense definition of traditional peacekeeping is "Deployment of a UN, regional organization, or coalition presence in the field with the consent of all the parties concerned, normally involving UN, regional organization, or coalition military forces, and/or police and civilians. Non-combat military operations (exclusive of self-defense) that are undertaken by outside forces with the consent of all major belligerent parties, designed to monitor and facilitate implementation of an existing truce agreement in support of diplomatic efforts to reach a political settlement to the dispute." *See also* AGGRAVATED PEACEKEEPING; FIRST GENERATION PEACEKEEPING; SECOND GENERATION PEACEKEEPING.

TRAINING AND EVALUATION SERVICE (TES). The Training and Evaluation Service (TES) is an organization within the **Department of Peacekeeping Operations** (DPKO) of the **United Nations** (UN). TES develops and provides standardized guidance to states wanting to contribute to UN peacekeeping operations. Two important initiatives of the organization are **Mission Training Cells** (MTC) and **Standardized Generic Training Modules** (SGTM).

TREATY OF GUARANTEE. Cyprus, **Great Britain**, Greece, and Turkey signed the Treaty of Guarantee on August 16, 1960. The treaty provided a measure of security for the Turkish and Greek Cypriots on the island. Great Britain played a role in the treaty since it was the former colonial holder of Cyprus. The treaty pledged Great Britain, Greece, and Turkey to consult each other on joint action during periods of crisis on Cyprus. However, if joint action could not be agreed upon, the treaty allowed each to unilaterally act to restore the status quo. In addition, the treaty forbade a union of Cyprus with any other state as well as partitioning the country along ethnic lines. The Turkish government used the Treaty of Guarantee as the legal basis for its invasion of Cyprus in 1974. The **United Nations Peacekeeping Force in Cyprus** (UNFICYP) currently observes the cease-fire line established following the Turkish invasion of Cyprus.

TREATY OF JOINT DEFENSE AND ECONOMIC COOPERA-TION. Members of the **League of Arab States** signed the treaty as a supplementary document to the Pact of the league. The treaty provides for the military cooperation of members if the territorial integrity, independence, or security of one state is threatened. The league has mandated its two peacekeeping missions based upon the provisions of this document. The treaty created a Permanent Military Commission and a Joint Defense Council to coordinate the military policies of member states. *See also* ARAB DETERRENT FORCE; ARAB LEAGUE FORCE IN KUWAIT; SYMBOLIC ARAB SECURITY FORCE.

TRIPARTITE MILITARY INTEGRATION COMMITTEE. The committee, chaired by a representative of the **United Nations Transitional Assistance Group** (UNTAG), had responsibility for developing an integrated Namibian national army following independence. The other members included South Africa and the South-West Africa Peoples' Organization. Kenya, which supplied one of the three combat battalions to UNTAG, kept its soldiers in Namibia for three months after independence under a bilateral agreement with the new Namibian government. The Kenyans assisted in the training and integration of the new Namibian national army.

TRUCE COMMISSION. The **United Nations** (UN) established the commission in April 1948 to oversee the cease-fire between Israel and its Arab neighbors. On May 21, 1948, the Truce Commission formally requested the Security Council to provide military observers to assist in the truce supervision. This request for observers developed into the formation of the **United Nations Truce Supervision Organization** (UNTSO).

– U –

UGANDA. *See* UNITED NATIONS OBSERVER MISSION UGANDA-RWANDA.

UNIFIED AFRICAN ACTION. On December 7, 1993, 11 members of the **Organization of African Unity** (OAU) held a mini summit in

Cairo, **Egypt**. The group signed what is known as the Mechanism for the Prevention, Management, and Settlement of African Disputes. The meeting and resulting declaration is often referred to as Unified African Action. The document re-examined the issue of peacekeeping under the auspices of the OAU. The OAU had exhibited a reluctance to mandate peacekeeping operations following the failure of its **Peacekeeping Force in Chad II** in 1982. In the report, the organization accepted the responsibility for funding peace-making measures, including peacekeeping. *See also* AFRICAN UNION.

UNIFIED TASK FORCE (UNITAF). The Unified Task Force (UNITAF), led by the **United States**, deployed to **Somalia** to assist the **United Nations Mission in Somalia I** (UNOSOM I) mission. The operation, mandated by **United Nations** (UN) Security Council Resolution 794 (1992) on December 3, 1992, was independent of the UNOSOM I units and consisted of approximately 37,000 personnel. Over 21,000 of these soldiers came from the United States. Contributing states, based upon the size of their contingents in descending order, included the United States, **France**, Italy, Morocco, Canada, Saudi Arabia, Belgium, Turkey, Botswana, **Egypt**, **Great Britain**, **Germany**, Kuwait, and New Zealand. Units assigned to UNITAF began arriving on December 9, 1992. UNITAF's mission included the stabilization of the conflict in Somalia to allow humanitarian agencies to carry out their duties in the country. UNITAF's methods included seizing arms, securing strategic points, and escorting convoys. Following the ambush deaths of 24 Pakistani peacekeepers at the hands of followers of **Mohammed Farah Aidid**, American forces assigned to UNITAF initiated a UN-backed hunt for the Somali leader. A firefight with Aidid's followers on October 3, 1993, resulted in the deaths of 18 American soldiers. Somali deaths are estimated to have been in the hundreds. The series of firefights prompted the United States and other Western states to withdraw their forces in early 1994 as UNOSOM I was transformed into the **United Nations Operation in Somalia II** (UNOSOM II).

UNITED NATIONS (UN). The **United Nations** (UN) has mandated and fielded more multinational peacekeeping operations than any other international organization. During the **Cold War**, most international disputes were debated at the UN despite the fact that the body prefers for them to be settled by regional or subregional organizations. Thus, nearly every peacekeeping operation mandated between 1948 and 1990 emerged from the UN. Regional and subregional organizations began to increase in their political and economic importance after the end of the Cold War. As a result, there has been a dramatic increase in peacekeeping missions mandated and fielded by these organizations. By 2003, over half of newly mandated peacekeeping operations were emerging from regional and subregional international organizations rather than the UN.

The Security Council, consisting of **France**, **Great Britain**, **People's Republic of China**, **Russia**, and the **United States** as well as ten rotating members, is the body within the UN that officially mandates, extends the mandates, and terminates peacekeeping operations. There is a provision known as the **Uniting for Peace Resolution** that permits the mandating of a peacekeeping operation to be shifted to the General Assembly if the Security Council is deadlocked by a veto from one of the five permanent members. The General Assembly, consisting of each UN member, officially funds peacekeeping operations via a formula that allocates a percentage of the total cost to each member state based upon its economic status in the world.

In recent years, the UN has been under considerable criticism from members such as the United States for its management of peacekeeping operations. The body has conducted several studies, including the **Panel on United Nations Peace Operations** and the **Independent Inquiry into the Actions of the United Nations During the 1994 Genocide in Rwanda**, in order to review its handling of peacekeeping missions and develop better methods for internal management and service in the field. *See also* other UNITED NATIONS entries.

UNITED NATIONS ADVANCE MISSION IN CAMBODIA (UNAMIC). The Secretary-General of the **United Nations** (UN) recommended on September 30, 1991, the formation of the United Nations Advance Mission in Cambodia (UNAMIC) to assist the belligerents in the Cambodian conflict. The UN envisioned UNAMIC as a means to help maintain a cease-fire until the fielding of the peacekeeping mission which would be known as the **United Nations Transitional**

Authority in Cambodia (UNTAC). The Security Council agreed and passed Resolution 717 (1991) on October 17, 1991. Later, the UN expanded UNAMIC's mission to include training the Cambodians in the clearance of mines. UNTAC absorbed UNAMIC on March 15, 1992.

UNITED NATIONS ANGOLA VERIFICATION MISSION I (UNAVEM I). Angola is a large country located on the central western coast of Africa. Portugal held the area as a colony until its independence in 1975. During the 1950s and 1960s, the Angolans formed several groups to resist the domination of Portugal. The largest of these were the Popular Movement for the Liberation of Angola (MPLA), the National Front for the Liberation of Angola (FNLA), and the National Union for the Total Independence of Angola (UNITA). Despite uneasy relations between the three groups, they were able to achieve limited successes against the Portuguese government and military.

In April 1974, a coup in Portugal brought a leftist oriented government to power, which made the decision to free the state's colonial possessions in Africa. An attempt at reconciliation between the three major resistance groups failed, and independence dawned amidst civil war conditions as the transitional government collapsed. The MPLA, with Cuban and Soviet support, seized the capital of Luanda and held it against the other groups. The Soviet Union increased military aid to the MPLA, and the Cubans dispatched combat units to Angola. Meanwhile, UNITA and the FNLA received increased CIA-supplied aid, while **South Africa** intervened militarily on their behalf. The civil war settled into a conflict between the MPLA and its Cuban allies and UNITA (with the support of South African military raids). By 1986, the **United States** began to openly channel military supplies to UNITA.

A costly military stalemate brought both sides to the negotiating table by the end of the 1980s. South Africa withdrew its remaining forces from Angola, and Cuba moved its forces away from the Namibian border. The diplomatic negotiations led to a two-part peace process whereby Namibia would become independent of South African control and Cuban army would withdraw from Angola, which would then conduct national elections. Despite UNITA opposition, which slowed the process, an agreement was signed between Angola, Cuba, and South Africa in 1988 with the assistance of the **United Nations** (UN), the United States, and the Soviet Union. Security Council Resolution 626 (1988) of December 20, 1988, established a peacekeeping operation known as the United Nations Angola Verification Mission I (UNAVEM I).

The Security Council mandate called for the peacekeeping operation to verify the redeployment and eventual withdrawal of the Cuban military from Angola. The schedule required Cuba to withdraw 3,000 soldiers by April 1, 1989; 25,000 by November 1, 1989; 33,000 by April 1, 1990; 38,000 by October 1, 1990; and the total 50,000 by July 1, 1990. UNAVEM I initially consisted of 70 unarmed peacekeepers from ten states (Algeria, Argentina, Brazil, Congo, Czechoslovakia, **India**, Jordan, Norway, Spain, and **Yugoslavia**). UNAVEM I also included 37 international and local civilian staff. There were no fatalities among UNAVEM I personnel between December 1988 and May 1991.

An advance party of 18 peacekeepers arrived in Angola on January 3, 1989, to verify the withdrawal of the first 450 Cuban soldiers. Following the arrival of the remaining 52 peacekeepers, the mission established its headquarters in Luanda and deployed to the ports of Cabinda, Lobito, Luanda, and Namibe as well as the airport at Luanda. The peacekeepers also established two mobile teams that could be used to verify the redeployment of Cuban soldiers northward away from the Namibian border. Following each official completion of a redeployment phase, the UNAVEM I mobile teams verified the process. The Cubans completed their northward redeployments on schedule by October 31, 1989, and in response UNAVEM I closed its observation mission in Namibe and reduced its overall strength to 60 (withdrawing one soldier from each contingent providing state). The Cubans withdrew ahead of schedule permitting the UN to terminate UNAVEM I on May 30, 1991.

The funding of the operation was through **Special Assessment**. The total cost between December 1988 and May 1991 was $16.4 million. The UN estimated the annual cost of UNAVEM I as approximately $9 million for the first 12 months and $9.8 million for the remaining 19 months ($18.8 million for 31 months). Approximately $1 million in savings materialized during the first year when the UN required the Angolan government to provide office and residence space for the operation headquarters in Luanda. Additional savings were realized due to the successful completion of the mission one month ahead of schedule. The cooperation extended by the Cuban and Angolan governments and military officials helped make UNAVEM I a successful mission, operating with relative ease despite strife and turmoil in the area since 1975. Following negotiations between the Angolan government and UNITA for national elections, the UN developed a new mandate and transformed UNAVEM I into the **United Nations Angola Verification Mission II** (UNAVEM II).

UNITED NATIONS ANGOLA VERIFICATION MISSION II (UNAVEM II). The United Nations Angola Verification Mission II (UNAVEM II) emerged after the successful completion of the **United Nations Angola Verification Mission I** (UNAVEM I). Following the completion of the Cuban military withdrawal from **Angola** in 1991, the belligerents in the civil war agreed to a cease-fire and national elections. **United Nations** (UN) Security Council Resolution 696 (1991) extended the mission of UNAVEM I, which became known as UNAVEM II. The peace plan called for UNAVEM II to be in place by June 30, 1991, and complete its mission following national elections in November 1992. The first elements of UNAVEM II arrived on June 2, 1991. The UNAVEM II mandate stated that the operation should verify the arrangements made by the Angolan belligerents—the Angolan government and the National Union for the Total Independence of Angola (UNITA) led by Jonas Savimbi. UNAVEM II would also monitor the Angolan police during the cease-fire. The peacekeepers kept track of the number of personnel reporting to designated assembly points; oversaw the storage of surrendered weapons; and investigated cease-fire violations. UNAVEM II also assumed a mission to provide oversight during the Angolan election process. Observers in the operation deployed to Luanda, Huambo, Lubango, Saurimo, Luena, and Mavinga. Full-time monitors were also deployed to 82 locations (23 assembly sites for UNITA, 27 assembly sites for government soldiers, and 32 critical points such as airports and ports) across Angola.

Logistical difficulties resulted in many government and UNITA soldiers deserting from assembly points. The cease-fire held despite many individual breaches. Jonas Savimbi of UNITA refused to accept defeat in the 1992 elections and renewed the civil war. Newly elected President Jose Eduardo dos Santos of Angola requested that the UN increase the size of its peacekeeping mission and support his government since it was UNITA that broke the cease-fire and refused to abide by the election results. Secretary-General **Boutros Boutros-Ghali** did not agree to the Angolan proposal and recommended that the Security Council reduce the size of the operation to a skeleton presence and move all personnel to the relative safety of Luanda since two-thirds of the assembly points were already abandoned due to the fighting. UNAVEM II remained on the ground in its reduced strength as negotiations continued between the belligerents. The various parties signed the Lusaka Protocol on October 31, 1994. The protocol was a comprehensive peace agreement that included a provision for a continued presence of UN military observers in the state. The UN Security Council mandated the **United Nations Angola Verification Mission III** (UNAVEM III) to replace UNAVEM II and oversee the implementation of the Lusaka Protocol. UNAVEM II officially ended its mission on February 8, 1995.

The maximum authorized strength of UNAVEM II consisted of 350 military observers, 126 police observers, and 96 international and local civilian staff. The operation's electoral monitoring division included a total of 400 observers. The strength of the operation decreased to 171 military observers, 122 civilian police, and an unlisted number of international and local civilians by the time the mission ended. There were five fatalities among UNAVEM II personnel between 1991 and 1995. Twenty-four countries provided the military and police observers assigned to UNAVEM II. All ten of the contingent providers of UNAVEM I contributed observers to UNAVEM II. The mission was funded by **Special Assessment** and cost approximately $175.8 million between 1991 and 1995.

UNITED NATIONS ANGOLA VERIFICATION MISSION III (UNAVEM III). The **United Nations** (UN) Security Council mandated the United Nations Angola Verification Mission III (UNAVEM III), with Resolution 976 (1995) of February 8, 1995, to replace the **United Nations Angola Verification Mission II** (UNAVEM II) and oversee the implementation of the Lusaka Protocol. The mistrust between the **Angolan** government and UNITA continued and prevented the fulfillment of the Lusaka Protocol's provisions. In October 1996, the UN warned both sides, but UNITA in particular, to end the delays. UNAVEM III prepared for a reduction in its strength and a withdrawal from Angola in light of the planned completion of its mandate. UNAVEM III officially withdrew on June 30, 1997. The Security Council voted to replace the operation with the **United Nations Observer Mission in Angola** (MONUA).

The maximum strength of UNAVEM III at the end of June 1997 was 3,649 soldiers, 283 military observers, and 288 civilian police. There were 32 fatalities among UNAVEM III personnel between February 1995 and June 1997. Thirty-one countries provided military personnel for UNAVEM III. The operation was funded by **Special Assessment**.

UNITED NATIONS ASSISTANCE MISSION IN RWANDA (UN-AMIR). The **United Nations** (UN) Security Council mandated the **United Nations Observer Mission Uganda-Rwanda** (UNOMUR) on June 22, 1993, to help stem the violence between the Hutu and Tutsi in **Rwanda.** UNOMUR observed the border between Uganda and Rwanda to prevent weapons from entering Rwanda.

The Security Council voted on October 5, 1993, to deploy a second peacekeeping operation, the United Nations Assistance Mission in Rwanda (UNAMIR), consisting of 2,500 soldiers and 331 military observers to the country of Rwanda. The warring factions agreed to a cease-fire in August 1993 and the Security Council mandated UN-AMIR with Resolution 872 (1993) on October 5, 1993. The peacekeeping operation was given the mission to retrain the Rwanda army, disarm irregular military units, assist in the return of refugees, add an element of protection in the capital, and help the state in election preparations. The UN added clearly defined timetables for the operation in an attempt to guarantee its prompt departure following the accomplishment of its duties.

The UN operation included observers from Belgium (the former colonial power), Bangladesh, Botswana, Brazil, Fiji, Ghana, Hungary, Netherlands, Senegal, Slovakia, and Zimbabwe. UNAMIR replaced the **Neutral Military Observer Group II** deployed by the **Organization of African Unity** (OAU) to oversee an earlier cease-fire. The peacekeepers began arriving on December 10, 1993, and established a demilitarized buffer zone approximately 100 miles long and 15 miles wide in northern Rwanda to separate the main rebel stronghold of Mulindi from the government-controlled south. The group also deployed observers to the airport at Kigali.

During the first week of April 1994, Presidents Juvenal Habyarimana of Rwanda and Cyprien Ntaryamira of Burundi died in a mysterious aircraft crash. Hutu extremists blamed the Tutsi and organized violence soon erupted across the country as Hutus began murdering Tutsis and fellow Hutus who supported the peace process. Over the next three months, approximately 800,000 people died as Hutus sought the genocidal extermination of Tutsi men, women, and children. The Hutu utilized modern weapons as well as machetes and farm tools to kill Tutsi. At the same time, the Tutsi dominated RPF launched a fresh offensive against the interim government of Rwanda. UNAMIR peacekeepers watched helplessly as the genocide erupted around them. The renewed ethnic fighting placed the operation in jeopardy when several Belgian peacekeepers were killed trying to prevent the murder of Rwandan Prime Minister Agathe Uwilingiyimana. Belgium unilaterally withdrew its contingent. The Belgians were followed by other contingent providers. Many peacekeepers attempted to fulfill their mandate but the belligerents were not willing to compromise or adhere to a cease-fire.

On April 21, 1994, the Security Council voted to reduce the size of UNAMIR from 2,548 to 270 and essentially left the Rwandans to themselves. UNAMIR became one of the most controversial UN peacekeeping missions in history. Many debated who and what was to blame for the failure to prevent the genocide. Two significant reviews investigated the events surrounding the massacre and UNAMIR's mandate. In 1999, the UN released the final report of the **Independent Inquiry into the Actions of the United Nations During the 1994 Genocide in Rwanda** and in 2000, the OAU released the results of the **International Panel of Eminent Personalities to Investigate the 1994 Genocide in Rwanda and the Surrounding Events**.

On May 17, 1994, the Security Council enlarged UNAMIR to 5,500 troops with Resolution 918 (1994). However, it took six months for member states to contribute contingents. Countries, remembering the experience of Belgium, did not want to send soldiers into an unstable area where they could become casualties. In the interim, the Security Council backed a French-led multinational mission to secure refugee camps in southwestern Rwanda. In July 1994, the RPF seized control of the capital and the government of Rwanda. UNAMIR departed on March 8, 1996.

The maximum authorized strength of UNAMIR before the massacre was 2,548 soldiers, 331 military observers, and 60 civilian police The maximum authorized strength after May 1994 was 5,500 soldiers and 90 civilian police. The strength at withdrawal was 1,200 troops, 200 military observers, and international and local civilian staff. There were 27 fatalities among UNAMIR personnel between October 1993 and March 1996. The UN funded UNAMIR with a **Special Assessment** and the total cost was $453.9 million. *See also* FRENCH PEACEKEEPING.

UNITED NATIONS ASSISTANCE MISSION IN SIERRA LEONE (UNAMSIL). The **United Nations** (UN) Security Council mandated the **United Nations Observer Mission in Sierra Leone** (UNOMSIL) to assist the **Economic Community of West African States Monitoring Group (ECOMOG) in Sierra Leone** with the disarming of combatants and restructuring the military of **Sierra Leone**. Following the signing of the Lome Peace Agreement, there was a need for a greater UN presence in Sierra Leone. ECOMOG forces were preparing to depart the country and a continued international military force was required to assist in the country's transition.

The Security Council mandated the United Nations Assistance Mission in Sierra Leone (UNAMSIL) on October 22, 1999, with Resolution 1270 (1999). UNAMSIL absorbed the mission and personnel of UNOMSIL. UNAMSIL's mandate includes assisting in the disarmament and demobilization process; ensuring freedom of movement of UN personnel; monitoring the cease-fire; facilitating the delivery of humanitarian assistance; and providing support for elections. The mandate was modified on February 7, 2000, with Resolution 1289 (2000). New tasks include providing security at key locations and government buildings; facilitating the free flow of people; providing security at disarmament and demobilization sites; assisting the civilian police force; and guarding weapons and ammunition collected at disarmament sites.

After the arrival of UNAMSIL, some of the peacekeepers were taken hostage by RUF fighters. In some areas, UNAMSIL personnel were left alone but their equipment was seized by RUF. UNAMSIL declared that their **rules of engagement** did not permit the peace-keeping force to launch an offensive or series of raids to rescue the peacekeepers being held by RUF. Great Britain, the former colonizer of Sierra Leone, dispatched a small military force to Sierra Leone in response to the RUF actions. London declared that its soldiers were not part of UNAMSIL and operated outside of the peacekeeping mandate. They quickly brought the situation under control and forced the release of the peacekeepers being held hostage.

UNAMSIL has steadily grown in size due to the situation in Sierra Leone. The original mandate of October 1999 authorized UNAMSIL to have 6,000 military personnel. The maximum authorized strength stood at over 17,000 peacekeepers, 87 civilian police, and 874 international and local civilian staff. Thirty-one countries, including the rare appearance of China in peacekeeping, have contributed military personnel to UNAMSIL. As of April 2003, there were 14,804 military personnel and 306 international civilians assigned to UNAMSIL. Eighteen states have contributed civilian police to the operation. UN-AMSIL personnel have suffered 108 fatalities in Sierra Leone between October 1999 and April 2003 making this one of the most costly UN peacekeeping operations in terms of human life. UNAM-SIL is funded by **Special Assessment** and costs approximately $717.6 million annually.

UNITED NATIONS CIVILIAN POLICE (UNCIVPOL). *See* UNITED NATIONS TRANSITION ASSISTANCE GROUP (UN-TAG).

UNITED NATIONS CIVILIAN POLICE MISSION IN HAITI (MIPONUH). The **United Nations** (UN) Security Council mandated the United Nations Civilian Police Mission in Haiti (MIPONUH) with Resolution 1141 (1997) on November 28, 1997, as a follow-on to the **United Nations Transition Mission in Haiti** (UNTMIH). MIPONUH's mission included the training and supervision of specialized Haitian police units. MIPONUH completed its mandate and departed Haiti in March 2000 and was replaced by the **International**

Civilian Support Mission in Haiti, a joint operation of the UN and the **Organization of American States** (OAS).

The maximum authorized strength of MIPONUH was 300 policemen and approximately 225 other international and local civilian personnel. Eleven states contributed personnel to MIPONUH and there were no fatalities between 1997 and 2000. MIPONUH was financed by **Special Assessment** and bilateral donor contributions. The total operation cost approximately $20.4 million.

Some scholars do not view MIPONUH as a peacekeeping operation. The Stockholm International Peace Research Institute (SIPRI) recognizes MIPONUH as a "peace operation" which the organization defines as either being an observer, peacekeeping, or peace building mission. The UN includes MIPONUH in its tally of peacekeeping operations. *See also* MULTINATIONAL FORCE IN HAITI; UNITED NATIONS MISSION IN HAITI; UNITED NATIONS SUPPORT MISSION IN HAITI.

UNITED NATIONS COMMISSION FOR INDIA AND PAKISTAN (UNCIP). Great Britain granted independence to **India** and Pakistan in 1947. The two states, divided by culture and religion, were in competition over the acquisition of the State of Jammu and Kashmir (often simply referred to as Kashmir). The latter held the right to join either of the two new states. A dispute over this issue erupted into open conflict at the end of 1947. The **United Nations** (UN) established the United Nations Commission for India and Pakistan (UNCIP) on January 20, 1948, through Security Council Resolution 39 (1948). UNCIP, composed of representatives of Czechoslovakia, Argentina, and the **United States**, represented the global body in the attempt to resolve the crisis between India and Pakistan. The commission recommended to the Secretary-General that he select and dispatch a military adviser, General Maurice Delvoie of Belgium, to the area. This military position evolved over time to become the commander of the future **United Nations Military Observer Group in India and Pakistan** (UNMOGIP). The UN extended the membership of the commission to include Columbia and Belgium.

The commission negotiated a cease-fire between India and Pakistan in their conflict over Jammu and Kashmir and offered neutral military observers to oversee the process. These neutral observers eventually formed the core of UNMOGIP. The tasks of the observers included the accompaniment of Indian and Pakistani military officials during the investigation of cease-fire violations and gathering their own information on such incidents. They were ordered to remain as neutral as possible in all discussions and investigations. UNCIP officials were instrumental in the negotiation of the Karachi Agreement, which officially established the cease-fire line between the two belligerents. UNCIP's mission was completed following the successful implementation of the Karachi Agreement and the group returned to New York to write its final report. UNMOGIP remained on the subcontinent to provide a continuing observation of the cease-fire.

UNITED NATIONS CONFIDENCE RESTORATION MISSION IN CROATIA (UNCRO). In the 1980s, **Yugoslavia** began showing serious strains between the various ethnic groups comprising the state. In June 1991, **Croatia** and Slovenia declared their independence from Serb-dominated Yugoslavia. The Serb minorities in the new states called for assistance and fighting erupted. The **European Community** failed in its efforts to halt the conflict, and the **United Nations** (UN) became actively involved in September 1991. The UN mandated the **United Nations Protection Force** (UNPROFOR) in February 1992 and deployed the operation by the summer of 1992. Hostilities continued and even spread.

The UN Security Council mandated the United Nations Confidence Restoration Mission in Croatia (UNCRO) on March 31, 1995, with Resolution 981 (1995). UNCRO's mission involved replacing the UNPROFOR personnel fielded in Croatia. UNCRO peacekeepers were deployed in the Serb-dominated regions of Western Slavonia, Krajina, and Eastern Slavonia and the operation was intended as a temporary measure to establish the conditions required for the reintegration of these areas with Croatia. Croatia reintegrated Western Slavonia and Krajina by force during the summer of 1995. UNCRO continued its mission in Eastern Slavonia while negotiations continued in that region. On November 12, 1995, an agreement provided for the peaceful integration of Eastern Slavonia, Baranja, and Western Sirmium into the country of Croatia. The UN Security Council established the **United Nations Transitional Administration in**

Eastern Slavonia, Baranja, and Western Sirmium (UNTAES) on January 15, 1996, to replace UNCRO.

UNCRO consisted of 6,775 military personnel and 296 civilian police along with international and local staff. There were 16 fatalities among UNCRO personnel between March 1995 and January 1996. UNCRO's expenditures were included in UNPROFOR's totals.

UNITED NATIONS DISENGAGEMENT OBSERVER FORCE (UNDOF). In October 1973, Syrian forces attacked Israeli military units located on the Golan Heights. **Israel** had originally seized the Golan Heights from Syria during the 1967 Six-Day War. The attack, in cooperation with Egyptian forces crossing the Suez Canal, penetrated the Israeli lines but quickly turned into a reversal of fortune as Israel counterattacked. Tensions remained high following a cease-fire partially arranged with the assistance of the **United Nations** (UN). Peacekeepers assigned to the **United Nations Truce Supervision Organization** (UNTSO) moved to the cease-fire area and established observation posts. In May 1974, **United States** Secretary of State **Henry Kissinger** persuaded the two belligerents to sign an Agreement on Disengagement between Israeli and Syrian Forces. The Protocol to this agreement called for the deployment of a neutral peacekeeping operation to oversee the cease-fire. This document, later endorsed by the UN in Security Council Resolution 350 (1974), established what has become known as the United Nations Disengagement Observer Force (UNDOF). The resolution called on UNDOF to supervise the cease-fire and redeployment of military forces as well as establish a neutral buffer zone between the belligerents.

Peacekeepers assigned to the **United Nations Emergency Force II** (UNEF II) in the Sinai formed the core of UNDOF. The UN transferred two battalions, one from Peru and one from Austria, from UNEF II to UNDOF. These peacekeepers joined the personnel from UNTSO who had already been on the ground for six months. The Canadian and Polish units assigned to UNEF II detached elements to provide logistical support to UNDOF. The Canadian detachment operated on the Israeli side of the cease-fire line, while the Polish detachment was located on the Syrian side. The peacekeeping mission patrols from within the buffer zone, which is known as the **Area of Separation**. Both sides extending from the neutral zone are known as the **Area of Limitation** since Israel and Syria are required to limit the size of forces and types of weapons located in the region. The UNDOF peacekeepers established a military unit known as the Rapid Reaction Group (RRG) to counter any potential violations of the cease-fire neutral zone. The UNDOF peacekeepers maintain observation posts and mobile patrols in the Area of Separation, while the personnel officially assigned to UNTSO verify the number of forces and weapons systems located in the two Areas of Limitation

The original maximum total strength of UNDOF was set at 1,250. Many states have contributed contingents to UNDOF for various lengths of service. Peru removed its battalion in 1975 and was replaced by Iran. Following the Iranian revolution in 1979, that state withdrew its personnel from UNDOF. Finland offered a battalion to replace the departing Iranian peacekeepers. As of April 2003, UNDOF consists of 1,042 peacekeepers from Austria, Canada, Japan, Poland, the Slovak Republic, and Sweden. It should be noted that UNDOF represents a rare appearance of peacekeepers from Japan, especially outside of Asia. Eighty UNTSO military observers assist UNDOF and the operation also employs 38 international civilians. There have been 40 fatalities between May 1974 and April 2003.

Financing UNDOF is through a unique arrangement. UNDOF's funds were provided from the appropriations collected for UNEF II. This arrangement resulted from a decision documented in General Assembly Resolution 301 (XXVII) of 1973. When UNEF II completed its mission in 1979, the account, rather than being closed, remained in place to continue channeling funds to UNDOF. UNDOF costs approximately $35.7 million annually.

UNITED NATIONS EMERGENCY FORCE I (UNEF I). Relations between **Israel** and **Egypt**, rocky since 1949, quickly collapsed when Gamal Abdel Nasser assumed power in the latter state during 1954. Nasser nationalized the Suez Canal, prompting resentment of Great Britain and **France**, and supported the raids of guerrillas into Israel. Great Britain, France, and Israel coordinated a joint attack on Egypt in 1956, with the former two states declaring their intentions of "protecting" the Suez Canal during an Israeli-Egyptian conflict. The **United Nations** (UN) Security Council met to review the crisis in

October 1956. However, the vetoes held by Great Britain and France prevented the Security Council from acting on the issue. The body moved discussion to the General Assembly under the **Uniting for Peace Resolution**. This body, meeting in its first emergency session, called for a cease-fire, the withdrawal of all forces to the 1949 armistice lines, and the reopening of the Suez Canal. Canada abstained during the vote and objected to the resolution due to the lack of enforcement procedures. **Lester Pearson** of Canada proposed the establishment of a neutral military force that could oversee the cease-fire and withdrawal of military units. The new resolution [Resolution 998(ES-I)] asked Secretary-General Trygve Lie to develop Pearson's plan into a workable scenario, prompting all four of the belligerents to abstain during the vote. The Secretary-General's reply resulted in the now famous Resolution 1000(ES-I), which officially mandated what became known as the United Nations Emergency Force I (UNEF I) and provided the operation with its mission.

Resolution 1001(ES-I) outlined the functions of the operation. The global body utilized the peacekeepers assigned to the **United Nations Truce Supervision Organization** (UNTSO) as the initial core of the new operation. Former UNTSO personnel were also used by UNEF I as liaison detachments headquartered in Cairo, Tel Aviv, Beirut, and Pisa. The latter unit assisted in the logistical coordination of the mission. The Chief of Staff of UNTSO, **E. L. M. Burns**, was named as the first **Force Commander** of UNEF I. The Secretary-General established an **Advisory Committee** to assist in the development of this new concept of peacekeeping. Earlier peacekeeping operations were observer missions. However, UNEF I can be seen as the first true **interposition force** fielded by either the League of Nations or UN.

Egypt agreed to accept the peacekeeping operation on its territory but wanted clarification of the rights and privileges of the personnel assigned to the mission. The resulting meetings produced what is known as a **Status of Force Agreement** between the Egyptian government and the UN. The Secretary-General sought contingents of battalion size to fill the ranks of UNEF I. His criteria included that each contingent must be acceptable to all parties involved in the conflict; neutral in the conflict; and represent a geographical balance of forces. Great Britain and France were denied their requests to participate in the contingent selection process. Afghanistan, Brazil,

Canada, Chile, Colombia, Czechoslovakia, Denmark, Ecuador, Ethiopia, Finland, India, Indonesia, Iran, Laos, Myanmar, New Zealand, Norway, Pakistan, Peru, Philippines, Romania, Sri Lanka, Sweden, and Yugoslavia volunteered contingents on their own initiative. The Secretary-General opted to select contingents from Brazil, Canada, Colombia, Denmark, Finland, India, Indonesia, Norway, Sweden, and Yugoslavia.

The Secretary-General decided to exclude any Middle Eastern states that chose to volunteer peacekeepers. Egypt rejected the participation of Pakistan due to the latter's recent critical remarks about the Egyptian government. Egypt initially rejected the inclusion of Canada, Norway, and Denmark since they are viewed as pro-Western members of the **North Atlantic Treaty Organization** (NATO). However, the Egyptian government relented and the Canadians deployed from the staging area in Naples, Italy. Opposition to the other two states was later dropped when Finland and Sweden refused to participate unless Norway and Denmark also contributed forces to UNEF I. Israel originally objected to countries that did not recognize it as a state. Indonesia withdrew its forces in September 1957; Finland in December 1957; and Colombia in October 1958. The other contingents remained until the operation was ordered out of Egypt in 1967. The maximum authorized strength of UNEF I was 6,073 military personnel accompanied by an international and civilian staff.

British and French forces departed the area by the end of 1956. Withdrawal of Israeli forces took longer and was conducted in stages across the Sinai. Israel evacuated the Sinai and Gaza Strip by March 1957. UNEF I moved into the Gaza Strip and along the 1949 armistice line and took up positions as an interposition force on the Egyptian side of the frontier since Israel refused to allow the peacekeepers on its side of the border. A UNEF I detachment remained in the town of **Sharm-el-Sheikh** to ensure Israeli passage through the Strait of Tiran. UNEF I operated static observation posts along the armistice line during the day and shifted to roving patrols at night. Peacekeepers from UNEF I assisted in the establishment of ONUC, the **United Nations Yemen Observation Mission** (UNYOM), and the **United Nations Temporary Executive Authority**. In fact, UNYOM was almost entirely constructed from the personnel and equipment assigned to UNEF I.

The peacekeeping operation remained at its positions until June 1967, when President Gamal Abdel Nasser ordered UNEF I to depart following increased tensions between Egypt and Israel. The Six-Day War erupted upon the departure of the peacekeepers who had not completed their total withdrawal from the area. Fifteen UNEF I peacekeepers died in the Gaza Strip fighting as they awaited removal from the area. A total of 107 UNEF I personnel died between November 1956 and June 1967.

Financing of the operation was handled through **Special Assessment**. This was the first time that the United Nations established a special assessment, outside of the regular budget, to fund a peacekeeping operation. Each contingent provider would cover the costs of equipment and normal salaries of its personnel. The United Nations would cover special costs such as transportation and logistics within the host state. General Assembly Resolution 1089(XI) modified this proposal to state that a country's payment of peacekeeper salaries was voluntary. If requested, the United Nations would provide the salaries of peacekeepers assigned to UNEF I. The Soviet Union refused to contribute to the Special Assessment. This action, along with opposition to financing the United Nations Truce Supervision Organization and the **United Nations Operation in the Congo**, led to the **Article 19 Crisis**. UNEF I's annual budget equaled one-third of the total UN annual regular budget. The total cost of UNEF I was $214.25 million. Many of the contingent providing states absorbed some of their personal costs in the operation and, thus, reduced the overall cost of UNEF I to the UN. See *also* BLUE HELMETS; GOOD FAITH AGREEMENT.

UNITED NATIONS EMERGENCY FORCE II (UNEF II). Following a period of increased tensions, **Egypt** and Syria launched a coordinated surprise attack on **Israel** in October 1973. Egyptian forces crossed the Suez Canal and in doing so overran observation posts manned by the **United Nations Truce Supervision Organization** (UNTSO). An Israeli counterattack in the Sinai trapped two Egyptian armies on the east bank of the Suez Canal and led to the establishment of an Israeli bridgehead on the west side of the waterway. The threat of Soviet military intervention led to the issue being considered by the **United Nations** (UN) Security Council on October 24, 1973. The next day, the Security Council passed Resolution 340 (1973), which called for an immediate cease-fire to the conflict, asked Secretary-General Kurt Waldheim to increase the number of UNTSO peacekeepers in the area of hostilities, and established a United Nations Emergency Force patterned on the operation fielded in 1956, the **United Nations Emergency Force** (UNEF) I.

UNEF II's mandate included supervising the cease-fire between the Egyptians and Israelis. After 1975, the mandate was modified to allow UNEF II to oversee the redeployment of Egyptian and Israeli military forces and man the neutral buffer zone between the two states as Israel returned territory in the Sinai to Egypt. UNEF II personnel also coordinated and provided drivers, in cooperation with the International Committee of the Red Cross, for the movement of humanitarian supplies to the Egyptian forces trapped on the east side of the Suez Canal.

The Secretary-General arranged for the immediate movement of military forces from Austria, Finland, and Sweden from the **United Nations Peacekeeping Force in Cyprus** (UNFICYP) to Egypt. The early deployers dispatched their personnel directly to the front lines between the Egyptians and Israelis. These peacekeepers, along with personnel assigned to UNTSO, became the initial core of what became known as the United Nations Emergency Force II (UNEF II). The Chief of Staff of UNTSO, Major-General Ensio P. H. Siilasvuo, was selected as the interim **Force Commander** of the new operation.

The UN estimated it needed approximately 7,000 soldiers for UNEF II and selected Ghana, Indonesia, Nepal, Panama, Peru, Canada, Ireland, and Senegal to join the previously mentioned states. The Soviet Union objected to the inclusion of Canada since the latter was a member of the **North Atlantic Treaty Organization** (NATO) and demanded inclusion of a Warsaw Pact country. In the compromise, Poland joined the mission and provided logistical support along with Canada. Several states withdrew their contingents between 1974 and 1979 as others arrived to join the operation. The Irish contingent is a good example. Ireland withdrew its battalion from UNEF II in order to provide home security following a series of terrorist bombings around Dublin. The Austrian and Peruvian elements transferred from UNEF II and became the core of the **United Nations Disengagement Observer Force** (UNDOF) in June 1974. The UN did not develop a

Status of Force Agreement for UNEF II but instead actually used the document developed for UNEF I.

Following a disengagement agreement in January 1974, UNEF II supervised the staged withdrawal of Israeli forces. UNEF II personnel manned the moving buffer zone between the belligerents, while the UNTSO peacekeepers were responsible for surveying and demarcating the buffer zones. Continued negotiations between Egypt and Israel led to more withdrawals eastward across the Sinai. An Egyptian-Israeli peace treaty, negotiated by the **United States**, was signed in March 1979. This agreement called for the continued observation of the border area by a peacekeeping operation. Although the signatories desired that UNEF II would continue this function, opposition arose from the Palestinian Liberation Organization, the Soviet Union, and many Arab states. The UN chose to allow the mandate of UNEF II to lapse on July 24, 1979, forcing the United States to enact an annex to the treaty, which called upon Washington to organize a new peacekeeping operation if UNEF II departed the area. The resulting mission is known as the **Multinational Force and Observers**. UNEF II personnel quickly left the Sinai following the lapse of their mandate, while those peacekeepers assigned to UNTSO remained to continue their mission.

The maximum strength of UNEF II was 6,973 military personnel supported by international and local civilian staff. There were 55 fatalities among the UNEF II personnel between October 1973 and July 1979. UNEF II was funded by **Special Assessment** and cost a total of $446.5 million.

UNITED NATIONS FORCE IN THE CONGO. *See* UNITED NATIONS OPERATION IN THE CONGO.

UNITED NATIONS GOOD OFFICES IN AFGHANISTAN AND PAKISTAN (UNGOMAP). The Soviet Union intervened in **Afghanistan** on December 27, 1979. The Security Council, deadlocked due to the veto of the Soviet Union, could not pass a resolution on the Soviet intervention. The General Assembly, using the **Uniting for Peace Resolution** of 1950, called for the withdrawal of all "foreign" forces from Afghanistan. Eight years of negotiations culminated in the signing of the Agreements on the Settlement of the

Situation Relating to Afghanistan on April 14, 1988. The agreements included four provisions, including the repatriation of refugees and a timetable for the withdrawal of Soviet forces from Afghanistan. The **United Nations** (UN) offered to field a peacekeeping mission to oversee the Agreements.

The mission, known as the United Nations Good Offices in Afghanistan and Pakistan (UNGOMAP), was mandated by Security Council Resolution 622 (1988) on October 31, 1988. The mandate authorized UNGOMAP to ensure Afghanistan and Pakistan did not interfere across their common border; oversee the withdrawal of Soviet forces from Afghanistan; and monitor the voluntary repatriation of refugees. UNGOMAP operated from two headquarters facilities, including one in Islamabad and the other in Kabul. Fifty peacekeepers were detached from existing UN operations, including the **United Nations Truce Supervision Organization** (UNTSO), the **United Nations Disengagement Observer Force** (UNDOF), and the **United Nations Interim Force in Lebanon** (UNIFIL), and reassigned to UNGOMAP. The transferred personnel represented Austria, Canada, Denmark, Fiji, Finland, Ghana, Ireland, Nepal, Poland, and Sweden. The initial element of UNGOMAP arrived on April 25, 1988. UNGOMAP set up three observation posts on the Afghan side of the border with the Soviet Union in order to observe compliance with the withdrawal timetables. These posts were located at Hayratan, Torghundi, and the air base at Shindand.

Withdrawal of the Soviet military proceeded smoothly and was completed in February 1989. UNGOMAP logged numerous complaints from Afghanistan and Pakistan against each other. In order to assist in the investigation of border incidents (including the smuggling of weapons), UNGOMAP established posts on the Pakistani side of the border at Peshawar, Quetta, Torkham, Teri Mangal, and Chaman. Following the refusal of signatories of the agreements to extend the mandate of UNGOMAP, the UN officially ended the operation on March 15, 1990. However, ten peacekeepers, one from each contributing country, remained in the area to serve as military advisers to the **Special Representative** of the Secretary-General.

UNGOMAP's maximum authorized strength was 50 military observers supported by international and local civilians. There were no UNGOMAP fatalities between May 1988 and March 1990. The total cost of UNGOMAP was $14 million. The UN financed UNGOMAP via its regular budget. Japan provided additional voluntary contributions for the operation.

UNITED NATIONS GUARDS CONTINGENT IN IRAQ (UNGCI). The **United Nations** (UN) established the contingent to replace allied soldiers who were protecting the Kurds in northern Iraq following the **Persian Gulf War** in 1991. This unit was assigned to provide limited security for the operations of the UN·suboffices and Humanitarian Centers program to coordinate the administration of aid to the Kurds. The mandate dictated that the total strength of the contingent could not exceed 500 soldiers, with no more than 150 assigned to any one particular region under UN protection. The guards in the contingent were authorized to carry small arms that were to be provided by the Iraqi government. The first ten guards arrived on May 19, 1991, and the remainder were on the ground by July 1991. The main headquarters was established in Baghdad. The mission of the unit included the protection of the individuals providing humanitarian relief to the Kurds as well as UN property and buildings. Funding of the operation has rested on appeals made by the United Nations Disaster Relief Organization and the International Committee of the Red Cross. The contingent eventually consisted of soldiers from 35 different countries.

UNITED NATIONS INDIA-PAKISTAN OBSERVATION MISSION (UNIPOM). An outbreak of hostilities between **India** and Pakistan in 1965 prompted the **United Nations** (UN) to mandate the United Nations India-Pakistan Observation Mission (UNIPOM). The Security Council developed this operation to supplement the **United Nations Military Observation Group in India and Pakistan** (UNMOGIP), which held the responsibility of overseeing a cease-fire in Kashmir since 1949. Rather than providing UNMOGIP with a new mandate to cover the Indian-Pakistani border south of Kashmir, the UN opted to establish a separate temporary peacekeeping mission. The Security Council mandated the mission with Resolution 211 (1965). The peacekeepers, the core of whom were detailed from UNMOGIP and the **United Nations Truce Supervision Organization** (UNTSO), began arriving on September 23, 1965.

The mission of UNIPOM included the supervision of the cease-fire outside of the Kashmir region as well as the oversight of the withdrawal of the belligerents to the prewar frontier. UNIPOM's maximum authorized strength was 96 military observers. The states that provided detached observers from UNTSO and UNMOGIP included Australia, Belgium, Canada, Chile, Denmark, Finland, Ireland, Italy, Netherlands, New Zealand, Norway, and Sweden. The observers specifically assigned to UNIPOM began arriving at the end of September 1965 and eventually included representatives from Brazil, Canada, Ethiopia, Ireland, Myanmar, Nepal, Netherlands, **Nigeria**, and Venezuela. In October 1965, the force reached its maximum strength. Following the successful implementation of the **Tashkent Agreement**, the UN terminated the mandate of UNIPOM on March 22, 1966. The peacekeeping mission was funded by the UN regular budget and cost the organization $1.7 million.

UNITED NATIONS INTERIM ADMINISTRATION IN KOSOVO (UNMIK). Kosovo is within the Federal Republic of **Yugoslavia**. The **North Atlantic Treaty Organization** (NATO) mandated and fielded an operation known as the **Kosovo Force** (KFOR) in 1999 to protect the ethnic Albanians from the Serbs within Yugoslavia. The **United Nations** (UN) Security Council, with Resolution 1244 (1999), endorsed KFOR and mandated the United Nations Interim Administration in Kosovo (UNMIK). One of KFOR's missions is to provide security for UNMIK. UNMIK's mandate includes performing basic civil administration functions; promoting the establishment of autonomy and self-government in Kosovo; coordinating humanitarian and disaster relief; maintaining civil law and order; promoting human rights; and ensuring the safe return of refugees. There have been 19 UNMIK fatalities between 1999 and 2002. Many scholars do not view UNMIK as a peacekeeping operation because of the administrative nature of its mandate. However, the UN includes UNMIK as one of its peacekeeping operations and the Stockholm International Peace Research Institute (SIPRI) labels the mission as a peace operation.

UNITED NATIONS INTERIM FORCE IN LEBANON (UNIFIL). **Lebanon**, a state with a diverse population divided along cultural and religious grounds, erupted into civil war in 1975. Despite an official end of the hostilities the following year and the dispatch of the Arab League's **Arab Deterrent Force**, the turmoil endured especially in southern Lebanon where Christian and Muslim militia continued to battle each other. The **Israelis** invaded Lebanon in March 1978 in retaliation for a Palestinian Liberation Organization attack on civilians near Tel Aviv. The Israeli forces quickly occupied all of Lebanon south of the **Litani River** except the city of Tyre. The Lebanese government protested the Israeli invasion at the **United Nations** (UN), prompting an American-led Security Council Resolution 425 (1978) calling for the withdrawal of the Israeli forces and the establishment of a United Nations Interim Force to replace them. The Security Council proposed that the new peacekeeping operation would verify the withdrawal of the Israeli military, restore international peace and security in the region, and assist the Lebanese government in its attempts to assert governmental authority over the area.

The Security Council officially named the operation the United Nations Interim Force in Lebanon (UNIFIL). The name offered an explicit declaration that the Security Council considered this operation a temporary mission to assist the Lebanese government. Peacekeepers assigned to the **United Nations Truce Supervision Organization** (UNTSO) were asked to assist UNIFIL while carrying out the mission of monitoring the **Armistice Declaration Line** between **Israel** and Lebanon. UNTSO also provided the initial core of peacekeepers until the arrival of soldiers who would be permanently assigned to the new mission. A company of Iranian peacekeepers assigned to the **United Nations Disengagement Observation Force** (UNDOF) and a company of Swedish soldiers from the **United Nations Emergency Force II** (UNEF II) were dispatched, with the approval of the home governments. Guidelines developed for the operation mirrored those written for UNEF II and UNDOF. Secretary-General Kurt Waldheim asked Major-General **Emmanuel Erskine**, the Chief of Staff of UNTSO, to serve as the first **Force Commander**. Erskine became the first African Force Commander of a UN peacekeeping operation outside of the African continent.

The UNIFIL composition of forces has frequently changed since 1978. For example, **France**, Iran, Nepal, Norway, and Sweden deployed units to Lebanon in support of UNIFIL. These units were joined by contingents from Fiji, Ireland, Nepal, Nigeria, and Senegal by the end of May 1978. Additional contingents included Finland (November 1982), Ghana (September 1979), Italy (July 1979), and the Netherlands (February 1979). Sweden removed its temporarily deployed infantry company during May 1978 and Iran did the same in March 1979. A Canadian logistics unit, detached from UNEF II, returned to its original assignment by October 1978. States that removed their contingents from UNIFIL include the Netherlands (October 1985), **Nigeria** (February 1983), Senegal (November 1984), and Ireland (November 2001). It is interesting to note that Nepal withdrew its peacekeepers in May 1980 and then returned them to Lebanon from June 1981 to November 1982 in response to the removal of the contingent from Senegal. The Nepalese combat units returned again in early 1985. The dispatch of troops from Finland covered the gap left by the departure of Nepalese troops in 1982. France, while always maintaining some type of presence in UNIFIL, removed its infantry battalion in March 1979 and then redeployed it from May 1982 to December 1986. At the same time, Ghana and Ireland increased the size of their infantry battalions. The Irish withdrew their battalion from UNIFIL at the end of 2001 as the UN prepared to make substantial cuts in UNIFIL's strength.

The maximum strength of UNIFIL stood at approximately 7,000 soldiers. UNIFIL consists of approximately 1,998 peacekeepers and 111 international civilians. Between March 1978 and April 2003, 246 UNIFIL personnel have died in Lebanon. UNIFIL peacekeepers have experienced many periods of tense relations with the Israelis and Lebanese. Many of the 246 deaths recorded since 1978 resulted from ambushes. In response to repeated attacks by Christian and Muslim militia in the region, UNIFIL set up a rapid response combat unit known as the **Force Mobile Reserve**. UNIFIL is funded by a **Special Assessment**. However, many states have refused to contribute to this fund due to political reasons. In response the Secretary-General established a special **Suspense Account** to allow states, other international organizations, and private sources to make voluntary contributions to UNIFIL. The mission costs approximately $144 million annually. *See also* KASMIYAH BRIDGE.

UNITED NATIONS INTERNATIONAL POLICE TASK FORCE (IPTF). The **United Nations** (UN) mandated the United Nations International Police Task Force (IPTF) in 1996 and attached it to the **United Nations Mission in Bosnia and Herzegovina** (UNMIBH). IPTF's mission included the implementation of reforms in the state police force and oversight of the police officers throughout the country. The organization consisted of approximately 1,500 officers and its funding came from the UNMIBH budget. On January 1, 2003, the **European Union Police Mission** (EUPM) replaced IPTF. There were six fatalities among IPTF personnel between 1996 and 2002.

UNITED NATIONS IRAN-IRAQ MILITARY OBSERVER GROUP (UNIIMOG). A conflict between Iran and Iraq erupted in 1980. Attempts by the **United Nations** (UN) to broker a peace plan failed for several years. In 1984, the belligerents agreed to allow a limited UN presence in their states. In June 1984, two teams of military observers arrived in the capitals of the states in order to oversee compliance with a call to cease launching attacks on population centers. The teams, each consisting of three officers, were detached from the **United Nations Truce Supervision Organization** (UNTSO). These teams would later become the core of a more traditional peacekeeping operation. Iran and Iraq agreed to accept a cease-fire during July 1988. In turn, the UN Security Council approved the fielding of the United Nations Iran-Iraq Military Observer Group (UNIIMOG) as a means of monitoring the cease-fire in the Iran-Iraq war. The mandate, Resolution 619 (1988), was approved on August 9, 1988. The peacekeepers were also given the mission of investigating alleged violations of the cease-fire; restoring the situation when a violation occurred; preventing changes in the status quo prior to the withdrawal of all forces to internationally recognized boundaries; supervising and verifying the withdrawal to these boundaries; and overseeing exchanges of prisoners.

The UN maintained a headquarters in the capital of each country and deployed peacekeepers to each side of the cease-fire line. Except for limited liaison meetings, the UNIIMOG peacekeepers were not allowed to cross the cease-fire line. The advance parties of UNIIMOG personnel arrived on August 19, 1988 joining the teams of military observers that were in the capitals since 1984. The Chief Military Observer and his staff spent alternate weeks in Baghdad and Tehran where the UN maintained headquarters led by Assistant Chief

Military Observers. Sector headquarters in Iran were located in Saqqez, Bakhtaran, Dexful, and Ahwaz. In Iraq, the UN sector headquarters were in Sulaymaniyah, Baqubah, and Basra. During the **Persian Gulf War**, all but three of the UNIIMOG personnel headquartered in Baghdad were moved to Iran. Mobile patrols were conducted by vehicle, aircraft, boat, foot with pack mules, and even skis.

The peacekeeping mission encountered many difficulties on the Iranian side of the border due to Tehran's distrust of foreign military personnel. For example, the Canadian communications unit was flown from Turkey to Iran on Soviet aircraft because of Iran's refusal to allow American military aircraft to enter the country. The Iranians also placed many restrictions on the movement of the peacekeeping personnel. On the other hand, the personnel assigned to the Iraqi side of the cease-fire line exercised greater freedom of movement. By the end of 1990, the cease-fire line developed into a one-kilometer neutral zone. Following successful negotiations between Iran and Iraq, UNIIMOG was withdrawn in February 1991.

UNIIMOG's maximum strength was 400 military observers as well as international and local civilian staff. The number of peacekeepers decreased during the mission due to operational constraints and Iraq's willingness to solve its problems with Iran in the wake of the Persian Gulf War. UNIIMOG suffered one fatality between 1988 and 1991. The operation was funded by a **Special Assessment** on all members and cost the global body approximately $177.9 million.

UNITED NATIONS IRAQ-KUWAIT OBSERVATION MISSION (UNIKOM). The **United Nations** (UN) deployed this observation mission to the Iraqi-Kuwaiti border following the conclusion of the **Persian Gulf War** in 1991. Security Council Resolution 689 (1991) mandated UNIKOM to monitor the Khor Abdullah waterway and a demilitarized zone extending along the Iraqi-Kuwaiti border; use its presence to deter violations of the **demilitarized zone**; and observe any hostile or potentially hostile acts mounted from the territory of either state. The demilitarized zone extended from the border to a depth of ten kilometers into Iraq and five kilometers into Kuwait. The two states, and not the UN, were responsible for humanitarian relief and law and order within their respective sides of the zone. The demilitarized zone was divided into three sectors within which can be found a headquarters location and six observation posts. Mobile foot and helicopter (provided by Chile) patrols are also carried out within the demilitarized zone

The Security Council envisioned the operation consisting of approximately 1,440 personnel. The maximum authorized strength as of July 2002 was 1,103 military personnel (905 soldiers and 198 military observers) and 222 international and local civilians. The UN initially deployed five infantry companies to establish the demilitarized zone in April 1991. Fiji, Ghana, and Nepal each provided a company from their contingents assigned to the **United Nations Interim Force in Lebanon** (UNIFIL), while an Austrian company and a Danish company arrived from the **United Nations Force Cyprus** (UNFICYP). A Swedish logistics company joined the operation from UNIFIL. All six companies returned to their original assignments when the UNIKOM peacekeepers arrived. The five permanent members of the Security Council (China, France, Great Britain, Russia, and the United States) each provided 20 military observers to the operation. After the initial deployment, the UN opted to replace the unarmed observers with 750 armed peacekeepers in response to Iraqi incursions along the border with Kuwait. A total of 32 states contributed personnel to UNIKOM. On March 17, 2003, the UN withdrew UNIKOM from the border region due to the impending American Coalition attack on Iraq. UNIKOM maintains a small 13-man headquarters in Kuwait and performs liaison duties between the UN and coalition forces in the area. This new mandate for UNIKOM extends to July 2003. Seventeen UNIKOM personnel have died between April 1991 and April 2003. UNIKOM is funded by a **Special Assessment**. The operation costs approximately $52.8 million annually prior to March 2003 when it was reduced in size. Kuwait pays two-thirds of UNIKOM's cost.

UNITED NATIONS MILITARY OBSERVER GROUP IN INDIA AND PAKISTAN (UNMOGIP). The **United Nations** (UN) established the **United Nations Commission for India and Pakistan** (UNCIP) as a means to assist in the peaceful negotiation of the conflict between **India** and Pakistan over Kashmir. Neutral military observers assigned to UNCIP eventually formed the nucleus of the newly deployed United Nations Military Observer Group in India and Pakistan (UNMOGIP). The Security Council mandated UN-MOGIP in Resolution 47 (1948). Following the successful implementation of the Karachi Agreement on a cease-fire in the Kashmir region, UNCIP departed the area. However, the Security Council, in Resolution 91 (1951), chose to retain UNMOGIP on the subcontinent as a tool in the continued oversight of the cease-fire between India and Pakistan. UNMOGIP headquarters alternates between Srinagar in Indian-controlled Kashmir (May–November) and Rawalpindi, Pakistan (November–May) in order to ensure the neutrality of the mission.

An outbreak of hostilities in 1965 between India and Pakistan taxed the resources of UNMOGIP, leading to the reinforcement of the unit by additional peacekeepers. As the war spread to areas outside of Kashmir, the UN opted to establish a new peacekeeping operation rather than assign UNMOGIP observers outside of Kashmir, which would have demanded a new mandate for the operation. The name given to this new mission was the **United Nations India-Pakistan Observation Mission** (UNIPOM). UNMOGIP's commander, Lieutenant-General Robert H. Nimmo, held the position of UNIPOM interim commander until the arrival of Major-General B. F. Macdonald of Canada in October 1965. In 1966, the Tashkent Agreement between India and Pakistan implemented a successful withdrawal of the belligerents to the prewar frontiers. UNMOGIP observed the withdrawal in the Kashmir region, while UNIPOM accomplished the same task along the border south of Kashmir. Following the completion of the withdrawal, the United Nations terminated UNIPOM and left UNMOGIP in place to continue its mission of overseeing the cease-fire in Kashmir.

In 1971, hostilities were renewed as the Indian military attacked Pakistani positions in the area that would later become independent Bangladesh. The conflict spread to Kashmir until the implementation of a cease-fire. Following the war, India and Pakistan agreed to minor changes in the cease-fire line and established what has become known as the **Line of Control** between the two belligerents. While Pakistan continues to use the UNMOGIP observers, India has not reported cease-fire violations to the peacekeepers since 1972, citing its view that the Karachi Agreement has lapsed. The Indians still allow the peacekeepers to operate along the eastern side of the Line of Control but restrict their movement. The UN is of the opinion that only the world body can terminate UNMOGIP. Therefore the peacekeeping operation is still in place in Kashmir.

The number of peacekeepers assigned to the operation fluctuates depending upon the needs of the Chief Military Observer. The maximum strength stood at 102 observers following an outbreak of hostilities in 1965. UNMOGIP's strength stands at approximately 44 military observers from nine countries and 64 international and local civilians. The original contingents in UNMOGIP came from Belgium, Canada, Mexico, Norway, and the **United States**. Mexico withdrew its peacekeepers during the same year of their arrival, the Canadians departed in 1979, the Norwegians left in 1952 (but returned in 1957), and the United States removed its observers in 1954. India demanded the departure of the American military observers following the extension of military aid from Washington to Pakistan. Thus, in the eyes of India, the United States had lost its neutrality in the conflict and should not participate in the UN operation to oversee the cease-fire in Kashmir. UNMOGIP has suffered nine fatalities between 1947 and April 2003. UNMOGIP, like the **United Nations Truce Supervision Organization** (UNTSO), is funded by the regular budget of the UN. The annual cost of the operation is approximately $6.2 million.

UNITED NATIONS MILITARY STAFF COMMITTEE. The committee, established in 1946 in accordance with Article 47 of the **United Nations** Charter, assists and advises the Security Council in military planning. The work of the committee includes advisement on peacekeeping operations. The group officially consists of the Chiefs of Staff of the five permanent members (**France**, **Great Britain**, **Peoples Republic of China**, **Russia**, and **United States**) of the Security Council although subordinate officers actually attend the sessions. The committee was not very effective due to tensions in the Cold War. Its future role has still not been fully determined.

UNITED NATIONS MISSION FOR THE REFERENDUM IN WESTERN SAHARA (MINURSO). The Western Sahara, previously known as the Spanish Sahara, is located between Morocco and Mauritania in Northwestern Africa. Spain held the region as a colony between 1884 and 1976. Spain, Morocco, and Mauritania secretly agreed to partition the area between the latter two states, which had militarily occupied the Western Sahara after the official withdrawal of Spain. The *Frente Popular para la Liberación de Saguia el-Hamra y de Rio de Oro* (POLISARIO), a political and military group organized in 1973 to resist Spain, attempted to prevent the occupation of the area by Morocco and Mauritania but were defeated by superior arms and air power. The POLISARIO and other Saharan refugees withdrew to Algeria where they proclaimed the formation of the Saharan Arab Democratic Republic and initiated a guerilla war against Morocco and Mauritania. Forces of the POLISARIO concentrated their efforts on Mauritania and compelled that state to relinquish its claims to the Western Sahara in 1979 following a three-year war of attrition. Morocco annexed the region of the Western Sahara previously held by Mauritania, increased the size of its armed forces in the region, and began construction of a sand wall teeming with electronic detection devices. Morocco scored military successes while the POLISARIO dominated the political victories in the conflict over the Western Sahara. By 1988, the two parties began direct negotiations on the issue of the Western Sahara which prompted Perez de Cuellar, the Secretary-General of the **United Nations** (UN), to offer his assistance with a referendum that would be supervised by a peacekeeping mission consisting of military observers and civilian election monitors.

The Security Council officially authorized the mission on April 29, 1991, with Resolution 690 (1991). The UN developed the United Nations Mission for the Referendum in Western Sahara (MINURSO) to oversee a referendum slated to determine the fate of the Western Sahara. Originally the organization envisioned the need to spend $260 million for an estimated 36-week operation. However, the UN was already $200 million behind in the collection of funding from member states for peacekeeping during a period when even more missions were being fielded in Kuwait, northern Iraq, and the former Yugoslavia. The budget for the operation in the Western Sahara was slashed to a total of $177 million as a result of these difficulties.

Moroccan referendum-delaying tactics prevented the full deployment of the operation to the Western Sahara. King Hassan of Morocco allowed a maximum of 200 personnel from the peacekeeping operation to deploy to the region in late 1991. By early 1992, he agreed to permit the entry of the communications, air, and medical units to the Western Sahara. As of 1993, there were only 228 military observers with MINURSO due to the delay in the referendum. The UN personnel established ten field sites, five on each side of the Moroccan sand wall. Moroccan soldiers have hampered UN patrols from these sites due to the failure to negotiate a **status of forces agreement** between the host state (officially Morocco) and the international organization. The POLISARIO have been cooperative with the UN personnel since they see the referendum as being their best chance for securing their aims. The identification of individuals in the area in order to determine eligibility for voting has proven to be difficult but was declared complete by 2000. Discussions continue on the appeals process for voter identification, the repatriation of refugees, and other issues in the peace plan.

The composition of the operation, as originally envisioned by the UN, totaled 3,295 individuals, including 1,695 military and 1,600 civilian personnel. Roughly one-third of the civilians would be selected from the UN staff; one-third from member states; and the final third from the local area. MINURSO consists of 255 military personnel and 166 international civilians. Twenty-four states, including a rare appearance by China in a peacekeeping operation, have provided military observers to MINURSO while ten countries have contributed civilian police to the mission. There have been ten fatalities between 1991 and April 2003. MINURSO is funded by **Special Assessment** and costs approximately $50.5 million annually.

UNITED NATIONS MISSION IN BOSNIA AND HERZEGOVINA (UNMIBH). The **United Nations** (UN) Security Council, with Resolution 1035 (1995), mandated the United Nations Mission in Bosnia and Herzegovina (UNMIBH) on December 21, 1995, to support the **Implementation Force** (IFOR) of the **North Atlantic Treaty Organization** (NATO). UNMIBH deployed to **Bosnia and Herzegovina** with IFOR.

UNMIBH's mandate included monitoring law enforcement activities; advising and training law enforcement personnel; coordinating humanitarian relief; coordinating demining operations; monitoring human rights; overseeing and advising on the election process; and assisting with the rehabilitation of the infrastructure. The **United Nations International Police Task Force** (IPTF) was part of UN-MIBH. UNMIBH worked closely with IFOR and its successor, the **Stabilisation Force** (SFOR). UNMIBH, a relatively unseen peace-keeping operation in terms of public knowledge, made international headlines on July 1, 2002, when the **United States** vetoed the extension of its mandate in response to the rejection of the **International Criminal Court** (ICC) to exempt American soldiers on peacekeeping duty from potential prosecution. The United States believed that American soldiers could be wrongfully prosecuted on political grounds. A compromise emerged on July 12, 2002, allowing for the extension of UNMIBH's mandate.

The maximum authorized strength of UNMIBH was 2,057 civilian police and five military liaison officers. The actual strength as of July 2002 was approximately 1,550 police, three military liaison officers, and 1,800 international and local civilians. Forty-three countries contributed civilian police for UNMIBH and the military liaison observers came from Denmark, Poland, and Russia. Eleven members of UNMIBH died between December 1995 and December 2002. UNMIBH was financed by **Special Assessment** and costs approximately $145 million annually. It should be noted that the **United Nations Mission of Observers in Prevlaka** (UNMOP) drew its funding from the UNMIBH budget and was, thus, also affected by the ICC controversy. The **European Union Police Mission** (EUPM) replaced UN-MIBH and IPTF on January 1, 2003.

UNITED NATIONS MISSION IN COTE D'IVOIRE (MINUCI). The **United Nations** (UN) mandated the United Nations Mission in Côte d'Ivoire (MINUCI) on May 13, 2003. Rebellious elements of the army in Côte d'Ivoire rose against the government in September 2002 following a move to dismiss a couple of hundred soldiers from the army. The country quickly split into two segments—the northern half controlled by the rebels and the southern half under the government. **French** troops, stationed in the country, established a barrier zone between the two areas and officially formed themselves into a peacekeeping operation. The French peacekeepers were later joined by a separate peacekeeping mission from the **Economic Community of West African States** (ECOWAS) referred to as the **Economic**

Community of West African States Peacekeeping Force in Côte d'Ivoire (ECOFORCE).

Following the signing of the Linas-Marcoussis Accord by the government and rebel factions, the UN agreed to form and dispatch a small military observer force to oversee the peace process in cooperation with France and ECOWAS. The task of the small 76-man UN mission is to facilitate the implementation of the accord; coordinate and ensure trust between rebel, government, French, and ECOWAS forces; and implement the disarmament and demobilization process. MINUCI is funded by **Special Assessment**.

UNITED NATIONS MISSION IN EAST TIMOR (UNAMET). In 1974, Portugal, the colonizer of East Timor, began preparations for the territory to determine its future status—an independent state or integration into Indonesia. Civil strife erupted between the opposing groups supporting the two options. The East Timorese are heavily Roman Catholic, and the Indonesians are predominantly Muslim. This cultural and religious difference helped fuel the conflict. In 1976, Indonesia unilaterally intervened with its military and annexed East Timor. The **United Nations** (UN) did not recognize this action. Continued discussions between Indonesia and Portugal led to an agreement on May 5, 1999, to allow the UN to conduct a referendum to determine the will of the East Timorese people. The Security Council mandated the United Nations Mission in East Timor (UN-AMET) on June 11, 1999, by Resolution 1246 (1999) to assist in this process.

UNAMET's mandate provided the operation with the mission to oversee the transition period as East Timor conducted a referendum to determine whether the people wanted special autonomy within the Republic of Indonesia. UNAMET personnel assisted with the registration of East Timorese voters. A large majority of the population rejected proposed autonomy within Indonesia and preferred independence. Pro-Indonesian militias, with some support from the Indonesian military, initiated a campaign of violence. Approximately half of the East Timorese population became internal refugees and many were killed. The majority of those serving in UNAMET were evacuated to Australia for safety. A small group of UNAMET personnel remained in their headquarters in the capital of Dili. UN negotiations with Indonesia resulted in an agreement on September 12, 1999, permitting the deployment of an international military force to assist in stabilizing the situation. The peacekeepers, known as the **International Force in East Timor** (INTER-FET), arrived on September 20, 1999. Additional discussions between the UN, Indonesia, and Portugal resulted in the transfer of the territory to UN administration. The Security Council opted to replace UNAMET with a new operation mandated to help the international organization administer the territory.

The maximum authorized strength of UNAMET included 50 military liaison officers, 271 police, 425 UN volunteers, 242 international civilians, and 668 local civilians. Fourteen countries provided military observers and 31 states dispatched civilian police officers to UNAMET. The operation cost approximately $100 million and was primarily funded by contributions from **Australia**, Finland, **Japan**, New Zealand, Norway, and Portugal.

UNITED NATIONS MISSION IN EL SALVADOR (MINUSAL). *See* UNITED NATIONS OBSERVER MISSION IN EL SALVADOR (ONUSAL).

UNITED NATIONS MISSION IN ETHIOPIA AND ERITREA (UNMEE). A border dispute between Ethiopia and Eritrea erupted into open warfare in May 1998. The **United Nations** (UN) and **Organization of African Unity** (OAU) immediately called for restraint and dispatched representatives to calm the crisis. Both states agreed at the annual OAU summit in July 1999 to abide by the Modalities for the Implementation of the OAU Framework Agreement. Both sides agreed to redeploy their military forces. Further discussion led to the signing of the Technical Arrangements for the Implementation of the OAU Framework Agreement and its Modalities. This document included a provision for the deployment of military observers to monitor the border area between the two states. Tensions remained high and the two parties began fighting again in May 2000 resulting in increased efforts of the UN and OAU to settle the crisis. The two belligerents signed a new document, the Agreement on Cessation of Hostilities Between Ethiopia and Eritrea, on June 18, 2000.

The UN Security Council originally mandated the United Nations Mission in Ethiopia and Eritrea (UNMEE) on June 31, 2000, by Resolution 1312 (2000). Like the **United Nations Organization Mission in the Democratic Republic of the Congo**, the UN planned to field UNMEE in stages based on acceptance of the belligerents of the cease-fire agreement. The first stage called for the deployment of observers to the capitals of the two states to serve as a military liaison. The UN provided UNMEE's first stage with a mandate to establish and maintain a liaison presence with both states; put into operation the mechanism for verifying the cessation of hostilities; prepare for the establishment of a Military Coordination Commission; and assist in planning for the later states of the UNMEE. The second stage involved dispatching approximately 100 military observers and additional civilian personnel. The third stage included the deployment of the main body of peacekeepers into a neutral demilitarized zone along the border and totaled approximately 4,300 soldiers.

The UN Security Council mandated the third stage of UNMEE on September 15, 2000, by Resolution 1320 (2000). UNMEE's new mission includes monitoring the cessation of hostilities; monitoring the redeployment of Ethiopian and Eritrean forces; ensuring the military forces of both states remain 25 kilometers apart; monitoring a temporary security zone between the two belligerents; providing technical assistance for humanitarian mine clearing; and assisting with human rights monitoring.

Ethiopia and Eritrea signed a peace agreement on December 12, 2000, in Algiers. The document provided for a Boundary Commission to examine the demarcation of the common border between Ethiopia and Eritrea. The commission concluded its review in April 2002 but the border situation was not fully settled at the same time. In May 2002, Ethiopia began restricting the movement of UNMEE personnel along the border. Political relations between UNMEE and Ethiopia have remained tense.

The maximum authorized strength of UNMEE is 4,200 soldiers and the operation includes approximately 500 international and local civilians. Forty-five countries, including **Switzerland**, have dispatched military personnel to UNMEE. The Swiss contribution is unique due to the neutrality of the state and the fact it did not become a full member of the UN until late 2002. Three peacekeepers died while serving in UNMEE between June 2000 and April 2003. UN- MEE is funded by a **Special Assessment** and costs approximately $206 million annually.

UNITED NATIONS MISSION IN HAITI (UNMIH). Haiti's demo- cratically elected president, Jean Bertrand Aristide, lost power to a military coup on September 30, 1991. Violence erupted across the country as supporters of the coup murdered backers of President Aristide and committed numerous human rights violations. The **United Nations** (UN) began debating how to handle the issue and eventually imposed an arms and oil embargo in June 1993. This act was suspended after successful negotiations to end the crisis. On Sep- tember 23, 1993, the Security Council passed Resolution 867 (1993) which mandated the United Nations Mission in Haiti (UNMIH). The mission was envisioned as a cooperative effort with the **Organiza- tion of American States** and would help modernize the Haitian mil- itary and establish a new police force. The peacekeeping mission did not have the authority to intervene in the civil crisis facing the island and did not have the unqualified acceptance of the military govern- ment in power.

The Haitian government refused to implement the peace agree- ment. In October 1993, the **United States** ship *Harlan County* at- tempted to land American and Canadian personnel to join peace- keepers who had previously arrived in the capital. Mobs organized by the government prevented the ship from docking. Following growing tensions, the remaining peacekeepers withdrew from Haiti in January 1994. By July 1994, the few UN observers in Haiti were ordered to depart the country. The Security Council, in Resolution 940 (1994), mandated the formation of a **Multinational Force in Haiti** (MNF) to topple the illegal Haitian government. The same resolution altered UNMIH's mandate and authorized the force to help provide a secure and stable environment and assist in the professionalization of the Haitian military and the establishment of a separate civilian police force.

The MNF deployed to Haiti on September 19, 1994, and secured the return of President Aristide on October 15, 1994. The MNF handed over security responsibility to UNMIH on March 31, 1995.

UNMIH remained in the country until June 30, 1996, when it transferred its responsibility to the **United Nations Support Mission in Haiti** (UNMIH). The maximum authorized strength of UNMIH was 1,200 military personnel, 300 civilian police, and 240 international and local civilians. Twenty-four countries contributed military personnel to UNMIH while 19 states provided civilian police. There were nine fatalities between 1993 and 1996. UNMIH was funded by **Special Assessment** and cost $315.8 million. *See also* UNITED NATIONS CIVILIAN POLICE MISSION IN HAITI; UNITED NATIONS OBSERVATION GROUP FOR THE VERIFICATION OF ELECTIONS IN HAITI; UNITED NATIONS TRANSITION MISSION IN HAITI.

UNITED NATIONS MISSION IN THE CENTRAL AFRICAN RE-PUBLIC (MINURCA). The **United Nations** (UN) recognized the inability of the African states in the **Inter-African Force in the Central African Republic** (MISAB) to continue the operation following the pending withdrawal of French troops and logistical support. In response, the Security Council passed Resolution 1159 (1998) on March 27, 1998, mandating the United Nations Mission in the Central African Republic (MINURCA). The global organization fielded MINURCA in April 1998. MINURCA's mandate called for the mission to assist in maintaining security and stability in and around the capital of Bangui; assist the national army to maintain law and order; supervise the disarmament process; assist in the short-term police trainer's program; and provide advice and support in the planned legislative elections. In July, the Security Council passed a resolution adding a mission to conduct limited-duration reconnaissance patrols outside of the capital. MINURCA successfully helped oversee the election process in the country and was phased out by the end of June 2000. The peacekeeping operation was replaced by the United Nations Peace-Building Support Office in the Central African Republic.

The maximum authorized strength of MINURCA was 1,350 troops and military support personnel, 24 civilian policemen, and up to approximately 250 civilian staff. Fourteen states (11 from Africa) contributed military personnel to MINURCA and there were two fatalities between 1998 and 2000. MINURCA was financed by a **Special Assessment** and the total operation cost approximately $101.3 million.

UNITED NATIONS MISSION OF OBSERVERS IN PREVLAKA (UNMOP). The **United Nations** (UN) Security Council mandated the **United Nations Confidence Restoration Mission in Croatia** (UNCRO) on March 31, 1995, to replace the **United Nations Protection Force** (UNPROFOR) personnel fielded in **Croatia**. UNCRO's mandate ended on January 15, 1996. However, the UN opted to maintain a presence to ensure the continued demilitarization of Croatia's Prevlaka peninsula. The United Nations Mission of Observers in Prevlaka (UNMOP) began operations on February 1, 1996, under a mandate in Security Council Resolution 1038 (1996) to fulfill this role. UNMOP's mandate included monitoring the demilitarization of the Prevlaka peninsula and of neighboring areas in Croatia and the Federal Republic of **Yugoslavia**. UNMOP conducted regular coordination meetings with the **Stabilisation Force** (SFOR) fielded in **Bosnia and Herzegovina**. The maximum authorized strength of UNMOP was 27 military observers, and 12 international and local civilians. Twenty-two states, including the traditionally neutral **Switzerland**, provided observers to UNMOP. UNMOP's funding was included in the budget of the **United Nations Mission in Bosnia and Herzegovina** (UNMIBH).

UNMOP and UNMIBH, relatively unseen peacekeeping operations in terms of public knowledge, made international headlines on July 1, 2002, when the United States vetoed the extension of UNMIBH's mandate in response to the rejection of the **International Criminal Court** (ICC) to exempt American soldiers on peacekeeping duty from potential prosecution. The United States believed that American soldiers could be wrongfully prosecuted on political grounds. A compromise emerged on July 12, 2002, allowing for the extension of the mandate. UNMIBH is financed by Special Assessment and costs approximately $145 million annually. It should be noted that since UNMOP draws its funding from the UNMIBH budget, the threat to UNMIBH's mandate during the ICC controversy had a direct impact on the resources required to continue UNMOP as a peacekeeping mission. UNMOP was terminated on December 15, 2002, two weeks prior to the **European Police Mission** replacing UNMIBH.

UNITED NATIONS MISSION OF OBSERVERS IN TAJIKISTAN (UNMOT). On September 24, 1993, the **Commonwealth of Inde-**

pendent States (CIS) mandated the **Commonwealth of Independent States Peacekeeping Force**. **United Nations** (UN) envoys and teams assisted in the negotiation process among the belligerents in Tajikistan that resulted in a cease-fire agreement in September 1994. Talks between the belligerents continued through the end of 1994. On December 14, 1994, the UN Security Council mandated the United Nations Mission of Observers in Tajikistan (UNMOT) with Resolution 968 (1994). The Mandate of UNMOT included monitoring the implementation of the cease-fire along the Tajik-Afghan border; investigating reports of cease-fire violations; maintaining liaison with the CIS and **Organization for Security and Cooperation in Europe** (OSCE) peace operations within Tajikistan; and providing support for the Secretary-General's envoy. A new opposition offensive nullified the cease-fire agreement by July 1996.

A second cease-fire was signed in December 1996 and a general peace agreement on June 27, 1997. The latter agreement initiated a transitional period that included the return of refugees and the demobilization of opposition fighters. The belligerents requested the UN to provide some form of oversight during the period. The Security Council expanded the mandate on November 14, 1997, with Resolution 1138 (1997), and provided UNMOT with the mission to monitor the assembly and disarmament of opposition fighters; coordinate UN assistance to Tajikistan; and provide good offices and advice. At the same time the UN increased the authorized size of UNMOT from 45 to 120 military observers. Tajikistan held legislative elections for its lower house on February 27, 2000, which were monitored by the UN and OSCE Joint Electoral Observation Mission. The Joint Mission noted that the elections did not meet minimum electoral standards. The upper house elections occurred on March 23, 2000. UN Secretary-General **Kofi Annan** announced that UNMOT had accomplished its mandate and the operation officially ended on May 15, 2000.

The maximum authorized strength of UNMOT was 120 military observers plus international and local civilian staff. The maximum deployed military strength only reached 81. Fifteen countries contributed military personnel to UNMOT and there were seven fatalities between 1994 and 2000. UNMOT was financed by a **Special Assessment** and the total operation cost approximately $64 million.

UNITED NATIONS MISSION OF SUPPORT IN EAST TIMOR (UNMISET). East Timor became an independent state on May 20, 2002, following years of being part of Indonesia. The **United Nations** (UN) played a significant role in negotiating between the two parties during the process. The UN fielded the **United Nations Transitional Administration in East Timor** (UNTAET) between 1999 and May 17, 2002. Just prior to East Timorese independence, the UN mandated and deployed a new peacekeeping operation, the United Nations Mission of Support in East Timor (UNMISET), on May 17, 2002. UNMISET's mandate includes providing assistance to the government to ensure political stability; maintaining interim law enforcement and public security; assisting in developing an East Timor Police Service; and contributing to the maintenance of the country's internal and external security. The initial maximum authorized strength of UNMISET is 5,000 peacekeepers and police along with over 1,000 international and local civilians. As of April 2003, there were 3,700 military personnel, 651 police, and 428 international civilians assigned to UNMISET. The intention is to slowly downsize the force between 2002 and 2004. Forty-six states contributed military personnel or civilian police to UNMISET, and ten UNMISET personnel have died between May 2002 and April 2003. UNMISET is financed by a **Special Assessment** and the annual operation costs approximately $316 million. *See also* INTERNATIONAL FORCE IN EAST TIMOR; UNITED NATIONS ASSISTANCE MISSION IN EAST TIMOR.

UNITED NATIONS OBSERVATION GROUP IN LEBANON (UNOGIL). Lebanon emerged from French colonial domination in 1943 with a constitution that divided the government among the dominant religious groups of the state. The Maronite Christians controlled the office of the presidency. However, each president could serve only one term. In May 1958, President Camille Cahmoun sought an amendment to the constitution that would allow him to seek a second term of office. This move prompted an armed uprising among Muslim elements of the country. The Lebanese executive branch of government charged that the United Arab Republic (**Egypt**) was supplying weapons to the rebels. In addition, the government accused armed personnel of entering Lebanon from Syria. Following a failure of the

League of Arab States to solve the crisis, the UN Security Council adopted Resolution 128 (1958) on June 11, 1958, calling for the dispatch of a neutral observation mission, which would be named the United Nations Observation Group in Lebanon (UNOGIL).

UNOGIL's mission in Lebanon involved the observation of the border with Syria to determine if armed personnel or weapons were crossing the frontier. The group did not have a mandate to halt any illegal movement of goods or personnel from Syria. Operations were carried out via daylight jeep patrols, the establishment of fixed observation posts, and flights of helicopters and light aircraft along the border. The peacekeepers began arriving on June 12, 1958. The initial personnel were detached from duty with the **United Nations Truce Supervision Organization** (UNTSO). UNOGIL reached a maximum strength of 591 military observers in November and consisted of personnel from 20 states.

Initially, the strength of UNOGIL stood at approximately 100 personnel. However, following a political crisis raised by the 1958 **United States** intervention in Lebanon and the dispatch of British paratroopers to Jordan, a Security Council compromise called for the increase in UNOGIL's size. The American and British troops departed the area, and the UN sent additional peacekeepers to Lebanon. Jordan refused to allow the establishment of a peacekeeping operation similar to UNOGIL on its territory. A few UNOGIL personnel were permitted to oversee the withdrawal of British forces from Jordan but returned to Lebanon after the evacuation. The election of a new President brought a truce to the fighting in Lebanon and better relations with the United Arab Republic. The Security Council accepted an UNOGIL recommendation that the operation be terminated due to the completion of the mandate. The last element of UNOGIL departed Lebanon on December 9, 1958. The UN funded UNOGIL through its regular budget and the total cost for the six-month operation came to $3.7 million.

UNITED NATIONS OBSERVER GROUP FOR THE VERIFICATION OF THE ELECTIONS IN HAITI (ONUVEH). The **United Nations** established the United Nations Observer Group for the Verification of the Elections in Haiti (ONUVEH) on October 10, 1990, under General Assembly Resolution 45/2 at an estimated cost of $6.5

million. The mission of ONUVEH included the monitoring of elections scheduled for Haiti. The operation was envisioned as including 193 observers from 43 countries, the core of which would be 39 peacekeepers selected from the **United Nations Transition Assistance Group** (UNTAG) and United Nations Observer Mission for the Verification of Elections in Nicaragua (ONUVEN). The chief election observer, Horacio Boneo, was the deputy chief election observer from ONUVEN. Initially, 64 security observers from Algeria, Canada, Colombia, **France**, Spain, and Venezuela were deployed to Haiti. The observers withdrew following the completion of the election process in Haiti. However, the military ousted President-Elect Jean Aristide of Haiti and returned the state to autocratic rule in September 1991. On September 23, 1993, the Security Council approved a new peacekeeping force for Haiti known as the **United Nations Mission in Haiti** (UNMIH).

UNITED NATIONS OBSERVER GROUP IN CENTRAL AMERICA (ONUCA). The United Nations Observer Group in Central America (ONUCA) resulted from a locally originated peace process. Colombia, Mexico, Panama, and Venezuela formed an informal organization known as the Contadora Group in 1983 in the attempt to settle the civil wars raging across Central America. The region had suffered from a very lengthy period of internal conflicts. The Presidents of Costa Rica, El Salvador, Guatemala, Honduras, and Nicaragua joined the Contadora Group, which developed the Procedure for the Establishment of a Firm and Lasting Peace in Central America in August 1987 in Esqupulas, Guatemala. The **Organization of American States** (OAS) and **United Nations** (UN) were requested to monitor the peace process and participate in the **International Verification and Follow-up Commission** (CIVS).

General Assembly Resolution 42/1 of October 7, 1987, confirmed the intention of the global body to assist the Central American states. A joint UN and OAS team visited the area in October 1987 to evaluate the security needs of the peace process. On February 8, 1989, UN Secretary-General Javier Perez de Cueller met with representatives of the five Central American states. The group issued what is known as the Costa del Sol Declaration to settle the crisis within Nicaragua. The Secretary-General fielded the United Nations Observer Mission to Verify the Electoral Process in Nicaragua (ONUVEN) on August 25, 1989. This civilian-manned mission oversaw the successful election process in Nicaragua. The United Nations and OAS also formed the **International Support and Verification Commission** (CIAV) to assist in the monitoring of the demobilization of Nicaraguan guerillas, also known as Contras. Brigadier-General Pericles Ferreira Gomes of Brazil, the Chief Military Observer for the **United Nations Angola Verification Mission I**, conducted a reconnaissance of the region between September 3 and 23, 1989. After reviewing the report submitted by Gomes, the Secretary-General recommended the deployment of ONUCA.

The mandate of ONUCA included the verification of the cessation of aid to irregular and insurrectionist forces and the non-use of the territory of one state to launch attacks on other states. ONUCA originally consisted of military observers and support personnel from Canada, Colombia, Ireland, Spain, and Venezuela, who were later joined by observers from Brazil, Ecuador, India, and Sweden. Argentina offered four patrol boats and crews for use in the Gulf of Fonseca. Canada contributed a helicopter unit and West Germany provided a civilian medical unit and civilian aircraft and crews. Venezuela dispatched a combat battalion between April and June 1990 for the purpose of demobilizing the Nicaraguan resistance.

An advance party of ONUCA peacekeepers arrived with Chief Military Observer Major-General Agustin Quesada Gomez of Spain on December 3, 1989. Gomez established his headquarters at Tegucigalpa, Honduras, and set up liaison units in the capital of the five Central American states. ONUCA dispatched patrols of ten military observers to oversee the peace process. ONUCA's mandate was expanded on March 27, 1990, via Security Council Resolution 650 (1990), to include the cease-fire and demobilization of irregular forces throughout the region as requested in the Declaration of San Isidro de Coronado. A battalion from Venezuela arrived to assist in the demobilization of the Nicaraguan resistance within the country of Honduras. The mandate was further expanded on April 20, 1990, via Security Council Resolution 653 (1990), to allow ONUCA to oversee the cease-fire and separation of forces inside Nicaragua itself. The personnel from ONUCA monitored five security zones in Nicaragua. Each security zone was surrounded by a 20-kilometer demilitarized zone for the safety of the demobilizing personnel. After a rocky beginning, ONUCA completed the demobilization process. ONUCA departed the area in January 1992.

ONUCA reached a maximum strength of 1,038 at the end of May 1989. This had been reduced to approximately 500 personnel by the end of 1991. ONUCA did not suffer any casualties during its deployment. The UN funded ONUCA by a **Special Assessment** on member states. The total cost between 1989 and 1992 amounted to $88.5 million.

UNITED NATIONS OBSERVER MISSION FOR THE VERIFICATION OF ELECTIONS IN NICARAGUA (ONUVEN). *See* UNITED NATIONS OBSERVER GROUP IN CENTRAL AMERICA (ONUCA).

UNITED NATIONS OBSERVER MISSION IN ANGOLA (MONUA). The **Angolan** government had faced opposition since independence from Portugal. After a series of truces verified by **United Nations** (UN) peacekeeping operations, the belligerents signed the Lusaka Protocol in November 1994. The protocol called for an integrated national army and police force as well as a reconciliation government. The **United Nations Angola Verification Mission III** departed the country in June 1997 after completing its mission associated with the protocol.

The UN Security Council mandated the United Nations Observer Mission Angola (MONUA) by Resolution 1118 (1997) on June 30, 1997, to assist Angola in the national reconciliation process. MONUA's multi-task mission included verifying the neutrality of the National Police; incorporating National Union for the Total Independence of Angola (UNITA) personnel into the National Police; quartering and deploying a rapid reaction police force; guaranteeing the free passage of civilians; protecting civil and political rights and freedoms; conducting joint patrols with the National Police; inspecting prisons; overseeing the disarmament process; providing security for UNITA leaders; overseeing human rights issues; verifying the ceasefire; investigating troop movements; and monitoring the integration of government and UNITA personnel into a national army.

The belligerents proved to be slow in enacting the provisions of the Lusaka Protocol. Disarmament of UNITA was difficult as both sides mistrusted each other. The UN imposed a series of sanctions against UNITA for its failure to comply with the protocol. The global body also recognized the need for the continuance of MONUA and extended its mandate yet reduced the size of its force. During the summer of 1998, UNITA stepped up its military operations frustrating the UN even further. **Special Representative** Beye of Mali died in an aircraft accident while consulting with regional leaders about the crisis. The military situation continued to deteriorate as UNITA forces increased their ambushes and incursions against government forces and civilian targets. Concern grew for MONUA personnel assigned in UNITA-held areas. On December 7, 1998, the UNITA leadership allowed UN aircraft to land and remove the MONUA peacekeepers. Two UN and four commercial aircraft were downed over UNITA territory by January 1999. The Security Council opted to not extend MONUA's mandate after its February 26, 1999, expiration date.

The maximum authorized strength of MONUA was 3,279 troops and military support personnel, 289 civilian police observers, and numerous civilian staff. Personnel assigned to MONUA steadily declined after July 1997 until the strength by the expiration of the mandate was 447 troops and 54 civilian police observers. Thirty-six states contributed military personnel to MONUA, and there were 17 total fatalities between 1997 and 2000. MONUA was financed by a **Special Assessment** and the total operation cost over $300 million. *See also* UNITED NATIONS ANGOLA VERIFICATION MISSION I; UNITED NATIONS ANGOLA VERIFICATION MISSION II.

UNITED NATIONS OBSERVER MISSION IN EL SALVADOR (ONUSAL). The ongoing civil war between the government and rebels in El Salvador moved towards settlement during the opening of the 1990s. On July 26, 1990, the various parties signed the Agreement on Human Rights in San Jose. The agreement included a provision for the fielding of an international observer force to verify the protection of human rights. The **United Nations** (UN) agreed to mandate a peacekeeping operation to perform this task. Eventually known as the United Nations Observer Mission in El Salvador (ONUSAL), the mission was the first military/civilian peacekeeping unit mandated solely to verify compliance with the protection of human rights. ONUSAL did not originally have a mandate to verify the cease-fire in the conflict. Later, the mandate was expanded to include cease-fire observation based on an agreement dated December 31, 1991. ONUSAL's additional mission included monitoring public order pending the organization of a new civilian police force. The Security Council originally mandated ONUSAL with Resolution 693 (1991) on May 20, 1991. ONUSAL completed its mission on April 30, 1995. When ONUSAL departed, a small group of civilians, known as the United Nations Mission in El Salvador (MINUSAL), remained to provided oversight for the remaining points of the agreements. ONUSAL's maximum authorized strength consisted of 380 military observers, 631 civilian police, and 320 international and local civilian staff. There were five fatalities among ONUSAL personnel between July 1991 and April 1995. The mission was funded by **Special Assessment** and cost $107 million. *See also* UNITED NATIONS OBSERVER GROUP IN CENTRAL AMERICA.

UNITED NATIONS OBSERVER MISSION IN GEORGIA (UNOMIG). The **United Nations** (UN) Security Council mandated the United Nations Observer Mission in Georgia (UNOMIG) with Resolution 850 (1993) on August 24, 1993. The purpose of the operation was to verify the cease-fire of July 27, 1993, between the government of Georgia and the province of Abkhazia. The cease-fire collapsed on September 16, 1993. The UN modified UNOMIG's mandate and directed the mission to maintain contact with the belligerents and a Russian military force in the state. The UN modified the mandate again on July 27, 1994, and asked UNOMIG to also monitor a new cease-fire agreement; observe the **Commonwealth of Independent States Peacekeeping Forces in Georgia**; monitor heavy weapons storage sites; monitor the withdrawal of Georgian troops beyond the boundaries of Abkhazia; and investigate violations of the cease-fire. The situation in Georgia has been unstable since 1994. UNOMIG patrols have been fired upon and several UN peacekeepers have been abducted and held for various lengths of time. On October 8, 2001, a UNOMIG helicopter was shot down with the loss of all on board, including four military observers. The operation consists of 116 military observers and 96 international civilian staff. Twenty-three states have contributed military personnel to UNOMIG and there have been seven fatalities among UNOMIG personnel between August 1993 and April 2003. UNOMIG is funded by **Special Assessment** and costs approximately $28 million annually.

UNITED NATIONS OBSERVER MISSION IN LIBERIA (UN-OMIL). The **United Nations** (UN) Security Council mandated the United Nations Observer Mission in Liberia (UNOMIL) on September 22, 1993, in Resolution 866 (1993) to support the **Economic Community of West African States Monitoring Group** (ECO-MOG) in the Liberian peace process. UNOMIL's mandate included investigating cease-fire violations; monitoring compliance with the peace agreement; verifying the election process; helping coordinate humanitarian assistance; training of ECOMOG engineers in demining operations; and coordinating with ECOMOG. Renewed fighting delayed implementation of the agreement and planned elections. Delays continued and new provisions were added to the peace agreement.

On November 10, 1995, the Security Council added several new missions to UNOMIL's mandate including providing good offices to support ECOMOG and the Liberian transitional government; assisting in the maintenance of demobilization sites; and monitoring compliance of the belligerents with the peace agreement. Liberia held elections in July 1997, and the Security Council terminated UNOMIL's mandate on September 30, 1997.

The maximum authorized strength of UNOMIL was 303 military observers, 65 other soldiers, and approximately 200 international and local personnel. Twenty-two states (including the rare participation of China) contributed personnel to UNOMIL without any fatalities. It is interesting to note that Zimbabwe refused an invitation to participate because it claimed it would not receive an adequate amount of cash from the UN as compensation for dispatching its soldiers to Liberia. UNOMIL was financed by **Special Assessment** and the total operation cost approximately $104 million.

UNITED NATIONS OBSERVER MISSION IN SIERRA LEONE (UNOMSIL). The **United Nations** (UN) Security Council mandated the **United Nations Observer Mission in Sierra Leone** (UNOM-SIL) on July 13, 1998, with Resolution 1181 (1998), to assist the **Economic Community of West African States Monitoring Group**

(ECOMOG) **in Sierra Leone** with the disarming of combatants and restructuring the military of Sierra Leone. UNOMSIL's mandate included monitoring the security situation in the country; overseeing the disarmament of former belligerents; and monitoring the role of ECOMOG within Sierra Leone. UNOMSIL included an authorized 70 military observers and approximately 120 other personnel. However, approximately half of this strength was not actually fielded until August 1999. Opposition forces launched a new offensive and captured over half of the country, including most of the capital, by January 1999 before succumbing to an ECOMOG counteroffensive in February. UNOMSIL personnel evacuated Sierra Leone and traveled to Guinea during this period. New negotiations between the belligerents began in May 1999 resulting in the Lome Peace Agreement in July. The Security Council authorized the expansion of UNOMSIL to 210 military observers in August 1999. On October 22, 1999, the Security Council mandated a new peacekeeping operation, the **United Nations Assistance Mission in Sierra Leone** (UNAMSIL), and ordered that the new organization absorb the mission and personnel of UNOMSIL.

The maximum fielded strength of UNOMSIL was 210 military observers and 142 other personnel. Twenty-five states (including the rare participation of China) contributed personnel to UNOMSIL without any fatalities. UNOMSIL was financed by **Special Assessment** and the total operation cost approximately $52.6 million.

UNITED NATIONS OBSERVER MISSION IN SOUTH AFRICA (UNOMSA). Although not a peacekeeping mission in the traditional sense of the term, the United Nations Observer Mission to South Africa (UNOMSA) was an observer operation fielded by the **United Nations** (UN) to monitor the political process in **South Africa's** transition to a democracy where all citizens, regardless of race, would have the opportunity to participate politically. Former **United States** Secretary of State Cyrus Vance and Secretary-General **Boutros Boutros-Ghali** recommended the deployment of the mission on behalf of the United Nations following an escalation of political violence in June 1992. The Security Council authorized 60 international observers for the operation in August 1992. The observers monitored political rallies and meetings throughout South Africa.

UNITED NATIONS OBSERVER MISSION UGANDA-RWANDA (UNOMUR). In 1991, Rwanda's seven million people were divided roughly into three groups—Hutu (90.4 percent), Tutsi (8.2 percent), and Twa (.4 precent). The differences between the Hutu and Tutsi are more social than ethnic but are still considerable. The Tutsi have faced discrimination within **Rwanda** for many decades. In 1990, a Tutsi exile group in Uganda, the Rwandan Patriotic Fund (RPF), invaded Rwanda in hope of toppling the Hutu-dominated government. African calls for a cease-fire met with limited success. The Rwandan government accused Uganda of supporting the RPF. In reply, the **United Nations** (UN) Security Council mandated the United Nations Observer Mission Uganda-Rwanda (UNOMUR) on June 22, 1993, with Resolution 846 (1993). UNOMUR's mandate included monitoring the border between Uganda and Rwanda to prevent weapons from entering Rwanda. The Security Council voted on October 5, 1993, to deploy a second peacekeeping operation, the **United Nations Assistance Mission in Rwanda** (UNAMIR), to oversee the cease-fire within Rwanda itself. UNAMIR absorbed UNOMUR for administration and funding on December 21, 1993, although UNOMUR did continue as a separate peacekeeping mission.

Following the Rwandan genocide, the Security Council terminated UNOMUR on September 21, 1994. UNAMIR remained in place until March 8, 1996. The maximum authorized strength of UNOMUR was 81 military observers supported by international and local civilians. There were not any fatalities during the mission. UNOMUR was funded by **Special Assessment** and cost $2.3 million from June 1993 to December 1993. From December 1993 to September 1994, UNOMUR was funded through the UNAMIR budget.

UNITED NATIONS OPERATION IN MOZAMBIQUE (ONUMOZ). Mozambique erupted into civil war following its independence from Portugal in 1975. The conflict, fanned by external sponsors, engulfed the entire society for two decades. A cease-fire agreement in the civil war allowed the **United Nations** (UN) to step in and propose a peacekeeping operation to oversee the cessation of hostilities, disarming of rebel forces, the integration of a new army, and the general election process. The Security Council mandated the United Nations Operation in Mozambique (ONUMOZ) on December

16, 1992, with Resolution 797 (1992). After several difficulties in negotiating the deployment of the peacekeepers, UN troops finally began arriving in Mozambique at the end of October 1993.

The peacekeepers were organized into five independent battalions of approximately 850 men each, three logistics companies, a headquarters company, and air and communications units. In addition, there were approximately 350 military observers. The peacekeepers carried out the additional mission of replacing the soldiers of Zimbabwe who guarded the Beria, Limpopo, and Nacal corridors as well as the national road in Tete Provence. The mandate of ONUMOZ formally ended on December 9, 1994, following successful elections in the country.

The maximum authorized strength was 6,625 soldiers, 354 military observers, 1,144 civilian police, and over 2,000 international and local civilians. By November 1994, ONUMOZ consisted of 3,941 soldiers, 204 military observers, and 918 civilian police. Twenty-five states contributed military personnel, and 28 countries provided civilian police to ONUMOZ between 1992 and 1994. There were 24 fatalities among ONUMOZ personnel. The mission was funded through a **Special Assessment** and cost a total of $486.7 million.

UNITED NATIONS OPERATION IN SOMALIA I (UNOSOM I).
Somalia, a country of one ethnic group but many clans, erupted in civil war as rivals of President Siad Barre moved to replace him. Following Barre's removal in January 1991, the country devolved into a state of anarchy and chaos with rival clans preying on each other. The inability of humanitarian organizations to curb the death rates from starvation and malnourishment led **United Nations** (UN) Secretary-General **Boutros Boutros-Ghali** to criticize the West for ignoring African problems while displaying concern for European crises such as the conflict in **Yugoslavia**. In response, the Security Council passed Resolution 751 (1992) on April 21, 1992, which mandated the United Nations Operation in Somalia I (UNOSOM I). The stated purpose of UNOSOM I was to facilitate an immediate and effective cessation of hostilities and the maintenance of a cease-fire throughout the country in order to promote the process of reconciliation and political settlement and to provide urgent humanitar-

ian assistance. UNOSOM I would accomplish its mission by visible patrols within Mogadishu, the capital. In addition the peacekeepers would accompany humanitarian aid convoys from the airport and port facilities of Mogadishu to the distribution points. It has been estimated that up to 40 percent of all food aid was being hijacked by the Somali factions.

The first peacekeepers, an unarmed advance group of 50 military personnel, arrived in August 1992. The first armed peacekeepers, a 40-man contingent from Pakistan, arrived on September 14, 1992, after the Somali factions granted grudging permission for the fielding of the operation. The remaining members of a 500-man Pakistani battalion arrived by the end of the month. Canada pledged a 750-man unit destined for the northeastern city of Bossaso. Other states offering 750-man peacekeeping contingents for UNOSOM I included Belgium, **Egypt**, and **Nigeria**. It is interesting to note that the new state of Eritrea, which had just won its independence from Ethiopia, offered to provide troops for UNOSOM I, but the UN declined the offer for political reasons.

The UN planned to establish four zones in the country and post a 750-man battalion into each including a civilian director of operations. Although the Security Council authorized up to 3,000 peacekeepers for UNOSOM I, the number of personnel never reached that amount due to harassment and opposition offered by the Somali factions. In particular, **Mohammed Farah Aidid**, the leader of the largest faction in Mogadishu, accepted the idea of the 500-man battalion but objected to the number of peacekeepers being increased to approximately 3,000 personnel.

The number of personnel assigned to UNOSOM I was frozen at 715 upon the arrival of the **Unified Task Force** (UNITAF) in December. The Pakistanis suffered greatly at the hands of the local factions. Reports indicate that Pakistani patrols were even robbed of money and clothing while performing their duties. Another report indicates that the Pakistani commander had to feed his troops by ordering food from home with a personal credit card while waiting for the UN to implement a logistical system in Somalia. Continued problems and the inability to deploy additional peacekeepers persuaded the **United States** to lead UNITAF into Somalia in December 1992. The **United Nations Operation in Somalia II** (UNOSOM II) officially replaced UNOSOM

I on May 4, 1993, following a stabilization of the situation in Somalia by UNITAF.

UNITED NATIONS OPERATION IN SOMALIA II (UNOSOM II).
The United Nations Operation in Somalia II (UNOSOM II) is actually a rebirth of the failed **United Nations Operation in Somalia I** (UNO-SOM I). Following the inability of UNOSOM I to accomplish its mission due to the opposition of the Somali factions, the **United States** led the **Unified Task Force** (UNITAF) into Somalia. After the stabilization of the political situation in and around Mogadishu, the **United Nations** (UN) moved to mandate a new peacekeeping operation to replace UN-OSOM I. The United States and the UN agreed to the replacement on February 1, 1993. The **Security Council** mandated UNOSOM II on April 24, 1992, with Resolution 751 (1992). UNOSOM II would monitor the cease-fire in Somalia and gradually replace UNITAF as well as escort humanitarian aid deliveries. The global body authorized UNO-SOM II to maintain and restore peace where required.

Lieutenant-General **Cevik Bir** of Turkey was selected as the first **Force Commander**. It has been reported that Bir was selected because the United States refused to serve under a commander who lacked significant **North Atlantic Treaty Organization** (NATO) experience. In other words, the Force Commander must come from a NATO member and not an African, Asian, or Latin American Third World state.

The UN authorized UNOSOM II's strength at up to 28,000 peacekeepers. Thirty-three states served as the initial contributors to UN-OSOM II. It is interesting to note that UNOSOM II marks the peacekeeping debut (armed personnel) for the states of Germany, Namibia, South Korea, and the United Arab Emirates. UNOSOM II also had a Quick Reaction Force consisting of 1,167 American soldiers. However, this unit was never officially a part of UNOSOM II. There were 143 fatalities among UNOSOM II personnel between March 1993 and March 1995.

After the 1994 withdrawal by most Western states, UNOSOM II's composition included approximately 20,000 personnel. Egypt, India, and Pakistan provided the bulk (approximately 15,000) of the assigned combat troops. Other combat contingents remaining with UN-OSOM II included Bangladesh, Botswana, Malaysia, Nepal, Nigeria, and Zimbabwe.

UNOSOM II and UNITAF are well known for their armed clashes with the forces of Mohammed Farah Aidid within Mogadishu. On June 5, 1993, 24 Pakistani peacekeepers died in an ambush initiated by Aidid's followers, which resulted in a UN-mandated manhunt for the Somali faction leader. On October 3, 1993, American forces clashed with Aidid's faction, leading to at least 18 battle deaths for the former and a reported figure for the latter in the hundreds. Peacekeeper deaths with UNOSOM II numbered 69 between May and October 1993 with an additional 200 personnel wounded. The ensuing controversy over casualties led to most Western states opting to withdraw from UNOSOM II from late 1993 to early 1994. On November 4, 1994, the Security Council voted to withdraw UNOSOM II by March 31, 1995, following the repeated refusal of the Somali factions to implement a cease-fire. In addition, the factions continued to ambush peacekeeper convoys and the mounting casualties, which numbered over 130 by the end of 1994, helped prompt the global body to remove the international force. The UN funded UNOSOM II through a **Special Assessment** and the total cost was $1.6 billion.

UNITED NATIONS OPERATION IN THE CONGO (ONUC). The Congo (current Democratic Republic of the Congo) emerged from colonization under Belgium in 1960. The new state gained independence with only a six-month period of preparation. A last minute political compromise established a government with Joseph Kasa Vubu as the President and Patrice Lumumba as the Prime Minister of the state. Belgium negotiated an agreement guaranteeing the former metropole an economic and military presence in the new country. On July 5, 1960, the Congolese soldiers of the new state's military mutinied against their Belgian commanders. Following attacks on European civilians, the Belgians asked Lumumba to request their military assistance. Lumumba refused and attempted a series of reforms in an attempt to Africanize the military. The Secretary-General of the **United Nations** (UN) persuaded the Congo to request assistance from the global body. However, before the assistance could materialize, the Belgians unilaterally intervened in the crisis. In turn, Lumumba and Kasa Vubu asked the UN to provide their state with military assistance.

Secretary-General **Dag Hammarskjöld** invoked Article 99 of the UN Charter to convene the Security Council. Hammarskjöld was the first Secretary-General to use this article, which allows the holder of his position to present an issue of international significance to the Security Council for deliberation. At the same time, Hammarskjöld recommended the deployment of a peacekeeping operation to assist the Congolese government. Originally referred to as the United Nations Force in the Congo, the mission later became known as the United Nations Operation in the Congo (ONUC). Hammarskjöld envisioned the force comprising a core of African contingents. Other non-African contingents would ensure an international mixture in ONUC. Ethiopia, Ghana, Guinea, Federation of Mali (present-day Mali and Senegal), Morocco, and Tunisia offered to provide soldiers for ONUC. The Secretary-General accepted the offers from all of the states except the Federation of Mali, whose troops he activated later. The original five African states provided the core of 4,000 peacekeepers. In addition, the global body sought contingents from three European, one Asian, and one Latin American state. **Ralph J. Bunche** accepted the post of Special Representative in the Congo, and **Lieutenant-General Carl C. von Horn** assumed the position as ONUC's first **Force Commander**.

Two existing peacekeeping operations provided assistance in the deployment of ONUC. General von Horn and his initial staff transferred to the Congo from the **United Nations Truce Supervision Organization** (UNTSO) and a Swedish battalion arrived from the **United Nations Emergency Force I** (UNEF I). Originally, the United Nations viewed ONUC's mission as a temporary security force that would remain neutral in the internal conflicts within the Congo. The **rules of engagement** called upon the peacekeepers to use force only in self-defense. This rule would be altered as the duration of ONUC lengthened. Tunisian soldiers were the first peacekeepers to arrive in the Congo. The Tunisians landed on July 15, 1960, and were followed within days by the other previously mentioned African contingents as well as combat units from India, Ireland, Liberia, and Sweden.

Although the mandate of ONUC can be traced through a series of resolutions, Security Council Resolution 143 (1960) is the first to authorize the Secretary-General to field a peacekeeping mission in the

Congo. The original objectives included oversight of the Belgian withdrawal and assistance to the Congolese government to maintain law and order in the state. By August 1960, UN soldiers replaced the Belgian military throughout the Congo except in two base areas and Katanga province, which had declared its secession from the state. Lumumba requested ONUC personnel to assist his government in subjugating Katanga. Further negotiations led to a peaceful entry of ONUC peacekeepers into Katanga and the bases to replace the Belgians. Political divisions within the Congo culminated with Kasa Vubu and Lumumba dismissing each other and the lack of an effective Congolese government for nearly one year. This incident led to coordination problems for ONUC, which was mandated to assist the Congolese government, an institution which was now difficult to identify.

Lumumba was murdered by political rivals in January 1961. In protest several states withdrew their contingents from ONUC. In addition, the Soviet Union demanded Hammarskjöld's resignation and refused to recognize his authority as Secretary-General. The Security Council dramatically altered the mandate of ONUC on February 15, 1961, when Resolution 161 (1961) authorized the operation to help prevent a civil war in the Congo. ONUC could use force in this mission but only as a last resort. The peacekeepers, who had been suffering casualties in the civil war, initiated their first limited offensive in Katanga in April 1961. Further attacks on ONUC personnel occurred at **Port-Francqui** and **Kindu** and later at **Niemb** and **Elisabethville**. Katanga ended its secession from the Congo by January 1963. The UN reduced the strength of ONUC throughout 1963 so that by December the total manpower equaled 6,535 peacekeepers. The General Assembly in Resolution 1885 (XVIII) of October 18, 1963, opted to fund ONUC until June 30, 1964. At the termination date, ONUC consisted of 3,297 peacekeepers.

The funding of ONUC resulted in a political controversy at the UN and the introduction of a novel way to finance the operation. Several member states refused to pay their portions of the assessment set by the General Assembly. The Soviet Union's refusal to pay its peacekeeping tab for ONUC, as well as the **United Nations Emergency Force I** (UNEF I) in the Sinai, led to what is often called the **Article 19 Crisis**. The cash shortfall of ONUC, which cost the global body $400 million between 1960 and 1964, led the UN to attempt a unique approach for financing a peacekeeping operation. The world body offered bonds for sale to countries across the globe. These notes were similar to bonds offered by the governments in member states when they needed to raise cash.

UNITED NATIONS ORGANIZATION MISSION IN THE DEMOCRATIC REPUBLIC OF THE CONGO (MONUC). A war involving military forces from the Democratic Republic of the Congo (DRC) and numerous neighboring states and internal groups lasted throughout the mid- and late 1990s. By the end of that decade, the conflict involved military forces from approximately ten African states with major units from Angola, Namibia, and Zimbabwe aiding the DRC against internal groups allied with Uganda and **Rwanda**. On July 10, 1999, the major states involved in the conflict and one major guerilla group signed what is known as the Lusaka Agreement. The document offered numerous provisions to stabilize the situation in eastern DRC and included the introduction of an unspecified "force" to be mandated and deployed by the **United Nations** (UN) to assist in the peace process.

The UN Security Council mandated the United Nations Organization Mission in the Democratic Republic of the Congo (MONUC) on August 6, 1999, with Resolution 1258 (1999). The UN opted to implement a new strategy in peacekeeping deployment. Rather than dispatching the entire operation immediately, the organization decided to send peacekeepers in stages. As the belligerents proved they were honestly willing to abide by the Lusaka Agreement, the UN gradually altered MONUC's mandate to increase its size and scope of mission. The first stage included the deployment of 90 military liaison personnel with civilian staff to the capitals of the states signing the Lusaka Agreement. The second stage, authorized by Security Council Resolution 1279 (1999), involved the dispatch of up to 500 military observers to the DRC. The third stage, authorized by Security Council Resolution 1291 (2000), permitted the expansion of MONUC to approximately 5,500 military personnel. A three-stage strategy was repeated with the **United Nations Mission in Ethiopia and Eritrea** (UNMEE). In May 2003, MONUC faced a crisis as renewed fighting and murders erupted in the northeast area of the country. Following the deaths of hundreds of civilians and two UN peacekeepers, the world body called upon France and other states to organize an international force to restore order and prevent a "second **Rwanda**."

MONUC's mandate includes provisions for the operation to monitor the cease-fire agreement; maintain liaison with the headquarters of all military forces involved in the agreement; assist in the exchange/release of prisoners of war and military captives; supervise the redeployment of military units; facilitate humanitarian assistance and human rights monitoring; and assist with the identification and clearing of land mines.

The maximum authorized strength of MONUC is 5,537 military personnel with additional civilian assistance. The maximum deployed strength as of April 2003 was 4,314 military personnel and 574 international civilians. MONUC personnel suffered 13 fatalities between November 1999 and April 2003. MONUC is financed by **Special Assessment** and the operation costs approximately $462.5 million annually. *See also* CONGO INTERNATIONAL FORCE; UNITED NATIONS OPERATION IN THE CONGO.

UNITED NATIONS PEACE FORCES (UNPF). On March 31, 1995, the **United Nations** (UN) Security Council, with Resolution 982 (1995), voted to restructure the **United Nations Protection Force** (UNPROFOR) peacekeeping operation in the former **Yugoslavia**. UNPROFOR, which had elements in **Croatia**, **Bosnia and Herzegovina**, and the Former Yugoslav Republic of **Macedonia**, ceased to exist, and the latter three missions became independent peacekeeping operations as the **United Nations Confidence Restoration Operation in Croatia** (UNCRO), **United Nations Protection Force (UNPROFOR) in Bosnia and Herzegovina**, and the **United Nations Preventive Deployment Force** (UNPREDEP). Each of the three missions was commanded by its own **Force Commander** and civilian Chief of Mission. At the same time, the Security Council established the United Nations Peace Forces (UNPF) in Zagreb, Croatia, as a theater headquarters to oversee all UN peacekeeping operations in the former Yugoslavia. The **Special Representative** and a Theater Force Commander resided with the UNPF headquarters. Essentially, UNPF was only a headquarters element and not a separate peacekeeping mission. UNPF ended its mission on January 31, 1996, following the withdrawal of most UN peace-keepers and the introduction of **North Atlantic Treaty Organization** (NATO) troops to Bosnia and Herzegovina.

UNPF's personnel authorization was combined with those of the other three missions for a total of 57,370 soldiers supported by international and local civilian staff. Nine UNPF headquarters staff died between March 31, 1995, and January 31, 1996. Funding for UNPF and the other three UN missions was included in a single budget estimate of $4.6 billion from January 12, 1992, to March 31, 1996.

UNITED NATIONS PEACEKEEPING FORCE IN CYPRUS (UN-FICYP). The **United Nations** (UN) deployed the United Nations Peacekeeping Force in Cyprus (UNFICYP) as a tool to help settle a civil war in Cyprus. UNFICYP is one of the three longest ongoing peacekeeping operations in the history of the UN. The two operations that have been on the ground longer than UNFICYP are the **United Nations Truce Supervision Organization** (UNTSO) and the **United Nations Military Observer Group in India and Pakistan** (UN-MOGIP). Great Britain granted Cyprus independence on August 16, 1960. The population at independence was approximately 80 percent Greek descent and 18 percent Turkish descent. The two groups exhibit vastly different and conflicting cultures. In addition, both Greece and Turkey maintained close relations with the population of Cyprus. Independence included a pledge that the island state would never unite with either Greece or Turkey in order to eliminate the fears of one group about being incorporated into a state hostile to its culture. The new Constitution guaranteed that the President would always be a Greek Cypriot, while the Vice-President would be a Turkish Cypriot. Each leader would be elected by his segment of the total Cypriot population. The Council of Ministers would consist of seven Greek Cypriots and three Turkish Cypriots.

In late 1963, President Archbishop Makarios of Cyprus proposed several amendments to the Constitution that would decrease the influence of the Turkish Cypriots in the government. In response to the resulting civil disturbances, Turkish forces, stationed in Cyprus under the Treaty of Guarantee, left their barracks in support of the Turkish Cypriot community on December 24, 1963. Great Britain, Greece, and Turkey arranged a cease-fire in Cyprus and persuaded the

Cypriot government to accept a "peace making" operation consisting of soldiers from the three former states to patrol a neutral zone between the Turkish and Greek Cypriots in the capital of Nicosia. This zone, known as the **Green Line**, was actually manned almost exclusively by British soldiers. Cyprus brought the issue to the United Nations during December 1963. Secretary-General U Thant appointed Lieutenant-General P. S. Gyani of India as his Special Representative on the Cyprus crisis. Gyani's mission included observing the peace process set up by Great Britain, Greece, and Turkey in Cyprus.

The situation in Cyprus continued to deteriorate despite the attempts to settle the conflict. On March 4, 1964, the Security Council adopted Resolution 186 (1964), which called for the establishment of the UNFICYP. The body presented UNFICYP with a mission of preventing a recurrence of fighting as well as maintaining law and order where necessary. The actual mandate for UNFICYP was vague in order to win the acceptance of the permanent members of the Security Council and avoid a battle over a potential veto. The original mandate envisioned a mission length of three months.

The first contingent, a Canadian unit, arrived in Cyprus on March 13, 1964. The original contingents of UNFICYP included Australia (police), Austria (police), Canada (infantry), Denmark (infantry and police), Finland (infantry), Great Britain (infantry from the units permanently stationed on Cyprus), Ireland (infantry), New Zealand (police), and Sweden (infantry and police). The Swedish military unit arrived after being detached from the **United Nations Operation in the Congo** (ONUC). UNFICYP represents the first UN peacekeeping mission where one of the permanent Security Council members, Great Britain, contributed a large military force. Usually the permanent members were excluded from peacekeeping operations until after 1989 due to the political complications of the **Cold War**.

The belligerents did not trust the **British** contingent to UNFICYP. An incident involving a British airman, not assigned to UNFICYP, running weapons to the Turkish Cypriots intensified Greek Cypriot mistrust of the British. (Members of the Swedish contingent were also caught attempting to smuggle weapons to the Turkish Cypriots at **Lefka** in Eastern Cyprus.) Anti-British feelings extended to the other contingents of the operation. The Canadians, concerned over being mistaken for British soldiers, repainted their vehicles and displayed their maple leaf national emblem on their equipment. The Irish and Finns also exhibited apprehension over serving with the British on Cyprus. As a result, the British reduced their contingent size on Cyprus. UNFICYP personnel were deployed to match the administrative divisions of the island state. The British and Finns, under Canadian command, moved into Nicosia. Contingents in the districts of Kyrenia and Lefka deployed along the dividing lines between Turkish and Greek Cypriots, while peacekeepers in the remaining districts established posts in areas where ethnic conflict seemed likely.

One of the missions of UNFICYP included the demarcation of the cease-fire line on the ground. In order to accomplish the mission, the peacekeepers resorted to tactics such as painting white lines within urban areas and even painting boulders in the rural areas. The peacekeepers of UNFICYP also assisted in restoring the Cyprus mail service. The UN police units, known as UNFICYP Civilian Police (UN-CIVPOL), conducted joint patrols with the Cyprus police as well as manning their own posts.

According to the UN, each belligerent in the civil crisis viewed the role of UNFICYP differently. The government, dominated by Greek Cypriots, saw UNFICYP as a tool to assist it in returning all territory to its sovereignty. The Turkish Cypriots viewed UNFICYP as a tool to assist them in returning the government of the island to the provisions of the 1960 Constitution. The Secretary-General rejected both views and declared the neutrality of the operation.

Ethnic conflict, which led to the loss of life of many peacekeepers, finally cooled by the end of December 1964. Fighting renewed itself with great intensity in November 1967. A UN-brokered agreement led to the removal of Greek national troops from Cyprus and a softening of the political crisis. On July 15, 1974, the Cyprus National Guard launched a coup against the Makarios government. The Turkish government initiated a large-scale military operation in northern Cyprus under what it declared as the terms of the Treaty of Guarantee and landed troops on the island on July 20th. In turn, the UN reinforced UNFICYP, which emerged as a major participant in the conduct of humanitarian operations throughout Cyprus. Great Britain, Greece, and Turkey, in consultation with the UN, agreed to establish a neutral security zone around the enclave carved out by Turkish forces. UNFICYP peacekeepers would be the only personnel authorized to enter the security zone. In addition, UNFICYP would replace Greek or Greek Cyprus forces within smaller Turkish enclaves. UNFICYP would also provide security to villages consisting of both Greek and Turkish civilians.

Since 1974, UNFICYP has observed a cease-fire and neutral buffer zone that covers the island from north to south. The buffer zone is seven kilometers at its widest point and only 20 meters at its narrowest point (within Nicosia). Patrolling the buffer zone still has its hazards as the peacekeepers are tested and taunted by the belligerents. This operation was the first UN peacekeeping mission to establish a rapid mobile force in order to quickly react to crisis situations. Originally, the Canadians, Danes, and Finns contributed personnel to the mobile force that used scout cars, armored cars, and jeeps mounting recoilless rifles to display UN determination within Nicosia.

UNFICYP achieved a maximum strength of 6,411 peacekeepers in June 1964. The strength of the operation in April 2003 is approximately 1,373 military personnel and 44 international civilian staff. Fourteen countries currently contribute military personnel to the operation. UNFICYP civilian police come from Australia and Ireland. It is interesting to note that the military contingent from Argentina is actually one of the composite units that is becoming more popular in UN peacekeeping. The "South American" contingent includes small groups of soldiers from Bolivia, Brazil, Chile, Paraguay, and Uruguay along with those of Argentina. There have been 170 fatalities among UNFICYP personnel since March 1964. It is also interesting to note that the contingents of UNFICYP originated predominantly from Western and neutral European states. Cyprus was seen as a dispute between two members of the **North Atlantic Treaty Organization** (NATO) and Cyprus. Thus, East European states were excluded from the operation.

Due to the controversy over funding the **United Nations Emergency Force I** (UNEF I) and ONUC, the UN originally opted to fund UNFICYP by billing the government of Cyprus and asking the contingent providers to cover their own costs. Funding by the Cypriots did not materialize in the early years. The contingent providers, with the exception of the Scandinavian states, covered the costs of their units, while the UN sought voluntary contributions from member states. The former Soviet Union, China, France, and India represent the many states that refused to contribute to UNFICYP's bills. Other states offered extremely small sums, including South Vietnam, which pledged only $1,000. Currently, Cyprus and Greece have enlarged their contributions to the operation. Recently, the Security Council approved a resolution to begin financing UNFICYP through a **Special Assessment** on all members of the organization and reduced the strength from 2,078 to 1,488. The annual cost of UNFICYP is $42.4 million with Cyprus contributing $13.6 million and Greece offering $6.5 million. UNFICYP is still in place with little chance of a settlement to the situation on Cyprus in the near future.

UNITED NATIONS PEACEKEEPING FORCE IN CYPRUS CIVILIAN POLICE (UNCIVPOL). *See* UNITED NATIONS PEACEKEEPING FORCE IN CYPRUS.

UNITED NATIONS PERMANENT STANDING FORCE. *See* STANDING ARMY.

UNITED NATIONS POLICE SUPPORT GROUP (UNPSG). The **United Nations** (UN) Security Council mandated the United Nations Police Support Group (UNPSG) on December 19, 1997, with Resolution 1145 (1997). In January 1998, UNPSG assumed the policing duties of the **United Nations Transitional Administration for Eastern Slovonia, Baranja, and Western Sirmium** (UNTAES). The UN authorized up to 180 policemen for UNPSG and presented it with the mission to monitor Croatian police activities in the Danube region. In particular, the UN wanted UNPSG to oversee the conduct of the Croatian police with returning displaced persons. UNPSG maintained three mobile patrols in the region and observed the Croatian police at 14 stations. One particular challenge involved working with Croatian authorities to increase the number of ethnic Serb police officers in the area.

The UN opted to phase out UNPSG following the determination that the Croatian police were handling issues within international standards. The UN coordinated its withdrawal with the **Organization for Security and Cooperation in Europe** (OSCE). UNPSG's mandate expired on October 15, 1998, and **the Organization for Secu-**

rity and Cooperation in Europe Mission to Croatia assumed the police monitoring duties the next day.

The maximum fielded strength of UNPSG was 114 policemen with international and local support personnel. Nineteen states contributed personnel to UNPSG without any fatalities. UNPSG was financed by **Special Assessment** and the total operation cost approximately $23 million

Some scholars do not view UNPSG as a peacekeeping operation due to its lack of military personnel and strictly police mission. The UN lists UNPSG as a "peacekeeping" operation and the Stockholm International Peace Research Institute (SIPRI) recognizes UNPSG as a "peace operation" which the organization defines as either being an observer, peacekeeping, or peace building mission.

UNITED NATIONS PREVENTIVE DEPLOYMENT FORCE (UNPREDEP). The **United Nations** (UN) fielded the **United Nations Protection Force** (UNPROFOR) in 1992 to provide security and monitor the conflict in areas of the former **Yugoslavia**. The UN Security Council mandated the United Nations Preventive Deployment Force (UNPREDEP) on March 31, 1995, with Resolution 983 (1995), to replace the **United Nations Protection Force in Macedonia**. UNPREDEP's mission involved replacing the UNPROFOR personnel fielded in the Former Yugoslav Republic of Macedonia (FYROM). UNPREDEP represents a unique type of peacekeeping where the UN deployed an operation in an area without a conflict in order to prevent an outbreak of possible violence. The mandate, adopted from the former UNPROFOR mission in the state, included monitoring the 420 kilometer border between FYROM and its neighbors, the Federal Republic of **Yugoslavia** and **Albania**; offering advice to the local communities; and providing humanitarian assistance as required. UNPREDEP manned 24 permanent and 33 temporary observation posts along the borders between the three countries. The peacekeepers remained on the Macedonian side of the borders.

In 1998, the UN increased the size of UNPREDEP to 1,050 observers due to increased tensions in the area. On February 28, 1999, the Security Council failed to extend the mandate of UNPREDEP and the mission officially ended. Due to international concerns about the **North Atlantic Treaty Organization** (NATO) campaign against the Federal Republic of Yugoslavia (Serbia), the **Russians** abstained in the vote and the **Chinese** opted to veto the resolution. A veto by a single permanent member of the council defeats a resolution. Officially, the Chinese complained that UN peacekeeping operations should not be open-ended missions and it was, thus, time to end the mandate of UNPREDEP.

The **United Nations Peace Force** (UNPF), headquartered in Zagreb, **Croatia**, served as the administrative and logistical center for UNPREDEP as well as the **United Nations Confidence Restoration Operation in Croatia** and the **United Nations Protection Force in Bosnia and Herzegovina**. During its four-year term, UNPREDEP coordinated its work with the **Organization for Security and Cooperation in Europe Monitor Mission in Skopje**, the **European Union Monitoring Mission in the Former Yugoslav Republic of Macedonia**, the **North Atlantic Treaty Organization Kosovo Verification Coordination Centre**, and the North Atlantic Treaty Organization Extraction Force.

The maximum authorized strength of UNPREDEP was approximately 1,050 soldiers and military observers as well as 26 civilian policemen. Twenty-seven states contributed personnel to UNPREDEP with four fatalities during the four years. UNPREDEP was financed by **Special Assessment** and the total operation cost approximately $166.5 million. Unpaid assessed contributions totaled approximately $20 million at the time of the operation's termination.

UNITED NATIONS PROTECTED AREAS (UNPA). The **United Nations Protection Force** (UNPROFOR) was originally mandated to safeguard three United Nations Protected Areas (UNPA) in **Croatia**. These geographical areas were populated by ethnic Serbs but located within the newly independent Croatia. The UNPAs included western Slavonia, Krajina, and Baranja and western Srem in eastern Slavonia. Prior to the arrival of UNPROFOR, Serbian forces moved into Croat areas adjacent to the UNPAs, which later became known as **pink zones**.

UNITED NATIONS PROTECTION FORCE (UNPROFOR). The United Nations Protection Force (UNPROFOR) can be one of the more challenging peacekeeping operations to follow throughout its life. UNPROFOR was originally deployed to the newly established state of **Croatia**, which seceded from the former **Yugoslavia** in 1991. As civil war spread throughout the area, the mission expanded as peacekeepers were dispatched to **Bosnia and Herzegovina** and then **Macedonia**. The peacekeepers in the former became the **United Nations Protection Force in Bosnia and Herzegovina**. The troops assigned to the latter were labeled as the **United Nations Protection Force in Macedonia**. All three of the UNPROFOR missions later evolved into separate UN peacekeeping operations with different names.

The term UNPROFOR has *three* possible meanings. First, it represented the entire **United Nations** (UN) peacekeeping mission in the former Yugoslavia between February 1992 and March 1995. The peacekeepers in Bosnia-Herzegovina and Macedonia officially fell under the command of UNPROFOR. Second, the title UNPROFOR represented the peacekeeping mission established within the borders of Croatia (the original mandate of the operation). Third, the term UNPROFOR is applied to the nine-month mission that replaced the UNPROFOR element in Bosnia and Herzegovina.

The fragile federation of states comprising Yugoslavia began breaking up following the death of Marshal Tito in 1980. In June 1991, Slovenia and Croatia seceded from Yugoslavia, later followed by **Bosnia and Herzegovina** and Macedonia. Vojvodina, Montenegro, and Kosovo then remained in a Yugoslavian federation with Serbia. The latter state objected to the secession movements and elected to aid the Serbian population living in the self-declared independent areas. Serbian efforts were directed against Croatia and, later, Bosnia-Herzegovina. On November 23, at a meeting in Geneva, the belligerents agreed to a cease-fire but it quickly collapsed (as would the many cease-fires to come). The Geneva meeting also gave birth to the idea of a UN-mandated peacekeeping operation to oversee a cease-fire in the former Yugoslavia. The European Community elected to recognize the independence of Croatia and Slovenia in January 1992. Following the dispatch of a UN advance team, the Security Council passed Resolution 743 (1992) on February 21, 1992, officially mandating UNPROFOR, which would enter Croatia and establish what became known as **United Nations Protected Areas** (UNPA). The latter were developed around pockets of the Serbian minority population in Croatia.

The UN envisioned an operation consisting of 14,000 armed and civilian personnel including up to 12 combat battalions, 530 police, and over 100 civilian administrators with an initial 12-month mandate. Combat battalions assigned to UNPROFOR and posted in Croatia included those from Argentina, Belgium, Canada, Czech Republic (originally fielded under the banner of Czechoslovakia), Denmark, **France**, Jordan, Kenya, Nepal, Poland, and **Russia**. Additional support personnel deployed from 18 other countries.

UNPROFOR's mission was based around the protection of three UNPAs, including western Slavonia, Krajina, and Baranja and western Srem in eastern Slavonia. UNPROFOR's problems developed early as the Serbs increased their holdings in Croatia prior to the arrival of peacekeepers to oversee the original UNPAs, while some areas of the zones were actually under the control of Croatian forces. Atrocities, "concentration" camps, and cease-fire failures continued to plague the peacekeepers after the official inauguration of the mission on March 15, 1992. During the next month, civil strife between Muslims, Croats, and Serbs erupted in Bosnia and Herzegovina. On April 27, 1992, Bosnian leaders requested the emergency deployment of UN peacekeepers to prevent a full-scale civil war from breaking out in the new state.

As cease-fires began to take hold in Croatia, global attention shifted to Bosnia and Herzegovina and the UN decision to deploy peacekeepers from Croatia to form the United Nations Protection Force in **Bosnia and Herzegovina**. Later, the UN would again expand the peacekeeping mission by posting combat personnel in Macedonia as a preventive move prior to any civil unrest. The Security Council altered the structure of UNPROFOR with Resolution 871 (1993) on October 4, 1993. The UN reorganized UNPROFOR into a headquarters with three subordinate operations under it— UNPROFOR Croatia, UNPROFOR Bosnia and Herzegovina, and UNRPOFOR Macedonia. The commanders of the three latter missions reported to the UNPROFOR **Force Commander** situated in Croatia. UNPROFOR Croatia carried out the mission originally given to UNPROFOR forces in the state prior to October 4, 1993.

UNPROFOR Croatia officially transitioned into the **United Nations Confidence Restoration Mission in Croatia** (UNCRO) on March 31, 1995. The UN mandated the **United Nations Peace Forces** (UNPF) to serve as a headquarters element for the newly established UNCRO, the United Nations Protections Force (UNPROFOR) in Bosnia and Herzegovina, and the **United Nations Preventive Deployment Force** (UNPREDEP).

Manpower for all three operations is officially rolled up into an UNPROFOR total of 38,599 military personnel, 803 civilian police, and 4,632 international and local civilian staff. The maximum authorized strength of UNPROFOR peacekeepers in Croatia prior to October 4, 1993, was 14,000 military and civilian personnel. There were 167 fatalities among UNPROFOR personnel in all three areas. UNPROFOR was funded through **Special Assessment**. However, it is difficult to determine the exact costs for each location due to UN insistence to include all three UNPROFOR missions, as well as their follow-on operations after 1995, in a single budgetary total. The UN reports the total cost between January 1992 and March 1996 as $4.6 billion. *See also* FRANCIS BRIQUEMONT; LEWIS MACKENZIE; PHILIPPE MORILLON; MICHAEL ROSE.

UNITED NATIONS PROTECTION FORCE (UNPROFOR) IN BOSNIA AND HERZEGOVINA. The **United Nations** (UN) Security Council altered the structure of the **United Nations Protection Force** (UNPROFOR) with Resolution 871 (1993) on October 4, 1993. The UN reorganized UNPROFOR into a headquarters with three subordinate operations under it—**United Nations Protection Force in Croatia**, United Nations Protection Force in Bosnia and Herzegovina, and **United Nations Protection Force in Macedonia**. The commanders of the three latter missions reported to the UNPROFOR **Force Commander** situated in Croatia. In February 1994, UN Secretary-General **Boutros Boutros-Ghali** requested and received the authorization to call for air strikes by the **North Atlantic Treaty Organization** (NATO) in support of peacekeepers. The air strikes resulted in limited damage to the Serbs and embarrassment for NATO and the UN. Occasional NATO air strikes in support of UNPROFOR continued throughout 1994 as Serb and Bosnian forces renewed their offensives and counter-offensives against each other. A series of large NATO air strikes against Serbian targets in November 1994 prompted the latter to hold several hundred peacekeepers as hostages. Personnel, including peacekeepers from Canada, **France**, **Great Britain**, Netherlands, **Russia**, and Ukraine, were either physically detained or prevented from leaving their garrisons as a means to force NATO to suspend air raids. At one airfield, peacekeepers were forced to lie on the runway in order to deter NATO bombing raids. Gradually, the peacekeepers were released or allowed to depart their garrisons.

On November 30, 1994, Secretary-General Boutros-Ghali announced that the UN might withdraw from the area unless a ceasefire was successfully implemented. At the same time the **United States** began backing away from its call for the use of force against the Serbs. NATO projected that it would need to deploy up to 50,000 soldiers to safely withdraw the 23,000 UN peacekeepers if they were ordered to depart the divided country. The Security Council established the mission as a separate peacekeeping operation on March 31, 1995, to be known as the United Nations Protection Force (UNPROFOR). This new operation should not be confused with the earlier operation operating under the same name between February 1992 and March 1995. The mission operated for nine months as an independent mission with its own Force Commander but reporting to a **Special Representative** and Theater Commander assigned to the **United Nations Peace Forces** (UNPF), a headquarters unit.

The UN peacekeepers faced many difficulties during their tenure in Bosnia and Herzegovina including fighting around **Bihac** and the massacre of Bosnian Muslim men and boys by Serbs in **Srebrenica**. Following the signing of the Dayton Accords, UNPROFOR in Bosnia and Herzegovina officially transitioned into the **United Nations Mission in Bosnia and Herzegovina** (UNMIBH) on December 20, 1995. NATO fielded the **Implementation Force** (IFOR) to take over the security duties of UNPROFOR in Bosnia and Herzegovina.

Manpower for all three UNPROFOR operations is officially rolled up into a total of 38,599 military personnel, 803 civilian police, and 4,632 international and local civilian staff. There were 167 fatalities among UNPROFOR personnel in all three areas. UNPROFOR was funded through **Special Assessment**. However, it is difficult to determine the exact costs for each location due to UN insistence to include all three UNPROFOR missions, as well as their follow-on operations after 1995, in a single budgetary total. The UN reports the total cost between January 1992 and March 1996 as $4.6 billion. *See also* FRANCIS BRIQUEMONT; LEWIS MACKENZIE; PHILIPPE MORILLON; MICHAEL ROSE; SAFE AREAS.

UNITED NATIONS PROTECTION FORCE (UNPROFOR) IN CROATIA. *See* UNITED NATIONS PROTECTION FORCE (UNPROFOR).

UNITED NATIONS PROTECTION FORCE (UNPROFOR) IN MACEDONIA. The **United Nations** (UN) originally deployed the **United Nations Protection Force** (UNPROFOR) in the newly established state of **Croatia**, which seceded from the former **Yugoslavia** in 1991. As civil war spread throughout the area, the mission expanded as peacekeepers were dispatched to **Bosnia and Herzegovina** and then **Macedonia**. The Security Council altered the structure of UNPROFOR with Resolution 871 (1993) on October 4, 1993. The UN reorganized UNPROFOR into a headquarters with three subordinate operations under it—**United Nations Protection Force in Croatia**, **United Nations Protection Force in Bosnia and Herzegovina**, and United Nations Protection Force in Macedonia. The commanders of the three latter missions reported to the UNPROFOR **Force Commander** situated in Croatia. UNPROFOR in Macedonia was unique in being the first to use what is known as **preventative peacekeeping**. The headquarters was located in Skopje.

UNPROFOR in Macedonia consisted of one battalion of approximately 700 personnel, 35 military observers, and 26 civilian police. The mission of the observers and combat unit was to patrol Macedonia's border with the new Yugoslavia to ensure that ethnic conflict did not spill over into the former state. The civilian police assigned with the operation monitor the Macedonian police. Company-sized contingents were initially provided by Finland, Norway, the United States, and Sweden. In 1994, the United States increased its contingent to allow the transfer of at least one Scandinavian company to the United Nations Protection Force in **Bosnia and Herzegovina**. The UN replaced UNPROFOR in Macedonia with the **United Nations**

Preventive Deployment Force (UNPREDEP) on March 31, 1995. UNPREDEP's Force Commander reported to the Special Representative and a Theater Commander with the **United Nations Peace Forces** (UNPF) headquarters in Croatia.

Manpower for all three UNPROFOR operations is officially rolled up into a total of 38,599 military personnel, 803 civilian police, and 4,632 international and local civilian staff. There were 167 fatalities among UNPROFOR personnel in all three areas. UNPROFOR was funded through **Special Assessment**. However, it is difficult to determine the exact costs for each location due to UN insistence to include all three UNPROFOR missions, as well as their follow-on operations after 1995, in a single budgetary total. The UN reports the total cost between January 1992 and March 1996 as $4.6 billion.

UNITED NATIONS SECURITY FORCE (UNSF). The **United Nations** (UN) established the **United Nations Temporary Executive Authority** (UNTEA) to administer West Irian (New Guinea), maintain law and order, and protect individual rights. At the same time, the Secretary-General developed the United Nations Security Force (UNSF) in order to provide security for UNTEA. UNSF consisted of 1,500 peacekeepers from Pakistan, as well as American aircraft and crews and Canadian support personnel. The mission of UNSF included maintaining law and order and building a new local police force. The advance contingent of UNSF, including 340 personnel, arrived in West Irian on October 3, 1962, followed by the remainder of the peacekeepers on October 5. After the successful completion of the mission, UNSF personnel were replaced by Indonesian soldiers during April 1963. UNSF, along with UNTEA, officially departed West Irian on May 1, 1963. Indonesia and the Netherlands financed UNSF and UNTEA. Taxes collected by UNTEA during the administration of the territory by the UN were applied to the funds owed by the two states.

UNITED NATIONS SPECIAL COMMITTEE ON PEACEKEEPING OPERATIONS. This group, also known as the Committee of Thirty-Four, is a committee of the General Assembly of the **United Nations** (UN). The committee, consisting of 34 member states, was established by Resolution 2006 (XIX) in 1965. The purpose of the organization is to review and provide advice to the General Assembly on the conduct and financing of peacekeeping operations.

UNITED NATIONS SPECIAL COMMITTEE ON THE BALKANS (UNSCOB). The Greek civil war, which began during World War II, intensified following Greece's liberation from the Germans as communist guerilla forces challenged the former government. The **United States** persuaded the **United Nations** (UN) to establish the United Nations Special Committee on the Balkans (UNSCOB). Although not a peacekeeping operation in the classic sense of the term, UNSCOB resembled several observation missions that would be fielded by the UN in future decades. The purpose of UNSCOB included observing whether Greece's communist neighbors were still providing aid to the rebel forces. The international organization envisioned the participants in UNSCOB as being from China, **France**, **Great Britain**, United States, and Soviet Union, along with Australia, Brazil, Mexico, Netherlands, Pakistan, and Poland. The Soviet Union and Poland declined to participate in UNSCOB due to the nature of the conflict. The remaining states deployed a total of approximately 40 observers to Greece. The observers were reduced and eventually withdrawn in 1954 following the resolution of the Greek civil war in favor of the pro-Western government.

UNITED NATIONS STAND BY ARRANGEMENTS SYSTEM (UNSAS). The United Nations Stand By Arrangements System (UNSAS) is a program of the **United Nations** (UN) to establish a **Rapid Reaction Force** for **peacekeeping** operations. UN member states participate at four different levels. At the first level, they list their military capabilities for peacekeeping support with the UN. The next level involves completing a detailed planning data sheet on their capabilities. The third level includes the signing of a memorandum of understanding between the UN and member states related to providing military units on short notice for peacekeeping missions. The fourth level, introduced for participation beginning in 2002, goes one step further than signing a memorandum by actually earmarking specific units and permitting UN reviews of their training and preparations for short notice deployments. During 2002, 24 states participated in level one, 12 in level two, 39 in level three, and only 2 (Jordan and Uruguay) in level four. *See also* PARTICIPATING STATE AGREEMENT.

UNITED NATIONS SUPPORT MISSION IN HAITI (UNSMIH). The **United Nations** (UN) Security Council mandated the United Nations Support Mission in Haiti (UNSMIH) on June 28, 1996, with Resolution 1063 (1996), to replace the **United Nations Mission in Haiti** (UNMIH). UNSMIH's mandate included helping the Haitian government professionalize its police force. The operation would also help ensure a stable and secure environment and assist with institution building and national reconciliation. UNSMIH began operations in June 1996 and was extended until June 1997 when it was replaced with the **United Nations Transition Mission in Haiti** (UNTMIH).

The maximum authorized strength of UNSMIH was 1,300 military personnel, 225 civilian policemen, and over 250 international and local civilian personnel. There were no fatalities between July 1996 and July 1997. UNSMIH was financed by **Special Assessment** and some voluntary donor contributions of personnel. The total operation cost approximately $56.1 million. *See also* MULTINATIONAL FORCE IN HAITI; UNITED NATIONS CIVILIAN POLICE MISSION IN HAITI; UNITED NATIONS OBSERVER GROUP FOR THE VERIFICATION OF ELECTIONS IN HAITI.

UNITED NATIONS TEMPORARY EXECUTIVE AUTHORITY (UNTEA). The Netherlands granted independence to Indonesia in 1949. However, a dispute remained over the sovereignty of West New Guinea, also known as West Irian. The two states brought the West Irian dispute to the **United Nations** (UN) in 1954. The debate continued without settlement until 1962 when Indonesia dispatched paratroopers to West Irian. All parties finally signed an agreement on August 15, 1962. The disputants agreed to allow the UN to assume the administration of West Irian until May 1, 1963. The global body would establish what became known as the United Nations Temporary Executive Authority (UNTEA) to administer the area, maintain law and order, and protect individual rights. At the same time, Secretary-General U Thant developed the **United Nations Security Force** (UNSF) in order to provide security for UNTEA. The Secretary-General also assigned military observers to assist UNTEA in its mission.

Major-General **Indar Jit Rikhye** of **India** was selected to head the military observers assigned to UNTEA. Rikhye arrived in West Irian with 21 military observers from six states (Brazil, India, Ireland, Nigeria, Sri Lanka, and Sweden). All of the observers were detached from duty with either the **United Nations Emergency Force I** (UNEF I) or the **United Nations Truce Supervision Organization** (UNTSO) and arrived within days of the signing of the original agreement. The observers assisted in the cease-fire and also helped resupply scattered Indonesian troops in the jungle. Collection of the Indonesian troops on West Irian was completed by September 21, 1962. Administrative transfer of West Irian to UNTEA occurred on October 1, 1962. The UN transferred administrative control of West Irian to Indonesia on May 1, 1963. The Netherlands and Indonesia split the costs for funding UNTEA. Taxes collected by UNTEA during the administration of the territory by the UN were applied to the funds owed by the two states.

UNITED NATIONS TRANSITION ASSISTANCE GROUP (UN-TAG). Following World War I, the victorious Allied powers stripped Germany of its colonies. **South Africa** assumed responsibility for the area known as South-West Africa. After World War II, the **United Nations** (UN) placed these former **German** colonies under its Trusteeship system. However, South Africa refused to comply with UN requirements to schedule South-West Africa for independence. The situation intensified as the local inhabitants formed the South West African People's Organization (SWAPO) and initiated a military campaign against the South African military from base camps in **Angola**. The Security Council passed Resolution 435 (1978) on September 29, 1978, which contained provisions for a settlement on Namibia developed by the Contact Group according to the terms of their "Proposal for a Settlement on the Namibian Situation." Besides calling for the independence of Namibia, the resolution also proposed the establishment of the United Nations Transition Assistance Group (UNTAG) with an initial 12-month mandate.

The Security Council envisioned using UNTAG to assist the Secretary-General's Special Representative in ensuring that the

Namibians were given the opportunity for free and fair elections. The original proposal for UNTAG estimated that its strength would include 7,500 personnel, which would consist of six combat battalions, each with three line companies. There would be one combat battalion in reserve. UNTAG would also have 200 military observers and 360 police monitors. The estimated cost was $700 million.

The 1978 peace proposals collapsed due to linkage with the Angolan civil war. In 1988, South Africa, Cuba, and Angola signed the Tripartite Agreement, witnessed by the **United States** and Soviet Union. This document linked the withdrawal of the Cubans from Angola with independence for Namibia. On January 16, 1989, the Security Council reaffirmed Resolution 435 (1978) and asked Secretary-General Kurt Waldheim to re-evaluate UNTAG for cost-cutting measures. The Secretary-General's response was approved by the Security Council in Resolution 632 (1989) on February 16. The 1989 proposal for UNTAG left the total strength at 7,500, but the UN would only deploy 4,650 personnel to Namibia. The combat elements would include three combat battalions, each consisting of five line companies. Four combat battalions would be held in reserve in their home countries. The reserve battalions account for the difference in the UNTAG total and deployed strength. Military observers would be increased to 300 while police monitors would be raised in number to 500. The Secretary-General estimated that the entire operation would cost $416 million. UNTAG's mission included monitoring the ceasefire, the reduction and withdrawal of the South African military from Namibia (Walvis Bay excluded), the return of SWAPO guerillas, the conduct of local security and police forces, and the election process.

UNTAG claimed manpower contributions from over 50 UN members. The combat battalions deployed to Namibia came from Finland, Kenya, and Malaysia. The Finns deployed to the northeast; the Malaysians to the northwest; and the Kenyans to the center and south. The reserve battalions were on alert in Bangladesh, Togo, Venezuela, and **Yugoslavia**. The reserve battalions were on a seven-day notice for deployment to Namibia in case they were needed. Military observers arrived from 14 countries; police monitors from 24 countries; and election observers from 28 countries. It is interesting to note that **Switzerland**, despite its strict neutrality, provided a civilian medical unit and three civilian aircraft with crews.

The military component of UNTAG included the combat battalions and the military observers. The three battalions provided an element of military security for UNTAG and the civilians of Namibia. The military observers actually monitored the cease-fire and the confinement of the South African military and SWAPO guerillas in base camps. UNTAG consisted of a civilian as well as military component. The two components reported to Special Representative Matti Ahtisaari of Finland and were considered equal in authority in the UN chain of command. The civilian component comprised six divisions, including the Special Representative's office, the United Nations Civilian Police (UNCIVPOL), an independent jurist, an office of the United Nations High Commissioner for Refugees (UNHCR), the electoral division, and an administrative division.

UNTAG divided Namibia into seven police districts within which UNCIVPOL manned 49 police stations. Nearly two-thirds of the UNCIVPOL personnel were posted in the northern areas of Namibia due to the intensity of the guerilla campaigns compared to southern areas of the state. The independent jurist's office provided advice on the release of political prisoners and detainees. UNHCR handled all issues dealing with the repatriation of refugees, including reception and resettlement. The electoral division coordinated the efforts to register voters and monitor the election process. Despite early breaches of the cease-fire, UNTAG's mission can be listed as an unqualified success. The funding of UNTAG resulted from a **Special Assessment** on the members of the United Nations. Despite the 1989 estimate of $416 million, cost-cutting measures and voluntary contributions resulted in a final tab of $383 million.

UNITED NATIONS TRANSITION MISSION IN HAITI (UNTMIH). The **United Nations** (UN) Security Council mandated the United Nations Transition Mission in Haiti (UNTMIH) on July 30, 1997, to replace the **United Nations Support Mission in Haiti** (UNSMIH). The mandate of the operation included assisting the Haitian National Police (HNP) in its efforts to professionalize itself. The UN envisioned UNTMIH as a tool for training the HNP in crowd control, rapid reaction, and government security. UNTMIH completed its mission in November 1997 and was replaced by the **United Nations Civilian Police Mission in Haiti** (MIPONUH).

The maximum authorized strength of UNTMIH was 250 civilian policemen and 50 military personnel. Eleven states contributed personnel to UNTMIH and there were no fatalities between August and November 1997. Canada and Pakistan provided the military personnel. UNTMIH was financed by **Special Assessment** and some voluntary donor contributions. The total operation cost approximately $20.6 million.

Some scholars do not view UNTMIH as a peacekeeping operation. The Stockholm International Peace Research Institute (SIPRI) recognizes UNTMIH as a "peace operation" which the organization defines as either being an observer, peacekeeping, or peace building mission. The UN includes UNTMIH in its tally of peacekeeping operations. *See also* MULTINATIONAL FORCE IN HAITI; UNITED NATIONS MISSION IN HAITI; UNITED NATIONS OBSERVER GROUP FOR THE VERIFICATION OF ELECTIONS IN HAITI.

UNITED NATIONS TRANSITIONAL ADMINISTRATION IN EAST TIMOR (UNTAET). The **United Nations** (UN) Security Council mandated the **United Nations Mission in East Timor** (UNAMET) on June 11, 1999, to assist the global body in conducting a referendum in East Timor. Following an outbreak of violence, the UN authorized the deployment of an international military force to assist in stabilizing the situation. The peacekeepers, known as the **International Force in East Timor** (INTERFET), arrived on September 20, 1999. Additional discussions between the UN, Indonesia, and Portugal resulted in the transfer of the territory to UN administration.

The Security Council mandated the United Nations Transitional Administration in East Timor (UNTAET) on October 25, 1999, with Resolution 1272 (1999) to replace UNAMET. UNTAET's broad mandate included providing security and maintaining law and order; establishing an effective governmental administration; assisting in the development of civil and social services; ensuring the coordination and delivery of humanitarian assistance; supporting the capacity-building for self-government; and assisting in the establishment of conditions for sustainable development.

In February 2000, INTERFET transferred command of military operations to UNTAET. The East Timorese voted on a Constituent Assembly on August 30, 2001, which then drafted a new constitution on March 22, 2002. East Timor became an independent state on May 20, 2002. The Security Council mandated a new peacekeeping operation, the **United Nations Mission of Support in East Timor** (UNMISET) on May 17, 2002, with a mandate to provide assistance to the government during a transitional period.

The maximum authorized strength of UNTAET was 9,150 soldiers, 1,640 civilian policemen, 118 military observers, and 2,482 international and local civilian staff. Thirty countries provided military personnel and 40 states provided policemen to UNTAET with 17 total fatalities during the duration of the operation. UNTAET was financed by **Special Assessment** and cost approximately $477 million annually.

UNITED NATIONS TRANSITIONAL ADMINISTRATION IN EASTERN SLAVONIA, BARANJA, AND WESTERN SIRMIUM (UNTAES). On November 12, 1995, an agreement provided for the peaceful integration of Eastern Slavonia, Baranja, and Western Sirmium into the country of Croatia. The **United Nations** (UN) Security Council established the United Nations Transitional Administration in Eastern Slavonia, Baranja, and Western Sirmium (UNTAES) on January 15, 1996. UNTAES was mandated to supervise and facilitate the demilitarization of the region; monitor the voluntary and safe return of refugees; contribute to peace in the region through its presence; establish a temporary police force; and organize and assist in the election process. UNTAES completed its mission in January 1998.

The maximum authorized strength of UNTAES was 2,346 soldiers, 97 military observers, and 404 civilian police. Thirty countries provided personnel for UNTAES. *See also* UNITED NATIONS CONFIDENCE RESTORATION MISSION IN CROATIA; UNITED NATIONS MISSION OF OBSERVERS IN PREVLAKA.

UNITED NATIONS TRANSITIONAL AUTHORITY IN CAMBODIA (UNTAC). The Cambodian civil war ravaged that country since 1970 when General Lon Nol ousted the government of Prince Norodom Sihanouk. In 1975, a group known as the Khmer Rouge, led by Pol Pot, forced Lon Nol to surrender the government to them. In 1978, the Vietnamese army intervened in Cambodia to help oust the Khmer Rouge, who were conducting massacres across the state. The civil crisis settled into a war between the Khmer Rouge and other rebel groups fighting against the Vietnamese-backed government. On October 23, 1991, the belligerents agreed to what is known as the Comprehensive Political Settlement of the Cambodia Conflict and also referred to as the Paris Agreement. The **United Nations** (UN) Security Council supported the agreement and proposed the fielding of a peacekeeping operation to oversee the disarming and election process. The world body envisioned a mission similar to the one carried out by the highly successful **United Nations Transition Assistance Group** (UNTAG) in Namibia. Initially, the organization deployed the **United Nations Advance Mission in Cambodia** (UN-AMIC) to begin the oversight of the peace process while Secretary-General Javier Perez de Cueller planned the larger operation. The Security Council approved the formation of the United Nations Transitional Authority in Cambodia (UNTAC) with Resolution 745 (1992) on February 28, 1992. UNTAC officially became operational on March 15, 1992, and absorbed UNAMIC.

In June 1993, UNTAC's maximum strength reached approximately 19,200 personnel, which included armed peacekeepers, police monitors, election observers, and civilian administrators. Combat battalions arrived from Bangladesh, Bulgaria, **France**, Ghana, India, Indonesia, Malaysia, Netherlands, Pakistan, Tunisia, and Uruguay. Other UNTAC personnel deployed from Algeria, Argentina, **Australia**, Austria, Belgium, Cameroon, Canada, Chile, **Germany**, **Great Britain**, Ireland, Italy, **Japan**, New Zealand, **People's Republic of China**, Philippines, Poland, **Russia**, Senegal, Singapore, Sweden, Thailand, and **United States**. UNTAC's seven-fold mission included the administration of Cambodia until the election, verification of the withdrawal of all "foreign forces" (meaning the Vietnamese army), supervision of the cease-fire, disarming factions, monitoring the police, repatriation of refugees, and the general rehabilitation of the country. Locating and removing mines fell under the latter category.

UNTAC's organization basically paralleled that of its predecessor, UNTAG. **Yasushi Akashi** served as the **Special Representative** and Lieutenant-General John Sanderson held the position of UNTAC **Force Commander**. Both men arrived in Cambodia on March 15,

1992. The UN divided the country into 11 sectors with a combat battalion assigned to each. The smallest sector, around Phnom Penh, hosted the battalion from Ghana and one from Indonesia. The latter battalion was designated as the Force Reserve for UNTAC. A second Indonesian battalion oversaw another sector to the north. The Indonesians, from March 2–13, 1992, were the first of the combat units to arrive in Cambodia. Deployment of the combat battalions continued through July 1992. UNTAC also contained a naval unit known as the Maritime Operational Group. The latter group included 137 naval observers who served on specially marked patrol boats of the Cambodian government. UNTAC established cantonment sites in Cambodia to host disarming factions.

The peacekeeping mission faced many difficulties, including the refusal of the Khmer Rouge to disarm, the assassination of UNTAC election observers, the detaining of observers, and the questionable performance of some of the contingents. In particular, the Japanese were criticized for desertion of their posts during periods of crisis. One Japanese team reportedly took its vehicle and drove to the Japanese embassy in Thailand. The Bulgarians have been accused of smuggling, aiding prostitution rings, drunkenness, and even excessively rowdy behavior on their return flights. One account relates that stewardesses had to seek refuge in the cockpit to escape from returning Bulgarian peacekeepers. Seventy-eight personnel died while carrying out UNTAC's mission. The election was completed in May 1993. Akashi and Sanderson departed in September 1993. Brigadier-General Tuswandi of India assumed command of the operation and the remaining contingents during the same month. UNTAC completed its withdrawal from Cambodia in November 1993. The United Nations funded UNTAC through a **Special Assessment** on all member states. UNTAC cost the global body approximately $2 billion between November 1991 and November 1993.

UNITED NATIONS TRUCE SUPERVISION ORGANIZATION (UNTSO). UNTSO is often credited with being the first **United Nations** (UN) peacekeeping operation—eight years before the mandating of the **United Nations Emergency Force I** (UNEF I). However, its originators did not intend to establish a peacekeeping operation as we now think of the term. The Truce Commission overseeing the cease-fire between Israel and its Arab neighbors requested the deployment of neutral military observers on May 21, 1948, to assist with monitoring the military situation. **Ralph Bunche** asked the UN to approve the dispatch of 21 observers from each of the member states (Belgium, **France**, and the **United States**) of the commission as well as five senior officers from Sweden. In addition, 51 guards from the UN headquarters in New York were also dispatched to assist the military observers, whose number was later increased to 93. A Soviet request for participation was denied. The military observers were unarmed and investigated alleged violations of the cease-fire between Israel and its neighbors.

The original group of observers departed the area at the end of a four-week cease-fire. Following renewed hostilities, a new cease-fire opened the way for a return of the neutral observers. Bunche, now the Acting Mediator following his predecessor's assassination by Jewish terrorists, concluded four armistice agreements between Israel and its neighbors. The Security Council, on August 11, 1949, adjusted the mandate of UNTSO to match these agreements and thus establish what became known as the **Mixed Armistice Commissions**. The commander of UNTSO was given the title of **Chief of Staff** and now responded directly to the Secretary-General. The headquarters for UNTSO was established in Jerusalem. Following the 1956 war, UNTSO personnel assisted the peacekeepers assigned to UNEF I. Due to their presence in the area, personnel from UNTSO acted as the initial contingent for UNEF I until the arrival of peacekeepers from states pledged to fill the new mission. General Burns, the Chief of Staff of UNTSO, was named by the Secretary-General as the first Force Commander of UNEF I.

By the Six-Day War in 1967, all four of the Mixed Armistice Commissions had been unilaterally renounced by Israel. However, the presence of the UNTSO peacekeepers on the Arab side of the borders provided the UN with personnel to immediately monitor the cease-fire at the conclusion of the conflict. The UNTSO personnel served as the only peacekeepers between Israel and its neighbors during the years between the Six-Day War and the Yom Kippur War of 1973. During the outbreak of the latter war, two peacekeepers in the Suez Canal area were killed in the Egyptian attack on Israeli forces. The UN dispatched the **United Nations Emergency Force II** (UNEF II) to the Sinai following the conclusion of a cease-fire between Egypt and Israel. UNTSO personnel, later organized as the Observer Group Egypt, were assigned to assist UNEF II in its duties. The Organization also organized the **Observer Group Golan** to assist the **United Nations Disengagement Observer Force**, the **Observer Group Lebanon** to support the **United Nations Interim Force in Lebanon** (UNIFIL), and the **Observer Group Beirut**. Following the withdrawal of UNEF II and its replacement by the **Multinational Force and Observers** (MFO), UNTSO remained in the Sinai to assist the latter peacekeeping organization. UNTSO operates six posts in the Sinai and one in Ismailia along the Suez Canal in Egypt. Because of their availability, UNTSO personnel have been used to help in the initial fielding of several other UN peacekeeping missions.

The strength of UNTSO as of April 2003 is 113 military observers and 103 international civilians. Twenty-three states provide observers for UNTSO and there have been 38 fatalities among UNTSO personnel between June 1948 and April 2003. UNTSO is one of only two current UN peacekeeping operations funded from the regular budget of the organization (the other mission is the **United Nations Military Observer Group in India and Pakistan**). UNTSO costs approximately $23 million annually.

UNITED NATIONS VERIFICATION MISSION IN GUATAMALA (MINUGUA). The Guatamalan government endured a lengthy conflict with *Unidad Revolucioniara Nacional Guatemalteca* (URNG) until successful negotiations brought a truce to the struggle in 1994. The General Assembly of the **United Nations** (UN) established the Human Rights Verification Mission in September 1994 to monitor human rights and refugee issues in Guatamala after the truce. In December 1996, the belligerents concluded a peace agreement. On January 20, 1997, the Security Council mandated the fielding of a small military observer group for attachment to the Human Rights Verification Mission by adopting Resolution 1094 (1997). The new combined mission received a new name—the United Nations Verification Mission in Guatamala (MINUGUA) on April 1, 1997. The military observers assigned to MINUGUA were tasked to verify the cease-fire agreement and were mandated for an initial three months.

The military observers deployed to six verification zones to monitor the demobilization of the URNG. The UN established two concentric circles around each URNG Assembly Point to separate the demobilizing forces from government troops. Individual MINUGUA peacekeepers were assigned to monitor government units. The peacekeepers successfully disarmed URNG fighters and reported their completed mission to the Guatamalan government on May 14, 1997. With the completion of its mandate, the military observers initiated a withdrawal from the country on May 17, 1997, and the last element departed ten days later.

The maximum authorized strength of MINUGUA was 145 military observers and 43 civilian policemen. Eighteen states contributed personnel to MINUGUA without any fatalities. MINUGUA was financed by **Special Assessment** and the total operation cost approximately $4.57 million.

UNITED NATIONS YEMEN OBSERVATION MISSION (UNYOM). A crisis erupted in Yemen following a coup against the Royal government of the state in September 1962. Yemen, which withdrew from a federation with **Egypt** in December 1961, faced a civil war situation with a new Revolutionary government backed by Egypt against the recently ousted guerilla forces of the former Royal government. The Soviet Union recognized the new government and Egypt dispatched a large military force to bolster the Revolutionary government in the civil war. Saudi Arabia, which shares a border with Yemen, opted to send support to the former Royalists. The **United Nations** (UN) tackled the problem when faced with the decision of whether to accept a Royalist or Revolutionary delegation at its headquarters in New York. King Hussein of Jordan recommended the deployment of a peacekeeping operation to the area. The King, naturally favoring a situation that could help another government based on royalty, had turned down an offer of peacekeepers in his own state only four years earlier. Secretary-General U Thant dispatched Undersecretary-General **Ralph J. Bunche** to the area. Yemen, Saudi Arabia, and Egypt agreed to accept the terms for a settlement offered by the UN. Saudi Arabia would end its aid to the Royalists and not permit the group to operate from Saudi territory. In return, Egypt would withdraw its forces from Yemen. The UN would then establish a demilitarized zone along the Saudi-Yemeni border. This zone would extend for 20 miles on each side of the border, and a peacekeeping operation would then assume observation of the area. Saudi Arabia and Egypt agreed to fund the operation.

The Security Council mandated the United Nations Yemen Observation Mission (UNYOM) in Resolution 179 (1963) on June 11, 1963, and the Secretary-General appointed Lieutenant-General Carl C. von Horn of Sweden to serve as the first **Force Commander** of the operation. Von Horn held the position of Chief of Staff of the **United Nations Truce Supervision Organization** (UNTSO) prior to his new assignment. The personnel assigned to UNYOM, which was envisioned as a short duration mission, were detailed from UNTSO and the **United Nations Emergency Force I** (UNEF I). A 114-man Yugoslav unit, dispatched from UNEF I, formed the core of the new operation. The other original peacekeepers of UNYOM represented Australia, Canada, Denmark, Ghana, Norway, and Sweden. In January 1964, additional personnel arrived from the states of India, Italy, Netherlands, and Pakistan. All of the contingents remained with UNYOM for its duration except Australia, which withdrew its military observers in November 1963. The UNYOM maximum strength was 189 personnel.

UNYOM conducted ground and air patrols of the demilitarized zone and set up checkpoints along the roads and trails crossing the area. The mandate of UNYOM permitted observation of the demilitarized zone but not the border between Yemen and the **British**-dominated South Arabian Federation or the undemarcated frontier between Yemen and Saudi Arabia. Arms continued to reach Royalist forces across these areas outside of UNYOM's mandate. In addition, Egypt did not completely remove its forces from Yemen. In August 1964, Saudi Arabia announced that it would cease funding its half of the UNYOM budget and Egypt agreed to the termination of the peacekeeping operation.

UNYOM officially ended its operations on September 4, 1964. The Royalist forces and the new government settled their problems after the withdrawal of UNYOM. The Yemen peacekeeping operation is interesting in UN history due to the methods of financing and staffing the mission. UNYOM was financed by the two states in the Middle East that had intervened in the Yemeni civil war. Non-UN funding makes peacekeeping more acceptable to the Security Council since most operations operate under deficit conditions. The total cost of UNYOM was $1.8 million. In addition, personnel assigned to UN-YOM were detailed from existing peacekeeping operations, allowing the Security Council to simply request a state's permission to transfer personnel and not supply additional soldiers to staff a UN peacekeeping force.

UNITED NATIONS ZIMBABWE FORCE. The **British** and **United States** governments recommended in 1977 the establishment of a **United Nations** (UN) peacekeeping operation to oversee a proposed peace process in Rhodesia/Zimbabwe. The force, included in the Anglo-American Proposals for a Settlement in Rhodesia, would supervise a cease-fire, support the civil authorities, and act as a liaison between the Rhodesian armed forces and the liberation forces of the Zimbabwe African People's Union (ZAPU) and Zimbabwe African National Union (ZANU). Andrew Young, American ambassador to the UN, David Owen, then British Foreign Secretary, and General Olusegun Obasanjo, then Nigerian Head of State, discussed the proposed force in a meeting held in Lagos where **Nigeria** agreed to supply the bulk of the peacekeeping contingent. The peacekeeping mission never deployed to Zimbabwe due to the failure of the peace process in the state. In 1979, the **Commonwealth Monitoring Force in Zimbabwe** deployed in response to a successful Commonwealth negotiated peace initiative and accomplished the mission originally detailed for the aborted UN operation.

UNITED STATES AND PEACEKEEPING. During the **Cold War** the United States, as well as the other four permanent members of the **United Nations** (UN) Security Council, provided very few soldiers to peacekeeping missions in order to maintain the perception of UN operational neutrality. For example, the **United Nations Truce Supervision Organization** (UNTSO) is one of the few UN peacekeeping missions fielded prior to 1990 with American soldiers on the ground as observers. However, during this period the United States offered significant transportation and logistical resources to UN peacekeeping operations and generally paid approximately 25 percent of nearly every mission due to the UN funding formula. This assistance led to a long feud with the UN over the peacekeeping funding issue. The United States has argued for decades that the cost of transporting peacekeepers from other countries should count toward its total funding assessment of an operation. Also, the United States has repeatedly declared that the peacekeeping funding formula is biased and not reflective of the economic growth in many Third World states. The United States did develop and/or contribute troops to several notable unilateral and non-international organization mandated peacekeeping operations during the Cold War including **Multinational Forces I** and **Multinational Forces II** in **Lebanon** and the **Multinational Force and Observers** between **Egypt** and **Israel**.

After the end of the Cold War, the United States became more involved in UN peacekeeping and provided considerable manpower to support operations in **Bosnia and Herzegovina**, **Macedonia**, and **Somalia**. However, the problems encountered by the UN in the former **Yugoslavia**, Somalia, and **Rwanda** between 1992 and 1995 persuaded American politicians to discontinue large-scale participation in UN peacekeeping missions. The United States provides small numbers of military observers to many UN peacekeeping operations but still refrains from dispatching large units. During the early 1990s, the United States turned more to regional peacekeeping operations. These missions are fielded by international organizations in which the United States has greater direct control over policy. For example, under the **North Atlantic Treaty Organization** (NATO), the United States has contributed large numbers of troops in support of the **Implementation Force** (IFOR), **Kosovo Force** (KFOR), and **Stabilisation Force** (SFOR) fielded in the former Yugoslavia. In April 2003, the United States began planning for the formation of the **Iraq Stabilization Force** to replace coalition soldiers after the removal of Saddam Hussein from power in that country.

UNITED STATES MULTINATIONAL FORCES (USMNF). *See* MULTINATIONAL FORCES I; MULTINATIONAL FORCES II.

UNITED STATES SINAI SUPPORT MISSION (USSSM). *See* MULTINATIONAL FORCE AND OBSERVERS.

UNITING FOR PEACE RESOLUTION. The official name of this **United Nations** (UN) General Assembly document is General Assembly Resolution 377(V) of November 3, 1950. This resolution cleared the way for important issues, deadlocked by a veto in the Security Council, to be considered by the General Assembly where the veto does not exist. Also known as the Acheson Plan, the resolution was first applied when the Security Council deadlocked on action during the **Korean War**. In 1956, **Great Britain** and **France** seized the Suez Canal, recently nationalized by Egypt, in cooperation with an attack by **Israel** across the Sinai. The **United States** and the Soviet Union drafted separate resolutions demanding the withdrawal of the invading forces. Great Britain and France elected to use their Security Council vetoes to block these resolutions. In turn, Yugoslavia suggested that the issue be moved to the General Assembly under the provisions of the 1950 resolution. The General Assembly, meeting for the first time in an emergency special session, passed Resolution 997(ES-1), which called for a cease-fire, the removal of all forces to the original armistice line, and the reopening of the Suez Canal. Further discussion between Secretary-General Trygve Lie and **Lester Pearson** of Canada led to the creation of the **United Nations Emergency Force I** (UNEF I) to support and monitor the cease-fire.

Following the successful deployment of UNEF I, use of this method is often known as the Uniting for Peace procedure. For example, the General Assembly applied this procedure on January 14, 1980, when the Security Council deadlocked on the issue of Afghanistan. The General Assembly asked for the withdrawal of all foreign (i.e., Soviet) troops from Afghanistan. The eventual peace process in Afghanistan, negotiated with the assistance of the United Nations, led to the establishment of the **United Nations Good Offices in Afghanistan and Pakistan** (UNGOMAP) in 1988. *See also* ADVISORY COMMITTEE.

URQUHART, BRIAN. Urquhart filled the post of Undersecretary-General for Special Political Affairs at the United Nations (UN) between 1971 and 1986. In this capacity, Urquhart headed the global organization's peacekeeping efforts. Before assuming his position in 1971, Urquhart worked under Ralph Bunche, who held the same post. Marrack Goulding succeeded Urquhart in the chief peacekeeping post in 1986.

– V –

VIETNAM. *See* INTERNATIONAL COMMISSION OF CONTROL AND SUPERVISION.

VILNA INTERNATIONAL FORCE. In October 1920, the **League of Nations** proposed the establishment of the Vilna International Force to help the Vilna Plebiscite Commission and the **Vilna Military Commission** prepare for the Vilna Plebiscite. Colonel Chardigny, the commander of the military commission, requested 1,000 soldiers from the league in order to maintain order in the area and guard railroad lines. **France, Great Britain**, and Spain immediately offered two companies of infantry and one machine-gun section apiece while Belgium stated that it would provide one infantry company and one machine-gun section on the condition that the force be truly international, with the costs borne by either the league or the **contingent** providers. The Secretary-General requested each member of the league's Council, except Brazil and Japan, to contribute to the international force. Each state was asked to provide two companies of infantry, one machine gun section, and officers with knowledge of Polish or Russian. He also agreed that the league should reimburse the contingents from the organization's 1922 budget. Lithuania and Poland would be requested to fund the civilian administrative related expenses of the force.

In November the league Council elected to increase the size of the operation to 1,800 personnel, selected Danzig as the logistics base for the mission, named Colonel Chardigny as the military commander, and expanded the request for military personnel by soliciting Denmark, Netherlands, Norway, and Sweden to each provide 100 soldiers and a machine-gun section. British soldiers serving with the **League of Nations Plebiscite Forces** in Danzig were earmarked for the operation along with French troops assigned to the league forces in Memel. The other contingents would arrive by sea at Danzig and then transfer overland to Vilna. Norway and Sweden agreed to participate on the condition that their soldiers volunteer for the assignment. Denmark and the Netherlands gave tentative approvals to the operation pending review by their parliaments. In addition, Spain confirmed its willingness to contribute a contingent, and Greece stepped forward to provide 50 soldiers for the international effort. The French government offered to handle the organization and logistics for the multinational unit.

Before the league could field the International Force, Lithuania withdrew its approval citing Soviet opposition to having soldiers of the former Allied powers so close to its border. The league canceled the Vilna International Force in accordance with Lithuania's demands. The Vilna International Force set a number of precedents for future peacekeeping operations. First, the Scandinavian states raised volunteer units and forwarded the tab to the league. Second, one state, France, dominated the logistics system. Third, the force faced "great power" opposition from **Russia** which ultimately doomed the operation.

VILNA MILITARY COMMISSION. The **League of Nations** appointed five military officers under the command of French Colonel Chardigny to form the Vilna Military Commission in 1920. Representatives from **Great Britain**, **France**, Italy, **Japan**, and Spain faced the task of overseeing the withdrawal of regular and irregular military forces from Vilna and preparing for the arrival of the aborted **Vilna International Force**. The commission was eventually responsible for two neutral zones between Polish and Lithuanian forces. The first extended 250-by-15 kilometers between the Lithuanians and irregular Polish soldiers, while the second stretched 100-by-10 kilometers between Lithuanian forces and the official Polish army. The commission remained in Vilna for a year to ensure calm after the plebiscite proposal was dropped.

VILNA PLEBISCITE. Following World War I, a dispute arose over whether the newly formed states of Poland or Lithuania should control the city of Vilna. Although Vilna was the historical capital of Lithuania, the majority of the city's population was ethnic Poles. To complicate matters, Lithuanian and Soviet troops occupied the city in July 1920 before the latter retired the next month in the wake of a Polish offensive during the Russian-Polish war. Poland addressed the issue to the **League of Nations**, which requested the neutralization of all Lithuanian territory in the Russian-Polish war, set a demarcation line that left Vilna in Lithuania (but did not settle the territorial issue) and created the **Vilna Military Commission** to oversee the withdrawal of both sides from the provisional line and to prepare the area for a plebiscite.

Polish irregular forces moved into Vilna despite the agreement and occupied the city in October. Clashes between the Polish and Lithuanian forces continued through November before the Vilna Military Commission persuaded the two parties to accept an armistice and withdraw behind a neutral zone. The League of Nations requested the two sides to accept a plebiscite and proposed the creation of a **Vilna International Force** to oversee the process. After the initial planning for the force, Lithuania withdrew its support for the multinational operation due to opposition from the Soviet Union, which did not want soldiers of the former Allied powers so close to its border. Without military support, the league dropped the idea of a plebiscite and returned the issue to the disputing parties and a mediator. Poland retained Vilna and renamed the city Wilno.

– W –

WEST EUROPEAN UNION (WEU). The West European Union (WEU) began as a grouping of the European members of the **North Atlantic Treaty Organization** (NATO). Although the WEU cooperates closely with NATO, it is a separate organization with its own agenda. The WEU signed a Memorandum of Understanding with Bulgaria, Hungary, and Romania on April 5, 1993, to assist the three states enforce the **United Nations** (UN)-imposed embargo on Serbia. The WEU provided ten patrol boats, manned by 270 personnel, to assist in embargo operations on the Danube River. Italy was selected to coordinate the WEU operation.

At the January 1994 NATO summit, attendees voted to give their support to the budding needs for strengthening European-led defense. The NATO members approved working with the WEU as the defense component of the new **European Union** (EU) and agreed to make NATO assets available to the organization. A Joint WEU/NATO exercise was first held in February 2000 to test the arrangements for WEU-led missions with NATO assets. The WEU lacks its own standing forces and military command structure. Members and associate members could designate conventional forces for use by the WEU during a crisis situation, including the deployment of peacekeepers. This list is known as the **Forces Answerable to the West European Union** (FAWEU). The EU will eventually absorb the WEU into its structure. *See also* AMSTERDAM TREATY; MULTINATIONAL PROTECTION FORCE; PETERSBERG MISSIONS.

WEST IRIAN. *See* UNITED NATIONS SECURITY FORCE; UNITED NATIONS TEMPORARY EXECUTIVE AUTHORITY.

WESTERN SAHARA. *See* UNITED NATIONS MISSION FOR THE REFERENDUM IN WESTERN SAHARA.

– Y –

YEMEN. *See* UNITED NATIONS YEMEN OBSERVATION MISSION.

YUGOSLAVIA. *See* BOSNIA AND HERZEGOVINA; CROATIA; EUROPEAN UNION MONITORING MISSION; MACEDONIA.

– Z –

ZAHLE. Zahle is located on the eastern edge of the Bekaa valley in eastern **Lebanon**. The town was the site of intense fighting between the Syrian elements of the **Arab Deterrent Force** (ADF) and Christian militia starting in December 1980. By April 1981, the ADF, consisting of 2,500 Syrian troops, initiated a siege of the town and its Christian forces. The **Israelis** became involved in the fighting by providing direct support to the Christian forces in Zahle. Two Syrian helicopters were shot down by the Israeli airforce near Zahle. In response, the Syrians moved antiaircraft batteries into the valley, a move that would lead to an intense confrontation during the Israeli invasion of Lebanon two months later. The Christian forces later departed Zahle following negotiations.

ZAIRE. *See* FRENCH PEACEKEEPING.

ZEPA. *See* SAFE AREAS.

ZIMBABWE. *See* COMMONWEALTH FORCE IN ZIMBABWE; COMMONWEALTH OBSERVER GROUP; UNITED NATIONS ZIMBABWE FORCE.

Appendix

EXAMPLES OF PEACEKEEPING MANDATES

1. United Nations Peacekeeping Force in Cyprus (1963–)
2. United Nations Observer Mission Uganda-Rwanda (1993–1994)
3. United Nations Mission in Ethiopia and Eritrea (2000–)

MANDATE OF THE UNITED NATIONS PEACEKEEPING FORCE IN CYPRUS

The Security Council,

Noting that the present situation with regard to Cyprus is likely to threaten international peace and security and may further deteriorate unless additional measures are promptly taken to maintain peace and to seek out a durable solution,

Considering the positions taken by the parties in relation to the Treaties signed at Nicosia on 16 August 1960,

Having in mind the relevant provisions of the Charter of the United Nations and its Article 2, paragraph 4, which reads: "All members shall refrain in their international relations from the threat or use of force against the territorial integrity or political independence of any State, or in any other manner inconsistent with the Purposes of the United Nations."

1. Calls upon all Member States, in conformity with their obligations under the Charter of the United Nations, to refrain from any action or threat of action likely to worsen the situation in the sovereign Republic of Cyprus, or to endanger international peace:
2. Asks the Government of Cyprus, which has the responsibility for the maintenance and restoration of law and order, to take all

additional measures necessary to stop violence and bloodshed in Cyprus;

3. Calls upon the communities in Cyprus and their leaders to act with the utmost restraint;

4. Recommends the creation, with the consent of the Government of Cyprus, of a United Nations peacekeeping force in Cyprus. The composition and size of the force shall be established by the Secretary General, in consultation with the Governments of Cyprus, Greece, Turkey, and United Kingdom. The commander of the force shall be appointed by the Secretary General and report to him. The Secretary General, who shall keep the Governments providing the force fully informed, shall report periodically to the Security Council on its operation;

5. Recommends that the function of the force should be, in the interest of preserving international peace and security, to use its best efforts to prevent a recurrence of fighting and, as necessary, to contribute to the maintenance and restoration of law and order and a return to normal conditions;

6. Recommends that the stationing of the force shall be for a period of three months, all costs pertaining to it being met, in a manner to be agreed upon by them, by the Governments providing the contingents and by the Government of Cyprus. The Secretary-General may also accept voluntary contributions for that purpose;

7. Recommends further that the Secretary General designate, in agreement with the Government of Cyprus and the Governments of Greece, Turkey, and the United Kingdom, a mediator, who shall use his best endeavours with the representatives of the communities and also with the aforesaid four Governments, for the purpose of promoting a peaceful solution and an agreed settlement of the problem confronting Cyprus, in accordance with the Charter of the United Nations, having in mind the well being of the people of Cyprus as a whole and the preservation of international peace and security. The mediator shall report periodically to the Secretary General on his efforts;

8. Requests the Secretary General to provide, from funds of the United Nations, as appropriate, for the renumeration and expenses of the mediator and his staff.

(*Source: United Nations Security Council Resolution 186 [1964]*)

MANDATE OF THE UNITED NATIONS
OBSERVER MISSION UGANDA-RWANDA

The Security Council,

Reaffirming its resolution 812 (1993) of 12 March 1993,

Taking note of the interim report of the Secretary General dated 20 May 1993 (S/25810 and Add 1),

Also taking note of the requests of the Governments of Rwanda and Uganda for the deployment of United Nations observers along their common border as a temporary confidence building measure (S/25355, S/25356, S/25797),

Emphasizing the need to prevent the resumption of fighting in Rwanda that could have adverse consequences on the situation in Rwanda and on international peace and security.

Stressing the need for a negotiated political solution, in the framework of the agreements to be signed by the parties in Arusha, in order to put an end to the conflicts in Rwanda,

Paying tribute to the efforts of the Organization of African Unity (OAU) and the Government of the United Republic of Tanzania to promote such a political solution,

Taking note of the joint request of the Government of Rwanda and the Rwandese Patriotic Front (RPF) concerning the establishment of a neutral force in Rwanda (S/25951),

Stressing the importance of the ongoing negotiations in Arusha between the Government of Rwanda and the RPF, and expressing its readiness to consider assistance to the OAU in the implementation of the agreements as soon as they are signed.

1. Welcomes with appreciation the report of the Secretary General (S/25810 and ADD.1);
2. Decides to establish the United Nations Observer Mission Uganda Rwanda (UNOMUR) that will be deployed on the Ugandan side of the border, for an initial period of six months, as set

out in the report of the Secretary General (S/25810 and ADD. 1), and subject to review every six months;

3. Decides that UNOMUR shall monitor the Uganda/Rwanda border to verify that no military assistance reaches Rwanda, focus being put primarily in this regard on transit or transport by roads or tracks which could accommodate vehicles of lethal weapons and ammunition across the borders, as well as any other material which could be of military use;

4. Requests the Secretary General to conclude with the Government of Uganda, before the full deployment of UNOMUR, a status of mission agreement including the safety, cooperation and support the Government of Uganda will provide to UNOMUR;

5. Approves the dispatching of an advance party within fifteen days of the adoption of this resolution or as soon as possible after the conclusion of the status of mission agreement and the full deployment within thirty days of the arrival of the advance party;

6. Urges the Government of Rwanda and the RPF strictly to respect the rules of international humanitarian law;

7. Further urges the Government of Rwanda and the RPF to refrain from any action that could contribute to tension;

8. Welcomes the decision of the Secretary General to support the peace efforts of the OAU by putting two military experts at its disposal with a view to assisting the Neutral Military Observer Group (NMOG), in particular through logistic expertise to help expedite deployment of the enlarged NMOG to Rwanda;

9. Urges the Government of Rwanda and the RPF to conclude quickly a comprehensive peace agreement;

10. Requests the Secretary General to report to the Council on the results of the Arusha peace talks;

11. Further requests the Secretary General to report on the contribution the United Nations could make to assist the OAU in the implementation of the above mentioned agreement and to begin contingency planning in the event that the Council decides such a contribution is needed;

12. Also requests the Secretary General to report to the council on the implementation of the present resolution within sixty days of the deployment of UNOMUR;

13. Decides to remain actively seized to the matter.

(*Source: United Nations Security Council Resolution 186 [1993]*)

MANDATE OF THE UNITED NATIONS
MISSION IN ETHIOPIA AND ERITREA

The Security Council,

Recalling resolutions 1298 (2000) of 17 May 2000 and 1308 (2000) of 17 July 2000 and all its previous resolutions and statements of its President pertaining to the Ethiopia-Eritrea conflict,

Commending the Organization of African Unity (OAU) for successfully facilitating the Agreement on Cessation of Hostilities between the Government of the Federal Democratic Republic of Ethiopia and the Government of the State of Eritrea (S/2000/601), signed in Algiers on 18 June 2000,

Recalling the official communications by the Government of Ethiopia (S/2000/627) and Eritrea (S/2000/612) of 30 and 26 June 2000 respectively to the Secretary-General requesting United Nations assistance in implementing the Cessation of Hostilities Agreement,

Recalling the relevant principles contained in the Convention on the Safety of United Nations and Associated Personnel adopted on 9 December 1994,

Welcoming the report of the Secretary-General of 30 June 2000 (S/2000/643), and *recalling* the letter of its President endorsing the Secretary-General's decision to dispatch reconnaissance and liaison teams to the region (S/2000/676),

1. *Decides* to establish the United Nations Mission in Ethiopia and Eritrea consisting of up to 100 military observers and the necessary civilian support staff until 31 January 2001, in anticipation of a peacekeeping operation subject to future Council authorization, and to undertake the following mandate:
   (a) to establish and maintain liaison with the parties;
   (b) to visit the parties' military headquarters and other units in all areas of operation of the mission deemed necessary by the Secretary-General;
   (c) to establish and put into operation the mechanism for verifying the cessation of hostilities;

(d) to prepare for the establishment of the Military Coordination Commission provided for in the Cessation of Hostilities Agreement;

(e) to assist in planning for a future peacekeeping operation as necessary;

2. *Welcomes* the discussions between the Secretariats of the United Nations and the OAU on cooperation in the implementation of the Cessation of Hostilities Agreement;

3. *Calls* on the parties to provide the Mission with the access, assistance, support and protection required for the performance of its duties;

4. *Requests* the parties to facilitate the deployment of mine action experts and assets under the United Nations Mine Action Service to further assess the mine and unexploded ordnance problem and to provide technical assistance to the parties to carry out emergency mine action required;

5. *Decides* that the measures imposed by paragraph 6 of its resolution 1298 (2000) shall apply to the sale or supply of equipment and related *materiel* for the use of the United Nations Mine Action Service, or to the provision of related technical assistance and training by that Service;

6. *Stresses* the importance of the rapid delimitation and demarcation of the common border between the parties in accordance with the OAU Framework Agreement (S/1998/1223, annex) and the Cessation of Hostilities Agreement;

7. *Requests* the Secretary-General to continue planning for a peacekeeping operation and to begin to take the administrative measures for assembling such a mission, which would be subject to future Council authorization;

8. *Requests* the Secretary-General to provide periodic reports, as necessary, on the establishment and work of the Mission;

9. *Decides* to remain actively seized of the matter.

(*Source: United Nations Security Council Resolution 1312 [2000]*)

Bibliography

TABLE OF CONTENTS

I. GENERAL

1. General Works on Peacekeeping

Abizaid, John P. "Lesson for Peacekeepers." *Military Review*, vol. 73, no. 3 (March 1993), pp. 11–19.

Baratta, Joseph Preston. *International Peacekeeping: History and Strengthening*. Washington, DC: The Center for UN Reform Education, 1989.

Beattie, Brigadier-General C. E. "Preparations for Peacekeeping at the National and International Level." *Canadian Defence Quarterly*, vol. 8, no. 2 (Autumn 1978), pp. 30–37.

Bloomfield, Lincoln. *International Military Forces*. Boston: Little, Brown and Co, 1964.

———. "Political Control of International Forces in Dealing with Problems of Local Instability." In *Quis Qustodiet?: Controlling the Police in a Disarmed World*. Washington, DC: Peace Research Institute, 1963.

Central Intelligence Agency Directorate of Intelligence. *Worldwide Peacekeeping Operations*. Report EUR 93 10008 (May 1993).

Charters, David A., ed. *Peacekeeping and the Challenge of Civil Conflict Resolution*. Fredericton, New Brunswick: Centre for Conflict Studies, 1994.

Diehl, Paul F. "Peacekeeping Operations and the Quest for Peace." *Political Science Quarterly*, vol. 103, no. 3 (Fall 1988), p. 485.

Durch, William J., ed. *The Evolution of UN Peacekeeping*. New York: St. Martin's Press, 1993.

Gordenker, Leon, and Thomas G. Weiss. *Soldiers, Peacekeepers, and Disasters*. London: Macmillan-International Peace Academy, 1991.

Greenwood, Christopher. "Is There a Right of Humanitarian Intervention?" *The World Today*, vol. 49, no. 2 (February 1993), pp. 34–40.

Gregory, Frank. *The Multinational Force: Aid or Obstacle to Conflict Resolution*. Conflict Study no. 170. Institute for the Study of Conflict. London: Eastern Press, 1984.

Haas, Ernst B. "Conflict Management and International Organizations, 1945–1981." In *The Politics of International Organizations*. Ed. by Paul F. Diehl. Chicago: Dorsey Press, 1989, pp. 189–223.

Henn, Brigadier F. R. "Guidelines on Peacekeeping: Another View." *British Army Review*, no. 67 (April 1981), pp. 31–39.

International Peace Academy. *Peacekeeper's Handbook*. New York: Pergamon Press, 1984.

Jones, Peter. "Peacekeepers and the Use of Force." *Peacekeeping and International Relations*, vol. 21, no. 2 (May–June 1992), p. 3.

Luard, Evan. "Collective Intervention." In *Intervention in World Politics*. Ed. by Hedley Bull. Oxford: Clarendon, 1984.

Menon, Bhaskar. "A Dangerous Time For Peacekeepers." *The Times of India*. Reprinted in *World Press Review* (October 1993), pp. 15–16.

Minear, Larry, and Thomas G. Weiss. *Humanitarian Action in Times of War: A Handbook for Practitioners*. Boulder, CO: Lynne Rienner Publishers, 1993.

Morrison, Alex, ed. *Peacekeeping, Peacemaking, or War: International Security Enforcement*. Toronto: The Canadian Institute of Strategic Studies, 1991.

"Peacekeeping: Norms, Policy, and Process." *Canadian Defence Quarterly*, vol. 23, no. 1 (Special no. 2, 1993).

Preparations for Peacekeeping: A Survey of Nine Nations. McLean, VA: Science Applications International Corporation, August 1993.

Rifkind, Malcolm. "Peacekeeping or Peacemaking? Implications and Prospects." *The RUSI Journal*, vol. 138, no. 2 (April 1, 1993), p. 1.

Rikhye, Indar Jit. *The Theory and Practice of Peacekeeping*. New York: St. Martin's Press, 1984.

Roos, John G. "The Perils of Peacekeeping: Tallying the Costs in Blood, Coin, Prestige, and Readiness." *Armed Forces Journal*, vol. 132, no. 5 (December 1993), pp. 13–17.

Weiss, Thomas G. *Humanitarian Emergencies and Military Help in Africa*. London: Macmillan-International Peace Academy, 1990.

2. Problems and Conditions for Success

Diehl, Paul F. "Conditions for Success in Peacekeeping Operations." In *The Politics of International Organizations*. Ed. by Paul F. Diehl. Chicago: Dorsey Press, 1989, pp. 173–188.

Nelson, C. "The Initiation of UN Peacekeeping Forces: Problems and Reform Proposals." *International Affairs Bulletin*, vol. 13, no. 1 (1989), p. 30.

Weber, Thomas. "The Problems of Peacekeeping." *Interdisciplinary Peace Research*, vol. 1, no. 2 (October 1, 1989), p. 3.

3. Financing

Christofides, Georg C. "Peacekeeping: Financial Aspects." In *The Cyprus Conflict and the Role of the United Nations*. Ed. by Kjell Skjelsbaek. Oslo: Norwegian Institute of International Affairs, Report no. 122 (1988), pp. 39–43.

Diehl, Paul F., and Elijah Pharaohkhan. "Financing UN Peacekeeping: A Review and Assessment of Proposals." *Policy Studies Review*, vol. 17, no. 1 (Spring 2000), pp. 71–105.

Dormoy, D. "Aspects Récents de la Question du Financement des Operations de Maintien de la Paix de l'Organisation des Nations Unies." *Annuaire Français de Droit International*, 1993, pp. 131–?.

Financing an Effective United Nations: A Report of the Independent Advisory Group on UN Financing. New York: Ford Foundation, April 1993.

Foran, Richard. "Peacekeeping Procurement and Financing: Challenges and Opportunities." In *The New Peacekeeping Partnership*. Ed. by Alex Morrison. Clementsport, NS: Canadian Peackeeping Press, 1995, pp. 26–29.

Gizewski, Peter, and Geoffrey Pearson. *The Burgeoning Cost of UN Peacekeeping: Who Pays and Who Benefits?* Aurora Papers no. 21. Ottawa: Canadian Centre for Global Security, 1993.

Green, David Michael, Chad Kahl, and Paul F. Diehl. "The Price of Peace: A Predictive Model of UN Peacekeeping Fiscal Costs." *Policy Studies Journal*, vol. 26, no. 4 (Winter 1998), pp. 620–623.

Kazimi, M. R. *Financing the United Nations Peacekeeping Operations*. New Delhi: Capital Publishing House, 1988.

Khanna, Jyoit. "Sharing the Financial Burden for UN and NATO Peacekeeping, 1976–1996." *Journal of Conflict Resolution*, vol. 42, no. 2 (April 1998), pp. 166–186.

Marnika, Maurice. "Dollars and Sense: Financing UN Peacekeeping." *Peacekeeping and International Relations*, vol. 25, no. 2 (March–April 1996), pp. 6–8.

McDermott, Anthony. "Peacekeeping Operations: Funding Problems and Solutions." In *Peacekeeping and the Challenge of Civil Conflict Resolution*. Ed. by David A. Charters. Fredericton, New Brunswick: Centre for Conflict Studies, 1994.

Mills, Susan R. *The Financing of the United Nations Peacekeeping Operations: The Need For a Sound Financial Basis*. New York: International Peace Academy. Occasional Papers on Peacekeeping no. 3, 1989.

Ogata, Shijuro, and Paul Volcker. *Financing an Effective United Nations: A Report of the Independent Advisory Group on UN Financing.* New York: Ford Foundation, April 1993.

Pagani, Fabrizio. "Financing Peacekeeping and Peace Related Operations: The UN and OSCE Practice." In *The OSCE in the Maintenance of Peace and Security.* Ed. by Michael Bothe, Natalino Ronzitti, and Allan Rosas. The Hague: Kluwar Law International, 1997, pp. 315–342.

Saito, Naoki. *Financing of UN Peacekeeping Operations: US and Japanese Responses.* Policy Paper no. 84E. Tokyo: International Institute for Global Peace, 1992.

4. Training

Cairns, P. W. "Maritime Training for Peacekeeping Operations." *NATO's Sixteen Nations,* vol. 1 (1994), pp. 17–20.

Doepfner, Andreas. "Training UN Peace Troops in Finland." *Swiss Review of World Affairs,* vol. 38, no. 12 (1989), pp. 11–13.

Freakle, Benjamin C., et al. "Training for Peace Support Operations." *Military Review,* vol. 78, no. 4 (July–August 1998), pp. 17–24.

Hessel, Friedrich. "Experience Gained in Leading and Training United Nations Troops." *Peacekeeping and International Relations,* vol. 20, no. 3 (May–June 1991), p. 3.

Langholtz, Harvey J. "The Training and Assessment of UN Peacekeepers With Distance-Education Pedagogy." *International Peacekeeping,* vol. 4, no. 5 (May–August 1998).

Miller, David. "Naval Training for Multinational Peacekeeping." *International Defense Review,* vol. 26 (December 1993), pp. 955–960.

Otte, John. "UN Concept for Peacekeeping Training." *Military Review,* vol. 78, no. 4 (July–August 1998), pp. 25–30.

Simpson, Stephen, and Steven Carlson. "Training for Measured Response." *US Naval Institute Proceedings,* vol. 124, no. 9 (September 1998), pp. 58–61.

Sevecke, Torsten. "The Training Unit of the United Nations Department of Peacekeeping Operations." *International Peacekeeping,* vol. 2, nos. 2–3 (February–May 1995).

5. Maritime Peacekeeping

Allison, Captain George. "The United States Navy and United Nations Peacekeeping Operations." *Naval War College Review,* vol. 46, no. 3 (Summer 1993), pp. 22–35.

Blackham, J. J. "Maritime Peacekeeping." *The RUSI Journal,* vol. 138, no. 4 (August 1, 1993), p. 18.

Cairns, P. W. "Maritime Training for Peacekeeping Operations." *NATO's Sixteen Nations,* vol. 1 (1994), pp. 17–20.

Day, Graham. "Naval Peacekeeping: A Practical Account." *Peacekeeping and International Relations*, vol. 22, no. 2 (March–April 1993), pp. 5–10.

Ginifer, Jeremy, and Eric Grove. "UN Management of Naval Operations." In *Maritime Security and Peacekeeping: A Framework for United Nations Operations*. Ed. by Michael Pugh. Manchester: Manchester University Press, 1994, pp. 126–144.

Griffiths, D. N. "The Maritime Force of Peacekeeping." *Canadian Defence Quarterly*, vol. 25, no. 1 (September 1995), pp. 12–16.

Grove, Eric. "Navies in Peacekeeping and Enforcement: The British Experience in the Adriatic Sea." *International Peacekeeping*, vol. 1, no. 4 (Winter 1994), pp. 462–471.

Hampson, Francoise J. "Naval Peacekeeping and the Law." In *Maritime Security and Peacekeeping: A Framework for United Nations Operations*. Ed. by Michael Pugh. Manchester: Manchester University Press, 1994, pp. 190–213.

Haydon, Peter. "Naval Peacekeeping: Multinational Considerations." In *The New Peacekeeping Partnership*. Ed. by Alex Morrison. Clementsport, NS: Canadian Peackeeping Press, 1995, pp. 105–124.

Miller, David. "Naval Training for Multinational Peacekeeping." *International Defense Review*, vol. 26 (December 1993), pp. 955–960.

Neves, J. C. "The Argentine Navy and UN Peacekeeping Operations in the Gulf of Fonseca." *Naval War College Review*, vol. 47, no. 1 (Winter 1994), pp. 40–67.

Oswald, Admiral of the Fleet Sir Julian. "UN Maritime Operations." *Naval War College Review*, vol. 46, no. 4 (Autumn 1993), pp. 124–129.

Pugh, Michael Charles. *Maritime Peacekeeping: Scope for Deep Blue Berets?* Working Paper no. 119. Canberra: Australian National University, 1992.

———. *Maritime Security and Peacekeeping: A Framework for United Nations Operations*. Manchester: Manchester University Press, 1994.

———. "Peacekeeping: A Role for Navies?" *Naval Forces*, vol. 22 (July–August 1993), pp. 13–15.

Pugh, Michael Charles, Jeremy Ginifer, and Eric Grove. "Sea Power, Security, and Peacekeeping After the Cold War." In *Maritime Security and Peacekeeping: A Framework for United Nations Operations*. Ed. by Michael Pugh. Manchester: Manchester University Press, 1994, pp. 10–31.

Simpson, Stephen, and Steven Carlson. "Training for Measured Response." *US Naval Institute Proceedings*, vol. 124, no. 9 (September 1998), pp. 58–61.

Smith, William. "Peacemaking From the Sea." *Proceedings*, vol. 119, no. 8 (August 1, 1993), p. 25.

Stanley, Robert Stephen II. *The Wave of the Future: The United Nations and Naval Peacekeeping*. Boulder, CO: Lynne Rienner Publishers, 1992.

Takai, Susumu. "Legal Aspects of Ocean Peacekeeping: A New Type of Confidence Building Measure." *Peacekeeping and International Relations*, vol. 26, no. 4–5 (July–October 1997), pp. 12–19.

6. Legal Issues

Baines, Thomas B. *The Laws of War and the Rules of Peace: Why Traditional Legal Models Do Not Work*. Pearson Papers no. 5. Clementsport, NS: Canadian Peacekeeping Press, 1999.

Bothe, Michael. "International Security and International Law." *International Peacekeeping*, vol. 2, no. 4 (June–July 1995).

Bowens, Glenn. "Legal Issues in Peace Operations." *Parameters*, vol. XXVIII, no. 4 (Winter 1998–1999), pp. 51–72.

Bratt, Duane. "Chapter VII: Peacekeeping and International Law." *Peacekeeping and International Relations*, vol. 26, no. 6 (November–December 1997), pp. 5–6.

Cassese, Antonio, ed. *The Current Legal Regulation of the Use of Force*. Dordrecht: Martinus Nijhoff Publishers, 1986.

Daalder, Ivo. "NATO, the UN and the Use of Force." *International Peacekeeping*, vol. 5, nos. 1–2 (January–April 1999).

Fleck, Dieter. "Conference on Contemporary Legal Issues: Legal Issues of European Regional Peace Operations." *International Peacekeeping*, vol. 6, no. 1 (January–February 2000).

Hampson, Francoise J. "Naval Peacekeeping and the Law." In *Maritime Security and Peacekeeping: A Framework for United Nations Operations*. Ed. by Michael Pugh. Manchester: Manchester University Press, 1994, pp. 190–213.

Kelly, Michael. *Peace Operations: Tackling the Military, Legal, and Policy Challenges*. Canberra: Australian Government Public Service, 1997.

Kirsch, Philippe. "The Legal Basis of Peacekeeping." *Canadian Defence Quarterly*, vol. 23, no. 1 (September 1993), pp. 18–23.

Kofour, K. O. "The Legality of the Intervention in the Liberian Civil War by the Economic Community of West African States." *African Journal of International and Comparative Law*, vol. 5 (1993), pp. 525–?.

Marnika, Maurice. "The Rules of the Game: The Three Guiding Legal Principles of Peacekeeping." *Peacekeeping and International Relations*, vol. 25, no. 1 (January–February 1996), pp. 3–4.

McCoubrey, Hilaire. "Kosovo, NATO, and International Law." *International Relations*, vol. XIV, no. 5 (August 1999), pp. 29–46.

McCoubrey, Hilaire, and Nigel White. *The Blue Helmets: Legal Regulation of UN Military Operations*. Dartmouth: Aldershot, 1996.
Takai, Susumu. "Legal Aspects of Ocean Peacekeeping." *Peacekeeping and International Relations*, vol. 26, nos. 4–5 (July–October 1997), pp. 12–16.
Teson, Fernando. *Humanitarian Intervention: An Inquiry into Law and Morality*. 2nd edition. Irvington on Hudson, NY: Transnational Publications, Inc., 1997.
Tuzmukhamedov, Bakthyar. "The Legal Framework of CIS Regional Peace Operations." *International Peacekeeping*, vol. 6, no. 1 (January–February 2000).
White, Nigel. "The UN Charter and Peacekeeping Forces: Constitutional Issues." *International Peacekeeping*, vol. 3, no. 4 (Winter 1996), pp. 43–63.
Williams, Paul R. "Legal Basis for NATO Military Action Taken Against Serbia/Montenegro." *International Peacekeeping*, vol. 5, nos. 1–2 (January–April 1999).

7. Intelligence Issues

Dorn, Walter, and J. H. Bell. "Intelligence and Peacekeeping: The UN Operation in the Congo, 1960–1964." *International Peacekeeping*, vol. 2, no. 1 (Spring 1995), pp. 11–33.
Dorn, Walter, and David A. Charters. *Intelligence in Peacekeeping*. Pearson Paper no. 4. Clementsport, NS: Canadian Peacekeeping Press, 1999.
Krepon, Michael, and Jeffrey P. Tracey. "'Open Skies' and United Nations Peacekeeping." *Survival*, vol. 32, no. 2 (May–June 1990), pp. 251–263.
Rehbein, Robert E. "On the Horns of a Dilemma: Intelligence Supports to UN Peacekeeping Operations." In *Peacekeeping at the Crossroads*. Ed. by S. Neil MacFarlane and Hans-Georg Ehrhart. Clementsport, NS: Canadian Peacekeeping Press, 1997, pp. 179–208.
Reunions, Bradley. "American and British Doctrine for Intelligence in Peace Operations." *Peacekeeping and International Relations*, vol. 24, no. 6 (November–December 1995), pp. 14–15.
Smith, Hugh. "Intelligence and United Nations Peacekeeping." *Survival*, vol. 36 (Autumn 1994), pp. 174–192.
Valimaki, Pasi. *Intelligence in Peace Support Operations*. Helsinki: National Defense College, 2000.

8. Non-Governmental Organizations

Kennedy, Kevin M. "The Relationship Between the Military and Humanitarian Organizations in Operation Restore Hope." *International Peacekeeping*, vol. 3, no. 1 (Spring 1996), pp. 92–112.

Lawrence, Tim. *Humanitarian Assistance and Peacekeeping: An Uneasy Alliance*. London: RUSI, 1999.

Rufini, Giovanni. "Peacekeeping and the Coming Age of NGOs." *Peacekeeping and International Relations*, vol. 24, no. 2 (March–April 1995), pp. 7–8.

———. "The Potential of Non-Governmental Organizations in Peacekeeping Negotiation and Mediation." *Peacekeeping and International Relations*, vol. 24, no. 3 (1995), pp. 5–6.

Steele, David B. "Securing Peace for Humanitarian Aid." *International Peacekeeping*, vol. 5, no. 1 (Spring 1998), pp. 66–88.

Tsitouris, Margaret G. "The Role of the NGO in Peacekeeping." In *Peacekeeping at the Crossroads*. Ed. by S. Neil MacFarlane and Hans-Georg Ehrhart. Clementsport, NS: Canadian Peacekeeping Press, 1997, pp. 34–39.

9. Humanitarian Intervention

Beigbeder, Yves. "The World Health Organization and Peacekeeping." *International Peacekeeping*, vol. 5, no. 4 (Winter 1998), pp. 31–48.

Collett, Stephen. "Humanitarian Peacekeeping: Ethical Considerations." In *The New Peacekeeping Partnership*. Ed. by Alex Morrison. Clementsport, NS: Canadian Peackeeping Press, 1995, pp. 159–168.

Connaughton, Richard. *Military Intervention and Peacekeeping: The Reality*. Burlington, VT: Ashgate, 2001.

Cooper, Robert, and Mats Berdal. "Outside Intervention in Ethnic Conflicts." *Survival*, vol. 35 (Spring 1993), pp. 118–142.

Dworken, Jonathon T. "What's So Special About Humanitarian Operations?" *Comparative Strategy*, vol. 8, no. 4 (October–December 1994), pp. 391–400.

Ero, C., and S. Long. "Humanitarian Intervention: A New Role for the United Nations." *International Peacekeeping*, vol. 2, no. 2 (Summer 1995), pp. 140–156.

Fisher, David. "The Ethics of Intervention." *Survival*, vol. 36, no. 1 (Spring 1994), pp. 51–59.

Harriss, John. *The Politics of Humanitarian Intervention*. New York: Pinter Publishers, 1995.

Knudson, Tonny Brems. "Humanitarian Intervention Revisited: Post-Cold War Responses to Classical Problems." *International Peacekeeping*, vol. 3, no. 4 (Winter 1996), pp. 146–165.

Lewy, Guenter. "The Case for Humanitarian Intervention." *Orbis*, vol. 37, no. 4 (Fall 1993), pp. 621–632.

Lucas, George. *Perspectives on Humanitarian Intervention*, Berkeley, CA: Berkeley Publications Policy Press, 2001.

Murphy, Sean. *Humanitarian Intervention: The United Nations in an Evolving World Order*. Philadelphia: University of Pennsylvania Press, 1996.

Natsios, Andrew S. "The International Humanitarian Response System." *Parameters*, vol. 25, no. 1 (Spring 1995), pp. 68–81.

O'Halloran, Patrick J. *Humanitarian Intervention and the Genocide in Rwanda*. Conflict Studies no. 277. London: Research Institute for the Study of Conflict and Terrorism, 1995.

———. "The Problem of Armed Intervention." *Peacekeeping and International Relations*, vol. 23, no. 5 (September–October 1994), pp. 5–6.

Phillips, Robert, and Duane Cody. *Humanitarian Intervention: Just War vs. Pacifism*. Lanham, MD: Rowman and Littlefield Publishers, Inc., 1996.

Roberts, Adam. "Humanitarian War: Military Intervention and Human Rights." *International Affairs*, vol. 69 (July 1993), pp. 429–449.

Russell, F. W. "The Dilemma of Humanitarian Assistance in Modern Peacekeeping." *Peacekeeping and International Relations*. vol. 25, no. 2 (March–April 1996), pp. 3–5.

Steele, David B. "Securing Peace for Humanitarian Aid." *International Peacekeeping*, vol. 5, no. 1 (Spring 1998), pp. 66–88.

10. Human Rights

Amnesty International. *Peacekeeping and Human Rights*. London: Amnesty International, 1994.

Beigbeder, Yves. "The World Health Organization and Peacekeeping." *International Peacekeeping*, vol. 5, no. 4 (Winter 1998), pp. 31–48.

Boekle, Henning. "The United Nations and the International Protection of Human Rights." *International Peacekeeping*, vol. 5, no. 6 (November–December 1999).

Clarence, W. "The Human Rights Field Operation in Rwanda: Protective Practice Evolves on the Ground." *International Peacekeeping*, vol. 2, no. 3 (Autumn 1995), pp. 291–308.

Hopkins, Raymond F. "Complex Emergencies, Peacekeeping, and the World Food Programme." *International Peacekeeping*, vol. 5, no. 4 (Winter 1998), pp. 71–91.

Newland, Kathleen, and Deborah W. Meyers. "Peacekeeping and Refugee Relief." *International Peacekeeping*, vol. 5, no. 4 (Winter 1998), pp. 15–30.

Roberts, Adam. "Humanitarian War: Military Intervention and Human Rights." *International Affairs*, vol. 69 (July 1993), pp. 429–449.

Sandoz, Yves. "The International Committee of the Red Cross and the Law of Armed Conflict Today." *International Peacekeeping*, vol. 4, no. 4 (Winter 1997), pp. 86–99.

Whitman, Jim. "The UN Specialized Agencies, Peacekeeping, and the Enactment of Values." *International Peacekeeping*, vol. 5, no. 4 (Winter 1998), pp. 120–137.

11. Rules of Engagement

Berkowitz, Bruce D. "Rules of Engagement for UN Peacekeeping Forces in Bosnia." *Orbis*, vol. 38, no. 4 (Fall 1994), pp. 635–646.

Dworken, Jonathon T. "Rules of Engagement: Lessons from RESTORE HOPE." *Military Review*, vol. 74, no. 9 (September 1994), pp. 26–34.

Liu, F. T. *United Nations Peacekeeping and the Non-Use of Force*. International Peace Academy Occasional Paper Series. Boulder, CO: Lynne Rienner, 1992.

12. Policing

Beaulac, Herman. "The Role of Police Forces in International Peacekeeping." In *The New Peacekeeping Partnership*. Ed. by Alex Morrison. Clementsport, NS: Canadian Peacekeeping Press, 1995, pp. 99–104.

Costa, G. "The United Nations and Reform of the Police in El Salvador." *International Peacekeeping*, vol. 2, no. 3 (Autumn 1995), pp. 365–390.

Hills, Alice. "International Peace Support Operations and CIVPOL: Should There Be a Permanent Global Gendarmerie?" *International Peacekeeping*, vol. 5, no. 3 (Autumn 1998), pp. 26–41.

13. Regional International Organizations

Bertin, Marc-Yves. "Strengthening Regional Support for Global Security." *Peacekeeping and International Relations*, vol. 23, no. 3 (May–June 1994), pp. 14–15.

Black, Davidson. "Widening the Spectrum: Regional International Organizations and Peacekeeping Operations." *Peacekeeping and International Relations*, vol. 25, no. 3 (May–June 1996), pp. 7–8.

Marnika, Maurice. "Regional Peacekeeping: The Case for Complementary Efforts." *Peacekeeping and International Relations*, vol. 25, no. 3 (May–June 1996), pp. 9–10.

McCoubrey, H., and Justin Morris. *Regional Peacekeeping in the Post-Cold War Era*. The Hague: Kluwar Law International, 2000.

14. Sociological/Psychological Issues

Applewhite, Larry, and David R. Segal. "Telephone Use by Peacekeeping Troops in the Sinai." *Armed Forces and Society*, vol. 17, no. 1 (Fall 1990), pp. 117–126.

Bramsen, Inge, Anja J. E. Dirkzwager, and Henk M. Van der Ploeg. "Predeployment Personality Traits and Exposure to Trauma as Predictors of Posttraumatic Stress Symptoms: A Prospective Study of Former Peacekeepers." *American Journal of Psychology*, vol. 157, no. 7 (July 2000), pp. 1115–1110.

Britt, Thomas W. "The Stigma of Psychological Problems in a Work Environment: Evidence From the Screening of Service Members Returning from Bosnia." *Journal of Applied Social Psychology*, vol. 30, no. 8 (August 2000), pp. 1599–?.

Dicks, Henry V. "The International Soldier: A Psychiatrist's View." In *International Military Forces: The Question of Peacekeeping in an Armed and Disarming World*. Ed. by L. P. Bloomfield. Boston: Little, Brown, and Co., 1964, pp. 236–256.

Harris, Jesse J., and David R. Segal. "Observations From the Sinai: The Boredom Factor." *Armed Forces and Society*, vol. 11 (Winter 1985), pp. 235–248.

Langholtz, Harvey J. *The Psychology of Peacekeeping*. Westport, CT: Praeger, 1998.

Olsson, Louise, and T. Tryggestand, eds. *Women and International Peacekeeping*. Portland: F. Cass, 2001.

Stiehm, Judith H. "Men and Women and Peacekeeping." *International Peacekeeping*, vol. 2, no. 4 (Winter 1995), pp. 564–569.

II. LEAGUE OF NATIONS PEACEKEEPING

1. General Works

Walters, F. P. *A History of the League of Nations*. London: Oxford University Press, 1952.

Zimmerman, Alfred, ed. *The League of Nations and the Rule of Law, 1918 1935*. London: Macmillan, 1936.

2. Vilna International Force

Wambaugh, Sarah. *Plebiscites Since the World War*. Washington, DC: Carnegie Endowment for International Peace, 1933.

3. Saar International Force

Burne, A. H. "British Bayonets on the Saar." *Fighting Forces*, vol. XII, no. 1 (April 1935), pp. 22–32.

Florinsky, Michael T. *The Saar Struggle*. New York: Macmillan Company, 1935.

Hill, C. J. "Great Britain and the Saar Plebiscite of 13 January 1935." *Journal of Contemporary History*, vol. 9, no. 2 (April 1974), pp. 121–142.

Russell, Frank M. *The Saar: Battleground and Pawn*. Stanford, CA: Stanford University Press, 1951.

Wambaugh, Sarah. *Plebiscites Since the World War*. Washington, DC: Carnegie Endowment for International Peace, 1933.

———. *The Saar Plebiscite*. Cambridge, MA: Harvard University Press, 1940.

III. UNITED NATIONS PEACEKEEPING

1. General Works

Bloomfield, Lincoln P., et al. *International Military Forces*. Boston: Little, Brown, and Co., 1964.

Bowett, Derek. *United Nations Forces*. London: Stevens, 1964.

Boyd, James M. *United Nations Peacekeeping Operations: A Military and Political Appraisal*. New York: Praeger, 1971.

Burns, Arthur Lee, and Nina Heathcote. *Peacekeeping by UN Forces*. New York: Praeger, 1963.

Davidson Smith, Lieutenant Colonel G. "UN Peacekeeping and the Role of Force." *RUSI Journal for Defence Studies*, vol. 130, no. 3 (September 1985), pp. 37–41.

Durch, William J., ed. *The Evolution of UN Peacekeeping: Case Studies and Comparative Analyses*. New York: St. Martin's Press, 1993.

Durch, William J., and Barry Blechman. *Keeping the Peace: The United Nations in the Emerging World Order*. Washington, DC: The Henry L. Stimson Center, 1993.

Fabian, Larry L. *Soldiers Without Enemies: Preparing the United Nations for Peacekeeping*. Washington, DC: The Brookings Institution, 1971.

Fetherston, A. B. *Toward a Theory of United Nations Peacekeeping*. Peace Research Report Number 31. Bradford, UK: University of Bradford, February 1993.

Garvey, Jack. "United Nations Peacekeeping and Host State Consent." *American Journal of International Law,* vol. 64, no. 1 (1970), pp. 241–269.

Grover, Eric. "UN Armed Forces and the Military Staff Committee: A Look Back." *International Security*, vol. 17, no. 4 (Spring 1993), pp. 172–182.

Hillen, John. *Blue Helmets: The Strategy of UN Military Operations*. Washington, DC: Brassey's, 2000.

Johansen, Robert C. "UN Peacekeeping: The Changing Utility of Military Force." *Third World Quarterly*, vol. 12, no. 2 (April 1, 1990), p. 53.

Lewis, Paul. "A Short History of United Nations Peacekeeping." *Military History Quarterly*, vol. 5, no. 1 (Fall 1992), p. 33.

Lewis, William H., and Thomas Julian, eds. *Military Implications of United Nations Peacekeeping Operations*. Washington, DC: National Defense University, 1992.

Liu, F. T. *United Nations Peacekeeping: Management and Operations*. Occasional Paper no. 4. New York: International Peace Academy, 1990.

———. *United Nations Peacekeeping and the Non Use of Force*. Boulder, CO: Lynne Rienner Publishers, 1992.

Morrison, David C. "Blue Helmet Blues." *National Journal,* vol. 25, no. 8 (February 20, 1993), p. 483.

Murphy, John F. *The United Nations and the Control of International Violence*. Totowa, NJ: Allanhead, Osmun, 1983.

Norton, Augustus Richard, and Thomas G. Weiss. *UN Peacekeepers: Soldiers with a Difference*. In Headline Series no. 292. New Tork: Foreign Policy Association, 1990.

Pelcovits, Nathan, and Kevin Kramer. "Local Conflict and UN Peacekeeping: The Uses of Computerized Data." *International Studies Quarterly*, vol. 20, no. 4 (1976), pp. 533–552.

Rosenau, James N. *The United Nations in a Turbulent World*. Boulder, CO: Lynne Rienner Publishers, 1992.

"UN Peacekeeping Efforts to Promote Security and Stability." *Foreign Policy Bulletin*, vol. 2, no. 6 (May 1, 1992), p. 5.

United Nations. *The Blue Helmets: A Review of United Nations Peacekeeping*. 2nd edition. New York: Department of Public Information, 1990.

United Nations, General Assembly. *Comprehensive Review of the Whole Question of Peacekeeping Operations in all Their Aspects*. Report of the Special Committee of Peacekeeping Operations. New York: United Nations, June 9, 1989.

Urquhart, Brian. *A Life in Peace and War*. New York: Harper and Row, 1987.

Verrier, Anthony. *International Peacekeeping: United Nations Forces in a Troubled World*. Harmondsworth, Great Britain: Penguin, 1981.

Weiss, Thomas. "New Challenges for UN Military Operations: Implementing an Agenda for Peace." *Washington Quarterly*, vol. 16, no. 1 (Winter 1993), pp. 51–66.

White, N. D. *Keeping the Peace: The United Nations and the Maintenance of International Peace and Security*. New York: St. Martin's Press, 1993.

Williamson, Richard S. *The United Nations: A Place of Promise and Mischief*. Lanham, MD: University Press of America, 1990.

Wilson, Brigadier-General A. J. *Some Principles for Peace-Keeping Operations: A Guide for Senior Officers*. Monograph Series no. 2. Paris: International Information Center on Peacekeeping Operations, 1967.

2. Role of the Secretary-General

Bailey, S. *The Secretariat of the UN*. London: Pall Mall Press, 1964.

Bingham, J. R. *U Thant of Burma*. London: Victor Gollancz Ltd., 1966.

Boutros-Ghali, Boutros. *An Agenda for Peace: Preventive Diplomacy, Peacemaking, and Peacekeeping*. New York: United Nations, 1992.

Dayal, Rajeshwar. *Mission for Hammarskjöld: The Congo Crisis*. London: Oxford University Press, 1976.

Franck, Thomas M. "The Good Offices Function of the UN Secretary General." In *United Nations, Divided World: The UN's Roles in International Relations*. Ed. by Adam Roberts and Benedict Kingsbury. Oxford: Clarendon Press, 1988, pp. 79–94.

Gavshon, Arthur L. *The Mysterious Death of Dag Hammarskjöld*. New York: Walker, 1962.

Gordenker, Leon. *The United Nations Secretary General and the Maintenance of Peace*. New York: Columbia University Press, 1967.

Hammarskjöld, Dag. *The International Civil Servant in Law and in Fact*. Oxford: Oxford University Press, 1961.

———. *Markings*. New York: Alfred A. Knopf, 1964.

Lash, J. P. *Dag Hammarskjöld: Custodian of the Brushfire*. New York: Doubleday, 1961.

Lie, Trygve. *In the Case of Peace*. New York: Macmillan Company, 1954.

Miller, R. I. *Dag Hammarskjöld and Crisis Diplomacy*. New York: Oceana Publications, 1962.

Newman, Edward. *The UN Secretary-General from the Cold War to the New Era: A Global Peace and Security Mandate?* New York: St. Martin's Press, 1998.

Nassif, Rames. *Thant in New York, 1961–1971: A Portrait of the Third UN Secretary General*. London: Hurst and Company, 1988.

Perez de Cuellar, Javier. "The Role of the UN Secretary-General." In *United Nations, Divided World: The UN's Roles in International Relations*. Ed. by Adam Roberts and Benedict Kingsbury. Oxford: Clarendon Press, 1988, pp. 61–77.

Sarooshi, Danesh. "The Role of the United Nations Secretary-General in United Nations Peacekeeping Operations." *Australian Yearbook of International Law*, vol. 20 (1999), pp. 279–297.

Thant, U. *View From the UN*. New York: Doubleday, 1978.

Thorpe, Deryck. *Hammarskjöld: Man of Peace*. Ilfracombe: Stockwell, 1969.

Urquhart, Brian. *Hammarskjöld*. New York: Knopf, 1972.

Waldheim, Kurt. *In the Eye of the Storm: The Memoirs of Kurt Waldheim*. London: Weidenfeld and Nicholson, 1985.

Zacher, Mark W. *Dag Hammarskjöld's United Nations*. New York: Columbia University Press, 1970.

3. Standing Forces and Stand By Arrangements

A. UN Permanent Standing Army

Dennehy, Captain Edward, et al. *A Blue Helmet Combat Force*. Harvard University, John F. Kennedy School of Government National Security Program Policy Analysis Paper 93–01, 1993.

Diehl, Paul F. "A Permanent UN Peacekeeping Force: An Evaluation." *Bulletin of Peace Proposals*, vol. 20, no. 1 (March 1, 1989), p. 27.

Harper, Captain Gregory. "Creating a U.N. Peace Enforcement Force: A Case for U.S. Leadership." *The Fletcher Forum of World Affairs*, vol. 18, no. 1 (Winter–Spring 1994), pp. 49–64.

Haynes, Lukas, and Timothy W. Stanley. "To Create a United Nations Fire Brigade." *Comparative Strategy*, vol. 14, no. 1 (January–March 1995), pp. 7–22.

Johnson, Edward. "A Permanent United Nations Force: British Thinking After Suez." *Review of International Studies*, vol. 17 (1991), pp. 251–266.

Kaysen, Carl, and George Rathjens. *Peace Operations by the United Nations: The Case for a Volunteer UN Military Force*. Cambridge, MA: American Academy of the Arts and Sciences, 1995.

Kinloch, Stephen P. "Utopian or Pragmatic? A UN Permanent Military Volunteer Force." *International Peacekeeping*, vol. 3, no. 4 (Winter 1996), pp. 166–190.

Lewy, Guenter. "The Case for Humanitarian Intervention." *Orbis*, vol. 37, no. 4 (Fall 1993), pp. 621–632.

Morrison, Alex. "A Standing United Nations Military Force: Future Prospects." In *Peacekeeping and the Challenge of Civil Conflict Resolution*. Ed. by David A. Charters. Fredericton, New Brunswick: Centre for Conflict Studies, 1994.

———. "The Fiction of a U.N. Standing Army." *The Fletcher Forum of World Affairs*, vol. 18, no. 1 (Winter–Spring 1994), pp. 83–96.

Rechner, Patrick A. "Should the United Nations Have Its Own Army?" *Peacekeeping and International Relations*, vol. 23, no. 2 (March–April 1994), pp. 4–5.

Rostow, Eugene V. "Should Article 43 of the United Nations Charter Be Raised from the Dead?" *Global Affairs*, vol. 8 (Winter 1993), pp. 109–124.

Siekmann, Robert. "Political and Legal Aspects of a Directly Recruited Permanent UN Force." *International Peacekeeping*, vol. 2, no. 4 (June–July 1995).

Urquhart, Brian. "Keeping the Peace: The Argument for a United Nations Volunteer Militia Force. *Social Education*, vol. 58, no. 7 (November–December 1994), pp. 410–412.

B. UN Stand By Arrangements

Cox, David, and Albert Legault, eds. *UN Rapid Reaction Capabilities: Requirements and Prospects.* Clemensport: Canadian Peacekeeping Press, 1995.

Faille, Maxime. "Towards a UN Rapid Reaction Capability: A Canadian Initiative." *Canadian Defence Quarterly,* vol. 25, no. 2 (December 1995), pp. 14–16.

Haynes, Lukas, and Timothy Stanley. "To Create a United Nations Fire Brigade." *Comparative Strategy,* vol. 14, no. 1 (January–March 1995), pp. 7–22.

Stenquist, Nils. *Swedish UN Stand by Force and Experience.* International Information Center on Peacekeeping Operations. Monograph no. 4 (August 1967).

4. Peacekeeping Operations

A. United Nations Truce Supervision Organization

Bailey, Sydney D. *How Wars End: The United Nations and the Termination of Armed Conflict 1946–1964.* 2 vols. Oxford: Clarendon Press, 1982.

Comay, Michael. *UN Peacekeeping in the Israeli Arab Conflict, 1948–1975: An Israeli Critique.* Jerusalem: Institute for International Relations, Hebrew University, 1976.

Fehrenbach, T. R. *The United Nations in War and Peace.* New York: Random House, 1968.

Fry, William R., ed. *A United Nations Peace Force.* New York: Oceana, 1957.

Harbottle, Michael. *The Blue Berets: The Story of the United Nations Peacekeeping Forces.* London: Leo Cooper, 1971.

Horn, Carl C. Von. *Soldiering for Peace.* New York: David McKay Company, Inc., 1967.

Hurewitz, Jacob C. "The Israeli-Syrian Crisis in the Light of the Arab-Israel Armistice System." *International Organization,* vol. 3 (August 1959), pp. 505–519.

———. "United Nations Conciliation Commission for Palestine." *International Organization,* vol. 7 (November 1953), pp. 482–495.

Hutchison, E. H. *Violent Truce.* London: John Calder, 1956.

Khouri, Fred J. "Friction and Conflict on the Israeli-Syrian Frontier." *The Middle East Journal,* vol. 17 (Winter 1963), pp. 14–31.

Leonard, Larry. "The United Nations and Palestine." *International Conciliation,* no. 454 (October 1949), pp. 607–786.

Nachmias, Nitza. "UNTSO: Obsolete Peacekeeping?" *Peacekeeping and International Relations,* vol. 25, no. 1 (January–February 1996), pp. 6–7.

Pelcovits, Nathan A. *The Long Armistice: UN Peacekeeping and the Arab-Israeli Conflict, 1948–1960*. Boulder, CO: Westview Press, 1993.

B. United Nations Special Committee on the Balkans

Frye, William R., ed. *A United Nations Peace Force*. New York: Oceana, 1957.
Higgins, Rosalyn. *United Nations Peacekeeping 1946–1967: Documents and Commentary*, vol. 4. London: Oxford University Press, 1981.

C. United Nations Military Observer Group in India and Pakistan

Bailey, Sydney D. *How Wars End: The United Nations and the Termination of Armed Conflict 1946–1964*. 2 vols. Oxford: Clarendon Press, 1982.
Dawson, Pauline. *The Peacekeeping of Kashmir: The United Nations Military Observer Group in India and Pakistan*. New York: St. Martin's Press, 1994.
Frye, William R., ed. *A United Nations Peace Force*. New York: Oceana, 1957.
Harbottle, Michael. *The Blue Berets: The Story of the United Nations Peace-keeping Forces*. London: Leo Cooper, 1971.
Hutter, Joachim. "United Nations Peacekeeping Operations." *Aussenpolitik*, vol. 36, no. 3 (1985), pp. 264–274.
Korbel, Josef. "The Kashmir Dispute After Six Years." *International Organization*, vol. 7, no. 4 (1953), pp. 498–510.
———. "The Kashmir Dispute and the United Nations." *International Organization*, vol. 3, no. 2 (1949), pp. 278–287.
Lourie, Sylvia. "United Nations Military Observation Group in India and Pakistan." *International Organization*, vol. 9, no. 1 (Fall 1955), pp. 19–31.
Millar, T. B. "Kashmir, the Commonwealth, and the United Nations." *Australian Outlook*, vol. 17, no. 1 (1963), pp. 54–73.
Moore, Raymond A. *Lessons of the Indo-Pakistan Dispute*. Columbia, SC: University of South Carolina, Institute of International Studies, 1966.
Parakatil, Francis. *India and United States Peacekeeping*. New Delhi: S. Chand, 1975.
Shahidul Alam, G. M. "Peacekeeping Without Conflict Resolution: The Kashmir Dispute." *Fletcher Forum of World Affairs*, vol. 6, no. 1 (1982), pp. 61–89.

D. United Nations Emergency Force I

Andrassy, Juraj. "Uniting for Peace." *American Journal of International Law*, vol. 50, no. 3 (1956), pp. 563–582.
Benton, Wilbourn E. *International Law and the Middle East Crisis*. New Orleans, LA: Tulane University Press, 1957.

Bowman, Edward H., and James E. Fanning. "The Logistics Problems of a UN Military Force." *International Organization*, vol. 17, no. 2 (1963), pp. 355–376.

Boyd, James M. *The United Nations Peacekeeping Operations: A Military and Political Appraisal*. New York: Praeger, 1971.

Burns, Arthur Lee, and Nina Heathcote. *Peacekeeping by UN Forces*. London: Pall Mall Press, 1963.

Chapman, Dudley H. "International Law—The United Nations Emergency Force: Legal Status." *Michigan Law Review*, vol. 62 (November 1958), pp. 56–81.

Cohen, Maxwell. "The United Nations Emergency Force: A Preliminary View." *International Journal*, vol. 12, no. 2 (1957), pp. 109–127.

Comay, Michael. *UN Peacekeeping in the Israel-Arab Conflict, 1948–1975: An Israeli Critique*. Jerusalem: Institute for International Relations, Hebrew University, 1976.

Elaraby, Nabil. "UN Peacekeeping: The Egyptian Experience." In *Peacekeeping: Appraisals and Proposals*. Ed. by Henry Wiseman. New York: Pergamon Press, 1983, pp. 65–92.

Goodrich, Leland M., and Gabriella Rosner. "The United Nations Emergency Force." *International Organization*, vol. 11, no. 3 (1957), pp. 413–430.

Harbottle, Michael. *The Blue Berets: The Story of the United Nations Peacekeeping Forces*. London: Leo Cooper, 1971.

Holm Johansen, Arne, and Odd Oeyen. "Experiences Related to Logistics in Gaza and the Congo." In *Peacekeeping: Experience and Evaluation*. Ed. by Per Frydenberg. Oslo: Norwegian Institute of International Affairs, 1964, pp. 163–172.

James, Alan. "UN Action for Peace: I. Barrier Forces." *World Today*, vol. 18, no. 11 (1962), pp. 478–486.

Kay, Zachariah. "The UN Force in Korea and Sinai." *International Relations*, vol. 2, no. 3 (1961), pp. 168–183.

Lal, Nand. *From Collective Security to Peacekeeping: A Study of India's Contribution to the United Nations Emergency Force, 1956–1967*. Calcutta: Minerva Associates, 1975.

Lauterpacht, E. *The UN Emergency Force: Basic Documents*. New York: Praeger, 1960.

Mason, Henry L. *The United Nations Emergency Force*. New Orleans, LA: Tulane University Press, 1957.

Pearson, Lester B. "Force for the UN." *Foreign Affairs*, vol. 35, no. 3 (1957), pp. 395–404.

Pelcovits, Nathan A. *The Long Armistice: UN Peacekeeping and the Arab Israeli Conflict, 1948–1960*. Boulder, CO: Westview Press, 1993.

Rosner, Gabriella. *The United Nations Emergency Force*. New York: Columbia University Press, 1963.

Solum, Ingebrigt. "Armed UN Action." In *Peacekeeping: Experience and Evaluation*. Ed. by Per Frydenberg. Oslo: Norwegian Institute of International Affairs, 1964, pp. 141–146.

Spry, Graham. "Canada, the United Nations Emergency Force, and the Commonwealth." *International Affairs*, vol. 33, no. 3 (1957), pp. 289–301.

Sundaram, J. *Operation Shanti: Indian Army Peace Mission in Egypt, 1956–1967*. New Delhi: Ministry of Defence, 1990.

Tsur, Yoel Arnon. "The United Nations Peacekeeping Operations in the Middle East From 1956 to 1976." In *United Nations Peacekeeping: Legal Essays*. Ed. by Antonio Cassese. Alphen aan den Rijn: Sijthoff and Noordhoff, 1978, pp. 183–213.

Urquhart, Brian. "United Nations Peacekeeping in the Middle East." *World Today*, vol. 36, no. 3 (1980), pp. 88–93.

Verrier, Anthony. *International Peacekeeping: United Nations Forces in a Troubled World*. Harmondsworth, Great Britain: Penguin Books, 1981.

E. United Nations Observation Group in Lebanon

Curtis, Gerald L. "The United Nations Observation Group in Lebanon." *International Organization*, vol. 18, no. 4 (1964), pp. 738–765.

Petersen, Keith S. "The Uses of the Uniting for Peace Resolution Since 1950." *International Organization*, vol. 13, no. 2 (1959), pp. 219–232.

Potter, Pitman B. "Legal Aspects of the Beirut Landing." *American Journal of International Law*, vol. 52, no. 3 (1958), pp. 727–730.

F. United Nations Operation in the Congo

Abi Saab, Georges. *The United Nations Operation in the Congo 1960–1964*. New York: Oxford University Press, 1978.

Amachree, Godfrey. "UN Civilian Operations in the Congo." In *Southern Africa in Transition*. Ed. by J. A. Davis and J. K. Baker. New York: Praeger, 1966, pp. 305–317.

Barton, G. P., and Derek W. Bowett. *United Nations Forces: A Legal Study of United Nations Practice*. London: Stevens, 1964.

Bilsen, A. A. J. Van. "Some Aspects of the Congo Problem." *International Affairs*, vol. 38, no. 1 (1962), pp. 41–51.

Bloomfield, Lincoln P. "Headquarters–Field Relations: Some Notes on the Beginning and End of ONUC." *International Organization*, vol. 17, no. 2 (1963), pp. 377–392.

——. "The United Nations in Crisis: The Role of the United Nations in United States Foreign Policy." *Daedalus,* vol. 91, no. 3 (1962), pp. 749–765.

Boulden, Jane. *Peace Enforcement: The UN Experience in Congo, Somalia, and Bosnia.* Westport, CT: Praeger, 2001.

Dayal, Rajeshwar. *Mission for Hammarskjöld: The Congo Crisis.* Princeton, NJ: Princeton University Press, 1976.

Findlay, Trevor. *Blue Helmets' First War? Use of Force by the UN in the Congo, 1960–1964.* Clementsport, NS: Canadian Peacekeeping Press, 1999.

Franck, Thomas M. "United Nations Law in Africa: The Congo Operation as a Case Study." *Law and Contemporary Problems,* vol. 27, no. 4 (Autumn 1962), pp. 632–652.

Galtung, Johan, and Helge Hveem. "Participants in Peacekeeping Forces." *Cooperation and Conflict,* no. 1 (1976), pp. 25–40.

Gibbs, David N. "The United Nations, International Peacekeeping, and the Question of 'Impartiality': Revisiting the Congo Operation of 1960." *The Journal of Modern African Studies,* vol. 38, no. 3 (September 2000), pp. 359–383.

Goode, Robert C. "Four African Views of the Congo Crisis." In *Footnotes to the Congo Story.* Ed. by Helen Kitchen. New York: Walker and Co., 1967, pp. 45–58.

Gordon, J. King. *The UN in the Congo.* New York: Carnegie Endowment for International Peace, 1962.

Harbottle, Michael. *The Blue Berets: The Story of the United Nations Peacekeeping Forces.* London: Leo Cooper, 1971.

Hoffmann, Stanley. "In Search of a Thread: The UN in the Congo Labyrinth." *International Organization,* vol. 16, no. 2 (Spring 1962), pp. 331–361.

Holm Johansen, Arne, and Odd Oeyen. "Experiences Related to Logistics in Gaza and the Congo." In *Peacekeeping: Experience and Evaluation.* Ed. by Per Frydenberg. Oslo: Norwegian Institute of International Affairs, 1964, pp. 163–172.

Horn, Carl C. Von. *Soldiering for Peace.* New York: David McKay Company, Inc., 1967.

Hoskyns, Catherine. *The Congo Since Independence.* Oxford: Oxford University Press, 1965.

House, Arthur H. *The UN in the Congo: The Political and Civilian Efforts.* Washington, DC: University Press of America, 1978.

Jacobsen, H. K. "ONUC's Civilian Operations: State Preserving and State Building." *World Politics,* vol. 17, no. 1 (October 1964), pp. 75–107.

James, Alan. *Britain and the Congo Crisis, 1960–1964.* London: MacMillan Press, Ltd., 1996.

Kitchen, Helen, ed. *Footnotes to the Congo Story.* New York: Walker and Co., 1967.

Lefever, Ernest W. *Crisis in the Congo: A United Nations Force in Action.* Washington, DC: The Brookings Institution, 1965.

——. *Uncertain Mandate: Politics of the United Nations Congo Operations.* Baltimore, MD: The Johns Hopkins University Press, 1967.

——. "United Nations Peace Forces and the Changing Globe." *International Organization*, vol. 17, no. 2 (Spring 1963), pp. 321–337.

Lefever, Ernest W., and Joshua Wynfred. *United Nations Peacekeeping in the Congo, 1960–1964.* vol. 3, Appendixes. Washington, DC: Brookings Institution, 1966.

Nimer, Benjamin. *The United Nations Force in the Congo: A Political Analysis.* Washington, DC: George Washington University, 1966.

Nkrumah, Kwame. *Challenge of the Congo.* New York: International Publishers, 1967.

O'Brien, Conor Cruise. *To Katanga and Back: A UN Case History.* London: Hutchinson, 1962.

O'Donovan, Patrick. "The Precedent of the Congo." *International Affairs*, vol. 37, no. 2 (April 1961), pp. 181–188.

Smith, Raymond. *The Fighting Irish in the Congo.* Dublin: Little and McClean, 1962.

Wainhouse, David W. *International Peacekeeping at the Crossroads: National Support-Experience and Prospects.* Baltimore, MD: Johns Hopkins University Press, 1973.

G. United Nations Security Force

Bailey, Sydney D. *How Wars End: The United Nations and the Termination of Armed Conflict 1946–1964.* 2 vols. Oxford: Clarendon Press, 1982.

Kroef, Justus M. van der. "The West New Guinea Settlement: Its Origins and Implications." *Orbis*, vol. 7, no. 1 (1963), pp. 120–149.

Leyser, Johannes. "Dispute and Agreement on West New Guinea." *Archiv des Volkerrechts*, vol. 10, no. 3 (1963), pp. 257–272.

Seyersted, Finn. *United Nations Forces in the Law of Peace and War.* Leyden, Netherlands: A. W. Sijtoff, 1966.

Taylor, Alastair M. *Indonesian Independence and the United Nations.* London: Stevens and Sons, 1960.

United Nations. *The United Nations in West New Guinea.* New York: United Nations, 1963.

Veur, Paul W. van der. "Political Awakening in West New Guinea." *Pacific Affairs*, vol. 36, no. 1 (1963), pp. 54–73.

——. "The UN and West Irian: A Critique." *International Organization*, vol. 18, no. 1 (1964), pp. 53–73.

H. United Nations Temporary Executive Authority

Leyser, Johannes. "Dispute and Agreement on West New Guinea." *Archiv des Völkerrechts*, vol. 10, no. 3 (1963), pp. 257–272.

Veur, Paul W. van der. "Political Awakening in West New Guinea." *Pacific Affairs*, vol. 36, no. 1 (1963), pp. 54–73.

———. "The UN and West Irian: A Critique." *International Organization*, vol. 18, no. 1 (1964), pp. 53–73.

I. United Nations Yemen Observation Mission

Bishku, Michael B. "The United States and the UN Yemen Observation Mission." In *Peacekeeping and the Challenge of Civil Conflict Resolution*. Ed. by David A. Charters. Fredericton, New Brunswick: Centre for Conflict Studies, 1994.

Jones, Peter. "UNYOM: The Forgotten Mission." *Canadian Defence Quarterly*, vol. 22, no. 1 (August 1992), pp. 18–23.

Strieff, Eric. "Problematic UN Mission in Yemen." *Swiss Review of World Affairs*, vol. 13, no. 7 (1967), pp. 5–6.

J. United Nations Peacekeeping Force in Cyprus

Barker, Barry, Gavin Brown, and Terry Burke. *Police as Peacekeepers: The History of the Australian and New Zealand Police Serving With the United Nations Force in Cyprus, 1964–1984*. Melbourne: UNCIVPOL, 1984.

Boyd, James M. "Cyprus: Episode in Peacekeeping." *International Organization*, vol. 20, no. 1 (Winter 1966), pp. 1–17.

———. *The United Nations Peacekeeping Operations: A Military and Political Appraisal*. New York: Praeger, 1971.

Carrion, Alejandro J. Rodriguez. "The United Nations Force in Cyprus: An Uncertain Case of Peacekeeping." In *United Nations Peacekeeping: Legal Essays*. Ed. by Antonio Cassese. Alphen aan den Rijn, Netherlands: Sijthoff and Noordhoff, 1978, pp. 155–182.

Castleberry, H. Paul. "Conflict Resolution and the Cyprus Problem." *Western Political Quarterly*, vol. 17, no. 3 (1964), pp. 118–130.

Coufoudakis, Van. "United Nations Peacekeeping and the Cyprus Question." *Western Political Quarterly,* vol. 29, no. 3 (1976), pp. 457–473.

Draper, G. I. A. D. "UN Force in Cyprus." *The Military Law and War Law Review*, vol. 6, no. 1 (1967), pp. 51–75.

Ertekun, Necati Munir. "The Role of the United Nations in the Search for a Political Settlement in Cyprus." In *The Cyprus Conflict and the Role of the United Nations*. Ed. by Kjell Skjelsbaek. Oslo: Norwegian Institute of International Affairs, Report no. 22, 1988.

Gordon, King. "The UN in Cyprus." *International Journal*, vol. 18, no. 3 (1964), pp. 326–347.

Higgins, Rosalyn. "Basic Facts on the UN Force in Cyprus." *World Today*, vol. 20, no. 8 (1964), pp. 347–350.

James, Alan. *Keeping the Peace in the Cyprus Crisis of 1963–64*. New York: Palgrave, 2001.

Martin, Paul. "UN Peacekeeping Operations in Cyprus." *External Affairs*, vol. 16, no. 4 (1964), pp. 130–135.

Mitchell, Robert B. "Military and Diplomatic Aspects of Peacekeeping." In *The Cyprus Conflict and the Role of the United Nations*. Ed. by Kjell Skjelsbaek. Oslo: Norwegian Institute of International Affairs, Report no. 22, 1988.

Skjelsbaek, Kjell, ed. *The Cyprus Conflict and the Role of the United Nations*. Oslo: Norwegian Institute of International Affairs, Report no. 22, 1988.

Sommereyns, Raymond. "United Nations Peacekeeping Forces in the Middle East." *Brooklyn Journal of International Law*, vol. 6 (Spring 1980), pp. 1–53.

Sowerwine, James S. "Conflict in Cyprus: The Turkish Dimension." In *Peacekeeping and the Challenge of Civil Conflict Resolution*. Ed. by David A. Charters. Fredericton, New Brunswick: Centre for Conflict Studies, 1994.

Soysal, Mumtaz. "Turkish Position on Cyprus." In *The Cyprus Conflict and the Role of the United Nations*. Ed. by Kjell Skjelsbaek Oslo: Norwegian Institute of International Affairs, Report no. 22, 1988.

Stegenga, James A. *The United Nations Force in Cyprus*. Columbus, OH: State University Press, 1968.

Venter, Al J. "Blue Helmets on the Green Line: The UN Peacekeeping Force in Cyprus." *International Défense Review*, vol. 22, no. 11 (1988), pp. 1431–1436.

K. United Nations India Pakistan Observation Mission

Parakatil, Francis. *India and United Nations Peacekeeping*. New Delhi: S. Chand, 1975.

Shahidul Alam, G. M. "Peacekeeping Without Conflict Resolution: The Kashmir Dispute." *Fletcher Forum of World Affairs*, vol. 6, no. 1 (1982), pp. 61–89.

L. United Nations Emergency Force II

Comay, Michael. *UN Peacekeeping in the Israeli-Arab Conflict, 1948–1975: An Israeli Critique*. Jerusalem: Institute for International Relations, Hebrew University, 1976.

Elaraby, Nabil. "UN Peacekeeping: The Egyptian Experience." In *Peacekeeping: Appraisals and Proposals*. Ed. by Henry Wiseman. New York: Pergamon Press, 1983, pp. 65–92.

Fabian, Larry. "Toward a Peacekeeping Renaissance." *International Organization*, vol. 30, no. 1 (1976), pp. 153–161.

Nelson, Richard W. "Multinational Peacekeeping in the Middle East and the United Nations Model." *International Affairs*, vol. 61, no. 1 (Winter 1984–1985), pp. 67–90.

———. "Peacekeeping Aspects of the Egyptian Israeli Peace Treaty and Consequences for United Nations Peacekeeping." *Denver Journal of International Law and Policy*, vol. 10 (Fall 1980), pp. 113–153.

Pelcovits, Nathan A. *Peacekeeping on Arab-Israeli Fronts: Lessons from Sinai and Lebanon*. Boulder, CO: Westview Press, 1984.

———. "UN Peacekeeping and the 1973 Arab-Israeli Conflict." *Orbis*, vol. 19 (Spring 1975), pp. 146–165.

Sommereyns, Raymond. "United Nations Peacekeeping Forces in the Middle East." *Brooklyn Journal of International Law*, vol. 6 (Spring 1980), pp. 1–53.

Stjernfelt, Bertil. *The Sinai Peace Front: UN Peacekeeping Operations in the Middle East, 1973–1980*. New York: St. Martin's Press, 1992.

Tsur, Yoel Arnon. "The United Nations Peacekeeping Operations in the Middle East From 1956 to 1976." In *United Nations Peacekeeping: Legal Essays*. Ed. by Antonio Cassese. Alphen aan den Rijn, Netherlands: Sijthoff and Noordhoff, 1978, pp. 183–213.

Urquhart, Brian. "United Nations Peacekeeping in the Middle East." *World Today*, vol. 36, no. 3 (1980), pp. 88–93.

Wiseman, Henry. "UNEF II: New Chance to Set Firm Peacekeeping Guidelines." *International Perspectives* (March–April 1974), pp. 42–48.

M. United Nations Disengagement Observer Force

Comay, Michael. *UN Peacekeeping in the Israel-Arab Conflict, 1948–1975: An Israeli Critique*. Jerusalem: Jerusalem Papers on Peace Problems, nos. 17–18, 1976.

James, Alan. *The UN on the Golan: Peacekeeping Paradox?* Oslo: Norwegian Institute of International Affairs, NUPI Report no. 100, 1986.

Mackinlay, John. *The Peacekeepers: An Assessment of Peacekeeping Operations at the Arab-Israeli Interface*. London: Unwin Hyman, 1989.

Pelcovits, Nathan A. "Uses of UN Peacekeeping on Arab-Israeli Fronts: Will Changing Power Relations Improve the Prospects?" *Jerusalem Journal of International Relations*, vol. 10, no. 1 (1988), pp. 77–113.

Siekmann, Robert C. R. "The Multinational Peacekeeping Force in the Sinai in the Light of the United Nations Practice on Peacekeeping Forces." *The Indian Journal of International Law*, vol. 24, no. 3 (1984), pp. 504–524.

Sommereyns, Raymond. "United Nations Peacekeeping Forces in the Middle East." *Brooklyn Journal of International Law*, vol. 6 (Spring 1980), pp. 1–53.

Tsur, Yoel Arnon. "The United Nations Peacekeeping Operations in the Middle East From 1956 to 1976." In *United Nations Peacekeeping: Legal Essays*. Ed. by Antonio Cassese. Alphen aan den Rijn, Netherlands: Sijthoff and Noordhoff, 1978, pp. 183–213.

Urquhart, Brian. "United Nations Peacekeeping in the Middle East." *World Today*, vol. 36, no. 3 (1980), pp. 88–93.

N. United Nations Interim Force in Lebanon

Boerma, Maureen. "The United Nations Interim Force in the Lebanon: Peacekeeping in a Domestic Conflict." *Millennium*, vol. 8, no. 1 (1979), pp. 51–63.

Comay, Michael. *UN Peacekeeping in the Israel-Arab Conflict, 1948–1975: An Israeli Critique*. Jerusalem: Jerusalem Papers on Peace Problems, nos. 17–18, 1976.

Dai, Poeliu. "The United Nations Interim Force in Lebanon and Canadian Participation." *The Canadian Yearbook of International Law*, vol. 17 (1979), pp. 304–313.

Goksel, Timur. "UNIFIL: Honour in Lebanon." *Army Quarterly* (October 1983), pp. 391–411.

Heilberg, Marianne. *Lebanon, Political Playground of the Middle East: The Role of Peacekeeping*. Oslo: Norwegian Institute of International Affairs, Paper no. 411, 1989.

———. *Observations on UN Peacekeeping in Lebanon*. Oslo: Norwegian Institute of International Affairs, Paper no. 305, 1984.

———. "Peacekeepers and Local Populations: Some Comments on UNIFIL." In *The United Nations and Peacekeeping: Results, Limitations, and Prospects*. Ed. by Indar Rikhye and Kjell Skjelsbaek. London: Macmillan, 1990, pp. 147–169.

———. "UNIFIL and the Lebanese." In *A Thankless Task: The Role of UNIFIL in Southern Lebanon*. Ed. by Anthony McDermott and Kjell Skjelsbaek. Oslo: Norwegian Institute of International Affairs, Report no. 123, 1988, pp. 70–94.

Holst, Johan J. "Peacekeeping: The Art and the Limits." In *A Thankless Task: The Role of UNIFIL in Southern Lebanon*. Ed. by Anthony McDermott and Kjell Skjelsbaek. Oslo: Norwegian Institute of International Affairs, Report no. 123, 1988, pp. 27–32.

Issele, Jean Pierre. "The French Position Towards UNIFIL: General Trends." In *A Thankless Task: The Role of UNIFIL in Southern Lebanon*. Ed. by Anthony McDermott and Kjell Skjelsbaek. Oslo: Norwegian Institute of International Affairs, Report no. 123, 1988, pp. 133–158.

James, Alan. *Interminable Interim: The UN Force in Lebanon*. London: Centre for Security and Conflict Studies, 1988.

———. "Painful Peacekeeping: The United Nations in Lebanon 1978–1982." *International Journal*, vol. 38, no. 4 (Autumn 1983), pp. 613–634.

Kazziha, Walid. "Syria, Lebanon, and UNIFIL." In *A Thankless Task: The Role of UNIFIL in Southern Lebanon*. Ed. by Anthony McDermott and Kjell Skjelsbaek. Oslo: Norwegian Institute of International Affairs, Report no. 123, 1988, pp. 123–132.

Levran, Aharon. "UNIFIL's Balance Sheet." In *A Thankless Task: The Role of UNIFIL in Southern Lebanon*. Ed. by Anthony McDermott and Kjell Skjelsbaek. Oslo: Norwegian Institute of International Affairs, Report no. 123, 1988, pp. 159–170.

Mackinlay, John. *The Peacekeepers: An Assessment of Peacekeeping Operations at the Arab-Israeli Interface*. London: Unwin Hyman, 1989.

McDermott, Anthony, and Kjell Skjelsbaek, eds. *A Thankless Task: The Role of UNIFIL in Southern Lebanon*. Oslo: Norwegian Institute of International Affairs, Report no. 123, 1988.

Ness, Martin Hjelmervik, and Kjell Skjelsbaek. *The Predicament of UNIFIL: Report on a Visit to Southern Lebanon and Israel, 1–11 November 1985*. Oslo: Norwegian Institute of International Affairs, Paper no. 343, 1985.

Parker, James. "UNIFIL and Peacekeeping—the Defence Forces Experiences." *Irish Studies in International Affairs*, vol. 2, no. 2 (1986), pp. 63–78.

Pelcovits, Nathan A. *Peacekeeping on Arab-Israeli Fronts: Lessons from Sinai and Lebanon*. Boulder, CO: Westview Press, 1984.

———. "Uses of UN Peacekeeping on Arab-Israeli Fronts: Will Changing Power Relations Improve the Prospects?" *Jerusalem Journal of International Relations*, vol. 10, no. 1 (1988), pp. 77–113.

Skogmo, Bjorn. *UNIFIL: International Peacekeeping in Lebanon, 1978–1988*. Boulder, CO: Lynne Rienner Publishers, 1988.

Thakur, Ramesh C. *International Peacekeeping in Lebanon: United Nations Authority and Multinational Force*. Boulder, CO: Westview Press, 1987.

———. "Ministate and Macrocooperation: Fiji's Peacekeeping Debut in Lebanon." *International Studies*, vol. 10 (October 1984), pp. 269–284.

Weinberger, Naomi J. "Peacekeeping Operations in Lebanon." *Middle East Journal*, vol. 37, no. 3 (Summer 1983), pp. 341–369.

Weisman, Henry. "Lebanon: The Latest Example of UN Peacekeeping Action." *International Perspectives* (January–February 1979), pp. 3–7.

O. United Nations Good Offices in Afghanistan and Pakistan

Eknes, Aage. *Revitalizing Peacekeeping: Old Constraints, New Challenges.* Oslo: Norwegian Institute of International Affairs, Paper no. 407, 1989.

Haq, Obaid ul. "The Regional Dimension: Pakistan and Afghanistan, the Gulf States, and the Iran-Iraq War." In *Afghanistan, Iran and Iraq: External Involvement and Multilateral Options.* Ed. by Indar Rikhye. New York: International Peace Academy, Report no. 31 (1989), pp. 30–59.

Leslie, D. S., and R. G. Elms. "United Nations Good Offices Mission in Afghanistan and Pakistan: Lessons from a Peacekeeping Experience." *Canadian Defence Quarterly,* vol. 19, no. 1 (August 1989), pp. 51–54.

Newell, Richard S. "Peacekeeping and the Role of the United Nations in Afghanistan." In *Peacekeeping and the Challenge of Civil Conflict Resolution.* Ed. by David A. Charters. Fredericton, New Brunswick: Centre for Conflict Studies, 1994.

Rikhye, Indar, ed. *Afghanistan, Iran and Iraq: External Involvement and Multilateral Options.* New York: International Peace Academy, Report no. 31, 1989.

P. United Nations Iran-Iraq Military Observer Group

Eknes, Aage. *From Scandal to Success: The United Nations and the Iran-Iraq War 1980–1988.* Oslo: Norwegian Institute of International Affairs, Paper no. 406, 1989.

Jones, Peter. "UNIIMOG and the Persian Gulf Crisis." *Peacekeeping and International Relations,* vol. 20, no. 2 (March–April 1991), pp. 7–8.

Leurdijk, D. A. "The Expediency and Effectiveness of UN Peacekeeping Operations." *Netherlands International Law Review,* vol. 35, no. 3 (1988), pp. 311–317.

Rikhye, Indar, ed. *Afghanistan, Iran and Iraq: External Involvement and Multilateral Options.* New York: International Peace Academy, Report no. 31, 1989.

Stone, Gary. "Peacekeeping on the Iran-Iraq Border." *Asia-Pacific Defence Reporter,* vol. 17 (October 1990), pp. 9–12.

Q. United Nations Angola Verification Mission I, II, and III

(1). General Works

Malaquias, Assis. "The UN In Mozambique and Angola." *International Peacekeeping,* vol. 3, no. 2 (Summer 1996), pp. 87–106.

Morel, Elenore, Charles Hucine, and Elenore Medrinal. *Angola (1988–1997) UNAVEM I, UNAVEM II, UNAVEM III.* Paris: Montchrestien, 1997.

(2). United Nations Angola Verification Mission I

Fortna, Virginia Page. "United Nations Angola Verification Mission I." In *The Evolution of UN Peacekeeping: Case Studies and Comparative Analysis.* Ed. by William J. Durch. New York: St. Martin's Press, 1993, pp. 377–387.

Krska, Vladimir. "Peacekeeping in Angola (UNAVEM I and II)." *International Peacekeeping*, vol. 4, no. 1 (Spring 1997), pp. 75–97.

Morel, Elenore, Charles Hucine, and Elenore Medrinal. *Angola (1988–1997) UNAVEM I, UNAVEM II, UNAVEM III.* Paris: Montchrestien, 1997.

(3). United Nations Angola Verification Mission II

Fornta, Virginia Page. "United Nations Angola Verification Mission II." In *The Evolution of UN Peacekeeping: Case Studies and Comparative Analysis.* Ed. by William J. Durch. New York: St. Martin's Press, 1993, pp. 389–405.

Krska, Vladimir. "Peacekeeping in Angola (UNAVEM I and II)." *International Peacekeeping*, vol. 4, no. 1 (Spring 1997), pp. 75–97.

Morel, Elenore, Charles Hucine, and Elenore Medrinal. *Angola (1988–1997) UNAVEM I, UNAVEM II, UNAVEM III.* Paris: Montchrestien, 1997.

"UNAVEM II Created to Verify Peaceful Transition." *UN Chronicle*, vol. 28, no. 3 (September 1991), pp. 27–28.

(4). United Nations Angola Verification Mission III

Lohmann, Torsten. "UNAVEM III: A New Sense of Realism?" *International Peacekeeping*, vol. 2, no. 2–3 (February–May 1995).

McQueen, Norrie. "Peackeeping by Attrition: The United Nations in Angola." *The Journal of Modern African Studies* (September 1998), pp. 399–401.

Morel, Elenore, Charles Hucine, and Elenore Medrinal. *Angola (1988–1997) UNAVEM I, UNAVEM II, UNAVEM III.* Paris: Montchrestien, 1997.

R. United Nations Transition Assistance Group

Chopra, J. *UN Authority in Cambodia.* Thomas Watson, Jr. Institute for International Studies Occasional Paper no. 15. Providence: Brown University, 1994.

Crocker, Chester. "Southern African Peace Making." *Survival*, vol. 31, no. 3 (May–June 1990), pp. 221–232.

Dale, Richard. "The UN and African Decolonization: UNTAG in Namibia." *Trans Africa Forum*, no. 8 (Fall 1991), pp. 31–48.

Fortna, Virginia Page. "United Nations Transition Assistance Group." In *The Evolution of UN Peacekeeping: Case Studies and Comparative Analysis*. Ed. by William J. Durch. New York: St. Martin's Press, 1993.

Hearn, Roger H. *United Nations Peacekeeping in Action: The Namibian Experience*. Commack, NY: Nova Sciences Publishers, 1999.

Jeffery, M. K. "The United Nations Transition Assistance Group (UNTAG) Namibia." *Canadian Defence Quarterly*, vol. 20, no. 6 (June 1991), pp. 7–11.

Thornberry, Cedric. *The UNTAG Experience in Namibia First Phase*. Johannesburg: South African Institute of International Affairs, 1990.

S. United Nations Observer Group in Central America

Baranyi, Stephen, and Lisa North. *Stretching the Limits of the Possible: United Nations Peacekeeping in Central America*. Ottawa: Canadian Centre for Global Security, 1992.

Hayes, Pat. "ONUCA Reconnaissance Mission." *An Cosantoir*, vol. 50, no. 2 (February 1990).

Joly, John D. "ONUCA: A Story of Success in the Quest for Peace." *Canadian Defence Quarterly*, vol. XX (June 1991), pp. 12–19.

Klepak, H. P. "Peacekeeping in Central America." In *Peacekeeping and the Challenge of Civil Conflict Resolution*. Ed. by David A. Charters. Fredericton, New Brunswick: Centre for Conflict Studies, 1994.

"Plan for UN Observers in Central America in Suspense." *UN Chronicle*, vol. 26, no. 3 (September 1989), pp. 13–14.

T. United Nations Mission for the Referendum in Western Sahara

Boudreau, Captain Brett. "The Great Berm of Western Sahara." *Sentinel*, vol. 28, no. 6 (December 1992–January 1993), pp. 4–7.

Damis, John. "The UN Settlement Plan for the Western Sahara: Problems and Prospects." *Middle East Policy*, vol. 1, no. 2 (1992), pp. 36–46.

Delaney, Trevor A. "Article 2(7) of the United Nations Charter: Hindrance to the Self Determination of the Western Sahara and Eritrea?" *Emory International Law Review*, vol. 4, no. 2 (Fall 1990).

Durch, William J. "Building on Sand: UN Peacekeeping in the Western Sahara." *International Security*, vol. 17, no. 4 (Spring 1993), p. 151.

———, ed. "United Nations Mission for the Referendum in Western Sahara." In *The Evolution of UN Peacekeeping: Case Studies and Comparative Analysis*. New York: St. Martin's Press, 1993, pp. 406–433.

Marauhn, Thilo. "Peacekeeping in a Critical Stage: The Operation in the Western Sahara." *International Peacekeeping*, vol. 2, no. 4 (June–July 1995).

U. United Nations Guards Contingent in Iraq

Abizaid, Colonel John P. "Lessons for Peacekeepers." *Military Review*, vol. 73, no. 3 (March 1993), pp. 11–19.

Gunter, Michael M. "The Kurdish Peacekeeping Operation in Northern Iraq, 1991." In *Peacekeeping and the Challenge of Civil Conflict Resolution*. Ed. by David A. Charters. Fredericton, New Brunswick: Centre for Conflict Studies, 1994.

V. United Nations Observer Mission in El Salvador

Doyle, Michael, Ian Johnstone, and Robert Orr, eds. *Keeping the Peace: Multidimensional UN Operations in Cambodia and El Salvador.* Cambridge: Cambridge University Press, 1997.

Flores, Tathiana. "ONUSAL: A Precedent for Future UN Missions?" *International Peacekeeping*, vol. 2, no. 1 (December 1994–January 1995).

Lawyer's Committee for Human Rights. *Improvising History: A Critical Evaluation of the UN Observer Mission in El Salvador*. New York: Lawyer's Committee for Human Rights, 1995.

Montgomery, Tommie Sue. "Getting to Peace in El Salvador: The Roles of the United Nations Secretariat and ONUSAL." *Journal of InterAmerican Studies and World Affairs*, vol. 37, no. 4 (Winter 1995), pp. 139–173.

W. United Nations Iraq-Kuwait Observer Mission

"UNIKOM." *Peacekeeping and International Relations*, vol. 20, no. 3 (May–June 1991), pp. 7–10.

X. United Nations Protection Force

(1). General Works

Fetherston, A. B., O. Ramsbotham, and T. Woodhouse. "UNPROFOR: Some Observations from a Conflict Resolution Perspective." *International Peacekeeping*, vol. 1, no. 2 (Summer 1994), pp. 179–203.

Halstead, John. "UN Peacekeeping: The Lessons of Yugoslavia." In *Peacekeeping at the Crossroads*. Ed. by S. Neil MacFarlane and Hans-Georg Ehrhart. Clementsport, NS: Canadian Peacekeeping Press, 1997, pp. 63–70.

Jacobi, Susanne. "UNPROFOR: Mission Impossible." *International Peacekeeping*, vol. 2, no. 2–3 (February–May 1995).

Klein, Edith. "Obstacles to Conflict Resolution in the Territories of the Former Yugoslavia." In *Peacekeeping and the Challenge of Civil Conflict Resolu-*

tion. Ed. by David A. Charters. Fredericton, New Brunswick: Centre for Conflict Studies, 1994.

MacInnis, John Archibald. "Lessons from UNPROFOR: Peacekeeping from a Force Commander's Perspective." In *The New Peacekeeping Partnership*. Ed. by Alex Morrison. Clementsport, NS: Canadian Peackeeping Press, 1995, pp. 178–188.

(2). United Nations Protection Force (Croatia)

James, Alan. "The UN in Croatia: An Exercise in Futility?" *The World Today* (May 1993), pp. 93–95.

Siekmann, Robert. "The Question of UNPROFOR's Withdrawal from Croatia." *International Peacekeeping*, vol. 2, no. 1 (December 1994–January 1995).

(3). United Nations Protection Force in Bosnia-Herzegovina

Boulden, Jane. *Peace Enforcement: The United Nations Experience in the Congo, Somalia, and Bosnia*. Westport, CT: Praeger, 2001.

Morillon, Philippe. "United Nations Operations in Bosnia: Lessons and Realities." *RUSI Journal*, vol. 88, no. 6 (December 1993), pp. 31–35.

Ripley, Tim. "Bosnia Mission Forces United Nations to Grow with the Times." *International Defence Review*, vol. 27 (May 1994), pp. 63–65.

"Vox Militaris." "Bosnia: 24 Nations Send Soldiers to UNPROFOR." *Army Defence Quarterly Journal*, vol. 123, no. 1 (January 1993), pp. 19–26.

Y. United Nations Operation in Somalia I and II

Arnold, S. L. "Somalia: An Operation Other Than War." *Military Review*, vol. 73 (December 1993), pp. 26–35.

Baroni, Claudia. "The Italian Participation in UNITAF and UNOSOM II." *Peacekeeping and International Relations*, vol. 22, no. 4 (July–August 1993), pp. 3–4.

———. "New Perspectives on UNOSOM II and the Italian Attitude." *Peacekeeping and International Relations*, vol. 23, no. 1 (January–February 1994), pp. 4–5.

Bolton, John R. "Wrong Turn in Somalia." *Foreign Affairs*, vol. 73, no. 1 (January/February 1994), pp. 56–66.

Boulden, Jane. *Peace Enforcement: The United Nations Experience in the Congo, Somalia, and Bosnia*. Westport, CT: Praeger, 2001.

Bridge, T. D. "Australia Commits 900 Soldiers to Restore Hope in Somalia." *Army Defence Quarterly Journal*, vol. 123, no. 1 (January 1993), pp. 5–7.

Bush, George. "Humanitarian Mission to Somalia." *United States Department of State Dispatch*, vol. 3, no. 49 (December 7, 1992), pp. 885–886.

Clark, Jeffrey. "Debacle in Somalia." *Foreign Affairs*, vol. 72, no. 1 (January–February 1993), pp. 102–123.

Clarke, Walter S. "Testing the World's Resolve in Somalia." *Parameters*, vol. 23, no. 4 (Winter 1993–1994), pp. 42–58.

Clarke, Walter S., and Jeffrey Herbst. "Somalia: Lessons from a Humanitarian Intervention." *Current*, no. 382 (May 1996), pp. 10–17.

Curtiss, Richard H. "Bosnia 1993: Showdown for US, UN and Shape of the New World Order." *The Washington Report on Middle East Affairs*, vol. 11, no. 8 (March 1993).

Diehl, Paul F. "With the Best Intentions: Lessons from UNOSOM I and II." *Studies in Conflict and Terrorism*, vol. 19, no. 2 (April–June 1996), pp. 153–178.

Freeman, Major General Waldo D., et al. "Operation Restore Hope: A US-CENTCOM Perspective." *Military Review*, vol. 73, no. 9 (September 1993), pp. 61–72.

Hirsch, John, and Robert Oakley. *Somalia and Operation Restore Hope*. Washington, DC: US Institute of Peace Press, 1995.

Hutchinson, Mark R. "Restoring Hope: UN Security Council Resolutions for Somalia and an Expanded Doctrine of Humanitarian Intervention." *Harvard International Law Journal*, vol. 34, no. 2 (Spring 1993), pp. 624–640.

Kochhar, M. R. *United Nations Peacekeeping and Operations in Somalia*. Gurgaon: Dipika Kochher, 2001.

Makinda, Samuel M. *Seeking Peace from Chaos: Humanitarian Intervention in Somalia*. Boulder, CO: Lynne Rienner Publishers, 1993.

Z. United Nations Transitional Authority in Cambodia

Akashi, Yasushi. "The Challenge of Peacekeeping in Cambodia." *International Peacekeeping*, vol. 1 (Summer 1994), pp. 204–215.

Babbage, R., and G. Klintworth. *Peacekeeping in Cambodia: An Australian Role?* Working Paper no. 179. Canberra: Strategic and Defence Studies Centre, 1989.

Dommen, Arthur J. "United Nations Bias and Cambodian Peace." *Global Affairs*, vol. 7 (Fall 1992), pp. 120–135.

Doyle, Michael W. *UN Peacekeeping in Cambodia: UNTAC's Civilian Mandate*. Boulder, CO: Lynne Rienner Publishers, 1994.

Doyle, Michael W., and Nishkala Suntharlingam. "The United Nations in Cambodia: Lessons for Complex Peacekeeping." *International Peacekeeping*, vol. 1, no. 2 (Summer 1994), pp. 117–147.

Farris, Karl. "United Nations Peacekeeping in Cambodia: On Balance, A Success." *Parameters*, vol. 24, no. 1 (Spring 1994), pp. 39–50.

Findlay, T. *Cambodia: The Legacy and Lessons of UNTAC*. Oxford: Oxford University Press and SIPRI, 1995.

Heiniger, Janet. *Peacekeeping in Transition: The UN in Cambodia*. New York: 20th Century Fund Press, 1994.

Jennar, Raoul M. "UNTAC: 'International Triumph' in Cambodia?" *Security Dialogue*, vol. 25 (June 1994), pp. 145–156.

Peou, Sorpong. "A Further Look at UNTAC's Performance and Dilemmas: A Review Article." *Contemporary Southeast Asia*, vol. 17, no. 2 (September 1995), pp. 207–224.

Saito, Jon. "UNTAC: A Success Story?" *Asian Defence Journal*, vol. 5 (May 1993), pp. 20–28.

Sanderson, John M. "Peacekeeping Operations in Cambodia." *RUSI Journal*, vol. 139, no. 6 (December 1994), pp. 20–26.

———. "UNTAC: Debriefing and Lessons—The Military Component View." *International Peacekeeping*, vol. 2, no. 2–3 (February–May 1995).

"World: A Peace Treaty Negotiated by the United Nations Will Give the World Body Effective Control Over Cambodia." *The New American*, vol. 7, no. 27 (December 31, 1991) .

AA. United Nations Observer Mission in South Africa

Goldstuck, Arthur. "United Nations Opens Mission to Aid South African Transition." *Africa News* (November 9–22, 1992), p. 7.

BB. United Nations Operation in Mozambique

Malaquias, Assis. "The UN in Mozambique and Angola." *International Peacekeeping*, vol. 3, no. 2 (Summer 1996), pp. 87–106.

Synge, Richard. *Mozambique: United Nations Peacekeeping in Action, 1992–1994*. Washington, DC: USIP Press, 1997.

CC. United Nations Assistance Mission Rwanda

Dallaire, Romeo, and Bruce Poulin. "Rwanda: From Peace Agreement to Genocide." *Canadian Defence Quarterly*, vol. 24, no. 3 (March 1995), pp. 7–11.

———. "UNAMIR: Mission to Rwanda." *Joint Force Quarterly*, vol. 7 (Spring 1995), pp. 66–71.

Jones, Bruce D. *Peacemaking in Rwanda: The Dynamics of Failure*. Boulder:

Lynne Rienner Publishers, 2001.

Mays, Terry M. *The 1999 United Nations and 2000 Organization of African Unity Formal Inquiries: A Retrospective Examination of Peacekeeping and the Rwandan Crisis of 1994*. Pearson Papers #7. Clementsport, NS: Canadian Peacekeeping Press, 2002.

DD. United Nations Mission in Haiti

Kurzidem, Thomas. "Haiti: The Different Mission." *International Peacekeeping*, vol. 3, no. 4–6 (June–December 1996).

EE. United Nations Preventive Deployment Force

Furlong, Bob. "Powder Keg of the Balkans: The United Nations Opts for Prevention in Macedonia." *International Defense Review*, vol. 26, no. 5 (May 1993), pp. 364–368.

Ostrowski, Stephen T. "Preventive Deployment of Troops as Preventive Measures: Macedonia and Beyond." *New York University Journal of International Law and Politics*, vol. 30, nos. 3–4 (Spring–Summer 1998), pp. 793–880.

Williams, Abiodun. *Preventing War: The United Nations and Macedonia*. Lanham, MD: Rowman and Littlefield, 2000.

FF. United Nations Civilian Police Mission in Haiti

Iweta, Tomoko. "The Extension of MIPONUH and Haiti's Democratization." *Peacekeeping and International Relations*, vol. 28, no. 1 (January–February 1999), pp. 8, 11, 22.

GG. United Nations Observer Mission in Angola

McQueen, Norrie. "Peacekeeping by Attrition: The United Nations in Angola." *The Journal of Modern African Studies* (September 1998), pp. 399–401.

HH. United Nations Transitional Administration in East Timor

Rolfe, Jim. "Operation East Timor: How Did We Do?" *Defence Quarterly*, vol. 29 (Winter 2000), pp. 2–4.

Strohmeyer, Hansjorg. "Collapse and Reconstruction of a Judicial System: The United Nations Missions in Kosovo and East Timor." *American Journal of International Law*, vol. 95, no. 1 (January 2001), pp. 46–63.

Wheeler, Nicolas J., and Tim Dunne. "East Timor and the New Humanitarian Intervention." *International Affairs*, vol. 77, no. 4 (October 2001), pp. 805–828.

IV. ORGANIZATION OF AFRICAN UNITY PEACEKEEPING

1. General Works

Berman, Eric, and Kaite Sams. *Peacekeeping in Africa: Capabilities and Culpabilities*. Geneva: UN Institute for Disarmament Research, 2000.

Coning, Cedric de. "The Role of the OAU in Conflict Management in Africa." In *Conflict Management, Peacekeeping, and Peacebuilding: Lessons from Africa*. Ed. by Mark Malan. ISS Monograph no. 10. Johannesburg: Institute for Security Studies, 1997.

Mulikita, Njunga. "The Peacekeeping Profile of the OAU: A Critical Assessment" *Peacekeeping and International Relations*, vol. 27, no. 6 (Nov./Dec. 1998), pp. 6–11.

Wiseman, Henry. "The OAU: Peacekeeping and Conflict Resolution." In *The OAU after Twenty Years*. Ed. by Yassim El Ayouty and I. William Zartman. New York: Praeger Publishers, 1984, pp. 123–154.

2. Organization of African Unity Peacekeeping Force in Chad I and II

Akinyemi, A. Bolaji. "Chad: The Lessons for Nigeria." *Nigerian Forum*, vol. 1, no. 1 (March 1981).

May, Roy, and Simon Massey. "The OAU Interventions in Chad: Mission Impossible or Mission Evaded?" *International Peacekeeping*, vol. 5, no. 1 (Spring 1998), pp. 46–65.

Mays, Terry M. *Africa's First Peacekeeping Operation: The OAU in Chad, 1981–1982*. Westport, CT: Praeger Publishers, 2002.

———. "Peacekeeping from a Realist Viewpoint: Nigeria and the OAU Operation in Chad." *Journal of Political Science*, vol. 25 (1997), pp. 59–74.

Ndovi, Victor. "Chad: Nation Building, Security, and OAU Peacekeeping." *Africa in World Politics: Changing Perspectives*. Ed. by Stephen Wright and Janice Brawfoot. London: Macmillan Press, Ltd, 1987, pp. 140–154.

Nwokedi, Emeka. "Sub-Regional Security and Nigerian Foreign Policy." *African Affairs*, vol. 84, no. 335, pp. 195–210.

Robinson, Pearl T. "Playing the Arab Card: Niger and Chad's Ambivalent Relations with Libya." In *African Security Issues: Sovereignty, Stability, and Solidarity*. Ed. by Bruce E. Arlinghaus. Boulder, CO: Westview Press, 1984, pp. 171–184.

Sesay, Amadu. "Peacekeeping by Regional Organizations: The OAU and ECOWAS Peacekeeping Forces in Comparative Perspective." In *Peacekeeping and the Challenge of Civil Conflict Resolution*. Ed. by David A. Charters. Fredericton, New Brunswick: Centre for Conflict Studies, 1994.

Sesay, Amadu, and Olusola Ojo. "The OAU Peacekeeping Force in Chad: An Analysis of Policy Implementation and Failure." In *A Nigerian Reader in the Policy Process*. Ed. by C. A. B. Olowu and Victor Ayeni. Ile Ife, Nigeria: University of Ife Press, 1986, pp. 1–18.

3. Neutral Military Observer Group

Stearns, Scott. "The OAU's Peacekeepers." *Africa Report*, vol. 39, no. 1 (January–February 1994), p. 35.

4. Organization of African Unity Liaison Mission in Ethiopia/Eritrea

"Towards New Peacekeeping Partnerships in Africa?: The OAU Liaison Mission in Ethiopia-Eritrea." *Africa Security Review*, vol. 10, no. 2 (2001), pp. 19–33.

V. ECONOMIC COMMUNITY OF WEST AFRICAN STATES PEACEKEEPING

1. General Works

Agyemfra, Francis A. "Regional Peacekeeping: The Economic Community of West African States Experiment in Liberia." In *Peacekeeping at the Crossroads*. Ed. by S. Neil MacFarlane and Hans-Georg Ehrhart. Clementsport, NS: Canadian Peacekeeping Press, 1997, pp. 61–67.

Berman, Eric, and Kaite Sams. *Peacekeeping in Africa: Capabilities and Culpabilities*. Geneva: UN Institute for Disarmament Research, 2000.

Niewkerk, Anthoni van. "Regionalism into Globalism? War into Peace? SADC and ECOWAS Compared." *African Security Review*, vol. 10, no. 2 (2001), pp. 7–18.

Olonisakin, Funmi. *Reinventing Peacekeeping in Africa: Conceptual and Legal Issues in ECOMOG Operations*. The Hague: Kluwar Law International, 2000.

2. Economic Community of West African States Monitoring Group–Liberia

Aboagye, Festus B. *ECOMOG: A Sub-Regional Experience in Conflict Resolution, Management and Peacekeeping in Liberia*. Accra, Ghana: Sedco Publishers Ltd., 1999.

Adebajo, Adekeye. *Liberia's Civil War: Nigeria, ECOMOG, and Regional Security in West Africa.* Boulder, CO: Lynne Rienner, 2002.

Cleaver, Gerry. "Liberia: Lessons for the Future from the Experience of ECOMOG." In *Peacekeeping in Africa.* Ed. by Oliver Furley and Roy May. Aldershot, UK: Ashgate, 1998, pp. 223–238.

Howe, Herbert. "Lessons of Liberia." *International Security*, vol. 21, no. 3 (1996), pp. 145–177.

Nolte, G. "Combined Peacekeeping: ECOMOG and UNOMIL in Liberia." *International Peacekeeping*, vol. 1, no. 2 (1994).

Sesay, Amadu. "Peacekeeping by Regional Organizations: The OAU and ECOWAS Peacekeeping Forces in Comparative Perspective." In *Peacekeeping and the Challenge of Civil Conflict Resolution.* Ed. by David A. Charters. Fredericton, New Brunswick: Centre for Conflict Studies, 1994.

Tart, S. Byron. "The ECOMOG Initiative in Liberia: A Liberian Perspective." *Issue: A Journal of Opinion*, vol. 21, nos. 1–2 (1993), pp. 74–83.

Walraven, Klass van. *The Pretense of Peacekeeping: ECOMOG, West Africa, and Liberia (1990–1998).* The Hague: Netherlands Institute of International Relations, 1999.

Yoroms, Gani J. "ECOMOG and West African Regional Security: A Nigerian Perspective." *Issue: A Journal of Opinion*, vol. 21, nos. 1–2 (1993), pp. 84–91.

VI. SOUTHERN AFRICAN DEVELOPMENT COMMUNITY PEACEKEEPING

1. General Works

Malan, Mark, ed. *Resolute Partners: Building Peacekeeping Capacity in Southern Africa.* ISS Monograph no. 21. Pretoria, South Africa: Institute for Security Studies, 1998.

Niewkerk, Anthoni van. "Regionalism into Globalism? War Into Peace? SADC and ECOWAS Compared." *African Security Review*, vol. 10, no. 2 (2001), pp. 7–18.

"Southern African Peacekeeping Exercise—a Great Success." *Army Quarterly and Defence Journal*, vol. 127, no. 3 (1997), pp. 299–302.

2. Lesotho

Whelan, Lawrence. "Questions Raised by Lesotho Intervention." *Jane's Intelligence Review*, vol. 11, no. 1 (January 1999), pp. 43–44.

VI. LEAGUE OF ARAB STATES PEACEKEEPING

1. Arab League Force

Hasou, Tawfig. Y. *The Struggle for the Arab World: Egypt's Nasser and the Arab League*. London: KPI, 1985.

Hassouna, Hussein A. *League of Arab States and Regional Disputes*. Dobbs Ferry, NY: Oceana Publications, 1975.

Pogany, Istvan. *The Arab League and Peacekeeping in the Lebanon*. Aldershot, Great Britain: Avebury, 1987.

2. Symbolic Arab Security Force—Arab Deterrent Force

Dawisha, A. I. *Syria and the Lebanese Crisis*. New York: St. Martin's Press, 1980.

Evron, Yair. *War and Intervention in Lebanon*. London: Croom Helm, 1987.

Hassouna, Hussein A. *League of Arab States and Regional Disputes*. Dobbs Ferry, NY: Oceana Publications, 1975.

Issele, J. P. "The Arab Deterrent Force in Lebanon." In *Current Legal Regulation on the Use of Force*. Ed. by A. Cassesse. Dordrecht, Netherlands: Martinus Nijhoff, 1986.

McCarthy, John T. "Lebanon and the Arab League: Success Story in the Making?" *Mediterranean Quarterly*, vol. 2, no. 1 (Winter 1991).

Pogany, Istvan. *The Arab League and Peacekeeping in the Lebanon*. Aldershot, Great Britain: Avebury, 1987.

———. "The Arab League and Regional Peacekeeping." *Netherlands International Law Review*, vol. 34, no. 1 (1987), pp. 54–75.

Zacher, Mark W. *International Conflicts and Collective Security, 1946–1977: The United Nations, Organization of American States, Organization of African Unity, and Arab League*. New York: Praeger, 1979.

VIII. ORGANIZATION OF AMERICAN STATES PEACEKEEPING

Child, Jack. "The Falklands-Malvinas Conflict and Inter-American Peacekeeping." *Conflict Quarterly*, vol. 3 (Winter 1983), pp. 5–20.

Fauriol, Georges, ed. "Latin America and Peacekeeping: Future Prospects." In *Peacekeeping, Peacemaking, or War: International Security Enforcement*. Ed. by Alex Morrison. Toronto: Canadian Institute of Strategic Studies, 1991.

Gordon, Dennis R. "The Paralysis of Multilateral Peacekeeping: International Organizations and the Falklands-Malvinas War." *Peace and Change*, vol. 12, nos. 1–2 (1987), pp. 51–63.

Greenberg, Lawrence M. "The US Dominican Intervention: Success Story." *Parameters*, vol. 17 (December 1987), pp. 18–29.

Heyer, Kent den, and Jeremy King. "Security and Peacekeeping: The Experience of the OAS." *Peacekeeping and International Relations*, vol. 25, no. 3 (MayJune 1996), pp. 15–16.

Klepak, H. P. "Peacekeeping in Central America." In *Peacekeeping and the Challenge of Civil Conflict Resolution*. Ed. by David A. Charters. Fredericton, New Brunswick: Centre for Conflict Studies, 1994.

Levin, Aida L. "The Organization of American States and the United Nations: Relations in the Peace and Security Field." In *Regionalism and the United Nations*. Ed. by Berhanykun Andemicael. New York: Oceana Publications, 1979, pp. 147–224.

Paz Barnica, Edgardo. "Peacekeeping Within the Inter-American System." In *Peacekeeping: Appraisals and Proposals*. Ed. by Henry Wiseman. New York: Pergamon Press, 1983, pp. 237–255.

Warschaver, Eduardo. *The Inter-American Military Force*. Brussels: Publications of the International Association of Democratic Lawyers, 1966.

Zacher, Mark W. *International Conflicts and Collective Security, 1946–1977: The United Nations, Organization of American States, Organization of African Unity, and Arab League*. New York: Praeger, 1979.

IX. ORGANIZATION OF EAST CARIBBEAN STATES PEACEKEEPING

Beck, R. J. "International Law and the Decision to Invade Grenada: A Ten Year Retrospective." *Virginia Journal of International Law*, vol. 33, no. 4, 1993, pp. 765–818.

Weiler, Joseph H. H. "Armed Intervention in a Dichotomized World: The Case of Grenada." In *The Current Legal Regulation of the Use of Force*. Ed. by Antonio Cassese. Dordrecht, Netherlands: Martinus Nijhoff Publishers, 1986, pp. 241–268.

X. COMMONWEALTH PEACEKEEPING

Acland, Major General J. H. B. "The Rhodesia Operation." *Guards Magazine* (Summer 1980), pp. 46–50.

Bailey, J. B. A. "Operation Agila–Rhodesia, 1979–1980." *British Army Review*, no. 66 (December 1980) .

Chan, Steven. *The Commonwealth Observer Group in Zimbabwe*. Gweru: Mambo Press, 1985.

Jones, R. J. Roderick. "The Commonwealth Ceasefire Monitoring Force in Rhodesia December 1979 to March 1980." *The Gauntlet*, 1980.

Kriger, Norma. "Zimbabwe's Peace Settlement: Re-evaluating Lancaster House." In *Peacekeeping in Africa*. Ed. by Oliver Furley and Roy May. Aldershot, England: Ashgate, 1998, pp. 83–104.

Learmont, J. H. "Reflections from Rhodesia." *RUSI Journal*, vol. 125, no. 4 (December 1980), pp. 47–55.

MacKinlay, John. "The Commonwealth Monitoring Force in Zimbabwe-Rhodesia, 1979–1980." In *Humanitarian Emergencies and Military Help in Africa*. Ed. by Thomas G. Weiss. New York: St. Martin's Press, 1990, pp. 38–60.

Southern Rhodesia Elections (February 1980): The Report of the Commonwealth Observer Group on Elections Leading to Independent Zimbabwe. London: Commonwealth Secretariat, 1980.

Stedman, Stephen John. *Peacemaking in Civil War: International Mediation in Zimbabwe, 1974–1980*. Boulder, CO: Lynne Rienner Publishers, 1990.

Verrier, A. "The Commonwealth Monitoring Force of Southern Rhodesia-Zimbabwe, 1979–1980." *International Peacekeeping*, vol. 1 (1994), pp. 440–461.

XI. NORTH ATLANTIC TREATY ORGANIZATION PEACEKEEPING

1. General Works

Ando, Salvo. "Preparing the Ground for an Alliance Peacekeeping Role." *NATO Review*, vol. 41, no. 2 (April 1993), p. 4.

Annan, Kofi A. "UN Peacekeeping Operations and Cooperation with NATO." *NATO Review*, vol. 41, no. 5 (October 1993), pp. 3–7.

Baxter, Laurence. "NATO and Regional Support Operations." *Peacekeeping and International Relations*, vol. 25, no. 6 (Nov./Dec. 1996), pp. 6–7.

Bono, Giovanna. *NATO's Peace Enforcement Tasks and Policy Communities*. Burlington, VT: Ashgate, 2002.

Chilton, D. C. F., and B. C. Hayes, eds. *NATO, Peacekeeping, and the United Nations*. London: British American Security Information Council, 1994.

Cragg, Anthony J. "The Role of NATO in Regional Peacekeeping." In *Peacekeeping at the Crossroads*. Ed. by S. Neil MacFarlane and Hans-Georg Ehrhart. Clementsport, NS: Canadian Peacekeeping Press, 1997, pp. 1–8.

Gilman, Ernest, and Detlef E. Herold. *Peacekeeping Challenges to Euro-Atlantic Security*. Rome: NATO Defense College, Monograph Series no. 2, 1994.

Khanna, Jyoit. "Sharing the Financial Burden for UN and NATO Peacekeeping, 1976–1996." *Journal of Conflict Resolution*, vol. 42, no. 2 (April 1998), pp. 166–186.

Kriendler, John. "NATO's Changing Role—Opportunities and Constraints for Peacekeeping." *NATO Review*, vol. 41, no. 4 (July 1993), pp. 16–22.

Lepgold, Joseph. "NATO's Post-Cold War Collective Action Problem." *International Security*, vol. 23, no. 1 (1998), pp. 78–106.

Manwaring, Max G. "Peace and Stability Lessons from Bosnia." *Parameters*, vol. 28, no. 4 (1998), pp. 28–38.

Rader, Steven. "NATO." In *Challenges for the New Peacekeeping*. Ed. by Trevor Findley. SIPRI Research Report no. 12. Oxford: Oxford University Press, 1996, pp. 142–158.

Schulte, L. "Former Yugoslavia and the New NATO." *Survival*, vol. 39, no. 1, 1997, pp. 19–42.

Weston, Sir John. "The Challenges to NATO: A British View." *NATO Review*, vol. 40, no. 6 (December 1992), pp. 9–14.

Zonnier, Lamberto. "Relations Between the OSCE and NATO with Particular Regard to Crisis Management and Peacekeeping." In *The OSCE and the Maintenance of Peace and Security*. Ed. by Michael Bothe, Natalino Ronzitti, and Allan Rosas. The Hague: Kluwar Law International, 1997, pp. 257–267.

2. Bosnia-Herzegovina

O'Brien, Kevin A. "NATO Air Strikes in Bosnia-Herzegovina." *Peacekeeping and International Relations*, vol. 23, no. 1 (February/January 1994), p. 8.

3. Implementation Force

Bose, Sumantra. *Bosnia After Dayton: Nationalist Partition and International Intervention*. New York: Oxford, 2002.

"IFOR's Air Components." *NATO's Sixteen Nations*, vol. 41, no. 2 (1996), pp. 89–90.

"IFOR's Ground Components." *NATO's Sixteen Nations*, vol. 41, no. 2 (1996), pp. 87–890.

"IFOR's Russian Forces." *NATO's Sixteen Nations*, vol. 41, no. 2 (1996), pp. 24–25.

Sheutsov, Leonity P. "Russian-NATO Military Cooperation in Bosnia: A Basis for the Future?" *NATO Review*, vol. 45, no. 2 (March 1997), pp. 17–20.

4. Stabilization Force

Cirafici, John L. "SFOR in Bosnia in 1997: A Watershed Year." *Parameters*, vol. XXIX (Spring 1999), pp. 80–91.

Clark, Wesley. "Building a Lasting Peace in Bosnia and Herzegovina." *NATO Review*, vol. 46, no. 1 (Spring 1998), pp. 19–22.

Manwaring, Max G. "Peace and Stability Lessons from Bosnia." *Parameters*, vol. XXVIII (Winter 1998–1999), pp. 28–38.

Phillips, William. "Civil-Military Cooperation: Vital to Peace Implementation in Bosnia." *NATO Review*, vol. 46, no. 1, pp. 22–25.

"SFOR Detachments Report." *NATO's Sixteen Nations*, vol. 42, no. 3 (1997), pp. 88–92.

Sheutsov, Leonity P. "Russian-NATO Military Cooperation in Bosnia: A Basis for the Future?" *NATO Review*, vol. 45, no. 2 (March 1997), pp. 17–20.

Shinseki, Eric K. "SFOR: We Stand for Peace." *NATO's Sixteen Nations*, vol. 42, no. 3 (1997), pp. 31–32.

Wilson, Gordon. "Post SFOR (Stabilisation Force): A European Security Solution?" *RUSI Journal*, vol. 143, no. 3 (June 1998), pp. 19–23.

5. Kosovo Force

Bothe, Michael. "Kosovo: Many Questions, Few Answers." *International Peacekeeping*, vol. 5, no. 1/2 (January–April 1999).

Cssurgai, Gyula. "Kosovo: A New War in the Balkans." *Peacekeeping and International Relations*, vol. 27, no. 2 (March/April 1998), pp. 3–4.

Leudijk, Dick. "NATO's Decision Making Towards Airstrikes on Kosovo." *International Peacekeeping*, vol. 5, no. 6 (November–December 1999).

McCoubrey, Hilaire. "Kosovo, NATO, and International Law." *International Relations*, vol. XIV, no. 5 (August 1999), pp. 29–46.

XII. EUROPEAN UNION (EU) PEACEKEEPING

1. West European Union

Eekelen, Willem Van. "WEU Prepares the Way for New Missions." *NATO Review*, vol. 41, no. 5 (October 1993), pp. 19–23.

Messervy-Whiting, Graham. "WEU Operational Development." *Joint Forces Quarterly*, no. 15 (Spring 1997), pp. 70–74.

Morales, Rafael de. "WEU's Multinational Advisory Police Element in Albania." *NATO's Sixteen Nations* (European Security Supplement 1998), pp. 59–61.

Vierucci, Luisa. "The Role of the West European Union (WEU) in the Maintenance of International Peace and Security." *International Peacekeeping*, vol. 2, no. 3 (1995), pp. 309–328.

2. European Union

Hillen, John. "After SFOR—Planning a European-Led Force." *Joint Forces Quarterly*, no. 15 (Spring 1997), pp. 75–79.

3. European Community/European Union Monitoring Mission

Griffiths, D. N. "Waging Peace in Bosnia." *Proceedings*, vol. 120 (January 1994), pp. 31–34.

XIII. COMMONWEALTH OF INDEPENDENT STATES PEACEKEEPING

1. General Works

Allison, R. *Peacekeeping and the Soviet Successor States.* Paris: Institute for Security Studies, Chaillot Papers No. 18, 1994.

Baev, Pavel K. "Russia's Experiments and Experience in Conflict Management and Peacemaking." *International Peacekeeping*, vol. 1, no. 3 (1994), pp. 245–260.

Croft, Michael. "Russia's Peacekeeping Policy, Part I: Domestic Imperatives and the Near Abroad." *Peacekeeping and International Relations*, vol. 25, no. 4 (1996), pp. 13–15.

———. "Russia's Peacekeeping Policy, Part II: Differences in Approach and Obstacles." *Peacekeeping and International Relations*, vol. 25, no. 5 (1996), pp. 5–8.

Crow, Suzanne. "Russia Seeks Leadership in Regional Peacekeeping." *RFE-RL Research Report*, vol. 2, no. 15 (April 9, 1993), pp. 28–32.

———. "Russian Peacekeeping: Défense, Diplomacy, or Imperialism?" *RFE-RL Research Report*, vol. 1, no. 37 (September 18, 1992), pp. 31–40.

———. "The Theory and Practice of Peacekeeping in the Former USSR." *RFE-RL Research Report*, vol. 1, no. 37 (September 18, 1992), p. 31.

Dailey, E. "Human Rights and the Russian Armed Forces in the Near Abroad." *Helsinki Monitor*, vol. 5, no. 2 (1994), pp. 11–19.

Facon, I. "La conception russe du maintien de la paix." *Defense nationale*, vol. 52 (1996), pp. 67–84.

Greene, James M. "Peacekeeping Doctrines of the CIS." *Jane's Intelligence Review*, vol. 5, no. 4 (April 1993), pp. 156–159.

Griffin, Stuart. "Peacekeeping, the United Nations, and the Future Role of the Commonwealth." *The Journal of Commonwealth and Comparative Studies*, vol. 39, no. 3 (November 2001), pp. 150–165.

Jonson, Lena, and Clive Archer, eds. *Peacekeeping and the Role of Russia in Euroasia.* Boulder, CO: Westview Press, 1996.

MacFarlane, S. Neil. "The CIS and Regional Security." In *Multilateralism and Regional Security*. Ed. by Michel Fortmann, S. Neil MacFarlane, and Stephane Roussel. Clementsport, NS: Canadian Peacekeeping Press, 1997, pp. 224–237.

O'Brien, Kevin. "Peacekeeping Forces in the Former Soviet Union" *Peacekeeping and International Relations*, vol. 23, no. 1 (1994), pp. 6–8.

2. Nagorno-Karabakh

Mihalka, Michael. "Nagorno-Karabakh and Russian Peacekeeping: Prospects for a Second Dayton." *International Peacekeeping*, vol. 3, no. 3 (1996), pp. 16–32.

3. Abkhazia

Lynch, Don. *The Conflict in Abkhazia: Challenges in Russian Peacekeeping Policy*. London: Royal Institute of International Affairs, Discussion Paper no. 77, 1998.

XIV. CONFERENCE ON SECURITY AND COOPERATION IN EUROPE (CSCE)/ ORGANIZATION FOR SECURITY AND COOPERATION IN EUROPE (OSCE)

1. Conference on Security and Cooperation in Europe General Works

Peel, D. "The Peacekeeping Role of the Conference on Security and Cooperation in Europe." In *The Changing Face of Peacekeeping*. Ed. by Alex Morrison. Toronto: 1993, pp. 51–?.

2. Organization for Security and Cooperation in Europe General Works

Burci, Gianluca. "Division of Labour Between the UN and OSCE in Connection with Peacekeeping." In *The OSCE in the Maintenance of Peace and Security*. Ed. by Michael Bothe, Natalino Ronzitti, and Allan Rosas. The Hague: Kluwar Law International, 1997, pp. 289–314.

Greco, Ettore. "Third Party Peacekeeping and the Interaction Between Russia and the OSCE in the CIS Area." In *The OSCE in the Maintenance of Peace and Security*. Ed. by Michael Bothe, Natalino Ronzitti, and Allan Rosas. The Hague: Kluwar Law International, 1997, pp. 267–288.

Nowak, Jerzy M. "OSCE." In *Challenges for the New Peacekeeping*. Ed. by Trevor Findley. SIPRI Research Report no. 12. Oxford: Oxford University Press, 1996, pp. 121–141.

"OSCE Peacekeeping: A Useful 'Harder' Option." *Helsinki Monitor*, vol. 7, no. 3 (1996), pp. 65–71.

Pagani, Fabrizio. "Financing Peacekeeping and Peace Related Operations: The UN and OSCE Practice." In *The OSCE in the Maintenance of Peace and Se-*

curity. Ed. by Michael Bothe, Natalino Ronzitti, and Allan Rosas. The Hague: Kluwar Law International, 1997, pp. 315–342.

Ronzitti, Natalino. "OSCE Peacekeeping." In *The OSCE in the Maintenance of Peace and Security.* Ed. by Michael Bothe, Natalino Ronzitti, and Allan Rosas. The Hague: Kluwar Law International, 1997, pp. 237–256.

Sica, Mario. "The Role of the OSCE in the Former Yugoslavia After the Dayton Peace Accord." In *The OSCE in the Maintenance of Peace and Security.* Ed. by Michael Bothe, Natalino Ronzitti, and Allan Rosas. The Hague: Kluwar Law International, 1997, pp. 479–494.

3. Organization for Security and Cooperation in Europe in Nagorno-Karabakh

Dehashti, Rexane. "Nagorno-Karabakh: A Case Study of OSCE Conflict Settlement." In *The OSCE in the Maintenance of Peace and Security.* Ed. by Michael Bothe, Natalino Ronzitti, and Allan Rosas. The Hague: Kluwar Law International, 1997, pp. 459–478.

4. Organization for Security and Cooperation in Europe in Kosovo

Greco, Ettore. "The OSCE's Kosovo Verification Mission: A Preliminary Assessment."*International Peacekeeping*, vol. 4, no. 5 (1998), pp. 115–117.

XV. UNITED STATES ORGANIZED MULTINATIONAL PEACEKEEPING

1. Multinational Forces I and II

Caligaris, Luigi. "Western Peacekeeping in Lebanon: Lessons of the MNF." *Survival,* vol. 26, no. 6 (1984), pp. 262–268.

Foley, Tom. "The Second Invasion of Lebanon." *Political Affairs*, vol. 63 (February 1984), pp. 24–31.

Hammel, Eric. *The Root: The Marines in Beirut (August 1982–February 1984).* Fort Worth: Harcourt Brace Jovanovich, 1985.

Heilberg, Marianne, and Johan J. Holst. Peacekeeping in Lebanon: Comparing UNIFIL and the MNF." *Survival,* vol. 28, no. 5 (1986), pp. 399–421.

Houghton, Robert B., and Frank G. Trinka. *Multinational Peacekeeping in the Middle East.* Washington, DC: United States Center for the Study of Foreign Affairs, 1985.

Mackinlay, John. "MNF2 in Beirut: Some Military Lessons for Peacekeepers." *Conflict Quarterly,* vol. 6 (Fall 1986), pp. 15–26.

McDermott, Anthony, and Kjell Skjelsbael, eds. *The Multinational Force in Beirut, 1982–1984.* Miami: Florida International University Press, 1991.

Murphy, Terrence. "The War Powers Resolution and US Involvement in Lebanon." *Search*, vol. 5 (December 1984), pp. 83–96.

Nelson, Richard W. "Multinational Peacekeeping in the Middle East and the United Nations Model." *International Affairs*, vol. 61, no. 1 (1985), pp. 67–89.

Osgood, Robert E. *The Case for the MNF: A Critical Evaluation.* Washington: North Atlantic Treaty Organization, 1982.

Schou, Arild. "The Breakdown of Conflict Management in Lebanon." *Bulletin of Peace Proposals*, vol. 20, no. 2 (1989), pp. 193–204.

Thakur, Ramesh. *International Peacekeeping in Lebanon: United Nations Authority and Multinational Force.* Boulder, CO: Westview Press, 1987.

———. "Peacekeeping in the Middle East From United Nations to Multinational Forces." *Australian Outlook*, vol. 38, no. 2 (1984), pp. 81–89.

———. "UN Authority and US Power." In *The Multinational Force in Beirut, 1982–1984.* Ed. by Anthony McDermott and Kjell Skjelsbael. Miami: Florida International University Press, 1991.

Weinberger, Naomi J. "Peacekeeping Options in Lebanon." *Middle East Journal*, vol. 37, no. 3 (1983), pp. 341–369.

Wood, Pia. "The Diplomacy of Peacekeeping: France and the Multinational Forces to the Lebanon, 1982–1984." *International Peacekeeping*, vol. 5, no. 2 (1998), pp. 19–37.

2. Multinational Force and Observers and United States Sinai Support Mission

Commonwealth Parliament Legislative Research Service. *The Middle East Conflict and the Proposed Sinai Peacekeeping Force.* Current Issues Brief no. 3, 1981.

Harris, Jesse J., and David R. Segal. "Observations From the Sinai: The Boredom Factor." *Armed Forces and Society*, vol. 11, no. 2 (1985), pp. 235–248.

Hofman, Cornelis. "MFO: Peacekeeping in the Middle East." *Military Review*, vol. 63, no. 9 (1983), pp. 2–12.

Houghton, Robert B., and Frank G. Trinka. *Multinational Peacekeeping in the Middle East.* Washington, DC: United States Center for the Study of Foreign Affairs, 1985.

James, Alan. "Symbol in Sinai: The Multinational Force and Observers." *Millenium: Journal of International Studies*, vol. 14, no. 3 (Winter 1985) .

Kinter, George L. *Peace in the Sinai: The United States Sinai Support Mission.* Washington, DC: United States Department of State, 1982.

Mandell, Brian S. *The Sinai Experience: Lessons in Multimethod Arms Control Verification and Risk Management.* Ottawa: Canadian Department of External Affairs, Arms Control and Verification Studies no. 3, 1987.

Pijpers, Alfred, ed. "European Participation in the Sinai Peacekeeping Force (MFO)." In *European Foreign Policy Making and the Arab Israeli Conflict*. Ed. by David Allen and Alfred Pijpers. The Hague: Martinus Nijhoff Publishers, 1984, pp. 211–223.

Pomerance, Michla. "The US Involvement in Sinai: 1975 as a Legal Political Turning Point." *Israel Law Review*, vol. 20, nos. 2–3 (1985), pp. 299–340.

Segal, David R., and Theodore P. Furukawa. "Light Infantry as Peacekeepers in the Sinai." *Armed Forces and Society*, vol. 16, no. 3 (Spring 1990), pp. 385–404.

Taboury, M. *The Multinational Force and Observers in the Sinai: Organization Structure and Function*. Boulder, CO: Westview Press, 1986.

Thakur, Ramesh. "Peacekeeping in the Middle East: From United Nations to Multinational Forces." *Australian Outlook*, vol. 38, no. 2 (August 1984).

———. "UN Authority and US Power." In *The Multinational Force in Beirut, 1982–1984*. Ed. by Anthony McDermott and Kjell Skjelsbael. Miami: Florida International University Press, 1991.

XVI. OTHER MULTINATIONAL PEACEKEEPING OPERATIONS

1. Temporary International Presence in Hebron

Pagani, Fabrizio. "The Temporary International Presence in Hebron: A New Type of Non-UN Observer Mission." *International Peacekeeping*, vol. 1, no. 3 (1994).

2. Operation Alba in Albania

Valpolini, Paolo. "Operation 'Alba' Lets Albania Go to the Polls." *Jane's Defence Weekly*, vol. 28, no. 1 (July 9, 1997), pp. 16–17.

3. Military Observer Mission Ecuador-Peru

Ide, Douglas. "MOMEP Spells Peace." *Soldiers*, vol. 51, no. 2 (February 1996), pp. 31–33.

Murphy, Brian. "On the Border." *Soldiers*, vol. 52, no. 5 (May 1997), p. 34.

4. International Forces in East Timor

Breen, Bob. *Mission Accomplished, East Timor: The Australian Defence Forces Part in the International Forces East Timor (INTERFET)*. St. Leonards: Allen and Unwin, 2000.

5. International Commission of Control and Supervision in Vietnam

Cox, David. "The International Commission of Control and Supervision in Vietnam, 1973." In *Peacekeeping: Appraisals and Proposals.* Ed. by Henry Wiseman New York: Pergamon Press, 1983, pp. 298–340.

Thakur, Ramesh. *Peacekeeping in Vietnam: Canada, India, Poland, and the International Commission.* Edmonton: University of Alberta Press, 1984.

XVII. INDIAN UNILATERAL PEACEKEEPING

1. Sri Lanka

Austin, Dennis, and Anirudha Gupta. *Lions and Tigers: The Crisis in Sri Lanka.* London: Centre for Security and Conflict Studies, 1988.

Bullion, Alan. "The Indian Peacekeeping Force in Sri Lanka." *International Peacekeeping*, vol. 1, no. 2 (1994), pp. 148–159.

Rupesinghe, Kumar. "Ethnic Conflicts in South Asia—The Case of Sri Lanka and the Indian Peacekeeping Force." *Journal of Peace Research*, vol. 25, no. 4 (1988), pp. 337–350.

2. Maldives

Tripathi, Deepak. "India's Maldives Mission and After." *The World Today*, vol. 45, no. 1 (January 1989).

XVIII. CONTINGENTS AND CONTINGENT PROVIDERS

1. General Works

Galtung, Johann, and Helge Hveem. *Participants in Peacekeeping Forces.* Oslo: University of Oslo Press, 1975.

Siekmann, Robert. *National Contingents in United Nations Peacekeeping Forces.* Dordrecht, Netherlands: M. Nijhoff, 1991.

2. Argentina

Huser, Herbert C. "Democratic Argentina's 'Global Reach': The Argentine Military in Peacekeeping Operations." *Naval War College Review*, vol. 51, no. 3 (Summer 1998), pp. 55–69.

Norden, Deborah L. "Keeping the Peace, Outside and In: Argentina's UN Missions." *International Peacekeeping*, vol. 2, no. 3 (Autumn 1995), pp. 330–349.

3. Australia

Austrailia. *Australia's Participation in Peacekeeping*. Parliamentary Joint Standing Committee on Foreign Affairs, Defence, and Trade. Parliamentary Paper no. 377. Canberra: Australian Government Publishing Service, 1994.

———. *Australia's Role in United Nations Peacekeeping*. 5 vols. Parliamentary Joint Standing Committee on Foreign Affairs, Defence, and Trade. Canberra: Australian Government Publishing Service, 1991.

———. *United Nations Peacekeeping and Australia*. Parliamentary Joint Standing Committee on Foreign Affairs, Defence, and Trade. Parliamentary Paper no. 140. Canberra: Australian Government Publishing Service, 1991.

Babbage, R., and G. Klintworth. *Peacekeeping in Cambodia: An Australian Role?* Working Paper no. 179. Canberra: Strategic and Defence Studies Centre, 1989.

Breen, Bob. *Mission Accomplished, East Timor: The Australian Defence Forces Part in the International Forces East Timor (INTERFET)*. St. Leonards: Allen and Unwin, 2000.

Hamilton-Smith, Martin. "Australians in the Multinational Force and Observers: An Alternative to the United Nations." *Australian Defence Forces Journal*, no. 104 (January–February 1994), pp. 68–82.

James, N. F. "A Brief History of Australian Participation on Multi-National Peacekeeping Operations." *Australian Defence Force Journal*, no. 84 (September 1, 1990), p. 47.

———. "A Brief History of Australian Peacekeeping." *Australian Defence Force Journal*, no. 104 (January–February 1994), pp. 3–18.

Klintworth, Gary, and Ross Babbage. *Peacekeeping in Cambodia: An Australian Role?* Canberra: Australian National University, Working Paper no. 179, 1989.

Miles, Tony. "Australian Peacekeeping Experiences Past, Present, and Future." *Asian Defence Journal*, no. 2 (February 1997), pp. 29–31.

Smith, Hugh, ed. *Australia and Peacekeeping*. Canberra: Australian Defence Studies Centre, 1990.

4. Austria

Krabbe de Suarez, Birte. *Contributions to United Nations Peacekeeping Operations: The Policy of Some Small Western European Countries*. Geneva: Institut Universitaire de Hautes Etudes Internationales, 1971.

5. Bangladesh

Shahed, Kalam. "Peacekeeping: Bangladesh's Experience in Bosnia." In *Peacekeeping at the Crossroads*. Ed. by S. Neil MacFarlane and Hans-Georg Ehrhart. Clementsport, NS: Canadian Peacekeeping Press, 1997, pp. 164–178.

6. Canada

Beattie, Brigadier General C. E. "Preparations for Peacekeeping at the National and International Level." *Canadian Defence Quarterly*, vol. 8, no. 2 (Autumn 1978), pp. 30–37.

Bratt, Duane. "Niche-Making and Canadian Peacekeeping." *Canadian Foreign Policy*, vol. 6, no. 3 (Spring 1999), pp. 73–84.

Byers, Rod B. "Peacekeeping and Canadian Défense Policy: Ambivalence and Uncertainty." In *Peacekeeping: Appraisals and Proposals*. Ed. by Henry Wiseman. New York: Pergamon Press, 1983, pp. 130–160.

"Canada and the Future of Peacekeeping." *Forum*, vol. 8, no. 2 (April 1993), pp. 49–51.

Canadian Institute of International Affairs. *Peacekeeping: International Challenge and Canadian Response*. Ontario: Canadian Institute of International Affairs, 1968.

Dai, Poeliu. "Canada and the Review of United Nations Peacekeeping Operations." *The Canadian Yearbook of International Law*, vol. 12 (1974), pp. 186–210.

———. "The United Nations Interim Force in Lebanon and Canadian Participation." *The Canadian Yearbook of International Law*, vol. 17 (1979), pp. 304–313.

Delvoie, Louis A. "Canada and Peacekeeping: A New Era?" *Canadian Defence Quarterly*, vol. 20, no. 2 (October 1990), pp. 9–14.

Dewitt, David. "Canadian Defence Policy: Regional Conflicts, Peacekeeping, and Stability Operations." *Canadian Defence Quarterly*, vol. 21, no. 1 (August 1991), pp. 40–51.

Eayrs, James. "Canadian Policy and Opinion During the Suez Crisis." *International Journal*, vol. 12, no. 1 (1957), pp. 97–108.

Granatstein, J. L. "Canada and Peacekeeping: Image and Reality." In *Canadian Foreign Policy*. Ed. by J. L. Granatstein. Toronto: Copp, Clark, and Pittman, Ltd., 1993, pp. 376–285.

Kirsch, Philippe. "Canada and International Security Enforcement." *In Peacekeeping, Peace Making, or War: International Security Enforcement*. Ed. by Alex Morrison and Susan McNish. Toronto: Canadian Institute of Strategic Studies, 1991, pp. 1–12.

Maloney, Sean M. "Insights into Canadian Peacekeeping Doctrine." *Military Review*, vol. 76, no. 2 (March–April 1996), pp. 12–23.

———. "Operation Bolster: Canada and the EC Monitor Mission in the Former Yugoslavia, 1991–1992." *International Peacekeeping*, vol. 4, no. 1 (Spring 1997), pp. 26–50.

Manson, Paul D. "Peacekeeping in Canadian Foreign and Defence Policy." *Canadian Defence Quarterly*, vol. 19, no. 1 (August 1989), pp. 7–10, 12.

Martin, Paul. "Canada's Role in Supporting United Nations Peacekeeping Efforts." In *Canada and the Quest for Peace*. Ed. by Paul Martin. New York: Praeger, 1967, pp. 1–32.

McLin, John B. *Canada's Changing Défense Policy, 1957–1963*. Baltimore, MD: The Johns Hopkins University Press, 1967.

Pearson, Geoffrey A. H. "Canadian Attitudes Toward Peacekeeping." In *Peacekeeping: Appraisals and Proposals*. Ed. by Henry Wiseman. New York: Pergamon Press, 1983, pp. 118–129.

Sparling, Tim. "Canada and International Peacekeeping." In *The New Peacekeeping Partnership*. Ed. by Alex Morrison. Clementsport, NS: Canadian Peackeeping Press, 1995, pp. 189–198.

Tackaberry, R.B. "Organizing and Training Peacekeeping Forces: The Canadian View." *International Journal*, vol. 22, no. 2 (Spring 1967), pp. 195–209.

Taylor, Alastair, et al. *Peacekeeping: International Challenge and Canadian Response*. Contemporary Affairs no. 39. Ontario: John Deyell Ltd., 1968.

7. China

Zhang, Yongjin. "China and UN Peacekeeping: From Condemnation to Participation." *International Peacekeeping*, vol. 3, no. 3 (Autumn 1996), pp. 1–15.

8. Czech Republic

Novotny, Jaromir. "The Czech Republic: An Active Partner with NATO." *NATO Review*, vol. 42, no. 3 (June 1994), pp. 12–15.

9. Denmark

"Danish Military Unit Melds Peacekeeping, Combat Arts." *Signal*, vol. 51, no. 10 (June 1997), pp. 81–84.

Haekkerup, Hana. "The Danish Approach to Peacekeeping." in *Peacekeeping by Proxy*. Ed. by Alex Morrison. Clementsport, NS: Canadian Peacekeeping Press, 1999, pp. 9–15.

Hoff, Ove Hoegh-Guldberg. "Lessons Learned from the IFOR Deployment: Danish Engagement in the former Yugoslavia." *NATO's Sixteen Nations*, vol. 42, no. 4 (1997), pp. 82–84.

Jakobsen, Peter Viggo. "The Danish Approach to UN Peace Operations after the Cold War: A New Model in the Making?" *International Peacekeeping*, vol. 5, no. 3 (Autumn 1998), pp. 106–123.

10. Egypt

Elaraby, Nabil. "UN Peacekeeping: The Egyptian Experience." In *Peacekeeping: Appraisals and Proposals*. Ed. by Henry Wiseman. New York: Pergamon Press, 1983, pp. 65–92.

11. Estonia

Oouel, Andrus. "Estonian Defense Policy: Independence and International Co-operation." *NATO Review*, vol. 44, no. 5 (September 1996), pp. 7–10.

12. Fiji

Fiji. *Review of Fiji's Peace Keeping Operations: Report of the Review Committee*. Suva: Government Printer, 1993.

Heilberg, Marianne. "Peacekeepers and Local Populations: Some Comments on UNIFIL." In *The United Nations and Peacekeeping: Results, Limitations, and Prospects*. Ed. by Indar Rikhye and Kjell Skjelsbaek. London: Macmillan, 1990, pp. 147–169.

Ishizuka, Katsumi. "Fiji: A Micro State and Its Peacekeeping Contribution." *Peacekeeping and International Relations*, vol. 28, no. 3 (May–June 1999), pp. 18–21.

Konrote, J. K. "The Fijian Perspective on Participation in United Nations Operations." In *Peacekeeping: Challenges for the Future*. Ed. by Hugh Smith. Canberra: Australian Defence Force Academy, Australian Defence Studies Centre, 1993, pp. 123–126.

Thakur, Ramesh. "Ministate and Macrocooperation: Fiji's Peacekeeping Debut in Lebanon." *International Studies*, vol. 10 (October 1984), pp. 269–284.

13. Finland

Doepfner, Andreas. "Training UN Peace Troops in Finland." *Swiss Review of World Affairs*, vol. 38, no. 12 (1989), pp. 11–13.

Heilberg, Marianne. "Peacekeepers and Local Populations: Some Comments on UNIFIL." In *The United Nations and Peacekeeping: Results, Limitations, and Prospects.* Ed. by Indar Rikhye and Kjell Skjelsbaek. London: Macmillan, 1990, pp. 147–169.

Lintula, Petri. "The Finnish Participation in Peacekeeping Operations." *International Peacekeeping*, vol. 2, nos. 2–3 (February–May 1995).

14. France

Guillot, Philippe. "France, Peacekeeping, and Humanitarian Intervention." *International Peacekeeping*, vol. 1, no. 1 (Spring 1994), pp. 30–43.

Heilberg, Marianne. "Peacekeepers and Local Populations: Some Comments on UNIFIL." In *The United Nations and Peacekeeping: Results, Limitations, and Prospects.* Ed. by Indar Rikhye and Kjell Skjelsbaek. London: Macmillan, 1990, pp. 147–169.

Issele, Jean Pierre. "The French Position Towards UNIFIL: General Trends." In *A Thankless Task: The Role of UNIFIL in Southern Lebanon.* Ed. by Anthony McDermott and Kjell Skjelsbaek. Oslo: Norwegian Institute of International Affairs, Report no. 123, 1988, pp. 133–158.

McDermott, Anthony, and Kjell Skjelsbaek. "The Ambiguous Role of France." In *The Multinational Force in Beirut, 1982–1984.* Ed. by Anthony McDermott and Kjell Skjelsbael. Miami: Florida International University Press, 1991.

McNulty, Mel. "France's Role in Rwanda and External Military Intervention: A Double Discrediting." *International Peacekeeping*, vol. 4, no. 3 (Autumn 1997), pp. 24–44.

15. Germany

Asmus, Ronald D. *Germany's Contribution to Peacekeeping: Issues and Outlook.* Santa Monica, CA: Rand Corporation, 1995.

Dorff, Robert H. "Germany and Peace Support Operations: Policy After the Karlsruhe Decision." *Parameters* (Spring 1996), pp. 73–90.

Ehrhart, Hans-Georg. "Germany." In *Challenges for the New Peacekeeping.* Ed. by Trevor Findley. SIPRI Research Report no. 12. Oxford: Oxford University Press, 1996, pp. 32–51.

Folgeoperation SFOR: Informationen uber die Beteiligung der Bundeswehr an die Stabilisierung des Friedens im Ehemaligen Jugoslawien. Bonn: Bundesministerium de Verteidigung, 1999.

Kamp, K. H. "The German Bundeswehr in Out-of-Area Operations: To Engage or Not to Engage?" *World Today*, no. 69 (August–September 1993), pp. 165–168.

Lefebvre, Stephane, and Ben Lombardi. "Germany and Peace Enforcement: Participating in IFOR." *European Security*, vol. 5, no. 4 (Winter 1996), pp. 564–587.

Thranert, Oliver. "Germans Battle Over Blue Helmets." *Bulletin of Atomic Scientists*, vol. 48, no. 8 (October 1, 1992), pp. 33–35.

Vogt, Wolf-Reinhard. "Peacekeeping: Germany's Balance Between Domestic Limitations, National Interests, and International Demands." In *Peacekeeping at the Crossroads*. Ed. by S. Neil MacFarlane and Hans-Georg Ehrhart. Clementsport, NS: Canadian Peacekeeping Press, 1997, pp. 71–98.

16. India

Bullion, Alan. "India and UN Peacekeeping Operations." *International Peacekeeping*, vol. 4, no. 1 (Spring 1997), pp. 98–114.

Lal, Nand. *From Collective Security to Peacekeeping: A Study of India's Contribution to the United Nations Emergency Force, 1956–1967*. Calcutta: Minerva Associates, 1975.

Parakatil, Francis. *India and United Nations Peacekeeping Operations*. New Delhi: S. Chand and Co., Ltd., 1975.

17. Indonesia

Haseman, John B. "Garuda XII: Indonesian Peacekeeping in Cambodia." *Joint Force Quarterly*, no. 12 (Summer 1996), pp. 89–94.

Mangindanna, E. E. "The Indonesian Perspective on Participation in United Nations Operations." In *Peacekeeping: Challenges for the Future*. Ed. by Hugh Smith. Canberra: Australian Defence Force Academy, Australian Defence Studies Centre, 1993, pp. 127–130.

18. Ireland

Heilberg, Marianne. "Peacekeepers and Local Populations: Some Comments on UNIFIL." In *The United Nations and Peacekeeping: Results, Limitations, and Prospects*. Ed. by Indar Rikhye and Kjell Skjelsbaek. London: Macmillan, 1990, pp. 147–169.

Kearsley, Harold J. "Blue Helmets of Ireland." *Army Quarterly and Defence Journal*, vol. 128, no. 4 (October 1990), pp. 390–395.

McDonald, Henry. *IRISHBATT*. Dublin: Gill and MacMillan, 1993.

MacDonald, Oliver. "Peacekeeping Lessons Learned: An Irish Perspective." *International Peacekeeping*, vol. 4, no. 3 (Autumn 1997), pp. 94–103.

Murphy, Ray. "Ireland: Legal Issues Arising from Participation in United Nations Operations." *International Peacekeeping*, vol. 1, no. 2 (March–May 1994).

———. "Ireland, the United Nations, and Peacekeeping Operations." *International Peacekeeping*, vol. 5, no. 1 (Spring 1998), pp. 22–45.

19. Italy

Angioni, Franco, and Maurizio Cremasco. "Italy's Role in Peacekeeping Operations." In *The Multinational Force in Beirut, 1982–1984*. Ed. by Anthony McDermott and Kjell Skjelsbael. Miami: Florida International University Press, 1991.

Grassi, Stefano. "The Italian Contribution to the UN's Stand-by Arrangements System." *International Peacekeeping*, vol. 5, no. 1 (Spring 1998), pp. 110–115.

Valpolini, Paolo. "Italian Army: Restructure Aims to Meet Changing Roles." *Jane's Defence Weekly*, vol. 29, no. 6 (February 11, 1998), pp. 22–25.

20. Japan

Harrison, Selig, and Masashi Nishihara. *UN Peacekeeping: Japanese and American Perspectives*. Washington, DC: Carnegie Endowment for International Peace, 1995.

"Japan to Participate in UN Peacekeeping Operations." *Peacekeeping and International Relations*, vol. 21, nos. 3–4 (1992), p. 15.

Kim, Andrew H. N. "Japan and Peacekeeping Operations." *Military Review*, vol. 74, no. 4 (April 1994), pp. 22–33.

Morrison, Alex, and James Kiras. *UN Peace Operations and the Role of Japan*. Clementsport, Canada: Canadian Peacekeeping Press, 1996.

Mulgan, Aurelia George. "International Peacekeeping and Japan's Role." *Asian Survey*, vol. 35, no. 12 (December 1995), pp. 1102–1118.

Owada, Hisashi. "Japan's Constitutional Power to Participate in Peacekeeping." *New York University Journal of International Law and Politics*, vol. 29, no. 3 (Spring 1997), pp. 271–284.

Richardson, Michael. "United Nations: Japan's Peacekeeping Dilemma." *Asia Pacific Defence Reporter*, vol. 19, no. 10–11 (April 1, 1993), p. 28.

Takahara, Takao. "Japan." In *Challenges for the New Peacekeeping*. Ed. by Trevor Findley. SIPRI Research Report no. 12. Oxford: Oxford University Press, 1996, pp. 52–67.

21. Malawi

Chirwa, Marcel R. D. "African Approaches to Peacekeeping: The Experience of Malawi in Rwanda." In *Peacekeeping at the Crossroads*. Ed. by S. Neil MacFarlane and Hans-Georg Ehrhart. Clementsport, NS: Canadian Peacekeeping Press, 1997, pp. 21–23.

22. Malaysia

Arshad, Mohammad. "Malaysian Participation in Peacekeeping." *Asian Defence Journal*, no. 11 (November 1997), pp. 43–44.

23. New Zealand

Barker, Barry, Gavin Brown, and Terry Burke. *Police as Peacekeepers: The History of the Australian and New Zealand Police Serving With the United Nations Force in Cyprus, 1964–1984.* Melbourne: UNCIVPOL, 1984.

Crawford, John. "New Zealand's Experience of Peacekeeping." *Asian Defence Journal,* no. 1 (January 1997), pp. 19–22.

Milburn, Thomas. "A Framework for Assessing New Zealand Peacekeeping." *Peacekeeping and International Relations,* vol. 26, no. 2 (March–April 1997), pp. 3–9.

24. Nigeria

Vogt, Margaret, and E. E. Ekoko, eds. *Nigeria in International Peacekeeping, 1960–1992.* Oxford: Malthouse, 1993.

25. Pakistan

Shah, G. Bokhari. "50 Years of Peacekeeping: The Pakistan Army in the Service of Peace." *Military Technology,* vol. 22, no. 3 (March 1998), pp. 17–20.

26. Philippines

Ceballos, Josefina V. *Philippine Perceptions of Peacekeeping: Filipinos in Blue Helmets.* Manila: Foreign Service Institute, 1996.

27. Poland

Zaccor, Albert M. *Polish Peacekeepers and Their Training.* Fort Leavenworth, KS: Foreign Military Studies Office, August 1993.

28. Portugal

Gama, Jaime. "Portugal and the Transformed NATO." *NATO Review,* vol. 44, no. 4, July 1996, pp. 3–6.

Ribeiro, Antonio Goncalves. "Portuguese Participation in Peacekeeping Operations." *NATO's Sixteen Nations,* Defence and Economics in Portugal Special Issue (1998), pp. 60–62.

29. Russia

Allison, Roy. "Russian Peacekeeping: Capabilities and Doctrine." *Jane's Intelligence Review,* no. 6 (December 1994), pp. 544–547.

Cherniavskii, Stanislav. "Russian Diplomacy in Transcaucasia." *Russian Politics and Law*, vol. 39, no. 3 (May–June 2001), pp. 5–20.

Croft, Michael. "Russia's Peacekeeping Policy, Part I: Domestic Imperatives and the Near Abroad." *Peacekeeping and International Relations*, vol. 25, no. 4 (July–August 1996), pp. 13–14.

———. "Russia's Peacekeeping Policy, Part II: Differences in Approach and Obstacles." *Peacekeeping and International Relations*, vol. 25, no. 5 (September–October 1996), pp. 5–6.

Crow, Suzanne. "Russian Peacekeeping: Défense, Diplomacy, or Imperialism?" *RFE-RL Research Report*, vol. 1, no. 37 (September 18, 1992) pp. 31–40.

Flikke, G. *Russia and International Peacekeeping*. NUPI Report no. 206. Oslo: Norwegian Institute of International Affairs, 1996.

Shashenkov, Maxim. "Russian Peacekeeping in the 'Near Abroad.'" *Survival*, vol. 36 (Autumn 1994), pp. 46–69.

Trenin, Dmitry. "Russia." In *Challenges for the New Peacekeeping*. Ed. by Trevor Findley. SIPRI Research Report no. 12. Oxford: Oxford University Press, 1996, pp. 68–84.

30. Scandinavian Region

Cordier, Sherwood. "The Scandinavian Role in International Peace Operations." *International Peacekeeping*, vol. 4, no. 6 (September–December 1998), pp. 150–152.

31. Singapore

Kah, Low Y. "Singapore's Perspective on Participation in United Nations Operations." In *Peacekeeping: Challenges for the Future*. Ed. by Hugh Smith. Canberra: Australian Defence Force Academy, Australian Defence Studies Centre, 1993, pp. 131–134.

32. South Africa

O'Brien, Kevin A. "Regional Security in Southern Africa: South Africa's National Perspective." *International Peacekeeping*, vol. 3, no. 3 (Autumn 1996), pp. 52–76.

Shaw, Mark, and Jakkie Cilliers. *South Africa and Peacekeeping in Africa*. Halfway House, SA: Institute for Defence Policy, 1995.

33. Soviet Union

Belonogov, Aleksander. "Soviet Peace-keeping Proposals." *Survival*, vol. 32, no. 3 (May–June 1990), pp. 206–211.

Geib, Peter J. *The Origins of the Soviet American Conflict Over United Nations Peacekeeping: 1942–1948*. Emporia: Kansas State Teacher's College, 1974.

34. Spaïin

Pardo, Victor Suanzes. "Spanish Contribution to Peace Operations." *NATO's Sixteen Nations*, vol. 42 (Defence in Spain Special Issue 1997), pp. 51–54.
"Spain's Blue Helmets." *International Defense Review*, vol. 24, no. 1 (January 1991), pp. 19–21.

35. Sweden

Johansson, Eva. "Role of Peacekeepers in the 1990's: Swedish Experience in UNPROFOR." *Armed Forces and Society*, vol. 23, no. 3 (Spring 1997), pp. 451–465.
Skold, Nils. *United Nations Peacekeeping After Suez: the Swedish Involvement*. New York: St. Martin's Press, 1996.
Thunborg, Anders. "Sweden and United Nations Peacekeeping Operations: Views on United Nations Peacekeeping Operations." *Australian Outlook*, vol. 30 (December 1976), pp. 363–370.

36. Thailand

Suksaichol, Pinit. "Thailand's Perspective on Participation in United Nations Operations." In *Peacekeeping: Challenges for the Future*. Ed. by Hugh Smith. Canberra: Australian Defence Academy, Australian Defence Studies Centre, 1993, pp. 135–137.

37. United Kingdom

Mackinlay, John, and Randolph C. Kent. "Complex Emergencies Doctrine: The British are Still the Best." *RUSI Journal*, vol. 142, no. 2 (April 1997), pp. 30–44.

38. United States

Abizaid, Colonel John P. "Lessons for Peacekeepers." *Military Review*, vol. 73, no. 3 (March 1993), pp. 11–19.
Allison, Captain George. "The United States Navy and United Nations Peacekeeping Operations." *Naval War College Review*, vol. 46, no. 3 (Summer 1993), pp. 22–35.
Allen, Colonel William W., et al. "Peacekeeping and Peace Enforcement Operations." *Military Review*, vol. 73, no. 10 (October 1993), pp. 53–61.

Bolton, John R. "United States Policy on the United Nations Peacekeeping: Case Studies in the Congo, Sierra Leone, Ethiopia-Eritrea, Kosova, and East Timor." *World Affairs*, vol. 163, no. 3 (Winter 2001), pp. 129–146.

Campbell, Kurt M. "Superpowers and UN Peacekeeping." *Harvard International Review*, vol. 12, no. 2 (Winter 1990), p. 22.

Cassese, Antonio. "Recent Trends in the Attitude of the Superpowers Towards Peacekeeping." In *United Nations Peacekeeping: Legal Essays*. Ed. by Antonio Cassese. Alphen aan den Rijn, Netherlands: Sijthoff and Noordhoff. 1978, pp. 223–244.

Claude, Inis L. "The OAS, the UN, and the United States." *International Conciliation*, no. 547 (March 1964), pp. 3–68.

———. "The United Nations, the United States, and the Maintenance of Peace." *International Organization*, vol. 23, no. 3 (1969), pp. 621–636.

Daniel, Donald. "United States." In *Challenges for the New Peacekeeping*. Ed. by Trevor Findley. SIPRI Research Report no. 12. Oxford: Oxford University Press, 1996, pp. 85–94.

Doll, William J., and Steven Metz. *The Army and Multinational Peace Operations: Problems and Solutions*. Strategic Studies Institute, US Army War College Special Report. Carlisle Barracks, Pennsylvania. November 29, 1993.

Evans, Ernest. "Peacekeeping: Two Views. The US Military and Peacekeeping Operations." *World Affairs*, vol. 155, no. 4 (Spring 1993), pp. 143–147.

———. "The US Military and Peacekeeping Operations." *World Affairs*, vol. 155, no. 4 (Spring 1993), p. 143.

———. *Wars Without Splendor: The US Military and Low Level Conflict*. Westport, CT: Greenwood Press, 1987.

Fleits, Frederick. *Peacekeeping Fiascoes of the 1990s: Causes, Solutions, and US Interests*. Westport, CT: Praeger, 2002.

Gruhn, Isebill. "The USA Peacekeeping Experience: An Assessment." In *The New Peacekeeping Partnership*. Ed. by Alex Morrison. Clementsport, NS: Canadian Peacekeeping Press, 1995, pp. 125–144.

Harper, Captain Gregory. "Creating a U.N. Peace Enforcement Force: A Case for U.S. Leadership." *The Fletcher Forum of World Affairs*, vol. 18, no. 1 (Winter–Spring 1994), pp. 49–64.

Harrison, Selig, and Masashi Nishihara. *UN Peacekeeping: Japanese and American Perspectives*. Washington, DC: Carnegie Endowment for International Peace, 1995.

Lowenthal, M. M. *Peacekeeping in Future US Foreign Policy*. Washington, DC: Congressional Research Service, 1994.

Mansel, Paul. *The Ambivalence of the US to United Nations Peacekeeping Operations*. London Defence Studies no. 24. London: Brassey's, 1994.

Peck, Steven. "US Peacekeeping Policy: An Update." *Peacekeeping and International Relations*, vol. 23, no. 1 (1994), pp. 10–11.

Pelcovits, Nathan A. "Should the US Police the Sinai?" *Midstream,* vol. 27, no. 6 (1981), pp. 13–20.

Powell, Colin L. "U.S. Forces: Challenges Ahead." *Foreign Affairs*, vol. 71, no. 5 (Winter 1992), p. 32.

Rosenau, William. "Non-Traditional Missions and the Future of the U.S. Military." *The Fletcher Forum of World Affairs*, vol. 18, no. 1 (Winter–Spring 1994), pp. 31–48.

Segal, David R., and Ronald B. Tiggle. "Attitudes of Citizen-Soldiers Toward Military Missions in the Post-Cold War World." *Armed Forces and Society*, vol. 23, no. 3 (Spring 1997), pp. 373–390.

Sewall, Sarah. "The Role of the United States in Peacekeeping." In *The New Peacekeeping Partnership*. Ed. by Alex Morrison. Clementsport, NS: Canadian Peacekeeping Press, 1995, pp. 145–152.

Snow, Donald M. *Peacekeeping, Peacemaking, and Peace Enforcement: The US Role in the New International Order*. Carlisle Barracks, PA: US Army War College, 1993.

Sokolsky, Joel J. "Clinton Administration and UN Peacekeeping." *Canadian Defence Quarterly*, vol. 26, no. 1 (Autumn 1996), pp. 6–13.

Summers, Harry G., Jr. "United States Participation in Peacekeeping Organizations." *Strategic Review*, vol. 21 (Fall 1993), pp. 69–72.

Thakur, Ramesh. "UN Authority and US Power." In *The Multinational Force in Beirut, 1982 1984*. Ed. by Anthony McDermott and Kjell Skjelsbael. Miami: Florida International University Press, 1991.

United States Government. "The Future of UN Peacekeeping Operations." Joint Hearing before the Subcommittee on International Operations and the Subcommittee on Human Rights and International Organizations of the Committee on Foreign Affairs, House of Representatives. One Hundred Second Congress. Second Session. March 25, 1992. Washington, DC: U.S. Government Printing Office.

Warrington, Robert. "The Helmets May be Blue, but the Blood's Still Red: The Dilemma of US Participation in UN Peace Operations." *Comparative Strategy*, vol. 14 (1995), pp. 23–34.

Weinrod, W. Bruce. "The US Role in Peacekeeping Related Activities." *World Affairs*, vol. 155, no. 4 (Spring 1993), p. 148.

XIX. THE FUTURE OF PEACEKEEPING

Bell, Peter D. "Getting Beyond New York: Reforming Peacekeeping in the Field." *World Policy Journal*, vol. 18, no. 3 (Fall 2001), pp. 41–47.

Berdel, Mats R. "Whither UN Peacekeeping?" *Adelphi Paper*, no. 281. London: International Institute for Strategic Studies, October 1993.

Blodgett, John Q. "Empowering the United Nations." *Foreign Affairs*, vol. 71, no. 5 (Winter 1992), p. 89.

———. "The Future of Peacekeeping." *The Washington Quarterly*, vol. 14, no. 1 (Winter 1991), p. 207.

Boutros-Ghali, Boutros. *An Agenda for Peace: Preventive Diplomacy, Peacemaking, and Peacekeeping*. New York: United Nations, 1992.

Bremmer, Colonel J. S., and Lieutenant-Colonel J. M. Snell. "The Changing Face of Peacekeeping." *Canadian Defence Quarterly*, vol. 22, no. 1. Special Issue no. 2 (1992), pp. 6–11.

"Bulletin Special: UN Secretary General's Plan to Enhance UN Preventive Diplomacy, Peacemaking, and Peacekeeping." *Foreign Policy Bulletin*, vol. 3, no. 2 (September 1, 1992), p. 1.

Cwerman, Ralph. "Management of Future of UN Peacekeeping." In *The New Peacekeeping Partnership*. Ed. by Alex Morrison. Clementsport, NS: Canadian Peacekeeping Press, 1995, pp. 165–168.

Goetze, Bernard A. "The Future of Peacekeeping: A Military View." In *Peacekeeping, Peacemaking, or War: International Security Enforcement*. Ed. by Alex Morrison. Toronto: Canadian Institute of Strategic Studies, 1991.

Hanning, Hugh, ed. *Peacekeeping and Technology: Concepts for the Future*. New York: International Peace Academy Report, 1983.

Jett, Dennis C. *Why Peacekeeping Fails*. New York: St. Martin's Press, 2000.

Krepen, Michael, and Jeffrey Tracey. "Open Skies and UN Peacekeeping." *Survival*, vol. 32, no. 3 (1990), pp. 251–263.

Lewis, William H. "Peacekeeping: The Deepening Debate." *Strategic Review*, vol. 21, no. 3 (Summer 1993), p. 26.

Loomis, Dan G. "Prospects for UN Peacekeeping." *Global Affairs*, vol. 8, no. 1 (Winter 1993), p. 141.

Mackinlay, John, and Jarat Chopra. "Second Generation Multinational Operations." *Washington Quarterly*, vol. 15, no. 3 (July 1993), pp. 451–464.

Metz, Steven. *The Future of the United Nations: Implications for Peace Operations*. Carlisle Barracks, PA: Strategic Studies Institute, US Army War College, October 1993.

Moore, John Norton. "Toward a New Paradigm: Enhanced Effectiveness in United Nations Peacekeeping, Collective Security, and War Avoidance." *Virginia Journal of International Law*, vol. 37, no. 4 (Summer 1997), pp. 811–890.

Morrison, Alex. *The Changing Face of Peacekeeping*. Toronto: Canadian Institute of Strategic Studies, 1993.

"New Peacekeeping After the Cold War: Multilateral Peacekeeping Problems." *International Spectator*, vol. 47, no. 11 (November 1993).

Renner, Michael. *Critical Juncture: The Future of Peacekeeping*. Washington, DC: Worldwatch Institute, 1993.

Rikhye, Indar Jit. *The Future of Peacekeeping*. New York: International Peace Academy, 1989.

Scheffer, David J. *Post Gulf War Challenges to the UN Collective Security System: Three Views on the Issue of Humanitarian Intervention*. Washington, DC: United States Institute of Peace, 1992.

"UN Reform, Peacekeeping, Collective Security." *Foreign Policy Bulletin*, vol. 4, no. 2 (September 1, 1993), p. 30.

Urquhart, Brian. "The Future of Peacekeeping." *Negotiation Journal*, vol. 5, no. 1 (January 1, 1989), p. 25.

Weiss, Thomas G., ed. *Collective Security in a Changing World*. Boulder, CO: Lynne Rienner, 1993.

———. "New Challenges for UN Military Operations: Implementing an Agenda for Peace."*The Washington Quarterly*, vol. 16, no. 1 (Winter 1993), pp. 51–66.

About the Author

Terry M. Mays (B.A. Auburn University; M.A. University of Southern California; Ph.D. University of South Carolina) is assistant professor of political science at The Citadel in Charleston, South Carolina, where he teaches in the field of international relations, including specialized courses on multinational peacekeeping and international organizations. He has conducted peacekeeping research at centers in Canada, Great Britain, Ireland, Nigeria, and Norway and visited the United Nations Disengagement Observation Force (UNDOF) and the Multinational Force and Observers (MFO) in the Middle East. Dr. Mays is the author of *Africa's First Peacekeeping Operation: The OAU in Chad, 1981–1982* and *The Historical Dictionary of the American Revolution* (Scarecrow Press). He is also the author of *The 1999 United Nations and 2000 Organization of African Unity Formal Inquiries: A Retrospective Examination of Peacekeeping and the Rwandan Crisis of 1994* with the Pearson Papers Monograph Series as well as several book chapters and journal articles on multinational peacekeeping. He and Mark W. DeLancey are also the authors of the *Historical Dictionary of International Organizations in Sub-Saharan Africa*, 2nd edition (Scarecrow Press).